MAIN LIBRARY

Bloom's Shakespeare Through the Ages

Antony and Cleopatra

As You Like It

Hamlet

Henry IV (Part I)

Julius Caesar

King Lear

Macbeth

The Merchant of Venice

A Midsummer Night's Dream

Othello

Romeo and Juliet

The Sonnets

The Taming of the Shrew

The Tempest

Twelfth Night

Bloom's Shakespeare Through the Ages

HENRY IV, PART I

Edited and with an introduction by
Harold Bloom
Sterling Professor of the Humanities
Yale University

Volume Editor
Neil Heims

Bloom's Shakespeare Through the Ages: Henry IV, Part I

Copyright © 2008 by Infobase Publishing

Introduction © 2008 by Harold Bloom

All rights reserved. No part of this publication may be reproduced or utilized in any form or by any means, electronic or mechanical, including photocopying, recording, or by any information storage or retrieval systems, without permission in writing from the publisher. For more information contact:

Bloom's Literary Criticism
An imprint of Infobase Publishing
132 West 31st Street
New York NY 10001

Library of Congress Cataloging-in-Publication Data
Henry IV, Part I / edited and with an introduction by Harold Bloom ; volume editor, Neil Heims.
  p. cm. — (Bloom's Shakespeare through the ages)
  This study guide contains a selection of criticism through the centuries on the play, plus an accessible summary, analysis of key passages, a comprehensive list of characters, and a biography of Shakespeare.
  Includes bibliographical references and index.
  ISBN 978-0-7910-9629-1 (hc : alk. paper) 1. Shakespeare, William, 1564–1616. King Henry IV. Part 1—Examinations—Study guides. 2. Henry IV, King of England, 1367–1413—In literature. I. Bloom, Harold. II. Heims, Neil.
  PR2810.H46 2008
  822.3'3—dc22   2007050856

Bloom's Literary Criticism books are available at special discounts when purchased in bulk quantities for businesses, associations, institutions, or sales promotions. Please call our Special Sales Department in New York at (212) 967-8800 or (800) 322-8755.

You can find Bloom's Literary Criticism on the World Wide Web at
http://www.chelseahouse.com

Series design by Erika K. Arroyo
Cover design by Ben Peterson
Cover photo © The Granger Collection, New York

Printed in the United States of America

Bang EJB 10 9 8 7 6 5 4 3 2 1

This book is printed on acid-free paper.

All links and Web addresses were checked and verified to be correct at the time of publication. Because of the dynamic nature of the Web, some addresses and links may have changed since publication and may no longer be valid.

CONTENTS

Series Introduction ix
Volume Introduction by Harold Bloom xi
Biography of William Shakespeare 1
Summary of *Henry IV, Part I* 5
Key Passages in *Henry IV, Part I* 23
List of Characters in *Henry IV, Part I* 41

CRITICISM THROUGH THE AGES 45
❖ *Henry IV, Part I* in the Seventeenth Century 47

    1601—W. J. *The Whipping of the Satyre* 49

    1667—Samuel Pepys, from *The Diary* 49

    1668—John Dryden, from "Of Dramatick Poesie" 50

    1698—Jeremy Collier, from *A Short View of the
    Immorality and Profaneness of the English Stage* 50

❖ *Henry IV, Part I* in the Eighteenth Century 53

    1702—John Dennis, from *A Large Account
    of the Taste in Poetry, and the Causes of the Degeneracy of It* 55

    1733—William Warburton, from *The Works of Shakespeare,
    Collated with the Oldest Copies, and Corrected, with Notes,
    Exemplary and Critical* 56

    1741—Corbyn Morris, from *An Essay towards
    Fixing the True Standards of Wit, Raillery, Satire, and Ridicule* ... 56

    1768—Samuel Johnson, from *Notes on Shakespeare's Plays* 59

1769—Elizabeth Montagu, from *An Essay on the Writings and Genius of Shakespear* ... 60

1774—Francis Gentleman, from *Bell's Edition of Shakespeare's Plays* ... 61

1777—Maurice Morgann, from *An Essay on The Dramatic Character of Falstaff* ... 61

1789—William Richardson, from *Essays on Shakespeare's Dramatic Character of Sir John Falstaff, and on His Imitation of Female Characters* ... 77

❖ *Henry IV, Part I* in the Nineteenth Century ... 79

1809—August Wilhelm Schlegel, from *Lectures on Dramatic Art and Literature* ... 81

1810-1811—Samuel Taylor Coleridge, from Coleridge's conversations on Shakespeare ... 83

1817—William Hazlitt, from "Henry IV" in *Characters in Shakespeare's Plays* ... 84

1819—Washington Irving. "The Boar's Head Tavern, Eastcheap: A Shakespearian Research," from *The Sketch Book* ... 88

1850—Henry Giles, from "Falstaff: A Type of Epicurean Life" in *Lectures and Essays* ... 96

1872—H. N. Hudson, from *Shakespeare: His Life, Art, and Characters* ... 103

1875—Edward Dowden, from *Shakespeare: A Critical Study of His Mind and Art* ... 104

1891—George Bernard Shaw, from *The Quintessence of Ibsenism* ... 107

❖ *Henry IV, Part I* in the Twentieth Century ... 109

1902—A. C. Bradley. "The Rejection of Falstaff," from *Oxford Lectures on Poetry* ... 112

1914—E. E. Stoll, from "Falstaff" in *Modern Philology* ... 129

1939—Mark Van Doren. "Henry IV," from *Shakespeare* ... 138

1951—Harold C. Goddard. "Henry IV," from *The Meaning of Shakespeare* ... 153

1953—William Empson. "Falstaff and Mr. Dover Wilson,"
from *The Kenyon Review* 167

1983—A. D. Nuttall. "*Henry IV*: Prince Hal and Falstaff,"
from *A New Mimesis: Shakespeare and the Representation
of Reality*... 200

1983—John W. Blanpied. "Rebellion and Design
in *Henry IV, Part One*," from *Time and the Artist
in Shakespeare's English Histories* 217

1985—E. Talbot Donaldson. "Sublimely Ridiculous:
The Wife of Bath and Falstaff," from *The Swan
at the Well: Shakespeare Reading Chaucer*.. 246

1986—C. L. Barber and Richard P. Wheeler.
"From Mixed History to Heroic Drama: The *Henriad*,"
from *The Whole Journey: Shakespeare's Power of Development* 255

1987—Harold Bloom. "Introduction," from
Henry IV, Part I (Bloom's Modern Critical Interpretations) 273

1992—Harold Bloom. "Introduction," from
Falstaff (Bloom's Major Literary Characters) 279

❖ *Henry IV, Part I* in the Twenty-first Century 285

2001—Hugh Grady. "Falstaff: Subjectivity between
the Carnival and the Aesthetic," from *The Modern
Language Review* 285

Bibliography 305
Acknowledgments 309
Index 311

Series Introduction

Shakespeare Through the Ages presents not the most current of Shakespeare criticism, but the best of Shakespeare criticism, from the seventeenth century to today. In the process, each volume also charts the flow over time of critical discussion of a particular play. Other useful and fascinating collections of historical Shakespearean criticism exist, but no collection that we know of contains such a range of commentary on each of Shakespeare's greatest plays and at the same time emphasizes the greatest critics in our literary tradition: from John Dryden in the seventeenth century, to Samuel Johnson in the eighteenth century, to William Hazlitt and Samuel Coleridge in the nineteenth century, to A.C. Bradley and William Empson in the twentieth century, to the most perceptive critics of our own day. This canon of Shakespearean criticism emphasizes aesthetic rather than political or social analysis.

Some of the pieces included here are full-length essays; others are excerpts designed to present a key point. Much (but not all) of the earliest criticism consists only of brief mentions of specific plays. In addition to the classics of criticism, some pieces of mainly historical importance have been included, often to provide background for important reactions from future critics.

These volumes are intended for students, particularly those just beginning their explorations of Shakespeare. We have therefore also included basic materials designed to provide a solid grounding in each play: a biography of Shakespeare, a synopsis of the play, a list of characters, and an explication of key passages. In addition, each selection of the criticism of a particular century begins with an introductory essay discussing the general nature of that century's commentary and the particular issues and controversies addressed by critics presented in the volume.

Shakespeare was "not of an age, but for all time," but much Shakespeare criticism is decidedly for its own age, of lasting importance only to the scholar who wrote it. Students today read the criticism most readily available to them, which means essays printed in recent books and journals, especially those journals made available on the Internet. Older criticism is too often buried in out-of-print books on forgotten shelves of libraries or in defunct periodicals. Therefore, many students, particularly younger students, have no way of knowing that some of the most profound criticism of Shakespeare's plays was written decades or centuries ago. We hope this series remedies that problem, and more importantly, we hope it infuses students with the enthusiasm of the critics in these volumes for the beauty and power of Shakespeare's plays.

INTRODUCTION BY
HAROLD BLOOM

I have taught this play so often, written so much about it, and reread it so frequently that at seventy-seven I feel the necessity of standing back to see if fresh perspectives suggest themselves to me. Though I have been criticized for neglecting Prince Hal and Hotspur, the rich complexity of the future Henry V and the captivating high spirit of Hotspur are not altogether lost upon me. But what chance have they against Shakespeare's grandest characterization, the immortal Sir John Falstaff?

Did Shakespeare ever again write a play as perfectly balanced as *Henry IV, Part 1*? There are *Macbeth* among the tragedies and *As You Like It* and *Twelfth Night* of the comedies. Even Shakespeare could not harmoniously measure out *Hamlet* and *King Lear*: their sublimity defies our ideas of order. *Antony and Cleopatra*, with its intercontinental scope, rivals Falstaff's play, while *A Midsummer Night's Dream* charmingly makes its mysterious fusion of rustics, mythic Athenians, fairies, and erotically crazed couples into a sweet discord.

Not just because I am a lifelong Falstaffian, I begin to believe that if we had to represent Shakespeare by only one play, it should be *Henry IV, Part 1*. The alternation between Eastcheap, the royal court, and the rebels is beyond the limits of art. So masterly is Shakespeare that the transitions hardly seem to be there.

In all of Western literature is there so persuasive a representation of ambivalences as in this play? Hal's affective responses to his father, King Henry IV, and to Hotspur, his rival for garnering "honor," are less complex than his stance towards Falstaff. His love for Falstaff, from the play's inception, is dead. Hal's imagination seems haunted by an image of Falstaff on the gallows, which few readers or playgoers could tolerate. Poor Bardolph is hanged by his king in *Henry V*, with no expressions even of regret. Had Falstaff not departed for Arthur's bosom, he would have dangled by Bardolph's side.

Though only a few Shakespearean scholars share Hal's murderous ambivalence towards Falstaff, I perpetually am astonished that most of them do not love the fat knight. One does not expect the greatest wit in literature to be chastised for his vices, all of which are open and self-acknowledged. Supreme wit is a cognitive power. Falstaff, as intelligent as Hamlet, is life's ambassador and not death's, unlike Hamlet. Is there another figure in world literature so vitalistic as Falstaff? Even the Panurge of Rabelais and Sancho Panza do not match up with the Sage of Eastcheap.

The essence of Falstaffianism is: *do not moralize*. No societal standards could survive Falstaff, if only because he is never a hypocrite. Do not bother to compute all of his flaws: he bulges with them. Falstaff is not so much a comic creation as he is a creator of comedy. And though he is supreme among comedians, his wisdom exceeds even his wit. The disreputable Falstaff is the Socrates of Eastcheap, essentially a teacher. Of what? Freedom, joy, the blessing of more life: these are the Falstaffian values. He would be invulnerable were it not that he loves Hal, who will destroy him at the close of *Henry IV, Part 2*.

Shakespeare's contemporaries did not moralize against Falstaff, who immediately became the most popular of all Shakespearean characters. A Falstaffian, I do not regard him as a masterwork of "transcendental subjectivity"—the usual dismissal of my idolatry—but as one of the crucial literary instances of what I urge us to call "immanent subjectivity.' Historicisms old and new rise and wane; they wash over Shakespeare and reveal nothing intrinsic to his heterocosm. Marlowe's protagonists never achieve subjectivity, nor do Ben Jonson's. Shakespeare's great originality is to bring upon stage what Machiavelli and Montaigne had investigated in the public and private spheres, respectively. The growing inner self, from which we cannot flee, is Shakespeare's domain, though others had to be there before him.

We come to know and understand Falstaff's inner self, to a degree unavoidable with any prior literary character. What makes this possible? Falstaff manifests both an excess of being and an excess of language, of "beautiful laughing speech" (Yeats). Overflow is the Falstaffian mode, and is not to be mistaken for hyperbole or overthrow. Hamlet contains a mystery: a recalcitrance in his spirit maintains his distance from us. Falstaff is up close; we could touch him if we dared.

I have celebrated Falstaff elsewhere, because he *is* celebration itself. The politics of the play do not much interest me. Falstaff is not a matrix where "social energies" mix and mingle. Rather, he is how human meaning starts. Defying time and our histories, indeed he is immortal.

Biography of William Shakespeare

WILLIAM SHAKESPEARE was born in Stratford-on-Avon in April 1564 into a family of some prominence. His father, John Shakespeare, was a glover and merchant of leather goods who earned enough to marry Mary Arden, the daughter of his father's landlord, in 1557. John Shakespeare was a prominent citizen in Stratford, and at one point, he served as an alderman and bailiff.

Shakespeare presumably attended the Stratford grammar school, where he would have received an education in Latin, but he did not go on to either Oxford or Cambridge universities. Little is recorded about Shakespeare's early life; indeed, the first record of his life after his christening is of his marriage to Anne Hathaway in 1582 in the church at Temple Grafton, near Stratford. He would have been required to obtain a special license from the bishop as security that there was no impediment to the marriage. Peter Alexander states in his book *Shakespeare's Life and Art* that marriage at this time in England required neither a church nor a priest or, for that matter, even a document—only a declaration of the contracting parties in the presence of witnesses. Thus, it was customary, though not mandatory, to follow the marriage with a church ceremony.

Little is known about William and Anne Shakespeare's marriage. Their first child, Susanna, was born in May 1583 and twins, Hamnet and Judith, in 1585. Later on, Susanna married Dr. John Hall, but the younger daughter, Judith, remained unmarried. When Hamnet died in Stratford in 1596, the boy was only 11 years old.

We have no record of Shakespeare's activities for the seven years after the birth of his twins, but by 1592 he was in London working as an actor. He was also apparently well known as a playwright, for reference is made of him by his contemporary Robert Greene in *A Groatsworth of Wit*, as "an upstart crow."

Several companies of actors were in London at this time. Shakespeare may have had connection with one or more of them before 1592, but we have no record that tells us definitely. However, we do know of his long association with the most famous and successful troupe, the Lord Chamberlain's Men. (When James I came to the throne in 1603, after Elizabeth's death, the troupe's name changed to the King's Men.) In 1599 the Lord Chamberlain's Men provided the financial backing for the construction of their own theater, the Globe.

The Globe was begun by a carpenter named James Burbage and finished by his two sons, Cuthbert and Robert. To escape the jurisdiction of the Corporation of London, which was composed of conservative Puritans who opposed the theater's "licentiousness," James Burbage built the Globe just outside London, in the Liberty of Holywell, beside Finsbury Fields. This also meant that the Globe was safer from the threats that lurked in London's crowded streets, like plague and other diseases, as well as rioting mobs. When James Burbage died in 1597, his sons completed the Globe's construction. Shakespeare played a vital role, financially and otherwise, in the construction of the theater, which was finally occupied sometime before May 16, 1599.

Shakespeare not only acted with the Globe's company of actors; he was also a shareholder and eventually became the troupe's most important playwright. The company included London's most famous actors, who inspired the creation of some of Shakespeare's best-known characters, such as Hamlet and Lear, as well as his clowns and fools.

In his early years, however, Shakespeare did not confine himself to the theater. He also composed some mythological-erotic poetry, such as *Venus and Adonis* and *The Rape of Lucrece*, both of which were dedicated to the earl of Southampton. Shakespeare was successful enough that in 1597 he was able to purchase his own home in Stratford, which he called New Place. He could even call himself a gentleman, for his father had been granted a coat of arms.

By 1598 Shakespeare had written some of his most famous works, *Romeo and Juliet*, *The Comedy of Errors*, *A Midsummer Night's Dream*, *The Merchant of Venice*, *Two Gentlemen of Verona*, and *Love's Labour's Lost*, as well as his historical plays *Richard II*, *Richard III*, *Henry IV*, and *King John*. Somewhere around the turn of the century, Shakespeare wrote his romantic comedies *As You Like It*, *Twelfth Night*, and *Much Ado About Nothing*, as well as *Henry V*, the last of his history plays in the Prince Hal series. During the next 10 years he wrote his great tragedies, *Hamlet*, *Macbeth*, *Othello*, *King Lear*, and *Antony and Cleopatra*.

At this time, the theater was burgeoning in London; the public took an avid interest in drama, the audiences were large, the plays demonstrated an enormous range of subjects, and playwrights competed for approval. By 1613, however, the rising tide of Puritanism had changed the theater. With the desertion of the theaters by the middle classes, the acting companies were compelled to depend more on the aristocracy, which also meant that they now had to cater to a more sophisticated audience.

Perhaps this change in London's artistic atmosphere contributed to Shakespeare's reasons for leaving London after 1612. His retirement from the theater is sometimes thought to be evidence that his artistic skills were waning. During this time, however, he wrote *The Tempest* and *Henry VIII*. He also wrote the "tragicomedies," *Pericles, Cymbeline*, and *The Winter's Tale*. These were thought to be inspired by Shakespeare's personal problems and have sometimes been considered proof of his greatly diminished abilities.

However, so far as biographical facts indicate, the circumstances of his life at this time do not imply any personal problems. He was in good health and financially secure, and he enjoyed an excellent reputation. Indeed, although he was settled in Stratford at this time, he made frequent visits to London, enjoying and participating in events at the royal court, directing rehearsals, and attending to other business matters.

In addition to his brilliant and enormous contributions to the theater, Shakespeare remained a poetic genius throughout the years, publishing a renowned and critically acclaimed sonnet cycle in 1609 (most of the sonnets were written many years earlier). Shakespeare's contribution to this popular poetic genre are all the more amazing in his break with contemporary notions of subject matter. Shakespeare idealized the beauty of man as an object of praise and devotion (rather than the Petrarchan tradition of the idealized, unattainable woman). In the same spirit of breaking with tradition, Shakespeare also treated themes previously considered off limits—the dark, sexual side of a woman as opposed to the Petrarchan ideal of a chaste and remote love object. He also expanded the sonnet's emotional range, including such emotions as delight, pride, shame, disgust, sadness, and fear.

When Shakespeare died in 1616, no collected edition of his works had ever been published, although some of his plays had been printed in separate unauthorized editions. (Some of these were taken from his manuscripts, some from the actors' prompt books, and others were reconstructed from memory by actors or spectators.) In 1623 two members of the King's Men, John Hemings and Henry Condell, published a collection of all the plays they considered to be authentic, the First Folio.

Included in the First Folio is a poem by Shakespeare's contemporary Ben Jonson, an outstanding playwright and critic in his own right. Jonson paid tribute to Shakespeare's genius, proclaiming his superiority to what previously had been held as the models for literary excellence—the Greek and Latin writers. "Triumph, my Britain, thou hast one to show / To whom all scenes of Europe homage owe. / He was not of an age, but for all time!"

Jonson was the first to state what has been said so many times since. Having captured what is permanent and universal to all human beings at all times, Shakespeare's genius continues to inspire us—and the critical debate about his works never ceases.

Summary of
Henry IV, Part I

History of England from 1367 to 1402, as Reconstructed by Shakespeare in His Plays

What follows is a brief and not entirely accurate history of England, as presented by Shakespeare in his *Henry IV* plays:

Richard II, born in 1367, was king of England from 1377 until he was deposed in 1400 by Henry Bolingbroke, who became Henry IV. Richard was the second son of Edward, the Black Prince, eldest son of Edward III. Richard's elder brother died in infancy and Richard became the royal successor, next in line after his father. His father died in 1376, and when Edward III died in 1377 Richard ascended to the English throne. Since he was a minor, Richard's rule was overseen by a group of nobles called the Lords Appellant, with whom Richard was in constant conflict for power. In 1397, Richard succeeded in freeing himself from the grip of the Lords Appellant by having a number of them murdered.

Although twice married, Richard was childless. The heir to the English throne, therefore, was Roger Mortimer, Earl of March. Roger Mortimer died in 1398, leaving his son Edmund Mortimer as his heir. (Shakespeare conflates this Edmund Mortimer and Roger's brother, also called Edmund Mortimer, into one person. He makes that composite Edmund Mortimer both the legitimate heir to the throne and the son-in-law of Henry's Welsh adversary, Owen Glendower.)

In 1399, as part of his plan to consolidate and fortify his power, Richard exiled Bolingbroke, son of John of Gaunt, one of Richard's father's younger brothers. When his Uncle Gaunt died that same year, Richard confiscated Gaunt's vast amount of land, depriving Bolingbroke of his inheritance.

When Richard made an expedition to Ireland that year in an attempt to fight an ultimately unsuccessful war, Bolingbroke returned to England with an army from France. His stated intention was to reclaim his inheritance and he vowed to demand no more than that. He drew many of the nobility to his cause, particularly the family of the Earl of Northumberland, Henry Percy, and his son, young Henry Percy, called Hotspur, whom Shakespeare makes younger than he actually was in order to set up a dramatic conflict between him and Prince

Hal, Bolingbroke's son. Despite his oath, and with the support of the nobility, Bolingbroke deposed Richard in 1400 and most likely had him murdered.

Once king, Henry was tormented by the insecurity of his hold on the English throne. Henry particularly feared Edmund Mortimer, young Percy's wife's brother, because of his stronger claim to the throne (he was the son of Edward III's third son, while Henry was the son of Edward III's fourth). Despite his greater entitlement, Mortimer had given his support to Henry; but when Glendower, Henry's Welsh adversary against whom Mortimer had fought in Henry's interest, captured Mortimer, Henry neglected to ransom him. Subsequently, Mortimer made peace with Glendower, married his daughter, and joined with him against the king who had, out of self-interest, betrayed his loyalty by refusing his ransom. Henry's failure to aid Mortimer or to allow Hotspur to keep for himself some of the prisoners he had taken in battle while in service to the king, as was the traditional custom, kindled the resentment of the Percy family and began a breach between the king and his former supporters that led to the battle of Shrewsbury, which concludes *Henry IV, Part I*.

Act I

The plot of *Henry IV, Part I* moves forward on parallel tracks. Structurally, the play is not composed of a main plot and a subplot but instead interweaves several strands that all come together at the battle of Shrewsbury.

As *Henry IV, Part I* begins, Henry is addressing his court. Attempting to fortify his legitimacy, he reports that with his ascension to the throne strife in England has come to an end and that he will now be turning his thoughts to Jerusalem, where he has vowed to lead a crusade in defense of Christianity. No sooner has he announced this plan than he adds he must postpone it. Contrary to what he has said about peace on home soil, the next order of business is a report on the war he is waging against Wales and Scotland for control of Britain. Westmoreland, a noble loyal to the king, reports that in one battle against the Welsh an army led by Mortimer was defeated and Mortimer was taken prisoner by Glendower. He further reports that young Henry Percy, also called Hotspur, was engaged in a great battle against the Scots, but he does not know the outcome. More news arrives with Sir Walter Blunt, who reports that Percy has been victorious and taken many prisoners. For Henry, however, there are two vexing aspects of Hotspur's victory: The first is Hotspur's refusal to yield his prisoners to the king; the second is that the battlefield hero is Harry Percy and not his own son, Harry the Prince of Wales, whom he considers stained by "riot and dishonor."

Scene 2 moves from the king's high chambers, where weighty military and political matters are being discussed, to the prince's lodgings in London, the scene of "riot and dishonor," where the prince is bantering with Falstaff, the old, fat knight who is commonly thought to be encouraging the prince to lead a life of dissipation. While Hal seems to display a familiar affection toward Falstaff in their conversation, there is also an element of unmistakable aggression, even unfriendliness. Their dialogue is most often marked by insults hurled by Hal and dodged by Falstaff. When Falstaff, waking from a doze, asks, "Now, Hal, what time of day is it, lad?" Hal won't give him a direct answer. Instead, he laces into him, beginning with his girth:

> Thou art so fat-witted, with drinking of old sack and unbuttoning thee after supper and sleeping upon benches after noon, that thou hast forgotten to demand that truly which thou wouldst truly know. What a devil hast thou to do with the time of the day? Unless hours were cups of sack and minutes capons and clocks the tongues of bawds and dials the signs of leaping-houses and the blessed sun himself a fair hot wench in flame-colored taffeta, I see no reason why thou shouldst be so superfluous to demand the time of the day. (I.ii.2-12)

There is more antagonism than affability in Hal's words, more condemnation of vice than regard for the man. Readers may wonder, when Hal's contempt seems so clear, what binds him to Falstaff other than a need for a subject for his mockery. Similarly, readers may wonder what gratifies Falstaff in his relationship with Hal if not delight in coming away unscathed from Hal's repeated jibes. Falstaff, whose main attributes are his huge body and his equally huge appetite, embodies need, and perhaps one of his needs is acceptance. Thus he insists on being continually, mischievously entertaining.

After Hal's reproaches, Falstaff concedes that the prince is right:

> Indeed, you come near me now, Hal; for we that take purses go by the moon and the seven stars, and not by Phoebus, he, that wandering knight so fair. And, I prithee, sweet wag, when thou art king, as, God save thy grace,—majesty I should say, for grace thou wilt have none,— (I.ii.13-18)

Falstaff does not apologize for his vices but instead turns them into accomplishments and matter for further teasing. He is as irreverent as Hal is aggressive. But his irreverence, rather than a form of aggression, is actually an invitation for reciprocation. He does not seem to suffer at all from the prince's sharp insults but turns them into a clever retort, accusing the prince of corrupting *him* and advising Hal how he should rule England once he becomes king.

When Poins appears on the scene, the stakes become raised, and the prince's debauchery turns from a matter of dissolute and irreverent conversation to actual illegal activity when Falstaff invites him to participate in a highway robbery.

Hal initially refuses, but Poins dismisses Falstaff and persuades Hal to join the mischief by putting a different spin on their plan. Falstaff's invitation to robbery, once Poins refines it, becomes an opportunity for further merrymaking at Falstaff's expense. Poins suggests to Hal that after Falstaff and his accomplices—Gadshill, Bardolph, and Peto—rob the carriers, Hal and Poins should turn the tables and rob the robbers. The joke will happen when Falstaff tries to explain his defeat to Hal and Poins.

While Poins lessens the degree of Hal's mischief, assuring that he will not participate directly in the crime, Hal is still taking part in the scheme. When Hal and Hotspur are compared, as the king does at the end of scene 1, what stands out is the wild and aggressive spirit that drives them both. They are not differentiated by temperament but by the object that engages them. Carnage and powermongering, moreover, are shown as honorable in the minds of both King Henry and Hotspur. Mischief-making of the sort that Hal undertakes in the company of Falstaff and against Falstaff, on the other hand, is invested with ignominy, as is the sensuous indulgence that characterizes Falstaff. The contrast between a life of aggressive discipline and a life of loose satisfaction, implicit in the comparison of Hotspur or Henry and Falstaff, thus becomes a basic theme that develops throughout the play and becomes overt on the battlefield at Shrewsbury, when Falstaff catechizes himself about honor.

Once Hal is alone at the end of Act I, scene 2, he delivers a soliloquy in which he puts his behavior into a different context from where it had appeared to be to the audience and to his father. Hal is as much a politician and a crafter of his public image as Henry. Just as Henry used Northumberland and his allies to gain power, Hal is using Falstaff and his group of friends, not to gain power, but to create low expectations for himself, which he will then confound when the time comes for him to assume his place as monarch. "I know you all," he says, distancing himself from his rough and dissolute companions, "and will awhile uphold / The unyoked humor of your idleness." He distresses his father deliberately with his dissipated and riotous behavior, sullying his reputation so that he may shine all the more brilliantly in the moment of his reformation:

> . . . herein will I imitate the sun,
> Who doth permit the base contagious clouds
> To smother up his beauty from the world,
> That, when he please again to be himself,
> Being wanted, he may be more wondered at,
> By breaking through the foul and ugly mists
> Of vapors that did seem to strangle him.
> . . . .
> So, when this loose behavior I throw off
> And pay the debt I never promised,

By how much better than my word I am,
By so much shall I falsify men's hopes;
And like bright metal on a sullen ground,
My reformation, glittering o'er my fault,
Shall show more goodly and attract more eyes
Than that which hath no foil to set it off.
I'll so offend, to make offence a skill;
Redeeming time when men think least I will.
          (I.ii.199-221)

This calculation shows Hal to be more cunning than his rival Hotspur. Hal truly is heir to his father's craft as well as to his throne. While Henry sees his son as an idler, he sees Hotspur as a hot-blooded, valiant, and dangerous adversary. As much as he deplores him, he envies Hotspur's father, Percy, for having such a son. Reader and spectator, however, can contrast Hal's subtle patience and Machiavellian cool with Hotspur's impetuosity, which will in the end prove much more deadly to himself than to the king.

In Act I, scene 3, Henry's determination to assert his authority as king is met by Hotspur's defiance of that authority. Henry tells the assembled Percy family,

My blood hath been too cold and temperate,
Unapt to stir at these indignities,
. . .
You tread upon my patience: but be sure
I will from henceforth rather be myself,
Mighty and to be feared. (I.iii.1-6)

When Worcester, Hotspur's uncle, responds with what can only be taken as a rebuke and the hint of a threat, "Our house, my sovereign liege, little deserves / The scourge of greatness to be used on it; / And that same greatness too which our own hands / Have holp to make so portly," Henry sees "[d]anger and disobedience in thine eye" and banishes him from his presence. Northumberland then attempts to placate the king, arguing that Hotspur did not deny turning over his prisoners to the king, and then Hotspur himself explains that the request took place right after the heat of battle and that the agent who demanded the prisoners of him was a foppish courtier whose manner infuriated him. But Henry remains firm and, despite all the offered explanations for Hotspur's disobedience, he argues, "Why yet he doth deny his prisoners / But with proviso and exception, / That we at our own charge shall ransom straight / His brother-in-law, the foolish Mortimer." Henry continues, accusing Mortimer of willfully betraying him and conspiring with Henry's Welsh enemy, Glendower. He refuses to ransom

Mortimer, demands that the prisoners be delivered to him, and leaves the stage with strongly worded admonitions, warning that he is to be obeyed or else.

Inflamed with anger, Hotspur begins to rage, and it is not easy for his father or his Uncle Worcester to calm him. When he finally settles down, the three forge a plan to ally themselves with Mortimer, Glendower, and the Archbishop of York against the king.

Act II

With the Prince of Wales among the robbers, the adventurous young hothead Harry Percy among his conspirators, and the exciting camaraderie of scheming evident in both endeavors, the line between the high seriousness of a political conspiracy and the low comedy of a robbery and counter-robbery begins to blur.

After presenting the clash of power-lusting men and their struggle for the position that can give one man command over many, Shakespeare turns in Act II, scene 1, to a group of common men who must cope with fleas and a lack of chamber pots waking at four in the morning to begin preparing to transport merchandise, livestock, and money to London. As they are preparing for the journey, the chamberlain of the inn at which they were staying tells Gadshill, one of Falstaff's associates, of a man bearing money who will be riding in their coach. Gadshill jests with the chamberlain about what he knows will happen: that the coach will undoubtedly be robbed. He promises the chamberlain a cut of their take for his information. Thus in this scene preceding the robbery, set among the common people, carriers, informants, thieves, and counter-thieves, Shakespeare mirrors and deflates the activity of the nobles.

As comical as the plot is and as much opportunity as it offers the actors for physical humor, the robbery itself is as chaotic as a battle, foreshadowing the battle at Shrewsbury, which, as serious as *it* is, is also grimly comic with its own chaos and the added presence of Falstaff. Sandwiched between the robbery and the confrontation between Falstaff, the prince, and Poins is a scene between Hotspur and his wife, Kate. If it had not yet been made clear, this scene makes it quite apparent that *Henry IV, Part I* is less a history than an anatomy of history, an examination of its human elements, of the persons who, in their actions and interactions, constitute and define the events of a historical era.

As far as it advances the plot of *Henry IV, Part I*, Act II, scene 3, the scene between Hotspur and his wife, like the two robbery scenes that precede it, seems unnecessary. While those scenes can be reduced to the narrative summary, "While Henry IV faces the threat of rebellion, the prince and his tavern companions play cops and robbers," this one can be reduced to "Hotspur parts from his wife without telling her where he is going, although she suspects it is off to war." However, those robbery scenes contain powerful representations of humanity that give essential meaning to the story. Similarly, in the scene between Hotspur and Kate, Shakespeare shapes Hotspur as a complex human character, impatient, charming, aloof, witty, and self-involved, loved by his wife despite his masculine detachment and his refusal to take her seriously because she is a woman. Making Hotspur a meaningful and affecting human character now ensures that his death in the fifth act, when Hal defeats him and Falstaff gives his corpse an extra wound for good measure, will also be meaningful and affecting, independent of what his death signifies for Hal's advancement toward respectability, honor, and authority.

After Hotspur leaves his wife, Shakespeare shifts to the tavern again in Act II, scene 4, where Hal's separation from Falstaff commences in earnest. The ambiguity over whether their relationship is based on a hostile affection or an affectionate hostility now begins to diminish. With grim and laconic resolve in four monosyllables comprising two sentences, Hal states his resolve to abandon Falstaff.

Act II, scene 4, is a long and revealing scene. It is actually made up of several smaller scenes that indirectly reveal much about Hal and Falstaff. The first scene presents the rather mean joke that Hal plays on Francis, the drawer (like a waiter) and for which he enlists Poins's cooperation as a coactor. What is particularly mean-spirited about this bit is that, unlike Falstaff, whom Hal and his cohorts had set up to be robbed after he had himself committed a robbery, Francis has committed no offense and is not of a mind-set to understand their teasing. Hal's practical joke involves having Poins call for Francis at the same time Hal is talking to him in order to hear Francis call "Anon, anon, sir," and then having them both call him, so that "the Drawer stands amazed, not knowing which way to go." Its significance is that Hal uses Francis to represent his own situation. Hal is, after all, a man pulled in two directions, caught between his father and Falstaff. Even though he has said his time spent with his low companions is designed to make a greater political impact later, it nevertheless also reflects some of Hal's deeper inclinations, which, although he will overcome them, are still a part of his true disposition.

Finished with Francis, Hal turns his thoughts to his rival, Percy. He mocks Percy's legendary savagery in an imagined conversation between Percy and his wife, in which Percy complains, "Fie upon this quiet life, I want work," after "he . . . kills me six or seven dozen of Scots at a breakfast." Through this little improvisation, Hal shows he is not very far removed from court concerns and also that he is not intimidated by Percy's reputation.

When Falstaff then enters the scene, Poins asks, "Where hast thou been?" and Falstaff begins a new interlude, not by answering the question, but by taking it as his cue to begin a typical Falstaffian act. As if inviting the accusation, Falstaff begins by hurling it: "A plague of all cowards," he says, demands a cup of sack, and proceeds to lament the "bad world" in which a "good" man like himself is forced to live. When the prince challenges him to explain himself, he continues with the taunts that he knows must ultimately be redirected against him: "A king's son!" he exclaims, "If I do not beat thee out of thy / kingdom with a dagger of lath, and drive all thy / subjects afore thee like a flock of wild-geese, / I'll never wear hair on my face more. You Prince of Wales!" To the prince's response of, "Why, you whoreson round man, what's the matter?" Falstaff retorts, "Are you not a coward? Answer me that—and Poins there?" He accuses them of running away during the robbery, leaving him alone to face the assailants, whose numbers he amplifies from two to 11 in buckram and three in "Kendall green." Hal and Poins encourage him in this fabrication until they finally confront him:

> We two saw you four set on four and bound them, and
> were masters of their wealth. Mark now, how a plain
> tale shall put you down. Then did we two set on you
> four; and, with a word, out-faced you from your
> prize, and have it; yea, and can show it you here in
> the house: and, Falstaff, you carried your guts
> away as nimbly, with as quick dexterity, and roared
> for mercy and still run and roared, as ever I heard
> bull-calf. What a slave art thou, to hack thy sword
> as thou hast done, and then say it was in fight!
> What trick, what device, what starting-hole, canst
> thou now find out to hide thee from this open and
> apparent shame?

But Falstaff is not thrown. "By the Lord," he responds, "I knew ye as well as he that made ye. . . . Was it for me to kill the heir apparent? . . . I am as valiant as Hercules, but beware instinct. The lion will not touch the true prince. . . . I was a coward on instinct. I shall think the better of myself and thee . . . I for a valiant lion, and thou for a true prince." Thus their interlude ends with Falstaff taking their term of abuse, "coward," upon himself and turning it inside out, fashioning it into the virtue of a valorous instinct. Happy, too, that they still have the booty, Falstaff suggests they "have a play extempore." Before they can begin, however, the hostess of the tavern announces that a nobleman wants to speak to the prince. Hal sends Falstaff to see what the messenger wants, and Falstaff returns with the news that Hal has been summoned to the court in the morning because Percy, Mortimer, Glendower, Northumberland, and Douglas are in league against his father, King Henry. Falstaff taunts Hal, saying, "Thou wilt be horribly chid tomorrow when thou comest to thy father," and suggests that Hal "practice an answer."

For this practice, Falstaff takes the part of Henry and Hal plays himself. As Henry, Falstaff delivers a lecture admonishing Hal for his behavior and for his choice of companions, yet praising "a virtuous man whom I have often noted in thy company," meaning Falstaff. Hal stops Falstaff midperformance, announcing that he will instead play his father and Falstaff can play him. Falstaff jokes that Hal is deposing him; the comment is somewhat ironic since this is a very true fear that will haunt the real king throughout this play and its sequel.

Just as Falstaff's performance was meant to praise his own character, the purpose of Hal's performance is to denigrate Falstaff through a cataloguing of his faults. As always, Falstaff responds to Hal's lambasting with a touching self-defense, and he concludes by saying,

>...banish Peto,
> banish Bardolph, banish Poins: but for sweet Jack
> Falstaff, kind Jack Falstaff, true Jack Falstaff,
> valiant Jack Falstaff, and therefore more valiant,
> being, as he is, old Jack Falstaff, banish not him
> thy Harry's company, banish not him thy Harry's
> company: banish plump Jack, and banish all the world.

And just as in these words Falstaff seems to have brought himself into his part, speaking what he wishes Hal would feel, so in response Hal seems to be voicing not his father's sentiments but his own with his icy, even sinister answer of "I do. I will." It is particularly eerie because he is not contradicting Falstaff; he does seem to feel what Falstaff wishes him to. Accepting that to banish him is also to banish "all the world," he resolves himself to triumph over the more dissolute parts of himself and to banish Falstaff and his corrupted world for the sake of his future reign.

As he finishes, Bardolph enters at a run. "O, my lord, my lord!" he cries, out of breath, "The sheriff with a most monstrous watch is at the door." The arrival of the sheriff signals the beginning of the rejection of Falstaff. Although Hal protects Falstaff from the sheriff, denying that he is present, Hal assumes the posture expected of him as Prince of Wales and assures the sheriff that "If he [Falstaff] have robbed these men, / He shall be answerable." At this worrisome moment, rather than being anxious over his own fate or the meaning of Hal's words, Falstaff is characteristically "fast asleep behind the arras, and snorting like a horse."

Act III

In Act III, scene 1, the scene shifts from a room in a London tavern to a room in Glendower's house in Wales where the rebels, Hotspur, Mortimer, Glendower, and Worcester have gathered in preparation for their battle against

Henry. They are full of optimism, and the particular business of their gathering is to outline the division of the kingdom after their victory. Hardly have they begun, however, when the discord between Hotspur and Glendower becomes apparent and Hotspur again shows his volatile and pugnacious personality. The contrast between Hotspur and Hal, which had before seemed to favor Hotspur, now begins to favor Hal, who has been revealed as patient and shrewd. Hotspur, although valiant and fierce in battle, has nevertheless shown himself to be unreliable and, as he shows in this scene, is ultimately unable to govern even himself.

Hotspur's first words in Act III, scene 1, "A plague upon it, I have forgot the map," reflect poorly on him and set the stage for his foul mood. To abate this, Glendower attempts to calm him with a friendly address:

> No, here it is. Sit, cousin Percy; sit, good cousin Hotspur, for by that
> name as oft as Lancaster doth speak of you, his cheek looks pale, and
> with a rising sigh he wisheth you in heaven.

("Lancaster" is the disrespectful name that Glendower uses for Henry.) Hotspur returns Glendower's praise with an ambiguous, "And you in hell, as oft as he hears Owen Glendower spoke of." Glendower, trying to make the best of a somewhat unpleasant conversation, responds,

> I cannot blame him: at my nativity
> The front of heaven was full of fiery shapes,
> Of burning cressets; and at my birth
> The frame and huge foundation of the earth
> Shaked like a coward.

But Percy is not content to leave it at that and turns the possibility of a quarrel into a full-blown argument with an insulting retort: "Why, so it would have done at the same season, if your mother's cat had but kittened, though yourself had never been born." Glendower insists, "The heavens were all on fire" and rages on in defense of his cosmically celebrated birth. This duel lasts for more than 20 lines as Hotspur continues his taunts and Glendower angrily responds, until their feud metamorphoses into a fight over the amount of land that Hotspur will be able to claim after their victory. In the interchanges between Hotspur and Glendower, the same dynamic that has been depicted in the exchanges between Hal and Falstaff is recapitulated. There is a brittle tension between the generations, with the young men showing contempt for their elders whom they guide into the role of buffoon. But while with Hal and Falstaff it is harmless play, in the case of Hotspur and Glendower it is a grandiose and dangerous posturing in preparation for war.

In Act III, scene 2, we finally see an encounter between Hal and his father, the king. After clearing the chamber of all the attendants, Henry addresses his son. "I know not whether God will have it so," he begins,

> For some displeasing service I have done,
> That, in his secret doom, out of my blood
> He'll breed revengement and a scourge for me;
> But thou dost in thy passages of life
> Make me believe that thou art only mark'd
> For the hot vengeance and the rod of heaven
> To punish my mistreadings. Tell me else,
> Could such inordinate and low desires,
> Such poor, such bare, such lewd, such mean attempts,
> Such barren pleasures, rude society,
> As thou art match'd withal and grafted to,
> Accompany the greatness of thy blood
> And hold their level with thy princely heart?

Unlike Falstaff's mock representation, Henry does not focus on Hal's companions, but rather first on himself and then on Hal. While Henry voices the common parental reproach, "What did I do to deserve a child like you?" his words are more than rhetoric. Because he is wracked by constant guilt and doubt over the way he acquired the throne, Henry suspects that Hal is fate's sly punishment for his usurpation.

It was clear from Hal's reply to Falstaff and from his subsequent behavior in the tavern that Hal intended to appease his father, but his initial reply in this scene shows just how thoroughly committed he is to doing so. His speech is filled with reverent courtesy. He accepts his father's indictment, admits his faults, and assures his father that he will purge himself of his dishonorable traits, begging him to "Find pardon on my true submission." His subordinating response allows Henry to vent his pent-up misery over Hal's previous defection as he compares Hal to those around him: to himself, as Hal seems not to have the dedication to his future and his reputation that Henry had; to Richard, as Hal seems nearer to Richard than to his own father as he wastes his resources in dissipation; and to Hotspur, who has gained renown for valor and leadership throughout the Christian world, the exact opposite of what Hal has spent his time doing. The king concludes,

> Why, Harry, do I tell thee of my foes,
> Which art my nearest and dearest enemy?
> Thou that art like enough, through vassal fear,
> Base inclination and the start of spleen

> To fight against me under Percy's pay,
> To dog his heels and curtsy at his frowns,
> To show how much thou art degenerate.

Such a spin on Hal's character gives the prince the opportunity to rival his father's painful eloquence with his own eloquent assertion of filial devotion. In response he neither compares himself to his father nor to Richard, but uses Hotspur as a standard against which to measure himself and which he vows to surpass:

> I will redeem all this on Percy's head
> And in the closing of some glorious day
> Be bold to tell you that I am your son;
> When I will wear a garment all of blood
> And stain my favors in a bloody mask,
> Which, washed away, shall scour my shame with it:
> And that shall be the day, whene'er it lights,
> That this same child of honour and renown,
> This gallant Hotspur, this all-praised knight,
> And your unthought-of Harry chance to meet.
> For every honor sitting on his helm,
> Would they were multitudes, and on my head
> My shames redoubled! for the time will come,
> That I shall make this northern youth exchange
> His glorious deeds for my indignities.
> Percy is but my factor, good my lord,
> To engross up glorious deeds on my behalf.

Hal ends by saying, "I will die a hundred thousand deaths/ Ere break the smallest parcel of this vow." His father responds by echoing Hal's rhetoric, saying, "A hundred thousand rebels die in this!" and adding, "Thou shalt have charge and sovereign trust herein," thus showing the two of them united not only in language but in purpose. Sir Walter Blunt then enters with the news that the rebels have assembled a mighty army at Shrewsbury. The king reviews the troops he has already set in the field and tells the prince, "On Wednesday next, you shall set forward; / On Thursday we ourselves will march."

The scene then shifts, not yet to the battlefield, but once again to the tavern where Falstaff is complaining of low spirits and asking Bardolph to "sing me a bawdy song, make me merry." As if he were an active participant in Hal's change of heart, he begins to tell himself that it is time to repent his vices. In his estimation, "Company, villainous company, hath been the spoil of me.... I was as virtuously given as a gentleman need be, virtuous enough." The ensuing catalogue Falstaff provides of his virtues shows how well he knows himself and with what ironic insight he is able to enjoy himself. He "swore little, diced not above seven times a week, went to a bawdy house not above once in a quarter of an hour; paid money that I borrowed, three of four times." But since falling on bad companions, Hal undoubtedly being chief among them in his inversion, "now I live all out of order, out of all compass."

When Hal and Poins come marching into the tavern playing the soldiers they shortly will be, they find Falstaff in the midst of an imbroglio with the Hostess, insisting that he has been robbed. Indeed, his pockets have been picked while he slept—Hal emptied them after he returned from his conversation with the sheriff at the end of Act II, scene 4. The joke made of it then was how little value there was in his pockets, and that his written accounts showed how much sack he drank and how little bread he ate. The joke now, typical of Falstaff, is his exaggeration of how much he has been robbed. When Hal confronts him about his lies and rebukes him more in rancor than in humor, Falstaff caves in wittily and winningly: "Dost thou hear, Hal? thou knowest in the state of innocency Adam fell; and what should poor Jack Falstaff do in the days of villainy? Thou seest I have more flesh than another man, and therefore more frailty." But the prince does not engage Falstaff in further antics. He tells him that he has returned the stolen money, which dismays Falstaff. Hal tells him that he is "good friends with my father, and may do anything," whereupon Falstaff exhorts him to "Rob me the exchequer." Hal ignores him except to tell him that he has put him at the head of a unit of foot soldiers. Giving a letter to Peto to bear to Prince John, Hal quits the tavern, rallying his ill-assorted comrades and crying, as if he were already Henry V, "The land is burning; Percy stands on high; / And either we or they must lower lie."

Act IV

As Act IV, scene 1, begins, Northumberland sends word to his son, Hotspur, that he is ill and will not be able to provide the troops that he has promised for the encounter with Henry's forces at Shrewsbury; nor will Glendower and his forces be available. Thus Hotspur and the Scot, Douglas, must face the massed forces of the king alone. Of particular interest to Hotspur is Hal's participation in the battle. Derisively he asks Vernon, who has brought news of the king's movements, "Where is his son, / The nimble-footed madcap Prince of Wales, / And his comrades, that daff'd the world aside, / And bid it pass?" Vernon's answer,

> All furnish'd, all in arms;
> ...
> I saw young Harry, with his beaver on,
> His cuisses on his thighs, gallantly armed
> Rise from the ground like feathered Mercury,

And vaulted with such ease into his seat,
As if an angel dropped down from the clouds,
To turn and wind a fiery Pegasus
And witch the world with noble horsemanship

disturbs and enflames Hotspur. "Worse than the sun in March," he frets, "This praise doth nourish agues," but he concludes, "Harry to Harry shall, hot horse to horse,/Meet, and ne'er part till one drop down a corse." Now roused and impassioned, Hotspur defies the disadvantage that his army faces and cries out, "Doomsday is near. Die all, die merrily."

As for the merriment in death, Shakespeare introduces Falstaff in the following scene as a gloss on Hotspur's recklessness. When Hotspur talks of all dying merrily, there is a heroic ring to his words. But when Falstaff responds to Hal's reproach over the condition of his rag-tag bunch of soldiers, saying, "Tut, tut, good enough to toss; food for powder, food for powder, they'll fill a pit as well as better. Tush, man, mortal men, mortal men," he is essentially portraying the same attitude as Hotspur, just in a more straightforwardly deplorable manner.

Despite the weakness of their battlefield position, Hotspur and Douglas are determined to fight. When Sir Walter Blunt comes from the king with an offer of peace and amnesty, Hotspur first rebuffs him, arguing with reasonable suspicion, "The king is kind; and well we know the King/ Knows at what time to promise, when to pay." He continues, recapitulating his family's past assistance to the king and what he considers the king's betrayal. Blunt dismisses Hotspur's long and defiant indictment, asking, "Shall I return this answer to the King?" Surprisingly, Hotspur says no. He asks for time to think and safe passage for the man he will send to the king's camp with his answer. Blunt is encouraged and says he hopes the rebels will "accept of grace and love," and Hotspur responds, "And may be so we shall."

Act V

When Worcester, who goes as the messenger to Henry's camp, returns reporting the opposite of what occurred there, Hotspur's quick temper is re-inflamed. In reality, the king repeated to Worcester Blunt's offer of amnesty for the rebels if they would yield to his authority, but upon his return from the king's camp, Worcester tells Sir Richard Vernon, "My nephew [Hotspur] must not know . . . /The liberal and kind offer of the King." His chief reason, suspicion of the king, does claim some merit. It is the same suspicion Hotspur expressed to Sir Walter Blunt that even if the king were to honor his word now, he would nevertheless always remain suspicious of them:

It is not possible, it cannot be,
The king should keep his word in loving us;

> He will suspect us still and find a time
> To punish this offence in other faults:
> Suspicion all our lives shall be stuck full of eyes;
> For treason is but trusted like the fox,
> Who, ne'er so tame, so cherished and locked up,
> Will have a wild trick of his ancestors.
> Look how we can, or sad or merrily,
> Interpretation will misquote our looks,
> And we shall feed like oxen at a stall,
> The better cherished, still the nearer death.

(A look forward to *Henry IV, Part II*, Act IV, scene 2, in which Prince John promises amity to the rebels but arrests them once their armies are dispersed, will show how well-founded is Worcester's suspicion.)

During Worcester's pre-battle interview with the king in his camp, Hal offers "to save the blood on either side," and challenges Hotspur to single combat. The king praises his offer but rejects it for unspecified "considerations infinite." As the king's forces await Worcester's response, Hal encounters Falstaff, who tells him that he would rather be going to bed than into battle. Hal responds, "Why, thou owest God a death," and leaves him. ("Death" was pronounced as if it ended with a "t" and not a "th," thus suggesting an identity with the word "debt.") "'Tis not due yet," Falstaff retorts once alone. "I would be loath to pay him before his day. What need I be so forward with him that calls not on me?" He then considers and comments on the accepted answer to his question, the same motive that inspired the battle-readiness of both Hal, Hotspur, and the majority of the combatants: honor. "Honor pricks me on," Falstaff says. But from his mouth this is a hypothesis, not a positive assertion. "But how if honor prick me off when I come on? How then?" Falstaff challenges the virtue of honor and questions the dedication of one's life to it. What, after all, does honor really offer?

> Can honour set to a leg? no: or
> an arm? no: or take away the grief of a wound? no.
> Honour hath no skill in surgery, then? no. What is
> honour? a word. What is in that word honour? what
> is that honour? air. A trim reckoning! Who hath it?
> he that died o' Wednesday. Doth he feel it? no.
> Doth he hear it? no. 'Tis insensible, then. Yea,
> to the dead. But will it not live with the living?
> no. Why? detraction will not suffer it. Therefore
> I'll none of it.

Falstaff concludes: "Honor is a mere scutcheon," a symbolic shield with a coat of arms, but worthless because it cannot protect one from physical harm.

In Act V, scene 3, the battle rages on. After the rebel Douglas kills Sir Walter Blunt, Hal and Falstaff meet on the battlefield. Falstaff tries to engage the prince in his usual way, first claiming that he has killed Hotspur. Hal contradicts him, telling him that Hotspur is still alive, and when Hal asks to borrow Falstaff's sword, Falstaff offers him his pistol but tosses him a bottle of sack in its place, getting in response only Hal's rebuke, "What, is it a time to jest and dally now?" After he leaves, Falstaff, referring to the corpse of Sir Walter Blunt, says, "I like not such grinning honor as Sir Walter hath. Give me life; which if I can save, so; if not, honor comes unlooked for, and there's an end." Falstaff defines honor not as the crown and glory of life but as the opposite of life, a function of death.

There are several challenges Hal faces on the battlefield by which he can redeem himself if he meets them successfully, asserting his valor and repairing his reputation. He engages in the first when he saves his father from Douglas, after which the king says, "Thou hast redeemed thy opinion, / And showed that mak'st some tender of my life / In this fair rescue thou hast brought to me." His use of the word "tender" to describe Hal's consideration of his life implies that Henry fears Hal may be concocting a plot of his own to depose him. The prince, shocked and indignant, responds:

> O God! they did me too much injury
> That ever said I hearken'd for your death.
> If it were so, I might have let alone
> The insulting hand of Douglas over you,
> Which would have been as speedy in your end
> As all the poisonous potions in the world
> And saved the treacherous labor of your son.

Thus does Hal justify his actions to his father, reassuring him that he has no desire to take the crown before his due time and that his filial devotion is genuine.

Hal's next challenge is his face-off with Hostpur, who has served as both his political rival and his father's standard of measure against which he has failed in comparison. When Hal finally meets Hotspur in combat, he vanquishes him, proving both his physical superiority and that of his reformed character. Occurring simultaneously is the fight between Falstaff and Douglas, during which Falstaff, in order to save himself, "falls down as if he were dead." After Hal delivers a farewell to the slain Hotspur and offers him the praise that he admits he would not utter were Hotspur still alive, the prince turns to see

Falstaff fallen. Thinking him dead, he delivers a farewell to him also, although hardly one of heartbreak:

> I could have better spared a better man:
> O, I should have a heavy miss of thee,
> If I were much in love with vanity!
> Death hath not struck so fat a deer to-day,
> Though many dearer, in this bloody fray.
> Embowell'd will I see thee by and by:
> Till then in blood by noble Percy lie.

Falstaff rises when Hal is gone, and he continues his meditations on honor, death, and life, that have been woven throughout the battle scenes. Explaining his feigned death, Falstaff says, "'twas time to counterfeit, or that hot termagant Scot had paid me scot and lot too." He does not only speak but also reflects on his own words: "Counterfeit? I lie, I am no counterfeit: to die is to be a counterfeit; for he is but the counterfeit of a man who hath not the life of a man: but to counterfeit dying, when a man thereby liveth, is to be no counterfeit, but the true and perfect image of life indeed." When he notices Hotspur lying dead nearby, he stabs him once more just in case Hotspur, too, should be counterfeiting. And then he plays an old Falstaffian trick and decides to claim Hotspur as his own prize. When Hal sees Falstaff again, the initial doubt he experiences over whether Falstaff is truly alive is quickly overtaken by his astonishment at Falstaff's claim to have killed Hotspur. Falstaff characteristically defends this claim through an inversion of reality before he offers his fantastic tale. "Lord, Lord," Falstaff says of the prince's claim to have killed Hotspur, "how this world is given to lying." But rather than engaging him now, Hal, who is with his brother, Prince John, humors Falstaff, demonstrating to John that he has become remote from Falstaff and from his own crude past. Now unwilling to play a part in Falstaff's game, Hal shows John that he is dedicated to his family and his future as king.

A major part of the rebellion crushed, *Henry IV, Part I* ends as the king sets forth to fight Hotspur's father and his allies.

KEY PASSAGES IN *HENRY IV, PART I*

Act I, i, 1-33

Henry: So shaken as we are, so wan with care,
Find we a time for frighted peace to pant,
And breathe short-winded accents of new broils
To be commenced in strands afar remote.
No more the thirsty entrance of this soil
Shall daub her lips with her own children's blood;
Nor more shall trenching war channel her fields,
Nor bruise her flowerets with the armed hoofs
Of hostile paces: those opposed eyes,
Which, like the meteors of a troubled heaven,
All of one nature, of one substance bred,
Did lately meet in the intestine shock
And furious close of civil butchery
Shall now, in mutual well-beseeming ranks,
March all one way and be no more opposed
Against acquaintance, kindred and allies:
The edge of war, like an ill-sheathed knife,
No more shall cut his master. Therefore, friends,
As far as to the sepulchre of Christ,
Whose soldier now, under whose blessed cross
We are impressed and engaged to fight,
Forthwith a power of English shall we levy;
Whose arms were molded in their mothers' womb
To chase these pagans in those holy fields
Over whose acres walked those blessed feet
Which fourteen hundred years ago were nailed
For our advantage on the bitter cross.
But this our purpose now is twelve month old,
And bootless 'tis to tell you we will go:
Therefore we meet not now. Then let me hear

> Of you, my gentle cousin Westmoreland,
> What yesternight our council did decree
> In forwarding this dear expedience.

These are the opening words of the play. Henry, the king, is addressing his court. A significant problem for some readers who are just beginning to get acquainted with Shakespeare is understanding the language his characters speak. The problem is not with the meaning of the words themselves but with hearing the voice that is speaking them and forming a sense of the speaking character, for in Shakespeare character is formed by speech. It is possible for new readers to find all of the characters' speeches blurring into one common pattern, which may be dismissed as a kind of difficult Elizabethan poetic language. But close observation shows that each character actually has his or her own characteristic voice. In the case of the present speech, this is Henry speaking, not Shakespeare.

Henry is a master rhetorician. The repetition of the word "so" in the very first line alerts readers to that: "*So* shaken as we are, *so* wan with care." By repeating this emphatic adjective, Henry is impressing the heavy weight of his responsibilities and suggesting the immense burden he must bear as a king. In the second line he reveals what everyone knows this burden to be: civil war. But rather than referring directly to war, Henry speaks of its counterpart, peace, calling it "frighted," for it has been frightened by war. Rhetorically this allows Henry to avoid the aggressive idea of war, keeping memories of brutal and bloody past events out of his listeners' minds, and to focus instead on the more fragile and comforting idea of peace. For now, he suggests, peace can catch its breath: "Find we a time for frighted peace to pant." The implication seems to be that war is now over and peace can breathe easy, but this is not so. In fact, peace will "breathe short-winded accents of new broils," indicating that new conflicts are on the horizon. But Henry promises that these new battles will be different from the ones he has implied are ended.

> No more the thirsty entrance of this soil
> Shall daub her lips with her own children's blood;
> Nor more shall trenching war channel her fields,
> Nor bruise her flowerets with the armed hoofs
> Of hostile paces.

The king is lamenting what has occurred, even though his rebellion against Richard II was the cause of it, and assuring his court that the battles soon to come will not be countryman against countryman, like those of the past. He refers to the past evils not as things that have happened, but as things that now will not happen. After discord and division, he promises unity:

"Opposed eyes . . . Shall . . . in mutual well-beseeming ranks / March all one way and be no more opposed / Against acquaintance, kindred, and allies." He does not speak of mortal men, many of whom have lost their lives in his war, but instead represents them with the more innocuous image of eyes that, once having faced each other in opposition, will now all face in the same direction. War itself becomes "an ill-sheathed knife" that he pledges to carry properly by shifting his energies from civil war to holy war and beginning a crusade. His rhetorical pitch then turns religious, turning the attention of his listeners from the recent civil war, which he instigated by deposing the rightful king to secure the throne for himself, to more righteous images of

> . . . pagans in those holy fields
> Over whose acres walked those blessed feet
> Which fourteen hundred years ago were nailed
> For our advantage on the bitter cross.

Here Henry is using the crucifixion, a very emotionally charged religious concept, to his own rhetorical advantage. He distracts his court from the truth of his own crimes by focusing their attention on crimes committed by others against their own personal salvations. His next utterance reinforces the emptiness of these words:

> But this our purpose now is twelve month old,
> And bootless 'tis to tell you we will go:
> Therefore we meet not now.

Directly after promising an end to civil war and a shift in focus to battles in which the people can fight united, Henry reveals that they are not going to make preparations for a holy war in Jerusalem after all. Westmoreland has just arrived in haste with news of the latest battle in the war's "trenching" channels in the English "fields," "daub[ing] her lips with her own children's blood," and "bruising her flowerets with the armed hoofs/Of hostile paces." In fact, Henry will be continuing the very same type of war that he has just assured the people was ended.

Through the devious rhetoric of this first speech, Shakespeare establishes the underhanded character of Henry IV, who uses false promises and redirection to camouflage his true objectives.

Act I, ii, 199-221

Hal: I know you all, and will awhile uphold
The unyoked humor of your idleness:

Yet herein will I imitate the sun,
Who doth permit the base contagious clouds
To smother up his beauty from the world,
That, when he please again to be himself,
Being wanted, he may be more wond'red at,
By breaking through the foul and ugly mists
Of vapors that did seem to strangle him.
If all the year were playing holidays,
To sport would be as tedious as to work;
But when they seldom come, they wished-for come,
And nothing pleaseth but rare accidents.
So, when this loose behavior I throw off
And pay the debt I never promised,
By how much better than my word I am,
By so much shall I falsify men's hopes;
And like bright metal on a sullen ground,
My reformation, glitt'ring o'er my fault,
Shall show more goodly and attract more eyes
Than that which hath no foil to set it off.
I'll so offend, to make offence a skill;
Redeeming time when men think least I will.

Although not his first utterance, this is the first speech from Henry's son Hal that shows his true self, a soliloquy in which he unveils his character to the audience, reveals the way he thinks, and shows his rhetorical brilliance. Admitting that he currently acts the role of a disreputable citizen and unfit heir, Hal explains how this marked reputation will only make his transformation into an honorable and upstanding king more admirable. This is the prince who, as King Henry V, will utter some of the most rousing, musical, martial, and magnificent speeches in all of Shakespeare. In this soliloquy, he shows himself to be the legitimate son of his father and his proper heir, displaying the same Machiavellian talent as his father, the same skill for manipulating his image. His father uses rhetoric to distract from his actual intentions, and Hal uses his behavior to the same end. No less aware than his father of their insecure hold on the throne, Hal has established a strategy of distraction, deliberately casting himself as a dissolute, irresponsible man unfit for ascension to the throne not because of the questionable way his father won it, but because of the insufficiency of his own character. Thus when the time comes for him to perform his reformation and take the throne, the issue at hand will not be the legitimacy of his crown but the awe-inspiring spectacle of his transformation.

Act I, iii, 158-255

Hotspur: But shall it be that you, that set the crown
Upon the head of this forgetful man
And for his sake wear the detested blot
Of murderous subornation, shall it be,
That you a world of curses undergo,
Being the agents, or base second means,
The cords, the ladder, or the hangman rather?
O, pardon me that I descend so low,
To show the line and the predicament
Wherein you range under this subtle king;
Shall it for shame be spoken in these days,
Or fill up chronicles in time to come,
That men of your nobility and power
Did gage them both in an unjust behalf,
As both of you—God pardon it!—have done,
To put down Richard, that sweet lovely rose,
An plant this thorn, this canker, Bolingbroke?
And shall it in more shame be further spoken,
That you are fooled, discarded and shook off
By him for whom these shames ye underwent?
No; yet time serves wherein you may redeem
Your banished honors and restore yourselves
Into the good thoughts of the world again,
Revenge the jeering and disdained contempt
Of this proud king, who studies day and night
To answer all the debt he owes to you
Even with the bloody payment of your deaths:
Therefore, I say—

Worcester: Peace, cousin, say no more:
And now I will unclasp a secret book,
And to your quick-conceiving discontents
I'll read you matter deep and dangerous,
As full of peril and adventurous spirit
As to o'er-walk a current roaring loud
On the unsteadfast footing of a spear.

Hotspur: If he fall in, good night! or sink or swim:
Send danger from the east unto the west,
So honor cross it from the north to south,

And let them grapple: O, the blood more stirs
To rouse a lion than to start a hare!

Northumberland: Imagination of some great exploit
Drives him beyond the bounds of patience.

Hotspur: By heaven, methinks it were an easy leap,
To pluck bright honor from the pale-faced moon,
Or dive into the bottom of the deep,
Where fathom-line could never touch the ground,
And pluck up drowned honor by the locks;
So he that doth redeem her thence might wear
Without corrival, all her dignities:
But out upon this half-faced fellowship!

Worcester: He apprehends a world of figures here,
But not the form of what he should attend.
Good cousin, give me audience for a while.

Hotspur: I cry you mercy.

Worcester: Those same noble Scots
That are your prisoners,—

Hotspur: I'll keep them all;
By God, he shall not have a Scot of them;
No, if a Scot would save his soul, he shall not:
I'll keep them, by this hand.

Worcester: You start away
And lend no ear unto my purposes.
Those prisoners you shall keep.

Hotspur: Nay, I will; that's flat:
He said he would not ransom Mortimer;
Forbad my tongue to speak of Mortimer;
But I will find him when he lies asleep,
And in his ear I'll holla 'Mortimer!'
Nay, I'll have a starling shall be taught to speak
Nothing but 'Mortimer,' and give it him
To keep his anger still in motion.

Worcester: Hear you, cousin; a word.

Hotspur: All studies here I solemnly defy,
Save how to gall and pinch this Bolingbroke:
And that same sword-and-buckler Prince of Wales,
But that I think his father loves him not
And would be glad he met with some mischance,
I would have him poisoned with a pot of ale.

Worcester: Farewell, kinsman: I'll talk to you
When you are better tempered to attend.

Northumberland: Why, what a wasp-stung and impatient fool
Art thou to break into this woman's mood,
Tying thine ear to no tongue but thine own!

Hotspur: Why, look you, I am whipped and scourged with rods,
Nettled and stung with pismires, when I hear
Of this vile politician, Bolingbroke.
In Richard's time,—what do you call the place?—
A plague upon it, it is in Gloucestershire;
'Twas where the madcap duke his uncle kept,
His uncle York; where I first bowed my knee
Unto this king of smiles, this Bolingbroke,—
'Sblood!—When you and he came back from Ravenspurgh.

Northumberland: At Berkley castle.

Hotspur: You say true:
Why, what a candy deal of courtesy
This fawning greyhound then did proffer me!
"Look, when his infant fortune came to age,"
And "gentle Harry Percy," and "kind cousin;"
O, the devil take such cozeners! God forgive me!
Good uncle, tell your tale; I have done.

Worcester: Nay, if you have not, to it again;
We will stay your leisure.

Hotspur: I have done, i' faith.

Hotspur's rant comes after Henry has demanded his prisoners but refused to ransom Mortimer, branding him a traitor. The sweep, imagination, and power of Hotspur's language place him in the ranks of the lead characters of the play. As well as advancing the psychology of the rebellion, Hotspur's resentments illuminate its true causes. Additionally, and perhaps most importantly, Hotspur's language presents his character. Unlike the king and the prince, he is not a deliberate speaker. He is impulsive; they are wily. He is direct; they are designing. Although he is plotting against the king, his speech is not planned, as are the words of both King Henry and Hal. The king and the prince deal in hypocrisy, pretending to be what they are not, but Hotspur simply is what he is.

As his nickname suggests, Hotspur is hot-tempered rather than temperate. He is spurred to action by the racing of his blood, and once it gets going neither he nor anyone else is able to restrain it, as the frustration of his father and his uncle shows. It is the mark of his heroism, but in the political context of such practiced masters of deception as the king and the prince, it is also his downfall. The surging energy that causes his mind to overrun his tongue, as is evidenced by his inability to recall the name of Berkley Castle, has often been presented on the stage by making Hotspur a stutterer.

Act II, iv, 466-502

Hal: [T]here is a devil haunts thee in the likeness of an
old fat man; a tun of man is thy companion. Why
dost thou converse with that trunk of humors, that
bolting-hutch of beastliness, that swollen parcel
of dropsies, that huge bombard of sack, that stuffed
cloak-bag of guts, that roasted Manningtree ox with
the pudding in his belly, that reverend vice, that
grey iniquity, that father ruffian, that vanity in
years? Wherein is he good, but to taste sack and
drink it? wherein neat and cleanly, but to carve a
capon and eat it? wherein cunning, but in craft?
wherein crafty, but in villainy? wherein villainous,
but in all things? wherein worthy, but in nothing?
. . . That villainous abominable misleader of youth,
Falstaff, that old white-bearded Satan.

. . .

Falstaff: But to say I know more harm in him than in myself,
were to say more than I know. That he is old, the
more the pity, his white hairs do witness it; but

that he is, saving your reverence, a whoremaster,
that I utterly deny. If sack and sugar be a fault,
God help the wicked! if to be old and merry be a
sin, then many an old host that I know is damned: if
to be fat be to be hated, then Pharaoh's lean kine
are to be loved. No, my good lord; banish Peto,
banish Bardolph, banish Poins: but for sweet Jack
Falstaff, kind Jack Falstaff, true Jack Falstaff,
valiant Jack Falstaff, and therefore more valiant,
being, as he is, old Jack Falstaff, banish not him
thy Harry's company, banish not him thy Harry's
company: banish plump Jack, and banish all the world.

Hal: I do, I will.

Together in the Boar's Head Tavern, Hal and Falstaff are imagining and rehearsing the encounter that Hal is going to have with Henry when he must account for his disreputable way of living. Hal is playing his father, while Falstaff mimes Hal's own princely self. Hal's depiction of Falstaff is made up of hard words, yet it is not much different from how the prince usually insults him, seemingly (but not quite surely) in jest with the intent of observing Falstaff's rebound.

In Falstaff's reply as the prince, he achieves a tenderness, which, while it seems to be self-reflective, is actually an expression of his affection for Hal. Falstaff's witty speech concludes with a suppressed but honest expression of sentiment. Because of that, Hal's laconic four-beat response, "I do. I will," is all the more affecting, even shocking. The reader is struck by the realization that Hal truly means what he says, that he has pried himself loose from the joking exchange and is saying flatly what will be, no matter what sentiment should stand against it

Act III, ii, 4-91

Henry: I know not whether God will have it so,
For some displeasing service I have done,
That, in his secret doom, out of my blood
He'll breed revengement and a scourge for me;
But thou dost in thy passages of life
Make me believe that thou art only marked
For the hot vengeance and the rod of heaven
To punish my mistreadings. Tell me else,
Could such inordinate and low desires,
Such poor, such bare, such lewd, such mean attempts,

Such barren pleasures, rude society,
As thou art matched withal and grafted to,
Accompany the greatness of thy blood
And hold their level with thy princely heart?

Hal: So please your majesty, I would I could
Quit all offences with as clear excuse
As well as I am doubtless I can purge
Myself of many I am charged withal:
Yet such extenuation let me beg,
As, in reproof of many tales devised,
which oft the ear of greatness needs must hear,
By smiling pick-thanks and base news-mongers,
I may, for some things true, wherein my youth
Hath faulty wandered and irregular,
Find pardon on my true submission.

The first encounter between the king and his son takes place not only in the context of the exchanges between Hal and Falstaff, but it also follows the duel of words in the previous scene between Hotspur and Glendower. That scene presents a model of discord and disrespect. Hotspur continually spurns and taunts Glendower, who repeatedly attempts to assert himself, maintain his sense of his own supernatural powers, and restrain his resentment against Hotspur's surly jibes. Their interaction mirrors more venomously the interactions between Hal and Falstaff.

Unlike Hal's stance in all his exchanges with Falstaff, the prince is neither ironic nor pugnacious when talking to his father. Nor is there a sign of that ambivalent affection he clearly feels for Falstaff. Hal's affection for Falstaff is a real affection that he continually suppresses as he expresses it through his taunts. With his father Hal presents a formal, courtly, and rock-solid filial devotion that is stronger than his character and that dominates him. When Hal speaks with Falstaff, his language is free and easy, full of fooling, spontaneous and rendered in prose. To his father he speaks inside the discipline of verse. The syntax of his sentences is complex, but he never loses control over its intricacy.

Theirs is a conversation between two master rhetoricians. By what Hal does not say he shows himself to perhaps even surpass his father in the art of self-creation. Henry's speech reveals his character as Hal's does not:

Henry: God pardon thee! yet let me wonder, Harry,
At thy affections, which do hold a wing
Quite from the flight of all thy ancestors.

Thy place in council thou hast rudely lost.
Which by thy younger brother is supplied,
And art almost an alien to the hearts
Of all the court and princes of my blood:
The hope and expectation of thy time
Is ruin'd, and the soul of every man
Prophetically doth forethink thy fall.
Had I so lavish of my presence been,
So common-hackney'd in the eyes of men,
So stale and cheap to vulgar company,
Opinion, that did help me to the crown,
Had still kept loyal to possession
And left me in reputeless banishment,
A fellow of no mark nor likelihood.
By being seldom seen, I could not stir
But like a comet I was wonder'd at;
That men would tell their children "This is he;"
Others would say "Where, which is Bolingbroke?"
And then I stole all courtesy from heaven,
And dress'd myself in such humility
That I did pluck allegiance from men's hearts,
Loud shouts and salutations from their mouths,
Even in the presence of the crowned king.
Thus did I keep my person fresh and new;
My presence, like a robe pontifical,
Ne'er seen but wondered at: and so my state,
Seldom but sumptuous, showed like a feast
And won by rareness such solemnity.
The skipping king, he ambled up and down
With shallow jesters and rash bavin wits,
Soon kindled and soon burnt; carded his state,
Mingled his royalty with capering fools,
Had his great name profaned with their scorns
And gave his countenance, against his name,
To laugh at gibing boys and stand the push
Of every beardless vain comparative,
Grew a companion to the common streets,
Enfeoff'd himself to popularity;
That, being daily swallow'd by men's eyes,
They surfeited with honey and began
To loathe the taste of sweetness, whereof a little
More than a little is by much too much.

So when he had occasion to be seen,
He was but as the cuckoo is in June,
Heard, not regarded; seen, but with such eyes
As, sick and blunted with community,
Afford no extraordinary gaze,
Such as is bent on sun-like majesty
When it shines seldom in admiring eyes;
But rather drowzed and hung their eyelids down,
Slept in his face and rendered such aspect
As cloudy men use to their adversaries,
Being with his presence glutted, gorged and full.
And in that very line, Harry, standest thou;
For thou has lost thy princely privilege
With vile participation: not an eye
But is a-weary of thy common sight,
Save mine, which hath desired to see thee more;
Which now doth that I would not have it do,
Make blind itself with foolish tenderness.

The king does not only tell Hal about the effect of Hal's recalcitrance upon him, but he also shares with him the strategies that he used to gain his power. He tells his son how he made the people admire him and want him as a leader. Hal never reveals to his father the content of his first soliloquy, in which he details his campaign to manipulate his image by appearing dissolute so that when he shakes off his youthful folly at the time of his coronation he will appear more wonderful. He withholds this so he can perform for his father the same metamorphosis he will perform for England.

Act IV, i, 59-82

Worcester: But yet I would your father had been here.
The quality and hair of our attempt
Brooks no division: it will be thought
By some, that know not why he is away,
That wisdom, loyalty and mere dislike
Of our proceedings kept the earl from hence:
And think how such an apprehension
May turn the tide of fearful faction
And breed a kind of question in our cause;
For well you know we of the offering side
Must keep aloof from strict arbitrement,
And stop all sight-holes, every loop from whence

> The eye of reason may pry in upon us:
> This absence of your father's draws a curtain,
> That shows the ignorant a kind of fear
> Before not dreamt of.
>
> *Hotspur:*   You strain too far.
> I rather of his absence make this use:
> It lends a luster and more great opinion,
> A larger dare to our great enterprise,
> Than if the earl were here; for men must think,
> If we without his help can make a head
> To push against a kingdom, with his help
> We shall o'erturn it topsy-turvy down.
> Yet all goes well, yet all our joints are whole.

Although the manifest content of this conversation is the fact that Northumberland, because he is ill, will not lead his forces with the rebels against the king in the battle of Shrewsbury, at its core is a discussion of how events can be variously interpreted—in modern jargon, what kind of "spin" can be put on them.

Worcester's regret at Northumberland's absence does not focus on their resulting weakened military force but rather on the fear that his absence "will be thought / By some, that know not why he is away, / That wisdom, loyalty and mere dislike / Of our proceedings kept the earl from hence." His greatest concern is that Northumberland's absence may reflect badly on their cause and encourage a scrutiny of their motives, which Worcester would rather not invite. It may even suggest that they are afraid.

Hotspur, on the other hand, "spins" it another way: "I rather of his absence make this use."

Characteristically, he finds in it a chance for greater honor and glory. It "lends a luster," shows their fight to be "a larger dare," and, he argues, suggests what they will be able to accomplish later when forces are joined if they can succeed now without full resources.

Their concern with how events may be variously interpreted suggests the complexity of human consciousness and perception and the power of rhetoric to control how things appear. It also signifies a concern for the opinion and favor of the people. Military might or assumed authority are not sufficient in themselves to cement any individual's or faction's hold on power. Such an observation had particular significance as the seventeenth century was approaching and England's sometimes unstable monarchy faced the moment in history when it would be toppled by a popular revolt in the 1640s.

Act IV, ii, 62-73

Hal: ... [T]ell me, Jack, whose fellows are these that come after?

Falstaff: Mine, Hal, mine.

Hal: I did never see such pitiful rascals.

Falstaff: Tut, tut; good enough to toss; food for powder, food
for powder; they'll fill a pit as well as better:
tush, man, mortal men, mortal men.

Westmoreland: Ay, but, Sir John, methinks they are exceeding poor
and bare, too beggarly.

Falstaff: Faith, for their poverty, I know not where they had
that; and for their bareness, I am sure they never learned that of me.

Falstaff's cavalier attitude here toward the sacrifice of human life to war seems bound to shock, and for the moralist it is particularly distressing. As much as one may approve his credo, "Give me life," proclaimed on the battlefield in the face of death at Act V, scene 3, line 59, this conversation with Hal as well as Falstaff's earlier confession, beginning at line 11 of Act IV, scene 2, makes it clear that this is an entirely egocentric creed. "If I be not ashamed of my soldiers, I am a soused gurnet," Falstaff says mischievously. But this is more than mischief: "I have misused the king's press damnably. I have got, in exchange of a hundred and fifty soldiers, three hundred and odd pounds. I press me none but good house-holders," men who can buy their way out of service. In their place he has drafted "slaves as ragged as Lazarus in the painted cloth." When questioned about them, his dismissal of their unworthiness as soldiers is that they are perfectly fit as cannon fodder. If this apparent disregard for humanity should press too heavily on our regard for Falstaff, Shakespeare does not leave it as Falstaff's last words. When Westmoreland challenges him, saying, "Ay, but, Sir John, methinks they are exceeding poor and bare, too beggarly," Falstaff springs back with an instance of his old, self-mocking wit, "Faith, for their poverty, I know not where they had that; and for their bareness, I am sure they never learned that of me."

What can be charged against Falstaff, then, is that he puts his interests above that of others, that he gains wealth through the exploitation of other men, and that the nature of that exploitation is to lead them to their death. Although two wrongs do not make a right, a mirror does reflect the figure of the world in front of it, and in this brutal reduction Falstaff is an exact mirror of the world of the king, the prince, and the rebels, however stripped of the decorations of honor, glory, and purpose that are used to obscure its clarity.

Act IV, iii, 112-113

Sir Walter Blunt: I would you would accept of grace and love.

Hotspur: And may be so we shall.

What Sir Walter wishes Hotspur would accept is the king's offer of conciliation and amnesty to the rebels before the battle. At line 41, Blunt reports,

> ... If that the king
> Have any way your good deserts forgot,
> Which he confesseth to be manifold,
> He bids you name your griefs; and with all speed
> You shall have your desires with interest
> And pardon absolute for yourself and these
> Herein misled by your suggestion.

Hotspur responds at length and wrathfully, first noting, "The King is kind; and well we know the King / Knows at what time to promise, when to pay." He then details Henry's offenses committed against the Percies and against Richard, "the king he deposed." After this long indictment, Sir Walter asks, reasonably, "Shall I return this answer [of defiance] to the King?" But Hotspur, uncharacteristically, says no, he will think about his response and send his answer by his uncle, Worcester, in the morning. It is then that Blunt offers his wish that Hotspur accept the king's terms and Hotspur says he may.

What happens after this conference, when seen in the context of Falstaff's cynicism regarding his recruits in the previous scene, shows how accurate a mirror Falstaff is. The king repeats his offer to Worcester. Worcester returns to Hotspur with a lie saying that the king offered only defiance and they must fight. The contempt for life that is involved in the practice of war and the exploitation of men for one's own gain, which Falstaff brings to the foreground in the previous comedic part of *Henry IV, Part I*, is repeated in this heroic section of the story without the comfort of comic relief.

Act V, i, 121-141

Falstaff: Hal, if thou see me down in the battle and bestride me, so; 'tis a point of friendship.

Hal: Nothing but a colossus can do thee that friendship. Say thy prayers, and farewell.

Falstaff: I would 'twere bed-time, Hal, and all well.

Hal: Why, thou owest God a death. *(Exit)*

Falstaff: 'Tis not due yet; I would be loath to pay him before his day. What need I be so forward with him that calls not on me? Well, 'tis no matter; honor pricks me on. Yea, but how if honor prick me off when I come on? how then? Can honour set to a leg? no: or an arm? no: or take away the grief of a wound? no. Honor hath no skill in surgery, then? no. What is honor? a word. What is in that word honor? what is that honor? air. A trim reckoning! Who hath it? he that died o' Wednesday. Doth he feel it? no. Doth he hear it? no. 'Tis insensible, then. Yea, to the dead. But will it not live with the living? no. Why? detraction will not suffer it. Therefore I'll none of it. Honor is a mere scutcheon: and so ends my catechism.

Falstaff's request comes after Henry has just finished his short speech sending his soldiers into battle. Falstaff asks Hal to look after him and protect him if Hal should find him fallen. However jokingly, the prince denies the request. Later, when Hal does see Falstaff fallen, in Act V, scene 4, he does not check to see if Falstaff is alive or dead but instead assumes he is dead and wonders with ironic detachment "could not all this flesh/Keep in a little life?"

After Hal rejects Falstaff's request for help on the battlefield, Falstaff says he wishes "'twere bedtime . . . and all well." The prince answers him without consolation, saying that he owes "God a death," with the word "death" also suggesting "debt." In response to that Falstaff begins his famous catechism on honor, reducing honor to a word that signifies nothing but a cheap decoration adorning a grave. The equation of death and honor is cemented shortly after, at the end of scene 3. Falstaff has failed to engage the prince in foolery as he formerly had been and, standing alone over the corpse of Sir Walter Blunt, he says, "I like not such grinning honor as Sir Walter hath. Give me life."

Act V, iv, 155-156

Hal: For my part, if a lie may do thee grace,
I'll gild it with the happiest terms I have.

Hal, in the company of his brother, Prince John, is speaking to Falstaff, whom he took for dead when last he saw him. Now Falstaff, very much alive, is lugging Hotspur's body and claiming that he has slain him, when in fact it was Hal who killed Hotspur in Act V, scene 4, beginning at line 58, one of the climactic moments of the play and a defining moment for Hal. By killing Hotspur, Hal redeems his own honor, glory, and reputation, not just by virtue of this victory but because this victory invests him with the honor, glory, and reputation that had belonged to Hotspur.

Hal's magnanimity to Falstaff when Falstaff is usurping Hal's definitive triumph seems to embody the sweetest disposition the prince has shown him throughout the play. There is no goading, teasing, or berating. When John comments that Falstaff's tall tale of his victory over Hotspur "is the strangest tale that ever I heard," Hal simply says to his brother, "This is the strangest fellow, brother John." Hal's willingness to "gild" Falstaff's tale with a lie if it will "do [him] grace" recalls Falstaff's first conversation with Hal in Act I, scene 2, at line 18, in which Falstaff predicted that when Hal becomes king "grace thou wilt have none . . . not so much as will serve to be prologue to an egg and butter." Hal now shows Falstaff that he does indeed have grace enough to expend some graciously on him. However, Hal's apparent magnanimity actually establishes a greater distance from Falstaff, as it differs so greatly from their previous interactions. While Falstaff continues to play, Hal does not, and thus this is less an act of friendship than any number of insults or derogations might be.

LIST OF CHARACTERS IN *HENRY IV, PART I*

Bardolph is one of Falstaff's companions, notable for how red his nose has become because of his drinking.

Sir Walter Blunt is a nobleman loyal to the king who conveys news of battles, advises the king, and negotiates with the rebels in the king's name.

The **carriers** are two coachmen setting out for London early in the morning carrying goods and passengers.

The **chamberlain** is a servant at an inn who tells Gadshill that one of the travelers in the coach will be carrying a sum of money, thus providing information for the robbery Falstaff is planning.

Archibald, Earl of Douglas is one of the rebels fighting against Henry.

Sir John Falstaff is the fat, old, dissolute, and disreputable knight who is Hal's companion. He is famous for his wit, intellectual dexterity, and profound love of life.

Francis is a waiter, or drawer, at the tavern whom Hal and Poins tease and confuse as he is trying to do his job.

Gadshill is an associate of Falstaff who joins him in the robbery of the carriers.

Owen Glendower is a Welsh adversary of the king, in league with the Percies, and Mortimer's father-in-law. Glendower is a colorful, almost comic figure who believes he is a magician with supernatural powers. Glendower does not take part in the battle at Shrewsbury for reasons never given.

Hal (Henry, Prince of Wales) is the son of King Henry IV and heir to the English throne. At the start of the play, Hal seems to be a rebellious and dissipated young man, spending his time in wild and even unlawful behavior and with low companions. By the end of the play, he redeems himself in his father's eyes and shows himself to be made of the same mettle as his father. He is both heroic in battle and politically adept.

King Henry IV known as Bolingbroke, is the son of John of Gaunt. Exiled by King Richard II, Bolingbroke deposed him after returning to England. Now king of England, Henry is at war on several fronts to protect his power. He is troubled not only by rebels against his rule, including some who once supported him, but also by the rebellion of his own son against his authority.

Hotspur (Henry Percy) is the son of Henry Percy, Earl of Northumberland. Hotspur is hot-tempered, valiant, and obsessed with honor. He seems to be the opposite of Prince Hal.

Prince John of Lancaster is Henry IV's second son, Hal's younger brother. Unlike Hal, he behaves as his station demands.

Edmund Mortimer, Earl of March is captured by Glendower while fighting against him for Henry. After Henry refuses to ransom him (most likely because Mortimer has a stronger claim to the throne than Henry), Mortimer marries Glendower's daughter and joins with him and the rebels against Henry.

Lady Mortimer is Owen Glendower's daughter and Edmund Mortimer's wife. She speaks no English and sings to her husband in Welsh.

Sir Michael is a friend of the Archbishop of York and the rebel faction.

Henry Percy, Earl of Northumberland is the father of Hotspur and a leader of the rebellion against Henry. He had been one of his strongest supporters when Bolingbroke returned from exile to reclaim his lawful title and inheritance after his father's death. Now he feels Henry has overstepped his proper limits, used the Percies, and proved ungrateful and untrustworthy.

Thomas Percy, Earl of Worcester is one of the leaders of the rebellious faction, brother to Henry Percy and uncle to Hotspur. Worcester is cunning where Hotspur is impulsive. Before the battle at Shrewsbury, he conveys false information to Hotspur, reporting that Henry is implacable when the king has actually offered terms of reconciliation.

Lady Percy, Kate, is Hotspur's wife and Edmund Mortimer's sister. She is a loving and sprightly wife even though her husband loves war and honor more than he loves her.

Peto is a companion of Falstaff's.

Ned Poins is one of Hal's tavern companions in mischief.

Mistress Quickly is the hostess at the tavern where the prince and Falstaff congregate. She is a comic character who speaks in malapropisms.

Richard Scroop is the Archbishop of York and a confederate of the Percies in the rebellion.

The **Sheriff** comes to the tavern to investigate charges that Falstaff has robbed some carriers but is appeased by Hal's promise to investigate and rectify the crime.

Sir Richard Vernon is one of the rebels.

Vintner is the tavern keeper who scolds Francis for not doing his job properly when Hal and Poins are both calling him and he doesn't know where to go.

Earl of Westmoreland is one of the nobles loyal to the king.

CRITICISM
THROUGH THE AGES

HENRY IV, PART I
IN THE SEVENTEENTH CENTURY
❧

The History of Henry IV—which is now known as *Henry IV, Part I*, since a sequel called *Henry IV, Part II* was printed in 1600—was probably written and first performed in 1596 or 1597. It was first performed at court on March 6, 1600, before the Flemish ambassador and later in 1612 and 1625. It was first entered into the Stationers Register by Andrew Wise on February 25, 1598, as "The historye of Henry the IIIJth with his battaile of Shrewsburye against Henry Hottspurre of the Northe with the conceipted mirth of Sir John Falstoff." Some time after, during 1598, a quarto (or unauthorized version) of the play was published, with the following on the title page:

THE HISTORY OF HENRIE THE FOVRTH; With the battell at Shrewsburie, *betweene the King and Lord* Henry Percy, surnamed Henrie Hotspur of the North. *With the humorous conceits of Sir* Iohn Falstalffe. AT LONDON, Printed by P. S. [Peter Short] for Andrew Wise, dwelling in Paules Churchyard, at the signe of the Angell. 1598.

Although this text is called the First Quarto, it is not the first quarto of *Henry IV, Part I* that was printed. There was an earlier quarto, but only four leaves from that quarto still exist, and that quarto is referred to as Q0. Q0, it appears, was the copy text for the First Quarto, which is believed to be a good quarto—that is, based on Shakespeare's own papers. From the start, *Henry IV, Part I* must have been a very popular play. It was reprinted four times, in 1599, 1604, 1608, and 1613, before it was printed in the First Folio of 1623, the collected works of Shakespeare published by John Hemings and Henry Condell, who had been partners with Shakespeare in their acting company, the King's Men.

One of the principal reasons for the popularity of *Henry IV, Part I* was the character of Sir John Falstaff. In 1702 John Dennis wrote that Queen Elizabeth herself was so pleased by him in the two Henry IV plays that she ordered Shakespeare to write another sequel, a comedy. In 1709, Nicholas Rowe added that Elizabeth had indicated that she wished to see Falstaff in love and that Shakespeare wrote *The Merry Wives of Windsor* in obedience—and quickly. Whether this story is true or not, it is certain that the character Falstaff was a great success and took on a life of his own. A passage from the series of insulting verses *The Whipping of the Satyre*, written in 1601 by someone only identified as W.J., features Shakespeare's Falstaff as a model for invidious comparison.

Even during the interregnum—that period after 1642, when the theaters were closed by the Puritan-controlled Parliament, until 1660, when the English monarchy was restored—Falstaff continued to be presented in "The Bouncing Knight," a farcical skit derived from the Henry IV plays. Such skits were called "drolls" and were performed secretly in defiance of the Puritan ban on theater. In 1662, after the restoration of the monarchy, twenty-six of these were published. In *Roscius Anglicanus, or an Historical review of the Stage from 1660 to 1706*, published in 1708, John Downes, who had worked in the post-Restoration theater run by Sir William Davenant, reported that after the Restoration, at the theater run by Davenant's rival, Thomas Killigrew, *Henry IV,* among other "Old Plays, [was] Acted but now and then" in its original version, and "being well Perform'd [was] very Satisfactory to the Town" (Vickers 2, 188). In fact, the Red Bull actors, a company comprising "the scattered Remnant" of several acting companies that were active before the theaters were shut down in 1642, performed *Henry IV, Part I* before Charles II relicensed the theater (Taylor, 21). Samuel Pepys noted in his diary that he saw the play five times between 1660 and 1669. (He did not like the play very much, however, and walked out twice before the end.)

The small amount of critical writing about *Henry IV, Part I* that began to appear after the Restoration focused on the character of Falstaff. In his essay "Of Dramatick Poesie" (1668), John Dryden offered a brief character analysis of Falstaff in his discussion of the resemblance of theatrical characters to actual persons. In 1698, the clergyman Jeremy Collier, in his popular and controversial *A Short View of the Immorality and Profaneness of the English Stage*, discussing how "stage-poets" reward or punish their characters in accord with the genre of the play in which they appear, offered a brief opinion about the character of Falstaff in the Henry plays and declared him a comic rather than a tragic figure.

Shakespeare's chief source for both the Henry IV plays and for *Henry V* was a popular anonymous play called *The Famous Victories of Henry the Fifth*, written before 1588. It was entered in the Stationers Register in 1594 and first printed, by Thomas Creede, in 1598, very likely to take advantage of the popularity of Shakespeare's *Henry IV, Part I*. It includes episodes recounting Prince Hal's youthful escapades, his reformation and reconciliation with his father, his disreputable companions, and the figure who will become Falstaff, Sir John

Oldcastle. Oldcastle was the name Falstaff originally bore in Shakespeare's Henry IV plays, as well.

There actually was a Sir John Oldcastle. A follower of the Protestant reformer John Wyclif, he was executed under Henry V in 1417 and died a martyr. Henry Brooke, Lord Cobham, who became Lord Chamberlain of England in 1598, and the titular head of Shakespeare's acting company at that time—they were called the Lord Chamberlain's Men before they became the King's Men under James I—was a descendent of Oldcastle and objected to the use of his name. Consequently, Shakespeare changed the name Oldcastle to Falstaff.

In writing the play, Shakespeare also consulted the sections on Henry IV in Volume III of Raphael Holinshed's *Chronicles of England, Scotland, and Ireland* (1577, 1586-87) and in Book III of Samuel Daniel's poem *The First Four Books of the Civil Wars between the Two Houses of Lancaster and York* (1595).

1601—W. J. *The Whipping of the Satyre*

The author known only as "W.J." wrote a series of insulting verses called *The Whipping of the Satyre*.

I dare here speake it, and my speech mayntayne,
That Sir John Falstaffe was not any way
More grosse in body, than you are in brayne.
But whether should I (helpe me nowe, I pray)
For your grosse brayne, you like J. Falstaffe graunt,
Or for small wit, suppose you John of Gaunt?

1667—Samuel Pepys, from *The Diary*

Samuel Pepys (1633–1703), Londoner and naval administrator, is most remembered today for his *Diary*, which gives a fascinating picture of the upper-class life of Restoration London.

November 2, 1667

. . . to the King's playhouse, and there saw *Henry the Fourth:* and contrary to expectation, was pleased in nothing more than in Cartwright's speaking of Falstaff's speech about 'What is Honour?'

1668—John Dryden, from "Of Dramatick Poesie"

John Dryden (1631-1700), an important poet, dramatist, and critic, was poet laureate and royal historiographer of England under Charles II.

I am assur'd from diverse persons, that *Ben. Johnson* was actually acquainted with such a man, one altogether as ridiculous as he (Morose in *The Silent Woman)* is here represented. Others say it is not enough to find one man of such an humor; it must be common to more, and the more common the more natural. To prove this they instance in the best of Comical Characters, Falstaff: There are many men resembling him; Old, Fat, Merry, Cowardly, Drunken, Amorous, Vain, and Lying: But to convince these people I need but tell them, that humor is the ridiculous extravagance of conversation, wherein one man differs from all others. If then it be common or communicated to many, how differs it from other men's? or what indeed causes it to be ridiculous so much as the singularity of it? As for Falstaffe, he is not properly one humor, but a Miscellany of Humors or Images, drawn from so many several men; that wherein he is singular in his wit, or those things he says, *praeter expectatum,* unexpected by the Audience; his quick evasions when you imagine him surpriz'd, which as they are extreamly diverting of themselves, so receive a great addition from his person; for the very sight of such an unwieldy old debauch'd fellow is a Comedy alone.

1698—Jeremy Collier, from *A Short View of the Immorality and Profaneness of the English Stage*

Jeremy Collier (1650-1726) was an English bishop of the nonjurors (clergy who refused to take the oaths of allegiance to William III and Mary II in 1689). He wrote a celebrated attack on the immorality of plays, actors, and playwrights.

Ben Jonson's Fox [or *Volpone*] is clearly against Mr. *Dryden,* and here I have his own Confession for Proof. He declares the *Poet's end in this Play was the Punishment of Vice, and the Reward of Virtue. Ben* was forced to strain for this piece of justice, and break through the *Unity of Design.* This Mr. *Dryden* remarks upon him: however he is pleased to commend the Performance, and calls it an excellent *Fifth Act.*

Ben Jonson shall speak for himself afterwards in the Character of a Critick, in the mean time I shall take a Testimony or two from *Shakespeare*. And here we may observe the admir'd *Falstaff* goes off in Disappointment. He is thrown out of Favor as being a *Rake,* and dies like a Rat behind the Hangings. The Pleasure he had given would not excuse him. The *Poet* was not so partial as to let his Humour compound for his Lewdness. If 'tis objected that this remark is wide of the Point because *Falstaff* is represented in Tragedy, where the Laws of Justice are more strictly observ'd: to this I answer, that you may call *Henry the Fourth* and *Fifth* Tragedies if you please, but for all that *Falstaff* wears no *Buskins,* his Character is perfectly comical from end to end.

HENRY IV, PART I IN THE EIGHTEENTH CENTURY

According to Samuel Johnson, "None of Shakespeare's plays are more read than the *First and Second Parts of Henry the Fourth*. Perhaps no author has ever in two plays afforded so much delight." The chief source of that delight and the chief reason for the unflagging popularity of those plays was Falstaff. As the century began, in 1700, *Henry IV, Part I* was on the stage at Lincoln's Inn Fields with a noted actor of the time, Thomas Betterton, playing Falstaff, and a new and inexpensive quarto edition had also just appeared.

In 1702, John Dennis's adaptation of *The Merry Wives of Windsor* was performed unsuccessfully. In "The Epistle Dedicatory to the Honorable George Granville, Esq.: 'A large account of the Taste in Poetry, and the Causes of the Degeneracy of it,'" Dennis explains how he set about making his adaptation and defending it against its detractors. In the course of his account, he compares Falstaff as he appears in the Henry IV plays and in *The Merry Wives*. Contrary to most later critical opinion, which deplored the Falstaff of *The Merry Wives* as an inferior version of the character, Dennis sees him to be the superior creation. Dennis prefers Falstaff in action, as he is in *The Merry Wives*, to the cynical and philosophical wit that he is in the Henry IV plays.

Some writers disapproved of the Henry IV plays entirely. Writing in 1706 in his thrice-weekly *Review of the State of the English Nation*, Daniel Defoe (the author of *Robinson Crusoe*) was not concerned with analyzing the construction or the characters in *Henry IV, Part I*. He was concerned instead with morality. Commenting on a recent performance of *Henry IV, Part I* at Oxford, Defoe asked rhetorically, "Is not that Play as full of prophane, immoral, and some blasphemous Parts, as most now extant? Is not Religion banter'd in it, the *Church* ridicul'd, and your Maker dishonor'd?" (Taylor 55). In 1710, Charles Gildon, in his *Remarks on the plays of Shakespeare*, praised the Falstaff of the first part of *Henry IV* but found him less winning in the sequel, and Gildon was also ambivalent toward Hotspur.

Tho' the Humour of *Falstaff* be what is most valuable in both these Parts yet that is far more excellent in the first, for Sir *John* is not near so Diverting in the second Part. *Hotspur* is the next in Goodness, but that wou'd have shew'd much more had it been in a regular Tragedy, where the Manners had not only been necessary but productive of Incidents Noble, and Charming. *Glendower* is fine for Comedy.

In 1733, Lewis Theobald put together an edition of Shakespeare and co-wrote the introduction with William Warburton, critic and clergyman, who would issue his own edition of Shakespeare's plays in 1747. In Theobald's edition, Warburton discussed the credibility of Hal's conversion at the end of *Henry IV, Part II*, with particular reference to his earlier, first-act soliloquy in *Henry IV, Part I*. Although Warburton's criticism is in many ways clumsy, it represents one of the first serious attempts to examine a character other than Falstaff.

Later in the century, Samuel Johnson acutely expressed the critic's paradoxical relation to Falstaff, seeing him as a figure of "vice" and of "sense" who might be "admired" but not "esteemed." In 1769, Elizabeth Montagu in "An essay on the Writings and Genius of Shakespeare," in considering the character of Falstaff, expressed a similar response to him that mingles moral rejection with human acceptance.

In 1774, Francis Gentleman, in his notes appended to John Bell's edition of Shakespeare's plays, praised the conflict between the characters of Prince Hal and Hotspur and also attacked Falstaff for coarse comedy. He thought the scene in which Falstaff counterfeits death at Shrewsbury was "too much in the stile of pantomime mummery."

A particular charge commonly brought against Falstaff was his perceived cowardice. Certainly, both Hal and Poins frequently accuse him of it, and both Falstaff's catechism on honor and his counterfeiting death to evade being killed by Douglas at Shrewsbury could be used to corroborate them. In 1777, Maurice Morgann undertook a defense of Falstaff in an important, long essay called "The Dramatic Character of Falstaff." Not only does Morgann endeavor to clear him of the imputation of cowardice, but he also argues that Falstaff was endowed with true courage. The essence of that courage was what the Protestant theologian Paul Tillich, a century and a half later, would call "the courage to be." The question of whether Falstaff is or is not a coward recurs throughout discussions of *Henry IV, Part I* through the present time. Morgann essentially argues that Falstaff's wit is its own end. Instead of being prostituted to the service of flattery, deception, self-interest, or advancement, it is dedicated to and an expression of an immediate joy of life.

The best writing about *Henry IV, Part I* for the rest of the century was primarily focused on Falstaff. Henry Mackenzie and Richard Cumberland both made his character the subject of an essay in 1786, as did William Richardson in 1789. They focus on Falstaff himself more than on his role and his meaning as a constituent element in a complex piece of literature. Richardson emphasizes Falstaff's "depravity" but still says the overall portrayal of the character is "delightful." Earlier, in 1744, Corbyn Morris had offered similar praise of Falstaff, saying that his combination of wit and cowardice makes it "impossible to avoid *loving* him."

In 1761, David Douglass brought his theater company to New York City, where *Henry IV, Part I* was performed for the first time in the United States (Dunn, 77). Thomas Jefferson, in his youth, copied out Falstaff's catechism on honor in one of his notebooks, unfortunately without commentary. President Lincoln saw the play performed in December 1863 at Ford's Theater in Washington, D.C.

1702—John Dennis, from *A Large Account of the Taste in Poetry, and the Causes of the Degeneracy of It*

John Dennis (1658–1734) was one of the major critics of his time, an opponent of more famous writers as Alexander Pope, Jonathan Swift, and Joseph Addison. This essay was appended to the publication of one of his plays, *The Comical Gallant, or the Amours of Sir John Falstaffe*, an adaptation of Shakespeare's *The Merry Wives of Windsor*.

... I had observed what success the Character of Falstaff had had, in the first part of *Henry IV*. And as the Falstaff in the *Merry Wives* is certainly superior to that of the second part of *Henry IV*, so it can hardly be said to be inferior to that of the first.

For in the second part of *Henry IV*, *Falstaff* does nothing but talk, as indeed he does nothing else in the third and fourth Acts of the first part. Whereas in the *Merry Wives* he everywhere Acts, and that action is more Regular and more in compass than it is in the first part of *Henry IV*. 'Tis true, what he says in *Henry IV* is admirable; but action at last is the business of the Stage. The Drama is action itself, and it is action alone that is able to excite in any extraordinary manner the curiosity of mankind....

1733—William Warburton, from *The Works of Shakespeare, Collated with the Oldest Copies, and Corrected, with Notes, Exemplary and Critical*

William Warburton (1698–1779) was a clergyman and a scholar, becoming bishop of Gloucester in 1759. He helped Lewis Theobald write the preface for Theobald's edition of Shakespeare.

. . . For what can be more ridiculous than, in our modern Writers, to make a debauch'd young Man, immers'd in all the Vices of his Age and Time, in a few hours take up, confine himself in the way of Honour to one Woman, and moralize in good earnest on the Follies of his past Behaviour? Nor can that great Exemplar of Comic Writing, *Terence*, be altogether excused in this Regard, who in his *Adelphi* has left *Demea* in the last Scenes so unlike himself: whom, as *Shakespeare* expresses it, *he has turn'd with the seamy Side of his Wit outward*. This Conduct, as Errors are more readily imitated than Perfections, *Beaumont* and *Fletcher* seem to have follow'd in a Character in their *Scornful Lady*. It may be objected, perhaps, by some who do not go to the Bottom of our Poet's Conduct, that he has likewise transgress'd against the Rule himself by making Prince *Harry* at once, upon coming to the Crown, throw off his former Dissoluteness and take up the Practice of a sober Morality and all the kingly Virtues. But this would be a mistaken Objection. The Prince's Reformation is not so sudden as not to be prepar'd and expected by the Audience. He gives, indeed, a Loose to Vanity and a light unweigh'd Behaviour when he is trifling among his dissolute Companions, but the Sparks of innate Honour and true Nobleness break from him upon every proper Occasion where we would hope to see him awake to Sentiments suiting his Birth and Dignity. And our Poet has so well and artfully guarded his Character from the Suspicions of habitual and unreformable Profligateness that even from the first shewing him upon the Stage, in the first Part of *Henry IV*, when he made him consent to join with Falstaff in a Robbery on the Highway, he has taken care not to carry him off the Scene without an Intimation that he knows them all, and their unyok'd Humour; and that, like the Sun, he will permit them only for a while to obscure and cloud his Brightness, then break thro' the Mist when he pleases to be himself again, that his Lustre, when wanted, may be the more wonder'd at.

1741—Corbyn Morris, from *An Essay towards Fixing the True Standards of Wit, Raillery, Satire, and Ridicule*

Corbyn Morris (1710–1779) was a customs official as well as a critic.

These seem to me to be the different Powers and Effects of HUMOUR and WIT. However, the most agreeable Representations or Compositions of all others, appear not where they *separately* exist, but where they are *united* together in the same Fabric; where HUMOUR is the *Ground-work* and chief Substance, and WIT happily spread, *quickens* the whole with Embellishments.

This is the Excellency of the *Character* of Sir *John Falstaff*; the Ground-work is *Humour*, or the Representation and Detection of a bragging and vaunting *Coward* in *real Life*; However, this alone would only have expos'd the *Knight*, as a meer *Noll Bluff*, to the Derision of the Company; And after they had once been gratify'd with his Chastisement, he would have sunk into Infamy, and become quite odious and intolerable: But here the inimitable *Wit* of Sir *John* come in to his Support, and gives a new *Rise* and *Lustre* to his Character; For the sake of his *Wit* you forgive his *Cowardice*; or rather, are fond of his *Cowardice* for the Occasions it gives to his *Wit*. In short, the *Humour* furnishes a Subject and Spur to the *Wit*, and the *Wit* again supports and embellishes the *Humour*.

At the *first* Entrance of the *Knight*, your good Humour and Tendency to *Mirth* are irresistibly excited by his jolly Appearance and Corpulency; you feel and acknowledge him, to be the fittest Subject imaginable for yielding *Diversion* and *Merriment*; but when you see him immediately set up for *Enterprize* and *Activity*, with his evident *Weight* and *Unweildiness*, your Attention is all call'd forth, and you are eager to watch him to the End of his Adventures; Your Imagination pointing out with a full Scope his future Embarrassments. All the while as you accompany him forwards, he *heightens* your Relish for his future Disasters, by his happy Opinion of his own Sufficiency, and the gay Vaunts which he makes of his Talents and Accomplishments; so that at last when he falls into a Scrape, your Expectation is exquisitely gratify'd, and you have the full Pleasure of seeing all his trumpeted Honour laid in the Dust. When in the midst of his Misfortunes, instead of being utterly demolish'd and sunk, he rises again by the superior Force of his *Wit*, and begins a *new* Course with fresh Spirit and Alacrity; This excites you the more to *renew* the Chace, in full View of his *second* Defeat; out of which he recovers again, and triumphs with new Pretensions and Boastings. After this he immediately starts upon a *third* Race, and so on; continually detected and caught, and yet constantly extricating himself by his inimitable *Wit* and *Invention*; this yielding a perpetual *Round* of Sport and Diversion.

Again, the genteel *Quality* of Sir *John* is of great Use in supporting his Character; It prevents his *sinking* too low after several of his Misfortunes; Besides, you allow him, in consequence of his *Rank* and *Seniority*, the Privilege to dictate, and take the Lead, and to rebuke others upon many Occasions; By this he is sav'd from appearing too *nauseous* and *impudent*. The good *Sense* which he possesses comes also to his Aid, and saves him from being *despicable*, by forcing your

Esteem for his real Abilities.—Again, the *Privilege* you allow him of rebuking and checking others, when he assumes it with proper Firmness and Superiority, helps to *settle* anew, and *compose* his Character after an Embarrassment; And reduces in some measure the *Spirit* of the Company to a proper *Level*, before he sets out again upon a fresh Adventure;—without this, they would be kept continually *strain'd*, and *wound up* to the highest Pitch, without sufficient Relief and Diversity.

It may also deserve to be remark'd of *Falstaff*, that the *Figure* of his *Person* is admirably suited to the *Turn* of his *Mind*; so that there arises before you a perpetual *Allusion* from one to the other, which forms an incessant Series of *Wit*, whether they are in *Contrast* or *Agreement* together.—When he pretends to *Activity*, there is Wit in the *Contrast* between his *Mind* and his *Person*,—And *Wit* in their *Agreement*, when he triumphs in *Jollity*.

To compleat the whole,—you have in this Character of *Falstaff*, not only a free Course of *Humour*, supported and embellish'd with admirable *Wit*; but this *Humour* is of a Species the most *jovial* and *gay* in all Nature.—Sir *John Falstaff* possesses Generosity, Chearfulness, Alacrity, Invention, Frolic and Fancy superior to all other Men:—The *Figure* of his Person is the Picture of Jollity, Mirth, and Good-nature, and banishes at once all other Ideas from your Breast; He is happy himself, and makes you happy.—If you examine him further, he has no Fierceness, Reserve, Malice or Peevishness lurking in his Heart; His Intentions are all pointed at innocent Riot and Merriment; Nor has the Knight any inveterate Design, except against *Sack*, and that too he *loves*.—If, besides this, he desires to pass for a Man of *Activity* and *Valour*, you can easily excuse so harmless a *Foible*, which yields you the highest Pleasure in its constant *Detection*.

If you put all these together, it is impossible to *hate* honest *Jack Falstaff*; If you observe them again, it is impossible to avoid *loving* him; He is the gay, the witty, the frolicksome, happy, and fat *Jack Falstaff*, the most delightful *Swaggerer* in all Nature.—You must *love* him for your *own* sake,—At the same time you cannot but *love* him for *his own* Talents; And when you have *enjoy'd* them, you cannot but *love* him in *Gratitude*;—He has nothing to disgust you, and every thing to give you Joy;—His *Sense* and his *Foibles* are equally directed to advance your Pleasure; And it is impossible to be tired or unhappy in his Company.

This *jovial* and *gay* Humour, without any thing *envious, malicious, mischievous,* or *despicable*, and continually *quicken'd* and adorn'd with *Wit*, yields that peculiar Delight, without any *Alloy*, which we all feel and acknowledge in *Falstaff*'s Company.

1768—Samuel Johnson, from *Notes on Shakespeare's Plays*

Samuel Johnson (1709-1784) is one of England's greatest literary figures, and some consider him the foremost literary critic of English literature. Although his edition of Shakespeare required further revisions by successors, his critical preface, as well as his many notes and observations for that edition, remain classical statements in the history of Shakespeare criticism. Included below is his "General Observation" on the Henry IV plays.

None of Shakespeare's plays are more read than the *First and Second Parts of Henry the Fourth.* Perhaps no author has ever in two plays afforded so much delight. The great events are interesting, for the fate of kingdoms depends upon them; the slighter occurrences are diverting and, except one or two, sufficiently probable; the incidents are multiplied with wonderful fertility of invention, and the characters diversified with the utmost nicety of discernment and the profoundest skill in the nature of man.

The Prince, who is the hero both of the comic and tragic part, is a young man of great abilities and violent passions, whose sentiments are right, though his actions are wrong; whose virtues are obscured by negligence, and whose understanding is dissipated by levity. In his idle hours he is rather loose than wicked; and when the occasion forces out his latent qualities, he is great without effort and brave without tumult. The trifler is roused into a hero, and the hero again reposes in the trifler. This character is great, original, and just.

Percy is a rugged soldier, choleric, and quarrelsome, and has only the soldier's virtues, generosity and courage.

But Falstaff, unimitated, unimitable Falstaff, how shall I describe thee? Thou compound of sense and vice; of sense which may be admired but not esteemed, of vice which may be despised but hardly detested. Falstaff is a character loaded with faults, and with those faults which naturally produce contempt. He is a thief and a glutton, a coward and a boaster, always ready to cheat the weak and prey upon the poor; to terrify the timorous and insult the defenseless. At once obsequious and malignant, he satirizes in their absence those whom he lives by flattering. He is familiar with the Prince only as an agent of vice, but of this familiarity he is so proud as not only to be supercilious and haughty with common men but to think his interest of importance to the Duke of Lancaster. Yet the man thus corrupt, thus despicable, makes himself necessary to the Prince that despises him, by the most pleasing of all qualities, perpetual gaiety, by an unfailing power of exciting laughter, which is the more freely indulged as his wit is not of the splendid or ambitious kind but consists in easy escapes and sallies of levity, which make sport but raise no envy. It must be observed that he is stained with no enormous or sanguinary crimes, so that his licentiousness is not so offensive but that it may be borne for his mirth.

The moral to be drawn from this representation is that no man is more dangerous than he that, with a will to corrupt, hath the power to please; and that neither wit nor honesty ought to think themselves safe with such a companion when they see Henry seduced by Falstaff.

1769—Elizabeth Montagu, from *An Essay on the Writings and Genius of Shakespear*

Elizabeth Montagu (1720–1800) was a writer and an intellectual hostess in London who established "conversation parties," during which literature was usually a topic.

Whether we consider the character of Falstaffe as adapted to encourage and excuse the extravagancies of the Prince, or by itself, we must certainly admire it, and own it to be perfectly original.

The professed wit, either in life or on the stage, is usually severe and satirical. But mirth is the source of Falstaffe's wit. He seems rather to invite you to partake of his merriment, than to attend to his jest; a person must be ill-natured, as well as dull, who does not join in the mirth of this jovial companion, who is in all respects the best calculated to raise laughter of any that ever appeared on a stage.

He joins the finesse of wit with the drollery of humour. Humour is a kind of grotesque wit, shaped and coloured by the disposition of the person in whom it resides, or by the subject to which it is applied. It is oftenest found in odd and irregular minds: but this peculiar turn distorts wit, and though it gives it a burlesque air, which excites momentary mirth, renders it less just, and consequently less agreeable to our judgments. Gluttony, corpulency, and cowardice, are the peculiarities of Falstaffe's composition, they render him ridiculous without folly, throw an air of jest and festivity about him, and make his manners suit with his sentiments, without giving to his understanding any particular bias. As the contempt attendant on these vices and defects is the best antidote against any infection that might be caught in his society, so it was very skilful to make him as ridiculous as witty, and as contemptible as entertaining. The admirable speech upon honour would have been both indecent and dangerous from any other person. We must every where allow his wit is just, his humour genuine, and his character perfectly original, and sustained through every scene, in every play, in which it appears.

1774—Francis Gentleman, from *Bell's Edition of Shakespeare's Plays*

Gentleman (1728-1784), an actor and a dramatist, wrote textual notes to John Bell's edition of Shakespeare's works.

[On Hal's victory over Hotspur, Henry Percy]

Though *Henry's* gallant behavior must give pleasure, yet we think every generous mind must feel for *Percy's* fall; as, though a rebel, he seems to act upon just principles and very aggravated provocation. It is a very nice, and almost unparalleled point, to bring two characters in mortal conflict on the stage where, as in the present case, we must rejoice at the success of one and grieve for the fate of the other.

. . .

[On Falstaff's faking his death at Shrewsbury]

The supposed dead man's rising is a most risible incident, and his soliloquy keeps pace with it; however, we conceive the son of sack's rolling and tumbling about the stage to get Hotspur on his back, is too much in the stile of pantomime mummery; it may, and certainly does, create laughter for the time; but such ludicrous attacks upon reason are beneath *Shakespeare* and the stage.

1777—Maurice Morgann, from *An Essay on The Dramatic Character of Falstaff*

Maurice Morgann (1726-1802) was a diplomat and writer of various literary and political tracts. He also wrote on *The Tempest*. Regarding *An Essay on The Dramatic Character of Falstaff*, Harold Bloom has said that "much of the subsequent major criticism of the sublime Falstaff can be read as a reply to this work."

The ideas which I have formed concerning the Courage and Military Character of the Dramatic Sir *John Falstaff*, are so different from those which I find generally to prevail in the world, that I shall take the liberty of stating my sentiments on the subject; in hope that some person as unengaged as myself, will either correct and reform my error in this respect; or, joining himself to my opinion, redeem me from, what I may call, the reproach of singularity.

I am to avow then, that I do not clearly discern that Sir *John Falstaff* deserves to bear the character so generally given him of an absolute Coward; or, in other words, that I do not conceive *Shakespeare* ever meant to make Cowardice an essential part of his constitution. (. . .)

It will scarcely be possible to consider the Courage of *Falstaff* as wholly detached from his other qualities: But I write not professedly of any part of his character, but what is included under the term, *Courage*; however I may incidentally throw some lights on the whole.—The reader will not need to be told that this Inquiry will resolve itself of course into a Critique on the genius, the arts, and the conduct of *Shakespeare*: For what is *Falstaff*, what *Lear*, what *Hamlet*, or *Othello*, but different modifications of *Shakespeare's* thought? It is true that this Inquiry is narrowed almost to a single point: but general criticism is as uninstructive as it is easy: Shakespeare deserves to be considered in detail;—a task hitherto unattempted.

It may be proper, in the first place, to take a short view of all the parts of *Falstaff*'s Character, and then proceed to discover, if we can, what *Impressions*, as to Courage or Cowardice, he had made on the persons of the Drama: After which we will examine, in course, such evidence, either of *persons* or *facts*, as are relative to the matter; and account as we may for those appearances, which seem to have led to the opinion of his Constitutional Cowardice.

The scene of the robbery, and the disgraces attending it, which stand first in the Play, and introduce us to the knowledge of *Falstaff*, I shall beg leave (as I think this scene to have been the source of much unreasonable prejudice) to reserve till we are more fully acquainted with the whole character of *Falstaff*; and I shall therefore hope that the reader will not for a time advert to it, or to the jests of the *Prince* or of *Poins* in consequence of that unlucky adventure.

In drawing out the parts of *Falstaff*'s character, with which I shall begin this Inquiry, I shall take the liberty of putting Constitutional bravery into his composition; but the reader will be pleased to consider what I shall say in that respect as spoken hypothetically for the present, to be retained, or discharged out of it, as he shall finally determine.

To me then it appears that the leading quality in *Falstaff*'s character, and that from which all the rest take their colour, is a high degree of wit and humour, accompanied with great natural vigour and alacrity of mind. This quality so accompanied, led him probably very early into life, and made him highly acceptable to society; so acceptable, as to make it seem unnecessary for him to acquire any other virtue. Hence, perhaps, his continued debaucheries and dissipations of every kind.—He seems, by nature, to have had a mind free of malice or any evil principle; but he never took the trouble of acquiring any good one. He found himself esteemed and beloved with all his faults; nay for his faults, which were all connected with humour, and for the most part, grew out of it. As he had, possibly, no vices but such as he thought might be openly professed, so he appeared more dissolute thro' ostentation. To the character of wit and humour, to which all his other qualities seem to have conformed themselves, he appears to have added a very necessary support, that of the profession of a *Soldier*. He had from nature, as I presume to say, a spirit of boldness and enterprise; which in a Military age, tho' employment was only occasional, kept him always above contempt, secured him an honourable reception among the Great, and suited best both with his particular mode of humour and of vice. Thus living continually in society, nay even in Taverns, and indulging himself, and being indulged by others, in every debauchery; drinking, whoring, gluttony, and ease; assuming a liberty of fiction, necessary perhaps to his wit, and often falling into falsity and lies, he seems to have set, by degrees, all sober reputation at defiance; and finding eternal resources in his wit, he borrows, shifts, defrauds, and even robs, without dishonour.—Laughter and approbation attend his greatest excesses; and being governed visibly by no settled bad principle or ill design, fun and humour account for and cover all. By degrees, however, and thro' indulgence, he acquires bad habits, becomes an humourist, grows enormously corpulent, and falls into the infirmities of age; yet never quits, all the time, one single levity or vice of youth, or loses any of that chearfulness of mind, which had enabled him to pass thro' this course with ease to himself and delight to others; and thus, at last, mixing youth and age, enterprize and corpulency, wit and folly, poverty and expence, title and buffoonery, innocence as to purpose, and wickedness as to practice; neither incurring hatred by bad principle, or contempt by Cowardice, yet involved in circumstances productive of imputation in both; a butt and a wit, a humourist and a man of humour, a touchstone and a laughing stock, a jester and a jest, has Sir *John Falstaff*, taken at that period of his life in which we see him, become the most perfect Comic character that perhaps ever was exhibited.

It may not possibly be wholly amiss to remark in this place, that if Sir *John Falstaff* had possessed any of that Cardinal quality, Prudence, alike the guardian of virtue and the protector of vice; that quality, from the possession or the absence of which, the character and fate of men in this life take, I think, their colour, and not from real vice or virtue; if he had considered his wit not as *principal* but *accessary* only; as the instrument of power, and not as power itself; if he had had much baseness to hide, if he had had less of what may be called mellowness or good humour, or less of health and spirit; if he had spurred and rode the world with his wit, instead of suffering the world, boys and all, to ride him;—he might, without any other essential change, have been the admiration and not the jest of mankind:—Or if he had lived in our day, and instead of attaching himself to one Prince, had renounced *all* friendship and *all* attachment, and had let himself out as the ready instrument and Zany of every successive Minister, he might possibly have acquired the high honour of marking his shroud or decorating his coffin with the living rays of an Irish at least, if not a British Coronet: Instead of which, tho' enforcing laughter from every disposition, he appears, now, as such a character which every wise man will pity and avoid, every knave will censure, and every fool will fear: And accordingly Shakespeare, ever true to nature, has made Harry desert, and Lancaster censure him:—He dies where he lived, in a Tavern, broken-hearted, without a friend; and his final exit is given up to the derision of fools. Nor have his misfortunes ended here; the scandal arising from the misapplication of his wit and talents seems immortal. He has met with as little justice or mercy from his final judges the critics, as from his companions of the Drama. With our cheeks still red with laughter, we ungratefully as unjustly censure him as a coward by nature, and a rascal upon principle: Tho', if this were so, it might be hoped, for our own credit, that we should behold him rather with disgust and disapprobation than with pleasure and delight.

But to remember our question—*Is Falstaff a constitutional coward?*

With respect to every infirmity, except that of Cowardice, we must take him as at the period in which he is represented to us. If we see him dissipated, fat,—it is enough;—we have nothing to do with his youth, when he might perhaps have been modest, chaste, '*and not an Eagle's talon in the waist*'. But *Constitutional Courage* extends to a man's whole life, makes a part of his nature, and is not to be taken up or deserted like a mere Moral quality. It is true, there is a Courage founded upon *principle*, or rather a principle independent of Courage, which will sometimes operate in spite of nature; a principle, which prefers death to shame, but which always refers itself, in conformity to its own nature, to the prevailing modes of honour, and the fashions of the age.—But Natural courage is another thing: It is independent of opinion; It adapts itself to occasions, preserves itself under every shape, and can avail itself of flight as well as of action.—In the last war, some Indians of America perceiving a line of Highlanders to keep their station under every disadvantage, and under a fire which they could not effectually return, were so miserably mistaken in our points of honour as to conjecture, from observation on the habit and stability of those troops, that they were indeed the women of England, who wanted courage to run away.—That Courage which is founded in nature and constitution, *Falstaff*, as I presume to say, possessed;—but I am ready to allow, that the principle already mentioned, so far as it refers to reputation only, began with every other Moral quality to lose its hold on him in his old age; that is, at the time of life in which he is represented to us; a period, as it should seem, approaching to *seventy*.—The truth is that he had drollery enough to support himself in credit without the point of honour, and had address enough to make even the preservation of his life a point of drollery. The reader knows I allude, tho' something prematurely, to his fictitious death in the battle of Shrewsbury. This incident is generally construed to the disadvantage of *Falstaff*: It is a transaction which bears the external marks of Cowardice: It is also aggravated to the spectators by the idle tricks of the Player, who practises on this occasion all the attitudes and wild apprehensions of fear; more ambitious, as it should seem, of representing a Caliban than a *Falstaff*, or indeed rather a poor unwieldy miserable Tortoise than either.—The painful Comedian lies spread out on his belly, and not only covers himself all over with his robe as with a shell, but forms a kind of round Tortoise-back by I know not what stuffing or contrivance; in addition to which, he alternately lifts up, and depresses, and dodges his head, and looks to the one side and to the other, so much with the piteous aspect of that animal, that one would not be sorry to see the ambitious imitator calipashed in his robe, and served up for the entertainment of the gallery.—There is no hint for this mummery in the Play: Whatever there may be of dishonour in *Falstaff*'s conduct, he neither does or says any thing on this occasion which indicates terror or disorder of mind: On the contrary, this very act is a proof of his having all his wits about him, and is a stratagem, such as it is, not improper for a buffoon, whose fate would be singularly hard, if he should not be allowed to avail himself of his Character when it might serve him in most stead. We must remember, in extenuation, that the executive, the destroying hand of *Douglas* was over him: '*It was time to counterfeit*, or *that hot termagant Scot had paid him scot and lot too.*' He had but one choice; he was obliged to pass thro' the ceremony of dying either in jest or in earnest; and we shall not be surprised at the event, when we remember his propensities to the former.—Life (and especially the life of *Falstaff*) might be a jest; but he could see no joke whatever in dying: To be chopfallen was, with him, to lose both life and character together: He saw the point of honour, as well as every thing else, in ridiculous lights, and began to renounce its tyranny.

But I am too much in advance, and must retreat for more advantage. I should not forget how much opinion is against me, and that I am to make my way by the mere force and weight of evidence; without which I must not hope to possess myself of the reader: No address, no insinuation will avail. To this evidence, then, I now resort. The Courage of *Falstaff* is my Theme: And no passage will I spare from which any thing can be inferred as relative to this point. It would be as vain as injudicious to attempt concealment: How could I escape detection? The Play is in every one's memory, and a single passage remembered in detection would tell, in the mind of the partial observer, for fifty times its real weight. Indeed this argument would be void of all excuse if it declined any difficulty; if it did not meet, if it did not challenge opposition. Every passage then shall be produced from which, in my opinion, any inference, favourable or unfavourable, has or can be drawn;—but not methodically, not formally, as texts for comment, but as chance or convenience shall lead the way; but in what shape soever, they shall be always distinguishingly marked for notice. And so with that attention to truth and candour which ought to accompany even our lightest amusements I proceed to offer such proof as the case will admit, that *Courage* is a part of *Falstaff*'s

Character, that it belonged to his constitution, and was manifest in the conduct and practice of his whole life.

Let us then examine, as a source of very authentic information, what Impressions *Sir John Falstaff* had made on the characters of the Drama; and in what estimation he is supposed to stand with mankind in general as to the point of Personal Courage. But the quotations we make for this or other purposes, must, it is confessed, be lightly touched, and no particular passage strongly relied on, either in his favour or against him. Every thing which he himself says, or is said of him, is so phantastically discoloured by humour, or folly, or jest, that we must for the most part look to the spirit rather than the letter of what is uttered, and rely at last only on a combination of the whole.

We will begin then, if the reader pleases, by inquiring what Impression the very Vulgar had taken of *Falstaff*. If it is not that of Cowardice, be it what else it may, that of a man of violence, or *a Ruffian in years*, as Harry calls him, or any thing else, it answers my purpose; how insignificant soever the characters or incidents to be first produced may otherwise appear;—for these Impressions must have been taken either from personal knowledge and observation; or, what will do better for my purpose, from common fame. Altho' I must admit some part of this evidence will appear so weak and trifling that it certainly ought not to be produced but in proof Impression only.

The Hostess *Quickly* employs two officers to arrest *Falstaff*. On the mention of his name, one of them immediately observes, '*that it may chance to cost some of them their lives, for that he will stab*'—'*Alas a day*', says the hostess, '*take heed of him, he cares not what mischief he doth; if his weapon be out, he will foin like any devil; He will spare neither man, woman, or child.*' Accordingly, we find that when they lay hold on him he resists to the utmost of his power, and calls upon *Bardolph*, whose arms are at liberty, to draw. '*Away, varlets, draw Bardolph, cut me off the villain's head, throw the quean in the kennel.*' The officers cry, a rescue, a rescue! But the Chief Justice comes in and the scuffle ceases. In another scene, his wench *Doll Tearsheet* asks him '*when he will leave fighting ****** and patch up his old body for heaven*'. This is occasioned by his drawing his rapier, on great provocation, and driving *Pistol*, who is drawn likewise, down stairs, and hurting him in the shoulder. To drive *Pistol* was no great feat; nor do I mention it as such; but upon this occasion it was necessary. '*A Rascal bragging slave,*' says he, '*the rogue fled from me like quicksilver.*' Expressions, which as they remember the cowardice of *Pistol*, seem to prove that Falstaff did not value himself on the adventure. Even something may be drawn from *Davy*, *Shallow*'s serving man, who calls *Falstaff*, in ignorant admiration, the *man of war*. I must observe here, and I beg the reader will notice it, that there is not a single expression dropt by these people, or either of *Falstaff*'s followers, from which may be inferred the least suspicion of Cowardice in his character; and this is I think such an *implied negation* as deserves considerable weight.

But to go a little higher, if, indeed, to consider *Shallow*'s opinion be to go higher. It is from him, however, that we get the earliest account of *Falstaff*. He remembers him a Page to *Thomas Mowbray, Duke of Norfolk*: '*He broke*', says he, '*Schoggan's head at the Court-Gate when he was but a crack thus high.*' *Shallow*, throughout, considers him as a great Leader and Soldier, and relates this fact as an early indication only of his future Prowess. *Shallow*, it is true, is a very ridiculous character; but he picked up these Impressions somewhere; and he picked up none of a contrary tendency.—I want at present only to prove that *Falstaff* stood well in the report of common fame as to this point; and he was now near seventy years of age, and had passed in a Military line thro' the active part of his life. At this period common fame may be well considered as the seal of his character; a seal which ought not perhaps to be broke open on the evidence of any future transaction.

But to proceed. *Lord Bardolph* was a man of the world, and of sense and observation. He informs *Northumberland*, erroneously indeed, that *Percy* had beaten the King at Shrewsbury. '*The King*', according to him, '*was wounded; the Prince of Wales and the two Blunts slain, certain Nobles*, whom he names, *had escaped by flight; and the Brawn Sir John Falstaff was taken prisoner.*' But how came *Falstaff* into this list? Common fame had put him there. He is singularly obliged to Common fame.—But if he had not been a Soldier of repute, if he had not been brave as well as fat, if he had been mere *brawn*, it would have been more germane to the matter if this lord had put him down among the baggage or the provender. The fact seems to be, that there is a real consequence about Sir *John Falstaff* which is not brought forward: We see him only in his familiar hours; we enter the tavern with *Hal and Poins*; we join in the laugh and *take a pride to gird at him*: But there may be a great deal of truth in what he himself writes to the Prince, that tho' he be '*Jack Falstaff with his Familiars, he is* Sir John *with the rest of Europe*'. It has been remarked, and very truly I believe, that no man is a hero in the eye of his valet-de-chambre; and thus it is, we are witnesses only of *Falstaff*'s weakness and buffoonery; our acquaintance is with *Jack Falstaff, Plump Jack*, and *Sir John Paunch*; but if we would look for *Sir John Falstaff*, we must put on, as *Bunyan* would have expressed it, the spectacles of observation. With respect, for instance, to his Military command at Shrewsbury, nothing appears on the surface but the Prince's familiarly saying, in the tone usually assumed when speaking of *Falstaff*, '*I will procure this fat rogue a Charge of* foot;' and in another place, '*I will procure thee Jack a Charge of foot; meet me to-morrow in the Temple Hall.*' Indeed we might venture to infer from this, that a Prince of so great ability, whose wildness was only external and assumed, would not have procured, in so nice and critical a conjuncture, a Charge of foot for a known Coward. But there was more it seems in the case: We now find from this report, to which *Lord Bardolph* had given full credit, that the world had its eye upon *Falstaff* as an officer of merit, whom it expected to find in the field, and whose fate in the battle was an object of Public concern: His life was, it seems, very material indeed; a thread of so much dependence, that fiction, weaving the fates of Princes, did not think it unworthy, how coarse soever, of being made a part of the tissue.

We shall next produce the evidence of the Chief Justice of England. He inquires of his attendant, '*if the man who was then passing him was* Falstaff; *he who was in question for the robbery*'. The attendant answers affirmatively, but reminds his lord '*that he had since done good service at Shrewsbury*'; and the Chief Justice, on this occasion, rating him for his debaucheries, tells him '*that his day's service at Shrewsbury had gilded over his night's exploit at Gads Hill*'. This is surely more than Common fame: *The Chief justice* must have known his whole character taken together, and must have received the most authentic information, and in the truest colours, of his behaviour in that action.

But, perhaps, after all, the Military men may be esteemed the best judges in points of this nature. Let us hear then *Coleville* of the dale, *a Soldier, in degree a Knight, a famous rebel, and* '*whose betters, had they been ruled by him, would have sold themselves dearer*': A man who is of consequence enough to be guarded by *Blunt and led to present execution*. This man yields himself up even to the very Name and Reputation of *Falstaff*. '*I think*', says he, '*you* are *Sir John Falstaff, and in that thought yield me.*' But this is but one only among the men of the sword; they shall be produced then by dozens, if that will satisfy. Upon the return of the King and Prince Henry from Wales, the prince seeks out and finds *Falstaff* debauching in a tavern; where Peto presently brings an account of ill news from the North; and adds, '*that as he came along he met or overtook a dozen Captains, bare-headed, sweating, knocking at the taverns, and asking every one for* Sir John Falstaff.' He is followed by *Bardolph, who informs Falstaff* that '*He must away to the court immediately; a dozen Captains stay at door for him.*' Here is Military evidence in abundance, and *Court evidence* too; for what are we to infer from *Falstaff*'s being sent for to Court on this ill news, but that his opinion was to be asked, as a Military man of skill and experience, concerning the defences necessary to be taken. Nor is *Shakespeare* content, here, with leaving us to gather up *Falstaff*'s *better character* from inference and deduction: He comments on the fact by making *Falstaff* observe that '*Men of merit are sought after: The undeserver may sleep when the man of action is called on.*' I do not wish to draw *Falstaff*'s character out of his own mouth; but this observation refers to the fact, and is founded in reason. Nor ought we to reject, what in another place he says to the Chief Justice, as it is in the nature of an appeal to his knowledge. '*There is not a dangerous action*', says he, '*can peep out his head but I am thrust upon it.*' The Chief Justice seems by his answer to admit the fact. '*Well, be honest, be honest, and heaven bless your expedition.*' But the whole passage may deserve transcribing.

> *Ch. Just.* Well, the King has severed you and Prince Henry. I hear you are going with Lord John of Lancaster, against the Archbishop and the Earl of Northumberland.
>
> *Fals.* Yes, I thank your pretty sweet wit for it; but look you pray, all you that kiss my lady peace at home, that our armies join not in a hot day; for I take but two shirts out with me, and I mean not to sweat extraordinarily: If it be a hot day, if I brandish any thing but a bottle, would I might never spit white again. There is not a dangerous action can peep out his head but I am thrust upon it. Well I cannot last for ever.—But it was always the trick of our English nation, if they have a good thing to make it too common. If you will needs say I am an old man you should give me rest: I would to God my name were not so terrible to the enemy as it is. I were better to be eaten to death with a rust than to be scour'd to nothing with perpetual motion.
>
> *Ch. Just.* Well be honest, be honest, and heaven bless your expedition.

Falstaff indulges himself here in humourous exaggeration:—these passages are not meant to be taken, nor are we to suppose that they were taken, literally;—but if there was not a ground of truth, if Falstaff had not had such a degree of Military reputation as was capable of being thus humourously amplified and exaggerated, the whole dialogue would have been highly preposterous and absurd, and the acquiescing answer of the *Lord Chief justice* singularly improper.—But upon the supposition of *Falstaff*'s being considered, upon the whole, as a good and gallant Officer, the answer is just, and corresponds with the acknowledgment which had a little before been made, '*that his day's service at Shrewsbury had gilded over his night's exploit at Gads Hill.—You may thank the unquiet time*, says the Chief Justice, *for your quiet o'erposting of that action*': agreeing with what *Falstaff* says in another place;—'*Well God be thanked for these Rebels, they offend none but the virtuous*: I laud them, *I praise them.*'—Whether this be said in the true spirit of a Soldier or not, I do not determine; it is surely not in that of a mere Coward and Poltroon.

It will be needless to shew, which might be done from a variety of particulars, that *Falstaff* was known, and had consideration at Court. *Shallow* cultivates him in the idea that *a friend at Court is better than a penny in purse: Westmorland speaks* to him in the tone of an equal: Upon *Falstaff*'s telling him, that he thought his lordship had been already at Shrewsbury, *Westmorland replies*,—'Faith Sir John, *'tis more than time that I were there, and* you *too; the King I can tell you looks for us all; we must away all to night.*'—*Tut*, says Falstaff, *never fear me, I am as vigilant as a cat to steal cream.*'—He desires, in another place, of my lord John of Lancaster, '*that when he goes to Court, he may stand in his good report.*' His intercourse and correspondence with both these lords seem easy and familiar. 'Go,' says he to the page, *'bear this to my Lord of Lancaster, this to the Prince, this to the Earl of Westmorland, and this* (for he extended himself on all sides), *to old Mrs. Ursula*', whom it seems, the rogue ought to have married many years before.—But these intimations are needless: We see him ourselves in the *Royal Presence*; where, certainly, his buffooneries never brought him; nor was the Prince of a character to commit so high an indecorum, as to thrust, upon a solemn occasion, a mere Tavern companion into his father's Presence, especially in a moment when he himself deserts his looser character, and takes up that of a *Prince indeed*.—In a very important scene, where *Worcester* is expected with proposals from *Percy*, and wherein he is received, is treated with, and carries back offers of accommodation from the King, the King's attendants upon the occasion are *the Prince of Wales, Lord John of Lancaster, the Earl of Westmorland, Sir Walter Blunt, and Sir John Falstaff*.—What shall be said to this? *Falstaff* is not surely introduced here in vicious indulgence to a mob audience;—he utters but one word, a buffoon one indeed, but aside and to the Prince only. Nothing, it should seem, is wanting, if decorum would here have permitted, but that he should have spoken one sober sentence in the Presence (which yet we are to suppose him ready and able to do if occasion should have required; or his wit was given him to little purpose) and Sir *John Falstaff might* be allowed to pass for an established Courtier and counsellor of state. '*If I do grow great,* says he, *I'll grow less, purge and leave sack, and live as a nobleman should do.*' Nobility did not then appear to him at an unmeasurable distance; it was, it seems, in his idea, the very next link in the chain.

But to return. I would not demand what could bring *Falstaff* into the Royal Presence upon such an occasion, or justify the Prince's so public acknowledgment of him, but an established fame and reputation of Military merit? In short, just the like merit as brought Sir *Walter Blunt* into the same circumstances of honour.

But it may be objected that his introduction into this scene is a piece of indecorum in the author. But upon what ground are we to suppose this? Upon the ground of his being a notorious Coward? Why this is the very point in question, and cannot be granted: Even the direct contrary I have affirmed, and am endeavouring to support. But if it be supposed upon any other ground, it does not concern me; I have nothing to do with Shakespeare's indecorums in general. That there are indecorums in the Play I have no doubt: The indecent treatment of Percy's dead body is the greatest:—the familiarity of the insignificant, rude, and even ill disposed *Poins*, with the Prince, is another;—but the admission of *Falstaff* into the Royal Presence (supposing, which I have a right to suppose, that his Military character was unimpeached) does not seem to be in any respect among the number. In camps there is but one virtue and one vice; Military merit swallows up or covers all. But, after all, what have we to do with indecorums? Indecorums respect the propriety or impropriety of exhibiting certain actions;

not their truth or *falsehood* when exhibited. *Shakespeare* stands to us in the place of truth and nature: If we desert this principle we cut the turf from under us; I may then object to the robbery and other passages as indecorums, and as contrary to the truth of character. In short we may rend and tear the Play to pieces, and every man carry off what sentences he likes best.—But why this inveterate malice against poor *Falstaff*? He has faults enough in conscience without loading him with the infamy of Cowardice; a charge, which, if true, would, if I am not greatly mistaken, spoil all our mirth.—But of that hereafter.

It seems to me that, in our hasty judgment of some particular transactions, we forget the circumstances and condition of his whole life and character, which yet deserve our very particular attention. The author, it is true, has thrown the most advantageous of these circumstances into the back ground, as it were, and has brought nothing *out of the canvass* but his follies and buffoonery. We discover however, that in a very early period of his life he was familiar with *John* of *Gaunt*; which could hardly be, unless he had possessed much personal gallantry and accomplishment, and had derived his birth from a distinguished at least, if not from a Noble family.

It may seem very extravagant to insist upon *Falstaff*'s birth as a ground from which, by an inference, Personal courage may be derived, especially after having acknowledged that he seemed to have deserted those points of honour, which are more peculiarly the accompanyments of rank. But it may be observed that in the Feudal ages rank and wealth were not only connected with the point of honour, but with personal strength and natural courage. It is observable that Courage is a quality, which is at least as transmissible to one's posterity as features and complexion. In these periods men acquired and maintained their rank and possessions by personal prowess and gallantry; and their marriage alliances were made, of course, in families of the same character: And from hence, and from the exercises of their youth, we must account for the distinguished force and bravery of our ancient Barons. It is not therefore beside my purpose to inquire what hints of the origin and birth of *Falstaff, Shakespeare* may have dropped in different parts of the Play; for tho' we may be disposed to allow that *Falstaff* in his old age might, under particular influences, desert the point of honour, we cannot give up that unalienable possession of Courage, which might have been derived to him from a noble or distinguished stock.

But it may be said that *Falstaff* was in truth the child of invention only, and that a reference to the Feudal accidents of birth serves only to confound fiction with reality: Not altogether so. If the ideas of Courage and *birth* were strongly associated in the days of *Shakespeare*, then would the assignment of high birth to *Falstaff* carry, and be intended to carry along with it, to the minds of the audience the associated idea of Courage, if nothing should be specially interposed to dissolve the connection;—and the question is as concerning this intention, and this effect. (. . .)

Let it not be here objected that *Falstaff* is universally considered as a Coward;—we do indeed call him so; but that is nothing, if the character itself does not act from any consciousness of this kind, and if our Feelings take his part, and revolt against our understanding.

As to the arts by which *Shakespeare* has contrived to obscure the vices of *Falstaff*, they are such, as being subservient only to the mirth of the Play, I do not feel myself obliged to detail.

But it may be well worth our curiosity to inquire into the composition of *Falstaff*'s character—Every man we may observe, has two characters; that is, every man may be seen externally, and from without;—or a section may be made of him, and he may be illuminated from within.

Of the external character of *Falstaff*, we can scarcely be said to have any steady view. *Jack Falstaff* we are familiar with, but *Sir John* was better known, it seems, to the rest of Europe, than to his intimate companions; yet we have so many glimpses of him, and he is opened to us occasionally in such various points of view, that we cannot be mistaken in describing him as a man of birth and fashion, bred up in all the learning and accomplishments of the times;—of ability and Courage equal to any situation, and capable by nature of the highest affairs; trained to arms, and possessing the tone, the deportment, and the manners of a gentleman:—but yet these accomplishments and advantages seem to hang loose on him, and to be worn with a slovenly carelessness and inattention: A too great indulgence of the qualities of humour and wit seems to draw him too much one way, and to destroy the grace and orderly arrangement of his other accomplishments;—and hence he becomes strongly marked for one advantage, to the injury, and almost forgetfulness in the beholder, of all the rest. Some of his vices likewise strike through, and stain his Exterior:—his modes of speech betray a certain licentiousness of mind; and that high Aristocratic tone which belonged to his situation was pushed on, and aggravated into unfeeling insolence and oppression. 'It is not a confirmed brow,' says the Chief Justice, '*nor the throng of words that come with such more than impudent sauciness from you, can thrust me from a level consideration:*' '*My lord,*' answers Falstaff, '*you call honourable boldness impudent sauciness. If a man will court'sie and say nothing, he is virtuous: No my lord, my humble duty remembered, I will not be your suitor. I say to you I desire deliverance from these officers, being upon hasty employment in the King's affairs.*' 'You speak', replied the Chief Justice, 'as *having power to do wrong.*'—His whole behaviour to the Chief Justice, whom he despairs of winning by flattery, is singularly insolent; and the reader will remember many instances of his insolence to others: Nor are his manners always free from the taint of vulgar society;—'*This is the right fencing grace, my lord,*' (says he to the Chief Justice, with great impropriety of manners) '*tap for tap, and so part fair:*' 'Now the lord lighten thee,' is the reflection of the Chief Justice, 'thou art a very great *fool,*'—Such a character as I have here described, strengthened with that vigor, force, and alacrity of mind, of which he is possessed, must have spread terror and dismay thro' the ignorant, the timid, the modest, and the weak: Yet is he however, when occasion requires, capable of much accommodation and flattery;—and in order to obtain the protection and patronage of the great, so convenient to his vices and his poverty, he was put under the daily necessity of practising and improving these arts; a baseness, which he compensates to himself, like other unprincipled men, by an increase of insolence towards his inferiors.—There is also a natural activity about *Falstaff*, which for want of proper employment, shews itself in a kind of swell or bustle, which seems to correspond with his bulk, as if his mind had inflated his body, and demanded a habitation of no less circumference: Thus conditioned he rolls (in the language of *Ossian*) like a *Whale of Ocean*, scattering the smaller fry; but affording, in his turn, noble contention to *Hal* and *Poins*; who, to keep up the allusion, I may be allowed on this occasion to compare to the Thresher and the Sword-fish.

To this part of *Falstaff*'s character, many things which he does and says, and which appear unaccountably natural, are to be referred.

We are next to see him *from within*: And here we shall behold him most villainously unprincipled and debauched; possessing indeed the same Courage and ability, yet stained with numerous vices, unsuited not only to his primary qualities, but to his age, corpulency, rank, and profession:—reduced by these vices to a state of dependence, yet resolutely bent to indulge them at any price. These vices have been already enumerated; they are many, and become still more intolerable by an excess of unfeeling insolence on one hand, and of base accommodation on the other.

But what then, after all, is become of *old jack?* Is this the jovial delightful companion—*Falstaff*, the favourite and the boast of the Stage?—by no means. But it is, I think however, the *Falstaff* of Nature; the very stuff out of which the Stage Falstaff is composed; nor was it possible, I believe, out of any other materials he could have been formed. From this disagreeable draught we shall be able, I trust, by a proper disposition of light and shade, and from the influence and compression of external things, to produce *plump Jack*, the life of humour, the spirit of pleasantry, and the soul of mirth.

To this end, *Falstaff* must no longer be considered as a single independent character, but grouped, as we find him shewn to us in the Play;—his ability must be disgraced by buffoonery, and his Courage by circumstances of imputation; and those qualities be thereupon reduced into subjects of mirth and laughter:—His vices must be concealed at each end from vicious design and evil effect, and must thereupon be turned into incongruities, and assume the name of humour only;—his insolence must be repressed by the superior tone of *Hal* and *Poins*, and take the softer name of spirit only, or alacrity of mind;—his state of dependence, his temper of accommodation, and his activity, must fall in precisely with the indulgence of his humours; that is, he must thrive best and flatter most, by being extravagantly incongruous; and his own tendency, impelled by so much activity, will carry him with perfect ease and freedom to all the necessary excesses. But why, it may be asked, should incongruities recommend *Falstaff* to the favour of the Prince?— Because the Prince is supposed to possess a high relish of humour and to have a temper and a force about him, which, whatever was his pursuit, delighted in excess. This, *Falstaff* is supposed perfectly to comprehend; and thereupon not only to indulge himself in all kinds of incongruity, but to lend out his own superior wit and humour against himself, and to heighten the ridicule by all the tricks and arts of buffoonery for which his corpulence, his age, and situation, furnish such excellent materials. This compleats the Dramatic character of *Falstaff*, and gives him that appearance of perfect good-nature, pleasantry, mellowness, and hilarity of mind, for which we admire and almost love him, tho' we feel certain reserves which forbid our going that length; the true reason of which is, that there will be always found a difference between mere appearances, and reality: Nor are we, nor can we be, insensible that whenever the action of external influence upon him is in whole or in part relaxed, the character restores itself proportionably to its more unpleasing condition.

A character really possessing the qualities which are on the stage imputed to *Falstaff*, would be best shewn by its own natural energy; the least compression would disorder it, and make us feel for it all the pain of sympathy: It is the artificial condition of *Falstaff* which is the source of our delight; we enjoy his distresses, we *gird* at *him* ourselves, and urge the sport without the least alloy of compassion; and we give him, when the laugh is over, undeserved credit for the pleasure we enjoyed. If any one thinks that these observations are the effect of too much refinement, and that there was in truth more of chance in the case than of management or design, let him try his own luck;—perhaps he may draw out of the wheel of fortune a *Macbeth*, an *Othello*, a *Benedict*, or a *Falstaff*.

Such, I think, is the true character of this extraordinary buffoon; and from hence we may discern for what special purposes *Shakespeare* has given him talents and qualities, which were to be afterwards obscured, and perverted to ends opposite to their nature; it was clearly to furnish out a Stage buffoon of a peculiar sort; a kind of Game-bull which would stand the baiting thro' a hundred Plays, and produce equal sport, whether he is pinned down occasionally by *Hal* or *Poins*, or tosses such mongrils as *Bardolph*, or the Justices, sprawling in the air. There is in truth no such thing as totally demolishing *Falstaff*; he has so much of the invulnerable in his frame that no ridicule can destroy him; he is safe even in defeat, and seems to rise, like another *Antaeus*, with recruited vigour from every fall; in this as in every other respect, unlike *Parolles* or *Bobadil*: They fall by the first shaft of ridicule, but *Falstaff* is a butt on which we may empty the whole quiver, whilst the substance of his character remains unimpaired. His ill habits, and the accidents of age and corpulence, are no part of his essential constitution; they come forward indeed on our eye, and solicit our notice, but they are second natures, not *first*; mere shadows, we pursue them in vain; *Falstaff* himself has a distinct and separate subsistence; he laughs at the chace, and when the sport is over, gathers them with unruffled feather under his wing: And hence it is that he is made to undergo not one detection only, but a series of detections; that he is not formed for one Play only, but was intended originally at least for two; and the author we are told, was doubtful if he should not extend him yet farther, and engage him in the wars with *France*. This he might well have done, for there is nothing perishable in the nature of *Falstaff*. He might have involved him, by the vicious part of his character, in new difficulties and unlucky situations, and have enabled him, by the better part, to have scrambled through, abiding and retorting the jests and laughter of every beholder.

But whatever we may be told concerning the intention of *Shakespeare* to extend this character farther, there is a manifest preparation near the end of the second part of Henry IV. for his disgrace: The disguise is taken off, and he begins openly to pander to the excesses of the Prince, intitling himself to the character afterwards given him of being *the tutor and the feeder of his riots*. '*I will fetch off*,' (says he) '*these Justices.—I will devise matter enough out of this* Shallow *to keep the prince in continual laughter the wearing out of six fashions.—If the young* dace *be a bait for the old* pike,' (speaking with reference of his own designs upon *Shallow*) '*I see no reason in the law of nature but I may snap at him*.'—This is showing himself abominably dissolute: The laborious arts of fraud, which he practices on *Shallow* to induce the loan of a thousand pound, create *disgust*: and the more, as we are sensible this money was never likely to be *paid back*, as we are told that was, of which the travellers had been robbed. It is true we feel no pain for *Shallow*, he being a very bad character, as would fully appear, if he were unfolded; but *Falstaff*'s deliberation in fraud is not on that account more excusable.—The event of the old King's death draws him out almost into detestation.—'*Master* Robert Shallow, *chuse what office thou wilt in the land,—'tis thine.—I am fortune's steward.—Let us take any man's horses.—The laws of England are at my commandment.—Happy are they who have been my friends;— and woe to my* Lord Chief Justice.'—After this we ought not to complain if we see Poetic justice duly executed upon him, and that he is finally given up to shame and dishonour.

But it is remarkable that, during this process, we are not acquainted with the success of *Falstaff*'s designs upon *Shallow 'till* the moment of his disgrace. '*If I had had time*,' (says he to *Shallow*, as the King is approaching,) '*to have made new liveries, I would have bestowed the thousand pounds I borrowed* of *you*';—and the first word he utters after this period, is, '*Master* Shallow, *I owe you a thousand pounds*': We may from hence very reasonably presume, that *Shakespeare* meant to connect this fraud with the punishment of *Falstaff*, as a more avowed ground of censure and dishonour: Nor ought the consideration that this passage contains the most exquisite comic humour and propriety in another view, to diminish the truth of this observation.

But however just it might be to demolish *Falstaff* in this way, by opening to us his bad principles, it was by no means *convenient*. If we had been to have seen a single representation of him only, it might have been proper enough; but as he was to be shewn from night to night, and from age to age, the disgust arising from the *close*, would by degrees have spread itself over the whole character; reference would be had throughout to his bad principles, and he would have become less acceptable as he was more known: And yet it was necessary to bring him, like all other stage characters, to some conclusion. Every play must be wound up by some event, which may shut in the characters and the action. If some hero obtains a crown, or a mistress, involving therein the fortune of others, we are satisfied;—we do not desire to be afterwards admitted of his council, or his bed-chamber: Or if through jealousy, causeless or well founded, another kills a beloved wife, and himself after,—there is no more to be said;— they are dead, and there an end; Or if in the scenes of Comedy, parties are engaged, and plots formed, for the furthering or preventing the completion of that great article Cuckoldom, we expect to be satisfied in the point as far as the nature of so nice a case will permit, or at least to see such a manifest *disposition* as will leave us in no doubt of the event. By the bye, I cannot but think that the comic writers of the last age treated this matter as of more importance, and made more bustle about it, than the temper of the present times will well bear; and it is therefore to be hoped that the Dramatic authors of the present day, some of whom, to the best of my judgment, are deserving of great praise, will consider and treat this business, rather as a common and natural incident arising out of modern manners, than as worthy to be held forth as the great object and sole end of the Play.

But whatever be the question, or whatever the character, the curtain must not only be dropt before the eyes, but over the minds of the spectators, and nothing left for further examination and curiosity.—But how was this to be done in regard to *Falstaff*? He was not involved in the future of the Play; he was engaged in no action which, as to him, was to be compleated; he had reference to no system, he was attracted to no center; he passes thro' the Play as a lawless meteor, and we wish to know what course he is afterwards likely to take: He is detected and disgraced, it is true; but he lives by detection, and thrives on disgrace; and we are desirous to see him detected and disgraced again. The *Fleet* might be no bad scene of further amusement;—he carries all within him, *and what matter* where, *if he be still the same*, possessing the same force of mind, the same wit, and the same incongruity. This, *Shakespeare* was fully sensible of, and knew that this character could not be compleatly dismissed but by death. 'Our author, (says the Epilogue to the Second Part of Henry IV.) will continue the story with Sir *John* in it, and make you merry with fair *Catherine of France*; where, for any thing I know, *Falstaff* shall dye of a sweat, unless already he be killed with your hard opinions.' If it had been prudent in *Shakespeare* to have killed *Falstaff* with *hard opinion*, he had the means in his hand to effect it;—but dye, it seems, he must, in one form or another, and a sweat would have been no unsuitable catastrophe. However we have reason to be satisfied as it is;—his death was worthy of his birth and of his life: '*He was born*', he says, '*about three o'clock in the afternoon with a white head, and something a round belly.*' But if he came into the world in the evening with these marks of age, he departs out of it in the morning in all the follies and vanities of youth;—'*He* was *shaked*' (we are told) 'of a *burning quotidian tertran;—the young King had run bad humours on the knight;—his heart was fracted and corroborate; and a' parted just between twelve and one, even at the turning of the tide, yielding the crow a pudding, and passing directly into* Arthur's *bosom, if ever man went into the bosom of* Arthur.'—So ended this singular buffoon; and with him ends an Essay, on which the reader is left to bestow what character he pleases: An Essay professing to treat of the Courage of *Falstaff*, but extending itself to his Whole character; to the arts and genius of his Poetic-Maker, SHAKESPEARE; and thro' him sometimes, with ambitious aim, even to the principles of human nature itself.

1789—William Richardson, from *Essays on Shakespeare's Dramatic Character of Sir John Falstaff, and on His Imitation of Female Characters*

William Richardson (1743–1814) was a poet, playwright, and professor at Glasgow University.

Thus Shakespeare, whose morality is no less sublime than his skill in the display of character is masterly and unrivalled, represents Falstaff, not only as a voluptuous and base sycophant, but totally incorrigible. He displays no quality or disposition which can serve as a basis for reformation. Even his abilities and agreeable qualities contribute to his depravity. Had he been less facetious, less witty, less dexterous, and less inventive, he might have been urged to self-condemnation, and so inclined to amendment. But mortification leads him to no conviction of folly, nor determines him to any change of life. He turns, as soon as possible, from the view given him of his baseness; and rattles as it were in triumph, the fetters of habituated and willing bondage.—Lear, violent and impetuous, but yet affectionate; from his misfortunes derives improvement. Macbeth, originally a man of feeling, is capable of remorse. And the understanding of Richard, rugged and insensible though he be, betrays his heart to the assault of conscience. But the mean sensualist, incapable of honorable and worthy thoughts, is irretrievably lost; totally, and for ever depraved. An important and awful lesson!

I may be thought perhaps to have treated Falstaff with too much severity. I am aware of his being a favorite. Persons of eminent worth feel for him some attachment, and think him hardly used by the King. But if they will allow themselves to examine the character in all its parts, they will perhaps agree with me, that such feeling is delusive, and arises from partial views. They will not take it amiss, if I say that they are deluded in the same manner with Prince Henry. They are amused, and conceive an improper attachment to the means of their pleasure and amusement. I appeal to every candid reader, whether the sentiment expressed by Prince Henry is not that which every judicious spectator and reader is inclined to feel.

I could have better spar'd a better man.

Upon the whole, the character of Sir John Falstaff, consisting of various parts, produces various feelings. Some of these are agreeable and some disagreeable; but, being blended together, the general and united effect is much stronger than if their impulse had been disunited: not only so, but as the agreeable qualities are brought more into view, for in this sense alone they can be said to prevail in the character; and as the deformity of other qualities is often veiled by the pleasantry employed by the poet in their display, the general effect is in the highest degree delightful.

Henry IV, Part I in the Nineteenth Century

The fascination with Falstaff that determined and dominated so much of eighteenth-century criticism of *Henry IV, Part I* persisted into the nineteenth century and deepened, reflecting the era's interest in the exploration of individual psychology and also its writers' concerns with the moral choices that each individual must make. One of the first important American writers, Washington Irving, summed up Falstaff's appeal in a passage in his *Sketch Book* (1819): "But, old Jack Falstaff!—kind Jack Falstaff! sweet Jack Falstaff!—has enlarged the boundaries of human enjoyment; he has added vast regions of wit and good-humor, in which the poorest man may revel, and has bequeathed a never-failing inheritance of jolly laughter, to make mankind merrier and better to the latest posterity." Along with Falstaff's merits and failings, the varieties of heroism embodied in Hal and Hotspur also occupied critics.

A. W. Schlegel set the keynote for much of the century's criticism of the play in 1809 in a commentary that concentrates on the morality and psychology of the major characters, exploring the ways in which they contrast and represent aspects of the human variety. Schlegel describes old John of Gaunt as "a model of chivalrous honor" who "stands there like a pillar of the olden time which he has outlived." In contrast, Schlegel sees his son, Henry IV, as "altogether unlike" his father, a "mixture of hardness, moderation, and prudence, . . . but without openness, without true cordiality, and incapable of noble ebullitions."

In his examination of Prince Hal and Hotspur, Schlegel sees character as the vehicle driving the drama of the play. He argues that Hotspur's character is his destiny, that his character is what defeats the rebellion, which Schlegel sees as justifiable. In the prince, Schlegel finds "amiability and attractiveness," saying "however familiar he makes himself with bad company, we can never mistake him for one of them: the ignoble does indeed touch, but it does not contaminate him." Schlegel's view of Hal seems similar to the idea Hal himself expresses in his first soliloquoy: "his wildest freaks appear merely as witty tricks, by which his restless mind sought to burst through the inactivity to which he was constrained, for on the first occasion which wakes him out of his unruly levity he distinguishes himself without effort in the most chivalrous guise."

In his discussion of Falstaff, Schlegel reveals one of the characteristic attitudes of nineteenth-century Shakespeare criticism—the sensitivity of the critic to the effect a character has upon him or her.

When the great poet and critic Samuel Taylor Coleridge thought about Falstaff in 1810, he very clearly brought one of his own lifelong preoccupations into his analysis, the conflict between intellect and sensibility. "Shakespeare," Coleridge said, "has shown us the defeat of mere intellect [as represented in Falstaff] by a noble feeling [as embodied in Hal], the Prince being the superior moral character who rises above his insidious companion." Some sixty years later the critic H. N. Hudson viewed the play similarly, but with greater emphasis on the play as morally instructive, suiting its characters in his moral categories: "[A]ll through the period of *King Henry the Fourth*, [Falstaff] keeps growing worse and worse, while the Prince is daily growing better. Out of their sport-seeking intercourse he [Falstaff] picks whatever is bad, whereas the other [Hal] gathers nothing but the good. . . . At the close of the First Part, . . . the Prince freely yields up to him the honor of Hotspur's fall; thus carrying home to him such an example of self-renouncing generosity as it would seem impossible for the most hardened sinner to resist. And the Prince appears to have done this partly in the hope that it might prove a seed of truth and grace in Falstaff. . . . "

This century's focus on character caused critics to regard the boundaries of the two Henry IV plays and *Henry V* as quite fluid, as they traced Hal's development through all three. As before, many critics continued to examine Falstaff across both Henry IV plays and even as his death is described in *Henry V*. The lecturer and essayist Henry Giles discussed Falstaff's character throughout the three works, with the premise that Falstaff is a true Epicurean. However, the inclusion of a character called Falstaff in another Shakespeare play, *The Merry Wives of Windsor*, caused a good deal of consternation to lovers of Falstaff who were distressed at his translation in that comedy into an ass. Some, like William Hazlitt and Edward Dowden, simply denied that the Falstaff of *The Merry Wives* was the same man. Dowden declared that "The Falstaff of *The Merry Wives of Windsor* is another person than the Sir John who is 'in Arthur's bosom, if ever a man went to Arthur's bosom'." (Critics such as Harold Bloom continue to agree with this sentiment today.)

In the last decade of the century, the famous playwright George Bernard Shaw, who often criticized Shakespeare, deplored the character of Falstaff in his typically prickly and witty manner: ". . . Falstaff develops into an enormous joke and an exquisitely mimicked human type. Only in the end the joke withers."

1809—August Wilhelm Schlegel, from *Lectures on Dramatic Art and Literature*

August Wilhelm Schlegel (1767–1845) was an influential German critic and poet and a key figure in the German Romantic movement. He translated a number of Shakespeare's plays into German.

. . . The old John of Gaunt is a model of chivalrous honor: he stands there like a pillar of the olden time which he has outlived. His son, Henry IV., was altogether unlike him: his character is admirably sustained throughout the three pieces in which he appears. We see in it that mixture of hardness, moderation, and prudence, which, in fact, enabled him to secure the possession of the throne which he had violently usurped; but without openness, without true cordiality, and incapable of noble ebullitions, he was so little able to render his government beloved, that the deposed Richard was even wished back again.

The *First Part of Henry the Fourth* is particularly brilliant in the serious scenes, from the contrast between two young heroes, Prince Henry and Percy (with the characteristical name of Hotspur). All the amiability and attractiveness is certainly on the side of the prince: however familiar he makes himself with bad company, we can never mistake him for one of them: the ignoble does indeed touch, but it does not contaminate him; and his wildest freaks appear merely as witty tricks, by which his restless mind sought to burst through the inactivity to which he was constrained, for on the first occasion which wakes him out of his unruly levity he distinguishes himself without effort in the most chivalrous guise. Percy's boisterous valor is not without a mixture of rude manners, arrogance, and boyish obstinacy; but these errors, which prepare for him an early death, cannot disfigure the majestic image of his noble youth; we are carried away by his fiery spirit at the very moment we would most censure it. Shakspeare has admirably shown why so formidable a revolt against an unpopular and really an illegitimate prince was not attended with success: Glendower's superstitious fancies respecting himself, the effeminacy of the young Mortimer, the ungovernable disposition of Percy, who will listen to no prudent counsel, the irresolution of his older friends, the want of unity of plan and motive, are all characterized by delicate but unmistakable traits. After Percy has departed from the scene, the splendor of the enterprise is, it is true, at an end; there remain none but the subordinate participators in the revolts, who are reduced by Henry IV., more by policy than by warlike achievements. To overcome this dearth of matter, Shakspeare was in the second part obliged to employ great art, as he never allowed himself to adorn history with more arbitrary embellishments than the dramatic form rendered indispensable. The piece is opened by confused rumors from the field of battle; the powerful impression produced by Percy's fall, whose name and reputation were peculiarly adapted to be the watchword of a bold enterprise, make him in some degree an acting personage after his death. The last acts are occupied with the dying king's remorse of conscience, his uneasiness at the behavior of the prince, and lastly, the clearing up of the misunderstanding between father and son, which make up several most affecting scenes. All this, however, would still be inadequate to fill the stage, if the serious events were not interrupted by a comedy which runs through both parts of the play, which is enriched from time to time with new figures, and which first comes to its catastrophe at the conclusion of the whole, namely, when Henry V., immediately after ascending the throne, banishes to a proper distance the companions of his youthful excesses, who had promised to themselves a rich harvest from his kingly favour.

Falstaff is the crown of Shakspeare's comic invention. He has, without exhausting himself, continued this character throughout three plays, and exhibited him in every variety of situation; the figure is drawn so definitely and individually, that even to the mere reader it conveys the clear impression of personal acquaintance. Falstaff is the most agreeable and entertaining knave that ever was portrayed. His contemptible qualities are not disguised: old, lecherous, and dissolute; corpulent beyond measure, and always intent upon cherishing his body with eating, drinking, and sleeping; constantly in debt, and anything but conscientious in his choice of means by which money is to be raised; a cowardly soldier, and a lying braggart; a flatterer of his friends before their face, and a satirist behind their backs; and yet we are never disgusted with him. We see that his tender care of himself is without any mixture of malice towards others; he will only not be disturbed in the pleasant repose of his sensuality, and this he obtains through the activity of his understanding. Always on the alert, and good-humored, ever ready to crack jokes on others, and to enter into those of which he is himself the subject, so that he justly boasts he is not only witty himself, but the cause of wit in others, he is an admirable companion for youthful idleness and levity. Under a helpless exterior, he conceals an extremely acute mind; he has always at command some dexterous turn whenever any of his free jokes begin to give displeasure; he is shrewd in his distinctions, between those whose favor he has to win and those over whom he may assume a familiar authority. He is so convinced that the part which he plays can only pass under the cloak of wit, that even when alone he is never altogether serious, but gives the drollest coloring to his love-intrigues, his intercourse with others, and to his own sensual philosophy. Witness his inimitable soliloquies on honor, on the influence of wine on bravery, his descriptions of the beggarly vagabonds whom he enlisted, of Justice Shallow, &c. Falstaff has about him a whole court of amusing caricatures, who by turns make their appearance, without ever throwing him into the shade. The adventure in which the Prince, under the disguise of a robber, compels him to give up the spoil which he had just taken; the scene where the two act the part of the King and the Prince;

Falstaff's behavior in the field, his mode of raising recruits, his patronage of Justice Shallow, which afterwards takes such an unfortunate turn:—all this forms a series of characteristic scenes of the most original description, full of pleasantry, and replete with nice and ingenious observation, such as could only find a place in a historical play like the present.

1810-1811—Samuel Taylor Coleridge, from Coleridge's conversations on Shakespeare

Samuel Taylor Coleridge (1772-1834) was a great poet and critic and, with William Wordsworth, one of the founders of English Romanticism. In collaboration with Wordsworth, he published *Lyrical Ballads*, which among other pieces contained his enduring poem "The Rime of the Ancient Mariner." His best-known critical work is *Biographia Literaria*. Much of his criticism of Shakespeare exists in the form of transcribed lectures and conversations.

[From a memorandum by H. C. Robinson of a conversation with Coleridge]
Falstaff Coleridge also considered as an instance of the predominance of intellectual power. He is content to be thought both a liar and a coward in order to obtain influence over the minds of his associates. His aggravated lies about the robbery are conscious and purposed, not inadvertent untruths. On my observing that this account seemed to justify Cooke's representation, according to which a foreigner imperfectly understanding the character would fancy Falstaff to be the designing knave who actually does outwit the Prince, Coleridge answered that in his own estimation Falstaff is the superior who cannot easily be convinced that the Prince has escaped him; but that as in other instances Shakespeare has shown us the defeat of mere intellect by a noble feeling, the Prince being the superior moral character who rises above his insidious companion.

[From a memorandum by J. P. Collier of a conversation with Coleridge]
... Falstaff was no coward, but pretended to be one merely for the sake of trying experiments on the credulity of mankind: he was a liar with the same object, and not because he loved falsehood for itself. He was a man of such preeminent abilities, as to give him a profound contempt for all those by whom he was usually surrounded, and to lead to a determination on his part, in spite of their fancied superiority, to make them his tools and dupes. He knew, however low he descended, that his own talents would raise him and extricate him from any difficulty. While he was thought to be the greatest rogue, thief, and liar, he still

had that about him which could render him not only respectable, but absolutely necessary to his companions. It was in characters of complete moral depravity, but of first-rate wit and talents, that Shakespeare delighted; and Coleridge instanced Richard the Third, Falstaff, and Iago.

1817—William Hazlitt, from "Henry IV" in *Characters in Shakespeare's Plays*

William Hazlitt (1778-1830) was an English essayist and one of the finest critics of the nineteenth century.

If Shakespeare's fondness for the ludicrous sometimes led to faults in his tragedies (which was not often the case), he has made us amends by the character of Falstaff. This is perhaps the most substantial comic character that ever was invented. Sir John carries a most portly presence in the mind's eye; and in him, not to speak it profanely, "we behold the fullness of the spirit of wit and humor bodily". We are as well acquainted with his person as his mind, and his jokes come upon us with double force and relish from the quantity of flesh through which they make their way, as he shakes his fat sides with laughter, or "lards the lean earth as he walks along". Other comic characters seem, if we approach and handle them, to resolve themselves into air, "into thin air"; but this is embodied and palpable to the grossest apprehension: it lies "three fingers deep upon the ribs," it plays about the lungs and the diaphragm with all the force of animal enjoyment. His body is like a good estate to his mind, from which he receives rents and revenues of profit and pleasure in kind, according to its extent, and the richness of the soil. Wit is often a meagre substitute for pleasurable sensation; an effusion of spleen and petty spite at the comforts of others, from feeling none in itself. Falstaff's wit is an emanation of a fine constitution; an exuberance of good-humor and good-nature; an overflowing of his love of laughter, and good-fellowship; a giving vent to his heart's ease and over-contentment with himself and others. He would not be in character, if he were not so fat as he is; for there is the greatest keeping in the boundless luxury of his imagination and the pampered self-indulgence of his physical appetites. He manures and nourishes his mind with jests, as he does his body with sack and sugar. He carves out his jokes, as he would a capon, or a haunch of venison, where there is cut and come again; and pours out upon them the oil of gladness. His tongue drops fatness, and in the chambers of his brain "it snows of meat and drink". He keeps up perpetual holiday and open house, and we live with him in a round of invitations to a rump and dozen.—Yet we are not to suppose that he was a mere sensualist. All this is as much in imagination as in reality. His sensuality does not engross and stupify his other faculties, but "ascends me into the brain, clears away all the dull, crude vapors that environ it, and makes it full of nimble, fiery, and delectable shapes". His imagination keeps up the ball after his senses have done with it. He seems to have even a greater enjoyment of the freedom from restraint, of good cheer, of his ease, of his vanity, in the ideal exaggerated descriptions which he gives of them, than in fact. He never fails to enrich his discourse with allusions to eating and drinking, but we never see him at table. He carries his own larder about with him, and he is himself "a tun of man". His pulling out the bottle in the field of battle is a joke to show his contempt for glory accompanied with danger, his systematic adherence to his Epicurean philosophy in the most trying circumstances. Again, such is his deliberate exaggeration of his own vices, that it does not seem quite certain whether the account of his hostess's bill, found in his pocket, with such an out-of-the-way charge for capons and sack with only one halfpenny-worth of bread, was not put there by himself as a trick to humor the jest upon his favorite propensities, and as a conscious caricature of himself. He is represented as a liar, a braggart, a coward, a glutton, &c., and yet we are not offended but delighted with him; for he is all these as much to amuse others as to gratify himself. He openly assumes all these characters to show the humorous part of them. The unrestrained indulgence of his own ease, appetites, and convenience, has neither malice nor hypocrisy in it. In a word, he is an actor in himself almost as much as upon the stage, and we no more object to the character of Falstaff in a moral point of view than we should think of bringing an excellent comedian, who should represent him to the life, before one of the police offices. We only consider the number of pleasant lights in which he puts certain foibles (the more pleasant as they are opposed to the received rules and necessary restraints of society) and do not trouble ourselves about the consequences resulting from them, for no mischievous consequences do result. Sir John is old as well as fat, which gives a melancholy retrospective tinge to the character; and by the disparity between his inclinations and his capacity for enjoyment, makes it still more ludicrous and fantastical.

    The secret of Falstaff's wit is for the most part a masterly presence of mind, an absolute self-possession, which nothing can disturb. His repartees are involuntary suggestions of his self-love; instinctive evasions of everything that threatens to interrupt the career of his triumphant jollity and self-complacency. His very size floats him out of all his difficulties in a sea of rich conceits; and he turns round on the pivot of his convenience, with every occasion and at a moment's warning. His natural repugnance to every unpleasant thought or circumstance of itself makes light of objections, and provokes the most extravagant and licentious answers in his own justification. His indifference to truth puts no check upon his invention, and the more improbable and unexpected his contrivances are, the more happily does he seem to be delivered of them, the anticipation of their effect acting as a stimulus to the gaiety of his fancy. The success of one adventurous sally gives him spirits to undertake another: he deals always in round numbers, and his exaggerations and excuses are "open, palpable, monstrous as the father that begets them". His dissolute carelessness of what he says discovers itself in the first dialogue with the Prince.

> Falstaff. By the lord, thou say'st true, lad; and is not mine hostess of the tavern a most sweet wench?
>
> P. Henry. As the honey of Hibla, my old lad of the castle; and is not a buff-jerkin a most sweet robe of durance?
>
> Falstaff. How now, how now, mad wag, what in thy quips and thy quiddities? what a plague have I to do with a buff-jerkin?
>
> P. Henry. Why, what a pox have I to do with mine hostess of the tavern?

In the same scene he afterwards affects melancholy, from pure satisfaction of heart, and professes reform, because it is the farthest thing in the world from his thoughts. He has no qualms of conscience, and therefore would as soon talk of them as of anything else when the humor takes him.

> Falstaff. But Hal, I pr'ythee trouble me no more with vanity. I would to God thou and I knew where a commodity of good names were to be bought: an old lord of council rated me the other day in the street about you, sir; but I mark'd him not, and yet he talked very wisely, and in the street too.
>
> P. Henry. Thou didst well, for wisdom cries out in the street, and no man regards it.
>
> Falstaff. O, thou hast damnable iteration, and art indeed able to corrupt a saint. Thou hast done much harm unto me, Hal; God forgive thee for it. Before I knew thee, Hal, I knew nothing, and now I am, if a man should speak truly, little better than one of the wicked. I must give over this life, and I will give it over, by the lord; an I do not, I am a villain. I'll be damn'd for never a king's son in Christendom,
>
> P. Henry. Where shall we take a purse to-morrow. Jack?

Falstaff. Where thou wilt, lad, I'll make one; an I do not, call me villain, and baffle me.

P. Henry. I see good amendment of life in thee, from praying to purse-taking.

Falstaff. Why, Hal, 'tis my vocation, Hal. 'Tis no sin for a man to labour in his vocation.

Of the other prominent passages, his account of his pretended resistance to the robbers, "who grew from four men in buckram into eleven" as the imagination of his own valor increased with his relating it, his getting off when the truth is discovered by pretending he knew the Prince, the scene in which in the person of the old king he lectures the prince and gives himself a good character, the soliloquy on honor, and description of his new-raised recruits . . . are all inimitable. Of all of them, the scene in which Falstaff plays the part, first, of the King, and then of Prince Henry, is the one that has been the most often quoted. . . .

The heroic and serious part of these two plays [Hazlitt has also been discussing the *Second Part of Henry IV*] founded on the story of Henry IV is not inferior to the comic and farcical. The characters of Hotspur and Prince Henry are two of the most beautiful and dramatic, both in themselves and from contrast, that ever were drawn. They are the essence of chivalry. We like Hotspur the best upon the whole, perhaps because he was unfortunate.—The characters of their fathers, Henry IV and old Northumberland, are kept up equally well. Henry naturally succeeds by his prudence and caution in keeping what he has got; Northumberland fails in his enterprise from an excess of the same quality, and is caught in the web of his own cold, dilatory policy. Owen Glendower is a masterly character. It is as bold and original as it is intelligible and thoroughly natural. The disputes between him and Hotspur are managed with infinite address and insight into nature. We cannot help pointing out here some very beautiful lines, where Hotspur describes the fight between Glendower and Mortimer.

> —When on the gentle Severn's sedgy bank,
> In single opposition hand to hand,
> He did confound the best part of an hour
> In changing hardiment with great Glendower:
> Three times they breath'd, and three times did they drink,
> Upon agreement, of swift Severn's flood;
> Who then affrighted with their bloody looks,
> Ran fearfully among the trembling reeds,
> And hid his crisp head in the hollow bank,
> Blood-stained with these valiant combatants.

The peculiarity and the excellence of Shakespeare's poetry is, that it seems as if he made his imagination the hand-maid of nature, and nature the plaything of his imagination. He appears to have been all the characters, and in all the situations he describes. It is as if either he had had all their feelings, or had lent them all his genius to express themselves. There cannot be stronger instances of this than Hotspur's rage when Henry IV forbids him to speak of Mortimer, his insensibility to all that his father and uncle urge to calm him, and his fine abstracted apostrophe to honor, "By heaven methinks it were an easy leap to pluck bright honor from the moon," &c. After all, notwithstanding the gallantry, generosity, good temper, and idle freaks of the mad-cap Prince of Wales, we should not have been sorry if Northumberland's force had come up in time to decide the fate of the battle at Shrewsbury. . . . The truth is, that we never could forgive the Prince's treatment of Falstaff; though perhaps Shakespeare knew what was best, according to the history, the nature of the times, and of the man. We speak only as dramatic critics. Whatever terror the French in those days might have of Henry V, yet to the readers of poetry at present, Falstaff is the better man of the two. We think of him and quote him oftener.

1819—Washington Irving. "The Boar's Head Tavern, Eastcheap: A Shakespearian Research," from *The Sketch Book*

Washington Irving (1783–1859), one of the first notable American writers, is best known for the classic tales "Rip Van Winkle" and "The Legend of Sleepy Hollow." Much of his most memorable essays and stories were presented in *The Sketch Book*.

> "A tavern is the rendezvous, the exchange, the staple of good fellows. I have heard my great-grandfather tell, how his great-great-grandfather should say, that it was an old proverb when his great-grandfather was a child, that 'it was a good wind that blew a man to the wine.'" —MOTHER BOMBIE.

IT IS a pious custom, in some Catholic countries, to honor the memory of saints by votive lights burnt before their pictures. The popularity of a saint, therefore, may be known by the number of these offerings. One, perhaps, is left to moulder in the darkness of his little chapel; another may have a solitary lamp to throw its blinking rays athwart his effigy; while the whole blaze of adoration is lavished at the shrine of some beatified father of renown. The wealthy devotee brings his huge luminary of wax; the eager zealot his seven-branched candlestick, and even the mendicant pilgrim is by no means satisfied that sufficient light is thrown upon the deceased, unless he hangs up his little lamp of smoking oil. The consequence is, that in the eagerness to enlighten, they are often apt to obscure; and I have occasionally seen an unlucky saint almost smoked out of countenance by the officiousness of his followers.

In like manner has it fared with the immortal Shakspeare. Every writer considers it his bounden duty to light up some portion of his character or works, and to rescue some merit from oblivion. The commentator, opulent in words, produces vast tomes of dissertations; the common herd of editors send up mists of obscurity from their notes at the bottom of each page; and every casual scribbler brings his farthing rushlight of eulogy or research, to swell the cloud of incense and of smoke.

As I honor all established usages of my brethren of the quill, I thought it but proper to contribute my mite of homage to the memory of the illustrious bard. I was for some time, however, sorely puzzled in what way I should discharge this duty. I found myself anticipated in every attempt at a new reading; every doubtful line had been explained a dozen different ways, and perplexed beyond the reach of elucidation; and as to fine passages, they had all been amply praised by previous admirers; nay, so completely had the bard, of late, been overlarded with panegyric by a great German critic, that it was difficult now to find even a fault that had not been argued into a beauty.

In this perplexity, I was one morning turning over his pages, when I casually opened upon the comic scenes of Henry IV., and was, in a moment, completely lost in the madcap revelry of the Boar's Head Tavern. So vividly and naturally are these scenes of humor depicted, and with such force and consistency are the characters sustained, that they become mingled up in the mind with the facts and personages of real life. To few readers does it occur, that these are all ideal creations of a poet's brain, and that, in sober truth, no such knot of merry roysterers ever enlivened the dull neighborhood of Eastcheap.

For my part I love to give myself up to the illusions of poetry. A hero of fiction that never existed is just as valuable to me as a hero of history that existed a thousand years since: and, if I may be excused such an insensibility to the common ties of human nature, I would not give up fat Jack for half the great men of ancient chronicle. What have the heroes of yore done for me, or men like me? They have conquered countries of which I do not enjoy an acre; or they have gained laurels of which I do not inherit a leaf; or they have furnished examples of hair-brained prowess, which I have neither the opportunity nor the inclination to follow. But, old Jack Falstaff!—kind Jack Falstaff! sweet Jack Falstaff!—has enlarged the boundaries of human enjoyment; he has added vast regions of wit and good humor, in which the poorest man may revel; and has bequeathed a never-failing inheritance of jolly laughter, to make mankind merrier and better to the latest posterity.

A thought suddenly struck me: "I will make a pilgrimage to Eastcheap," said I, closing the book, "and see if the old Boar's Head Tavern still exists. Who knows but I may light upon some legendary traces of Dame Quickly and her guests; at any rate, there will be a kindred pleasure, in treading the halls once vocal with their mirth, to that the toper enjoys in smelling to the empty cask once filled with generous wine."

The resolution was no sooner formed than put in execution. I forbear to treat of the various adventures and wonders I encountered in my travels; of the haunted regions of Cock Lane; of the faded glories of Little Britain, and the parts adjacent; what perils I ran in Cateaton-street and old Jewry; of the renowned Guildhall and its two stunted giants, the pride and wonder of the city, and the terror of all unlucky urchins; and how I visited London Stone, and struck my staff upon it, in imitation of that arch rebel, Jack Cade.

Let it suffice to say, that I at length arrived in merry Eastcheap, that ancient region of wit and wassail, where the very names of the streets relished of good cheer, as Pudding Lane bears testimony even at the present day. For Eastcheap, says old Stowe, "was always famous for its convivial doings. The cookes cried hot ribbes of beef roasted, pies well baked, and other victuals: there was clattering of pewter pots, harpe, pipe, and sawtrie." Alas! how sadly is the scene changed since the roaring days of Falstaff and old Stowe! The madcap roysterer has given place to the plodding tradesman; the clattering of pots and the sound of "harpe and sawtrie," to the din of carts and the accursed dinging of the dustman's bell; and no song is heard, save, haply, the strain of some siren from Billingsgate, chanting the eulogy of deceased mackerel.

I sought, in vain, for the ancient abode of Dame Quickly. The only relic of it is a boar's head, carved in relief in stone, which formerly served as the sign, but at present is built into the parting line of two houses, which stand on the site of the renowned old tavern.

For the history of this little abode of good fellowship, I was referred to a tallow-chandler's widow, opposite, who had been born and brought up on the spot, and was looked up to as the indisputable chronicler of the neighborhood. I found her seated in a little back parlor, the window of which looked out upon a yard about eight feet square, laid out as a flower-garden; while a glass door opposite afforded a distant peep of the street, through a vista of soap and tallow candles: the two views, which comprised, in all probability, her prospects in life, and the little world in which she had lived, and moved, and had her being, for the better part of a century.

To be versed in the history of Eastcheap, great and little, from London Stone even unto the Monument, was doubtless, in her opinion, to be acquainted with the history of the universe. Yet, with all this, she possessed the simplicity of true wisdom, and that liberal communicative disposition, which I have generally remarked in intelligent old ladies, knowing in the concerns of their neighborhood.

Her information, however, did not extend far back into antiquity. She could throw no light upon the history of the Boar's Head, from the time that Dame Quickly espoused the valiant Pistol, until the great fire of London, when it was unfortunately burnt down. It was soon rebuilt, and continued to flourish under the old name and sign, until a dying landlord, struck with remorse for double scores, bad measures, and other iniquities, which are incident to the sinful race of publicans, endeavored to make his peace with heaven, by bequeathing the tavern to St. Michael's Church, Crooked Lane, towards the supporting of a chaplain. For some time the vestry meetings were regularly held there; but it was observed that the old Boar never held up his head under church government. He gradually declined, and finally gave his last gasp about thirty years since. The tavern was then turned into shops; but she informed me that a picture of it was still preserved in St. Michael's Church, which stood just in the rear. To get a sight of this picture was now my determination; so, having informed myself of the abode of the sexton, I took my leave of the venerable chronicler of Eastcheap, my visit having doubtless raised greatly her opinion of her legendary lore, and furnished an important incident in the history of her life.

It cost me some difficulty, and much curious inquiry, to ferret out the humble hanger-on to the church. I had to explore Crooked Lane, and divers little alleys, and elbows, and dark passages, with which this old city is perforated, like an ancient cheese, or a worm-eaten chest of drawers. At length I traced him to a corner of a small court surrounded by lofty houses, where the inhabitants enjoy about as much of the face of heaven, as a community of frogs at the bottom of a well.

The sexton was a meek, acquiescing little man, of a bowing, lowly habit: yet he had a pleasant twinkling in his eye, and, if encouraged, would now and then hazard a small pleasantry; such as a man of his low estate might venture to make in the company of high churchwardens, and other mighty men of the earth. I found him in company with the deputy organist, seated apart, like Milton's angels, discoursing, no doubt, on high doctrinal points, and settling the affairs of the church over a friendly pot of ale—for the lower classes of English seldom deliberate on any weighty matter without the assistance of a cool tankard to clear their understandings. I arrived at the moment when they had finished their ale and their argument, and were about to repair to the church to put it in order; so having made known my wishes, I received their gracious permission to accompany them.

The church of St. Michael's, Crooked Lane, standing a short distance from Billingsgate, is enriched with the tombs of many fishmongers of renown; and as every profession has its galaxy of glory, and its constellation of great men, I presume the monument of a mighty fishmonger of the olden time is regarded with as much reverence by succeeding generations of the craft, as poets feel on contemplating the tomb of Virgil, or soldiers the monument of a Marlborough or Turenne.

I cannot but turn aside, while thus speaking of illustrious men, to observe that St. Michael's, Crooked Lane, contains also the ashes of that doughty champion, William Walworth, knight, who so manfully clove down the sturdy wight, Wat Tyler, in Smithfield; a hero worthy of honorable blazon, as almost the only Lord Mayor on record famous for deeds of arms:—the sovereigns of Cockney being generally renowned as the most pacific of all potentates.[14]

Adjoining the church, in a small cemetery, immediately under the back window of what was once the Boar's Head, stands the tombstone of Robert Preston, whilom drawer at the tavern. It is now nearly a century since this trusty drawer of good liquor closed his bustling career, and was thus quietly deposited within call of his customers. As I was clearing away the weeds from his epitaph, the little sexton drew me on one side with a mysterious air, and informed me in a low voice, that once upon a time, on a dark wintry night, when the wind was unruly, howling, and whistling, banging about doors and windows, and twirling weathercocks, so that the living were frightened out of their beds, and even the dead could not sleep quietly in their graves, the ghost of honest Preston, which happened to be airing itself in the church-yard, was attracted by the well-known call of "waiter" from the Boar's Head, and made its sudden appearance in the midst of a roaring club, just as the parish clerk was singing a stave from the "mirre garland of Captain Death;" to the discomfiture of sundry train-band captains, and the conversion of an infidel attorney, who became a zealous Christian on the spot, and was never known to twist the truth afterwards, except in the way of business.

I beg it may be remembered, that I do not pledge myself for the authenticity of this anecdote; though it is well known that the church-yards and by-corners of this old metropolis are very much infested with perturbed spirits; and every one must have heard of the Cock Lane ghost, and the apparition that guards the regalia in the Tower, which has frightened so many bold sentinels almost out of their wits.

Be all this as it may, this Robert Preston seems to have been a worthy successor to the nimble-tongued Francis, who attended upon the revels of Prince Hal; to have been equally prompt with his "anon, anon, sir;" and to have transcended his predecessor in honesty; for Falstaff, the veracity of whose taste no man will venture to impeach, flatly accuses Francis of putting lime in his sack; whereas honest Preston's epitaph lauds him for the sobriety of his conduct, the soundness of his wine, and the fairness of his measure.[15] The worthy dignitaries of the church, however, did not appear much captivated by the sober virtues of the tapster; the deputy organist, who had a moist look out of the eye, made some shrewd remark on the abstemiousness of a man brought up among full hogsheads; and the little sexton corroborated his opinion by a significant wink, and a dubious shake of the head.

Thus far my researches, though they threw much light on the history of tapsters, fishmongers, and Lord Mayors, yet disappointed me in the great object of my quest, the picture of the Boar's Head Tavern. No such painting was to be found in the church of St. Michael. "Marry and amen!" said I, "here endeth my research!" So I was giving the matter up, with the air of a baffled antiquary, when my friend the sexton, perceiving me to be curious in every thing relative to the old tavern, offered to show me the choice vessels of the vestry, which had been handed down from remote times, when the parish meetings were held at the Boar's Head. These were deposited in the parish club-room, which had been transferred, on the decline of the ancient establishment, to a tavern in the neighborhood.

A few steps brought us to the house, which stands No. 12 Miles Lane, bearing the title of The Mason's Arms, and is kept by Master Edward Honeyball, the "bully-rock" of the establishment. It is one of those little taverns which abound in the heart of the city, and form the centre of gossip and intelligence of the neighborhood. We entered the bar-room, which was narrow and darkling; for in these close lanes but few rays of reflected light are enabled to struggle down to the inhabitants, whose broad day is at best but a tolerable twilight. The room was partitioned into boxes, each containing a table spread with a clean white cloth, ready for dinner. This showed that the guests were of the good old stamp, and divided their day equally, for it was but just one o'clock. At the lower end of the room was a clear coal fire, before which a breast of lamb was roasting. A row of bright brass candlesticks and pewter mugs glistened along the mantelpiece, and an old-fashioned clock ticked in one corner. There was something primitive in this medley of kitchen, parlor, and hall, that carried me back to earlier times, and pleased me. The place, indeed, was humble, but every thing had that look of order and neatness, which bespeaks the superintendence of a notable English housewife. A group of amphibious-looking beings, who might be either fishermen or sailors, were regaling themselves in one of the boxes. As I was a visitor of rather higher pretensions, I was ushered into a little misshapen backroom, having at least nine corners. It was lighted by a skylight, furnished with antiquated leathern chairs, and ornamented with the portrait of a fat pig. It was evidently appropriated to particular customers, and I found a shabby gentleman, in a red nose and oil-cloth hat, seated in one corner, meditating on a half-empty pot of porter.

The old sexton had taken the landlady aside, and with an air of profound importance imparted to her my errand. Dame Honeyball was a likely, plump, bustling little woman, and no bad substitute for that paragon of hostesses, Dame Quickly. She seemed delighted with an opportunity to oblige; and hurrying up stairs to the archives of her house, where the precious vessels of the parish club were deposited, she returned, smiling and courtesying, with them in her hands.

The first she presented me was a japanned iron tobacco-box, of gigantic size, out of which, I was told, the vestry had smoked at their stated meetings, since time immemorial; and which was never suffered to be profaned by vulgar hands, or used on common occasions. I received it with becoming reverence; but what was my delight, at beholding on its cover the identical painting of which I was in quest! There was displayed the outside of the Boar's Head Tavern, and before the door was to be seen the whole convivial group, at table, in full revel; pictured with that wonderful fidelity and force, with which the portraits of renowned generals and commodores are illustrated on tobacco-boxes, for the benefit of posterity. Lest, however, there should be any mistake, the cunning limner had warily inscribed the names of Prince Hal and Falstaff on the bottoms of their chairs.

On the inside of the cover was an inscription, nearly obliterated, recording that this box was the gift of Sir Richard Gore, for the use of the vestry meetings at the Boar's Head Tavern, and that it was "repaired and beautified by his successor, Mr. John Packard, 1767." Such is a faithful description of this august and venerable relic; and I question whether the learned Scriblerius contemplated his Roman shield, or the Knights of the Round Table the long-sought sangreal, with more exultation.

While I was meditating on it with enraptured gaze, Dame Honeyball, who was highly gratified by the interest it excited, put in my hands a drinking cup or goblet, which also belonged to the vestry, and was descended from the old Boar's Head. It bore the inscription of having been the gift of Francis Wythers, knight, and was held, she told me, in exceeding great value, being considered very "antyke." This last opinion was strengthened by the shabby gentleman in the red nose and oil-cloth hat, and whom I strongly suspected of being a lineal descendant from the valiant Bardolph. He suddenly roused from his meditation on the pot of porter, and, casting a knowing look at the goblet, exclaimed, "Ay, ay! the head don't ache now that made that there article!"

The great importance attached to this memento of ancient revelry by modern churchwardens at first puzzled me; but there is nothing sharpens the apprehension so much as antiquarian research; for I immediately perceived that this could be no other than the identical "parcel-gilt goblet" on which Falstaff made his loving, but faithless vow to Dame Quickly; and which would, of course, be treasured up with care among the regalia of her domains, as a testimony of that solemn contract.[16]

Mine hostess, indeed, gave me a long history how the goblet had been handed down from generation to generation. She also entertained me with many particulars concerning the worthy vestrymen who have seated themselves thus quietly on the stools of the ancient roysterers of Eastcheap, and, like so many commentators, utter clouds of smoke in honor of Shakspeare. These I forbear to relate, lest my readers should not be as curious in these matters as myself. Suffice it to say, the neighbors, one and all, about Eastcheap, believe that Falstaff and his merry crew actually lived and revelled there. Nay, there are several legendary anecdotes concerning him still extant among the oldest frequenters of the Mason's Arms, which they give as transmitted down from their forefathers; and Mr. M'Kash, an Irish hair-dresser, whose shop stands on the site of the old Boar's Head, has several dry jokes of Fat Jack's, not laid down in the books, with which he makes his customers ready to die of laughter.

I now turned to my friend the sexton to make some further inquiries, but I found him sunk in pensive meditation. His head had declined a little on one side; a deep sigh heaved from the very bottom of his stomach; and, though I could not see a tear trembling in his eye, yet a moisture was evidently stealing from a corner of his mouth. I followed the direction of his eye through the door which stood open, and found it fixed wistfully on the savory breast of lamb, roasting in dripping richness before the fire.

I now called to mind that, in the eagerness of my recondite investigation, I was keeping the poor man from his dinner. My bowels yearned with sympathy, and, putting in his hand a small token of my gratitude and goodness, I departed, with a hearty benediction on him, Dame Honeyball, and the Parish Club of Crooked Lane;—not forgetting my shabby, but sententious friend, in the oil-cloth hat and copper nose.

Thus have I given a "tedious brief" account of this interesting research, for which, if it prove too short and unsatisfactory, I can only plead my inexperience in this branch of literature, so deservedly popular at the present day. I am aware that a more skilful illustrator of the immortal bard would have swelled the materials I have touched upon, to a good merchantable bulk; comprising the biographies of William Walworth, Jack Straw, and Robert Preston; some notice of the eminent fishmongers of St. Michael's; the history of Eastcheap, great and little; private anecdotes of Dame Honeyball, and her pretty daughter, whom I have not even mentioned; to say nothing of a damsel tending the breast of lamb, (and whom, by the way, I remarked to be a comely lass, with a neat foot and ankle;)—the whole enlivened by the riots of Wat Tyler, and illuminated by the great fire of London.

All this I leave, as a rich mine, to be worked by future commentators; nor do I despair of seeing the tobacco-box, and the "parcel-gilt goblet," which I have thus brought to light, the subjects of future engravings, and almost as fruitful of voluminous dissertations and disputes as the shield of Achilles, or the far-famed Portland vase.

NOTES

14. The following was the ancient inscription on the monument of this worthy; which, unhappily, was destroyed in the great conflagration.

> Hereunder lyth a man of Fame,
> William Walworth callyd by name;
> Fishmonger he was in lyfftime here,
> And twise Lord Maior, as in books appere;
> Who, with courage stout and manly myght,
> Slew Jack Straw in Kyng Richard's sight.
> For which act done, and trew entent,
> The Kyng made him knyght incontinent;
> And gave him armes, as here you see,
> To declare his fact and chivaldrie.
> He left this lyff the yere of our God
> Thirteen hundred fourscore and three odd.

An error in the foregoing inscription has been corrected by the venerable Stowe. "Whereas," saith he, "it hath been far spread abroad by vulgar opinion, that the rebel smitten down so manfully by Sir William Walworth, the then worthy Lord Maior, was named Jack Straw, and not Wat Tyler, I thought good to reconcile this rash-conceived doubt by such testimony as I find in ancient and good records. The principal leaders, or captains, of the commons, were Wat Tyler, as the first man; the second was John, or Jack, Straw," etc., etc. —STOWE'S LONDON.

15. As this inscription is rife with excellent morality, I transcribe it for the admonition of delinquent tapsters. It is, no doubt, the production of some choice spirit, who once frequented the Boar's Head.

> Bacchus, to give the toping world surprise,
> Produced one sober son, and here he lies.
> Though rear'd among full hogsheads, he defy'd
> The charms of wine, and every one beside.
> O reader, if to justice thou'rt inclined,
> Keep honest Preston daily in thy mind.
> He drew good wine, took care to fill his pots,
> Had sundry virtues that excused his faults.
> You that on Bacchus have the like dependance,
> Pray copy Bob in measure and attendance.

16. Thou didst swear to me upon a parcel-gilt goblet, sitting in my Dolphin chamber, at the round table, by a sea-coal fire, on Wednesday, in Whitsunweek, when the prince broke thy head for likening his father to a singing man at Windsor; thou didst swear to me then, as I was washing thy wound, to marry me, and make me my lady, thy wife. Can'st thou deny it?—Henry IV., Part 2.

1850—Henry Giles, from "Falstaff: A Type of Epicurean Life" in *Lectures and Essays*

Henry Giles (1809–1882), an Irish-born preacher, essayist, and lecturer, immigrated to America in 1840. His volume *Lectures and Essays* covers a range of topics, from literature to Irish history. His most popular book was *Human Life in Shakespeare* (1868).

Falstaff is an Epicurean, after the lowest interpretation of Epicurus; and such is the least evil form of character, which springs from mere intellect combined with the senses. Where moral principles and sympathy are inactive, it is well that irritable and ambitious passions should be so likewise, or a great intellect would become a great scourge. Indolence, therefore, and self-indulgence, sets limits to energies which would scarcely be used aright, and the love of ease becomes a safeguard against talents which the love of power would make a curse. Falstaff is of those who value each moment by what it confers of palpable enjoyment; of those who say, Let us eat and drink, for to-morrow we die; and he acted out his philosophy consistently and completely. He is true to his creed, and his practice fulfills it to the letter. He is honest and open, too, in its profession. Beyond the boundary of the actual, Falstaff discerns no reality. Out from the region of the senses he appreciates no means of happiness. Within this boundary all being exists for him; beyond it are only emptiness and death. A spiritual order of things has no hold on his convictions; and the future, which is to survive his animal economy, has no influence on his feelings. He has therefore no sentiment. He laughs at it. He derides it. Chivalry is to him mere vanity; glory a worthless phantom. Daring, in his view is hot-brained folly. Danger is always to be avoided, and never to be sought. After feigning death at Shrewsbury, he thus soliloquizes: "Counterfeit? I lie. I am no counterfeit; for he is but the counterfeit of a man, who has not the life of a man; but to counterfeit dying when a man thereby liveth, is to be no counterfeit, but the true and perfect image of life indeed. The better part of valor is discretion; in the which better part I have saved my life." His reflections upon "honor" are conceived in the same absorbing materialism: "Can honor set a leg? No. Honor hath no skill in surgery, then. What is honor? A word. What is in that word honor? Air; a trim reckoning. Who hath it? He that died o' Wednesday. Doth he feel it? No. Doth he hear it? No. Is it insensible, then? Yea, to the dead. But will it not live with the living? No. Why? Detraction will not suffer it. Therefore, I'll none of it."

Falstaff has little sympathy. He loves none, and he cares for few. He is luxuriously selfish. Constant indulgence of the passions blunts every finer sensibility, and extinguishes generosity of character. The affections are narrowed by depravity, and all that corrupts the moral nature, contracts the social. The voluptuary is by necessity selfish, and the gifted voluptuary effectively so. The voluptuary of talents is selfish by instinct, and selfish by ability; by instinct he pursues merely his own gratification, and by ability he makes others the instruments of it. Thus it is with Falstaff. All are for his use, and, except for that, he esteems them of no value. The prince is to supply his money; Dame Quickly is to provide his food; the page is for his service; and Bardolf for his jests.

Seeing that so much of the selfish and the heartless enters into this character, why is it not more odious to us? The fact is, the brilliant qualities alone of Falstaff render him attractive; and his vicious ones are not directly or aforethought inhuman. He is not in earnest for any thing; he has no enthusiasm; he admires nothing; he covets merely to live jovially, and to live at ease. Companions to his wish around him, fare to his taste before him; plenty of sack, and a sea-coal fire; no disturbances from justices or duns; and he would have the best Elysium he could conceive or picture. He does not love any, neither does he hate any. If he is wanting in affection, he is also void of malice. It is from this conviction that we tolerate him; that we laugh at his jokes, and revel in the prodigality of his fancy. Did we feel in him any positive inhumanity, his jokes would disgust, and his fancy would revolt us. And, besides, selfish though he be, there is a sort of rude friendliness about him. Though he uses Bardolf, he does not abuse him. Even when he is most exacting, he pays back more than he receives, in the humor and the wit by which he diversifies the lives of those who serve him; and this he seems to know most thoroughly, and not to set it any whit below its value. He is often grotesque, but he is never tryannical; and between himself and the page there goes on a strain of playfulness, in which his rollicking jokes appear to conceal an underlying vein of gentleness and tenderness. He is a big, fat, easy-going, easy-living man; who is not unkind, but will be indulged; who can bear much scolding, and yet is liked by those who scold him the loudest and with the most justice; a jovial, joyous, care-hating man, who will not beg pardon of the world for being in it; and who, moreover, thinks that the world ought to keep him well while it has him.

As it is, then, we take him for what he is, and accept the pleasure he affords. He does not arouse our antipathies, and he does not falsify our expectations. He is open and clear to our view, and we know him as he is; we do not look for moral greatness in him, as we do not require him to walk a thousand miles successively in a thousand hours. We should never mistake him for a peripatetic philosopher, and we feel no anger because he is not. As little should we mistake him for a patriot or a philanthropist. We should have had no hope, did he live in our age, to see him volunteer in the Greek war, or a missionary to the heathens of India. We should despair to move his heart to subscribe to the Bible Society. Believing merely in this world, he would have no care beyond his own term of possession. With the Irishman in the house on fire, he would probably exclaim, What is it to me? I am but a tenant. Go to, go to, (he would say,) annoy me not with these vain disturbances; let your melancholy bipeds take such things in charge; let your lean folks see to them; "let your restless, attenuated apologies for humanity, that have no appetite and no digestion, busy themselves with your spiritual irritations; but leave an honest man in peace, who understands what is good, and who knows how to use it.

To lay aside levity of expression, earnest purpose is foreign to characters of the Falstaff order. Seriousness, for good or evil, is no part of their nature; and if we laugh at their wit, it is with no approbation of their vices. We may relax with the indolent, and yet not depart from the worthy; we may contemplate a phase of human nature, and though we do not resist the mirth which it excites, neither need we turn from it without some addition to our wisdom.

And this remark applies, I think, with very peculiar force to any intelligent reflection on the character of Falstaff. What a mornful condition of humanity is presented to us in the debasement of talent to the appetites! Behold it in the picture set before us in Falstaff! Look at that gray-headed, gray-bearded old man, lolling, bloated on the dregs of life; the desires insatiate as strength declines; the senses gross, while a brilliant imagination flows in radiance over them, as the sun upon a morass; abilities, which might have exalted empires, devoted to the cooking of a capon or the merits of a sack posset; eloquence and wit lavished upon blackguards; law, honor, courage, chastity, made a jest. Laugh, it is true, you must; but, when you have laughed, turn back and think; and after thinking, you will admit that tragedy itself has not any thing more sad.

In the character of Falstaff there is a foregone conclusion, upon which every thoughtful mind will dwell. He is presented to us an old man, "written down old, with all the characters of age." We have, therefore, before us the last stage of a life, and we have its ultimate result. Were we to meet, in actual intercourse, a man with the genius and habits of Falstaff, we would know that a miserable experience lay behind it. The brilliant wit of the antiquated libertine might, for a moment, cause us to forget the purpose of existence, but soon, the bloated spectre would become to us its most solemn memento. Much, we would know, of excellent living material had been spoiled, ere the ruin which we gazed on, could exist. There was a youth to this old age. We are sure that commanding abilities enriched it, for, even in their last abuse, these abilities are yet commanding; and truth, as it is now, could not always have been a jest. By what process, we would ask, has the noble been changed into the base? By a process, alas, too often repeated ever to be strange! There was fine judgment, but it was not under the guidance of rectitude. There was imagination, but it was not chastened by purity. There was sensibility, but it fell amidst grosser pleasures, and among them it was smothered. The merely intellectual faculties kept their supremacy, and the passions went from strength to strength. In the midst of boon companions, the royalty of sheer mind was acknowledged. The discourse of a strong reason compelled respect, even through the shoutings of revelry. The corruscations of a fire-lit fancy played among the broken clouds of nightly orgies, and tinted their ragged fringes with golden light. Days there were, which excitement shortened, and nights which gaiety prolonged. While the senses had the delusion of an immortality in youth, pleasure appeared perennial; it seemed to have a fairness which could never wither, to flourish with a summer bloom which no frost could chill. Years wore on, the physical powers grew sluggish, and the mental powers selfish. At this stage of his course, let us suppose that we have such a person in the character of Falstaff. He has come to a dishonored and to a comfortless age. The world owes him no reverence. Mankind is indebted to such a man for nothing but his example; and, for his example, only as a warning. He has been untrue to the affections, and now he has no affections true to him. Old, unwieldy, infirm, wifeless, childless, friendless, he is at last alone, among the dishonest and the false.

A sad life is that which is called a life of pleasure; and it is immeasurably sad when the sons of genius enslave themselves to it. How often must remorse appal them! What alternations to them of anguish and lassitude! What nights of madness, and what days of sorrow! Oh, how terrible to think of the past, when the past is an ocean overhung with darkness, and the shipwrecked faculties tossed in fragments upon its waves! Take into your mental view some voluptuary, who might have been an ornament to his species, but whom the infatuation of the senses has destroyed. Behold him in a moment of repentance, and in solitude. Mark the wretchedness of his face, and the convulsions of his breast. Look at him in his joyless home, where ruin is gathering to its last desolation, where hearts are throbbing which must soon be broken. For a little, the man, the generous, the loving man, seems to triumph in his nature; a new life seems to spring forth in his weeping, the return of an alienated heart to its allegiance, of a wandering soul to its peace, and a light of joy begins to overspread his dwelling. Watch him again encircled by his companions; watch him, amused by the clashings of intoxicated eloquence; whirled in the mazes of a delirious imagination; the fatal spell comes over him again; he gives himself to the trance with his eyes open, and the next time he awakes, he awakes to his perdition.

The law of compensation operates with certainty, and it operates impartially. To this solemn fact our great dramatist is ever faithful. This august poet of conscience and the heart, this wonderful revealer of the passions and their struggles, this moralist of insight, almost of inspiration, never forgets the eternal principles of right and wrong. In Falstaff, even as in Macbeth, Shakspeare vindicates these principles. Falstaff is loosely related to other men; other men are, therefore, loosely related to him. He does not reap attachment where he has only sown indifference. His creed is turned on himself. He has no faith in excellence, and he gets no credit for possessing any. His practice is retorted as well as his creed. He uses his inferiors, and his superiors use him. They give him their presence when it is their desire to be amused, but they discard him as a worn rag when gaiety is no longer seemly. Falstaff occasions mirth, but does not gain esteem. He adds to the brightness of the revel, but when the revel is over he is paid by no gratitude. For the vile there can be no esteem. Esteem cannot be where there is no confidence; and there can be no confidence where there is no respect. The pure cannot have respect for the vicious; and the vicious have no respect for each other. Their association precludes all reverence, for it is a cohesion in common infamy. They tolerate each other upon a mutual suppression of moral distinctions; but there are times, when the bad appear to the bad more detestable than they possibly can to the upright. The upright look not on the worst of their brethren without a touch of mercy; but the bad, under the laceration of their crimes, glare upon their compeers with unmitigated horror. The bonds which keep them together are as fragile as they are corrupt, and when low interest or depraved gratification is exhausted, always easy to be severed. The vicissitude which breaks up the combination finds in every brother of it a traitor or an enemy. When once, therefore, a man plunges into a gross existence, he will, in time, discover that even the lowest will not do him reverence. He will be rejected by the persons who basked in the radiance of his fancy, and who were electrified by the flashes of his wit. Approbation is not for great talents, but for good works. Wages belong to the laborer, not to the idler, and much less to the spendthrift. It is no matter for praise that a man has a strong intellect, which is active only in debasement; that he has an affluence of imagination, which is squandered in corruption; that he has a rich faculty of eloquence, which is dumb on every generous theme; and absent from all worthy places, which is only to be heard among inebriate debaters, and is only to be aroused by maudlin applause. No glory is for this man but shame, and shame the more burning for his genius.

The end of Falstaff may stand as a type for the close of every such life. It was without regret and without honor. There is no life so melancholy in its close, as that of a licentious wit. The companions with whom he jested abandon him; the hope of the visible world is gone, and, in the spiritual, he has no refuge. Utterly impoverished in all means of amusement and comfort, he is thrown entirely on himself; and, when he can least bear to be alone, he is delivered over to unmitigated solitude. Pleasure was the bond by which he held his former associates, and by affliction that bond is broken. The gay assembly takes no thought of him, and the place therein shall know him no more. Instead of the hilarious looks which were wont to beam around him, a crowd of ghastly images are flitting in his solitary room; instead of a board groaning under the weight of the feast, a couch is made hard with the pressure of disease; instead of the blaze of many lights, there is the dimness of a single taper; and for the song and the viol, there are the moanings of death.

Laurence Sterne had sentiment, which was often expressed with the most delicate tenderness, but he debased the finest of humor by the grossest of ribaldry. He scattered about him the wit of Rabelais, and his filth also; but when his brilliant career was run, there were none to cheer him at the end. "The last offices," Sir Walter Scott tells us, "were rendered him, not in his own house, or by kindred affection, but in an inn, and by strangers." Sir Walter also remarks, that Sterne's death strikingly resembled Falstaff's. Brinsley Sheridan was, like Falstaff, companion to a Prince of Wales. He was, also, like Falstaff, "a fellow of infinite jest, of most excellent fancy." He lavished upon this heir of kings the bounties of his humor and his eloquence, and in return for such wealth, the heir of kings abandoned the donor. When the lights went out upon the banquet, the man who threw the glory over it was no more remembered. But, when the frame sickened and the soul drooped, no royalty was at hand; when the eye had no more the lustre of wit, it looked in vain for brothers of the feast; when lips, from which there once flew winged words, feebly stammered titled names, none who bore those names were present to hear. The spendthrift, both in property and talents, was left alone with fate; and while eternity was opening for his spirit, the bailiffs were watching for his corpse.

The late Theodore Hook had vast capacities for amusing, and he, too, was a favorite with nobles and with princes. His repartees banished dullness from their parties, and his pen was the slave of their order. He was equally the champion of their politics, and the glory of their dinner tables. He was, in fact, a wit of all-work in aristocratic houses. He played, jested, conversed; tried, by every device, to make himself generally useful to his entertainers, and he was not unsuccessful. His brain was a storehouse of combustibles, out of which he played off intellectual fire-works in every caprice of oddity; his listless spectators gazed and admired, retired when the exhibition was over, and forgot the show. Meanwhile, secret wretchedness was devouring this man's life, and outward ruin was collecting on his head. He had gone through the experience of his class; he outran his means, depended on those whom he had amused, and found it was reliance upon a vapor. His comicry was all they wanted; they could afford him laughter, but not sympathy; they could join in his merriment, but they had no concern in his distress. His death was sudden, it was silent, and it was in poverty; "He died, and made no sign!"

This class is well embodied in Falstaff, in his life, also in his death. No death in Shakspeare is more sadly impressive to me than that of Falstaff. In the other deaths there is the sweetness of innocence, or the force of passion. Desdemona expires in her gentleness; Hamlet, with all his solemn majesty about him; Macbeth reels beneath the blow of destiny; Richard, in the tempest of his courage and his wickedness, finds a last hour conformable to his cruel soul; Lear has at once exhausted life and misery; Othello has no more for which he can exist; but the closing moments of Falstaff are gloomy without being tragic; they are dreary and oppressive, with little to relieve the sinking of our thoughts, except it be the presence of humanity in the person of Mrs. Quickly. When prince and courtier had forsaken their associate, this humble woman remained near him. The woman, whose property he squandered, and whose good name he did not spare; this woman, easily persuaded and easily deceived, would not quit even a worthless man in his helpless hour, nor speak severely of him when that hour was ended. Here is the greatness of Shakspeare: he never forgets our nature, and in the most unpromising circumstances he compels us to feel its sacredness. The last hours even of Falstaff he enshrouds in the dignity of death; and, by a few simple and pathetic words in the mouth of his ignorant but charitable hostess, he lays bare the mysterious struggles of an expiring soul. "A parted," she says, "even just between twelve and one, e'en at the turning o' the tide; for after I saw him fumble with the sheets, and play with flowers, and smile upon his finger ends, I knew there was but one way, for his nose was sharp as a pen, and a babbled of green fields. How now, Sir John, quoth I? What, man, be of good cheer! So 'a cried out, God! God! God! three or four times; then all was cold."

Thus, as Shakspeare pictures, a man of pleasure died. Even upon him nature again exerts her sway; the primitive delights of childhood revisit his final dreaming; and he plays with flowers, and he babbles of green fields. And that voice of an eternal Power, which was lost in the din of the festival, must have utterance in the travail of mortality; and exclamations, which falter to the silence of the tomb, make confession of a faith which all the practice had denied.

1872—H. N. Hudson, from *Shakespeare: His Life, Art, and Characters*

Henry Norman Hudson (1814–86) was an American essayist and Shakespearean scholar. According to *The Cambridge History of English and American Literature*, his criticism was "popular rather than scholarly" and of the Romantic tradition of Coleridge in that it "endeavours to set forth Shakespeare's inwardness, and pays comparatively little attention to his outwardness."

. . . [A]ll through the period of King Henry the Fourth, [Falstaff] keeps growing worse and worse, while the Prince is daily growing better. Out of their sport-seeking intercourse he [Falstaff] picks whatever is bad, whereas the other [Hal] gathers nothing but the good. As represented in the Comedy he [Falstaff] seems to be in the swiftest part of this worsening process. At the close of the First Part of the History, the Prince freely yields up to him the honor of Hotspur's fall; thus carrying home to him such an example of self-renouncing generosity as it would seem impossible for the most hardened sinner to resist. And the Prince appears to have done this partly in the hope that it might prove a seed of truth and grace in Falstaff, and start him in a better course of life. But the effect upon him is quite the reverse. Honor is nothing to him but as it may help him in the matter of sensual and heart-steeling self-indulgence. And the surreptitious fame thus acquired, instead of working in him for good, merely serves to procure him larger means and larger license for pampering his gross animal selfishness.

His thoughts dwell not at all on the Prince's act of magnanimity, which would shame his egotism and soften his heart, but only on his own ingenuity and success in the stratagem that led to that act. So that the effect is just to puff him up more than ever with vanity and conceit of wit, and thus to give a looser rein and a sharper stimulus to his greed and lust; for there is probably nothing that will send a man faster to the Devil than that sort of conceit. The result is, that Falstaff soon proceeds to throw off whatever of restraint may have hitherto held his vices in check, and to wanton in the arrogance of utter impunity. As he then unscrupulously appropriated the credit of another's heroism; so he now makes no scruple of sacrificing the virtue, the honor, the happiness of others to his own mean and selfish pleasure.

1875—Edward Dowden, from *Shakespeare: A Critical Study of His Mind and Art*

Edward Dowden (1843–1913) was an Irish critic, university lecturer, and poet.

Shakespeare has judged Henry IV., and pronounced that his life was not a failure; still it was at best partial success. Shakespeare saw, and he proceeded to show to others, that all which Bolingbroke had attained, and almost incalculably greater possession of good things could be attained more joyously, by nobler means. The unmistakable enthusiasm of the poet about his Henry V. has induced critics to believe that in him we find Shakspere's ideal of manhood. He must certainly be regarded as Shakspere's ideal of manhood in the sphere of practical achievement, the hero, and central figure therefore of the historical plays.

The fact has been noticed that with respect to Henry's youthful follies, Shakspere deviated from all authorities known to have been accessible to him. "An extraordinary conversion was generally thought to have fallen upon the Prince on coming to the crown,—insomuch that the old chroniclers could only account for the change by some miracle of grace or touch of supernatural benediction." Shakspere, it would seem, engaged now upon historical matter and not the fantastic substance of a comedy, found something incredible in the sudden transformation of a reckless libertine (the Henry described by Cagton, by Fabyan and others) into a character of majestic force, and large practical wisdom. Rather than reproduce this incredible popular tradition concerning Henry, Shakspere preferred to attempt the difficult task of exhibiting the Prince as a sharer in the wild frolic of youth, while at the same time he was holding himself prepared for the splendid entrance upon his manhood, and stood really aloof in his inmost being from the unworthy life of his associates.

The change which effected itself in the Prince, as represented by Shakspere, was no miraculous conversion, but merely the transition from boyhood to adult years, and from unchartered freedom to the solemn responsibilities of a great ruler. We must not suppose that Henry formed a deliberate plan for concealing the strength and splendour of his character, in order afterwards to flash forth upon men's sight and overwhelm and dazzle them. When he soliloquizes (1 Henry IV., Act i., Scene 2), having bid farewell to Poins and Falstaff,

> I know you all, and will awhile uphold
> The unyoked humour of your idleness:
> Yet herein will I imitate the sun,
>> Who doth permit the base contagious clouds
>> To smother up his beauty from the world,
>> That, when he please again to be himself,
>> Being wanted, he may be more wonder'd at,
>> By breaking through the foul and ugly mists
>> Of vapours, that did seem to strangle him.

—when Henry soliloquises thus, we are not to suppose that he was quite as wise and diplomatical as he pleased to represent himself, for the time being, to his own heart and conscience. The Prince entered heartily and without reserve into the fun and frolic of his Eastcheap life; the vigour and the folly of it were delightful; to be clapped on the back, and shouted for as "Hal," was far better than the doffing of caps and crooking of knees, and delicate, unreal phraseology of the court. But Henry, at the same time, kept himself from subjugation to what was really base. He could truthfully stand before his father (1 Henry IV., Act iii., Scene 2), and maintain that his nature was substantially sound and untainted, capable of redeeming itself from all past, superficial dishonour.

Has Shakspere erred? Or is it not possible to take energetic part in a provisional life, which is known to be provisional, while at the same time a man holds his truest self in reserve for the life that is best, and highest, and most real? May not the very consciousness, indeed, that such a life is provisional, enable one to give oneself away to it, satisfying its demands with scrupulous care, or with full and free enjoyment, as a man could not if it were a life which had any chance of engaging his whole personality, and that finally? Is it possible to adjust two states of being, one temporary and provisional, the other absolute and final, and to pass freely out of one into the other? Precisely because the one is perfect and indestructible, it does not fear the counter life. May there not have been passages in Shakspere's own experience which authorised him in his attempt to exhibit the successful adjustment of two apparently incoherent lives?

The central element in the character of Henry is his noble realisation of fact. To Richard II life was a graceful and shadowy ceremony, containing beautiful and pathetic situations. Henry IV saw in the world a substantial reality, and he resolved to obtain mastery over it by courage and by craft. But while Bolingbroke with his caution and his policy, his address and his ambition, penetrated only a little way among the facts of life, his son, with a true genius for the discovery of the noblest facts, and of all facts, came into relation with the central and vital forces of the universe, so that, instead of constructing a strong but careful life for himself, life breathed through him, and blossomed into a glorious enthusiasm of existence. And therefore from all that was unreal, and from all exaggerated egoism, Henry was absolutely delivered. A man who firmly holds, or rather is held by the beneficent forces of the world, whose feet are upon a rock, and whose goings are established, may with confidence abandon much of the prudence, and many of the artificial proprieties of the world. For every unreality Henry exhibits a sovereign disregard—for unreal manners, unreal glory, unreal heroism, unreal piety, unreal warfare, unreal love. The plain fact is so precious it needs no ornament.

From the coldness, the caution, the convention of his father's court (an atmosphere which suited well the temperament of John of Lancaster), Henry escapes to the teeming vitality of the London streets, and the tavern where Falstaff is monarch. There, among ostlers, and carriers, and drawers, and merchants, and pilgrims, and loud robustious women, he at least has freedom and frolic. "If it be a sin to covet honour," Henry declares, "I am the most offending soul alive." But honour that Henry covets is not that which Hotspur is ambitious after:

> By heaven, methinks it were an easy leap
> To pluck bright heaven from the pale-faced moon.

The honor that Henry covets is the achievement of great deeds, not the words of men which vibrate round such deeds. Falstaff, the despiser of honor, labors across the field bearing the body of the fallen Hotspur, the impassioned pursuer of glory, and in his fashion of splendid imposture or stupendous joke, the fat knight claims credit for the achievement of the day's victory. Henry is not concerned on this occasion to put the old sinner to shame. To have added to the deeds of the world a glorious deed is itself the only honor that Henry seeks. Nor is his heroic greatness inconsistent with the admission of very humble incidents of humanity. ... [Dowden continues to discuss Hal's character as it develops in *Henry IV, Part I and Henry V, Part II.*]

1891—George Bernard Shaw, from *The Quintessence of Ibsenism*

> George Bernard Shaw was a playwright and critic. He often expressed his ambivalence toward Shakespeare. Some of his greatest works include *Saint Joan, Pygmalion* (later adapted into the musical and film *My Fair Lady*), *Man and Superman,* and *Caesar and Cleopatra.*

Don Quixote and Mr Pickwick are recognized examples of characters introduced in pure ridicule, and presently gaining the affection and finally the respect of their authors. To them may be added Shakespear's Falstaff. Falstaff is introduced as a subordinate stage figure with no other function than to be robbed by the Prince and Poins, who was originally meant to be the *raisonneur* of the piece, and the chief figure among the prince's dissolute associates. But Poins soon fades into nothing, like several characters in Dickens's early works; whilst Falstaff develops into an enormous joke and an exquisitely mimicked human type. Only in the end the joke withers. The question comes to Shakespear: *Is* this really a laughing matter? Of course there can be only one answer; and Shakespear gives it as best he can by the mouth of the prince become king, who might, one thinks, have had the decency to wait until he has redeemed his own character before assuming the right to lecture his boon companion. Falstaff, rebuked and humiliated, dies miserably. His followers are hanged, except Pistol, whose exclamation "Old do I wax; and from my weary limbs honor is cudgelled" is a melancholy exordium to an old age of beggary and imposture.

But suppose Shakespear had begun where he left off! Suppose he had been born at a time when, as the result of a long propaganda of health and temperance, sack had come to be called alcohol, alcohol had come to be called poison, corpulence had come to be regarded as either a disease or a breach of good manners, and a conviction had spread throughout society that the practice of consuming "a half-pennyworth of bread to an intolerable deal of sack" was the cause of so much misery, crime, and racial degeneration that whole States prohibited the sale of potable spirits altogether, and even moderate drinking was more and more regarded as a regrettable weakness! Suppose (to drive the change well home) the women in the great theatrical centres had completely lost that amused indulgence for the drunken man which still exists in some out-of-the-way places, and felt nothing but disgust and anger at the conduct and habits of Falstaff and Sir Toby Belch! Instead of *Henry IV* and *The Merry Wives of Windsor*, we should have had something like Zola's *L'Assommoir.* Indeed, we actually have Cassio, the last of Shakespear's gentleman-drunkards, talking like a temperance reformer, a fact which suggests that Shakespear had been roundly lectured for the offensive vulgarity of Sir Toby by some woman of refinement who refused to see the smallest fun in giving a knight such a name as Belch, with characteristics to correspond to it. Suppose, again, that the first performance of *The Taming of the Shrew* had led to a modern Feminist demonstration in the theatre, and forced upon Shakespear's consideration a whole century of agitatresses, from Mary Wollstonecraft to Mrs Fawcett and Mrs Pankhurst, is it not likely that the jest of Katharine and Petruchio would have become the earnest of Nora and Torvald Helmer?

HENRY IV, PART I
IN THE TWENTIETH CENTURY

In the twentieth century, the character of Falstaff continued to attract critics, though often in more complex ways. At the same time, Hal, Hotspur, and the king, as well as subsidiary figures like Sir Walter Blunt, were also important subjects of criticism, both as characters themselves and as elements of significant interactions between characters. As with many of Shakespeare's plays, important twentieth-century criticism of *Henry IV* begins with A. C. Bradley. Bradley's critical method essentially continues the nineteenth-century focus on character. In "The Rejection of Falstaff," Bradley discusses Falstaff's character in relation to other persons of the play, especially in relation to Hal, considering character then as an element of the play. Bradley uses Falstaff to explain Hal. Regarding Hal's final rejection of Falstaff, Bradley writes, "I am suggesting that our fault lies not in our resentment at Henry's conduct, but in our surprise at it; that if we had read his character truly in the light that Shakespeare gave us, we should have been prepared for a display both of hardness and of policy at this point in his career."

The American critic E. E. Stoll, however, attacked Bradley and other critics, such as Hazlitt, for having "sentimentalized" Falstaff. With a practical acidity characteristic of him, Stoll argues that Falstaff is a version of the *miles gloriosus*, the boastful warrior who gets his comeuppance, a dramatic convention that drove Shakespeare's construction of him.

One of the century's finest Shakespearian critics, Harold C. Goddard, took a different view. He finds in Falstaff a man who "plays," explaining what he means as follows:

> Play is not sport. The confusion of the two is a major tragedy of our time. A crowd of fifteen-year-old schoolboys "playing" football on a back lot are indulging in sport. They are rarely playing. The one who is playing is the child of five, all alone, pretending that a dirty rag doll is the rich mother of a dozen infants—invisible to the naked eye. Even

boys playing war, if they are harmonious and happy, are conducting an experiment in peace. Play is the erection of an illusion into a reality. It is not an escape from life. It is the realization of life in something like its fullness.

Goddard sets this character, the playful character of Falstaff, against Henry IV, with Hal as a mediating term between them, and then asks, "Of the two, which was the better man?" He answers,

> ... take Falstaff at his worst. He was a drunkard, a glutton, a profligate, a thief, even a liar if you insist, but withal a fundamentally honest man. He had two sides like a coin, but he was not a counterfeit. And Henry? He was a king, a man of "honour," of brains and ability, of good intentions, but withal a "vile politician" and respectable hypocrite. He was a counterfeit.

Goddard concludes with a question, "Which, if it comes to a choice, is the better influence on a young man?" His question shows that he has moved in his essay from character criticism to criticism designed to address the education of character. More recently, the scholar A. D. Nuttall also explored the complex relationship between Falstaff and Prince Hal.

Goddard's 1951 reading of King Henry is far from Mark Van Doren's 1939 reading of the same character. Where Goddard's reading emphasizes the hypocrisy in Henry, Van Doren's is free of such criticism. "Henry wears his robes regally," Van Doren writes, "and his sighs because they weigh him down are dignified and sonorous. One of his cares is that domestic rebellion keeps him from Jerusalem," where, according to Van Doren, he sincerely wishes to venture on a holy crusade. Goddard's reading implies, on the other hand, that Henry's talk of crusade is the pure politics of an anxious king who on his death bed will advise his son to make foreign wars in order to distract his subjects.

In his 1983 essay, "Rebellion and Design in *Henry IV, Part One*," John W. Blanpied moves from what seems to be a study of King Henry's character to the world of the play. According the Blanpied, the play opens as Henry is addressing his court, but then there is

> an explosion, and suddenly a world appears, densely and diversely peopled, and already in full motion. It is a truly spontaneous world, its life a matter of internal and native growth, its free-speaking citizens all intricately related, not by the invisible webs of a plotting playwright, but through the verisimilitude of contending strengths.

The play's form is not imposed, but emerges from the cross-hatching rhythms of instinctive opposition to imposed control.

Characters as they interact create theme—which, in this play, is rebellion in many forms.

In his essay on Falstaff, the important critic William Empson considers Falstaff's role in both Henry IV plays and in *Henry V.* He argues that the ambiguity built into a reader's or viewer's understanding of Falstaff—Is he a coward? Is he aware that Poins and the Prince are setting him up in the robbery? Is he deliberate in his serial exaggeration of the episode at Gadshill?—is an ambiguity that permeates the play and is important for an understanding of Hal's character, too. Empson also argues, boldly, that in creating Falstaff, Shakespeare created a scandalous character with whom he could identify, that Falstaff was "a secret come-back against aristocratic patrons," who "liberated" Shakespeare and gave him the power to write the great works that followed. Empson's essay is a response to J. Dover Wilson's 1943 study of Falstaff, whom Dover Wilson sees as representing vanity within a drama about "human salvation." In his book *Shakespeare: The Invention of the Human*, Harold Bloom commends Empson's essay as brilliant and "sensible" but also disagrees with it: "Empson sees Falstaff as a potential mob leader—charismatic, unscrupulous, and able to sway people. . . . But does that not wholly decenter the magnificent Falstaff?" A 1986 essay by C. L. Barber and Richard Wheeler also discusses Falstaff across the Henry IV plays, and in a somewhat similar vein, emphasizing, as Harold Bloom describes their piece, "Falstaff's aura of freedom."

Other critics in the century examined the connections between the play and the character of Falstaff in particular to other literary works. The noted Chaucerian scholar E. Talbot Donaldson published an important essay on the relationship between Falstaff and Chaucer's famous character the Wife of Bath. Harold Bloom, who finds Falstaff one of the most magnificent of Shakespeare's creations, compares him to Hamlet: "[I]s not Falstaff, like Hamlet, so original a representation that he originates much of what we know or expect about representation? We cannot see how original Falstaff is because Falstaff *contains* us; we do not contain him. And though we love Falstaff, he does not need our love any more than Hamlet does."

On stage and on film, some of the twentieth century's finest actors have appeared in *Henry IV*, including Ralph Richardson as Falstaff on the stage and Orson Welles on the screen. In the same Old Vic stage production in which Richardson played Falstaff, Laurence Olivier played Hotspur. John Gielgud played Henry IV in Welles' film, and Richardson served as the voice of an off-screen narrator.

1902—A. C. Bradley. "The Rejection of Falstaff," from *Oxford Lectures on Poetry*

A. C. Bradley (1851–1935) was a professor at Oxford and other institutions. His book *Shakespearean Tragedy* was one of the most significant works of Shakespeare criticism of the twentieth century.

The Rejection of Falstaff[1]

Of the two persons principally concerned in the rejection of Falstaff, Henry, both as Prince and as King, has received, on the whole, full justice from readers and critics. Falstaff, on the other hand, has been in one respect the most unfortunate of Shakespeare's famous characters. All of them, in passing from the mind of their creator into other minds, suffer change; they tend to lose their harmony through the disproportionate attention bestowed on some one feature, or to lose their uniqueness by being conventionalised into types already familiar. But Falstaff was degraded by Shakespeare himself. The original character is to be found alive in the two parts of *Henry IV.*, dead in *Henry V.*, and nowhere else. But not very long after these plays were composed, Shakespeare wrote, and he afterwards revised, the very entertaining piece called *The Merry Wives of Windsor*. Perhaps his company wanted a new play on a sudden; or perhaps, as one would rather believe, the tradition may be true that Queen Elizabeth, delighted with the Falstaff scenes of *Henry IV.*, expressed a wish to see the hero of them again, and to see him in love. Now it was no more possible for Shakespeare to show his own Falstaff in love than to turn twice two into five. But he could write in haste—the tradition says, in a fortnight—a comedy or farce differing from all his other plays in this, that its scene is laid in English middle-class life, and that it is prosaic almost to the end. And among the characters he could introduce a disreputable fat old knight with attendants, and could call them Falstaff, Bardolph, Pistol, and Nym. And he could represent this knight assailing, for financial purposes, the virtue of two matrons, and in the event baffled, duped, treated like dirty linen, beaten, burnt, pricked, mocked, insulted, and, worst of all, repentant and didactic. It is horrible. It is almost enough to convince one that Shakespeare himself could sanction the parody of Ophelia in the *Two Noble Kinsmen*. But it no more touches the real Falstaff than Ophelia is degraded by that parody. To picture the real Falstaff befooled like the Falstaff of the *Merry Wives* is like imagining Iago the gull of Roderigo, or Becky Sharp the dupe of Amelia Osborne. Before he had been served the least of these tricks he would have had his brains taken out and buttered, and have given them to a dog for a New Year's gift. I quote the words of the impostor, for after all Shakespeare made him and gave to him a few sentences worthy of Falstaff himself. But they are only a few—one side of a sheet of notepaper would contain them. And yet critics have solemnly debated at what period in his life Sir John endured the gibes of Master Ford, and whether we should put this comedy between the two parts of *Henry IV.*, or between the second of them and *Henry V*. And the Falstaff of the general reader, it is to be feared, is an impossible conglomerate of two distinct characters, while the Falstaff of the mere playgoer is certainly much more like the impostor than the true man.

The separation of these two has long ago been effected by criticism, and is insisted on in almost all competent estimates of the character of Falstaff. I do not propose to attempt a full account either of this character or of that of Prince Henry, but shall connect the remarks I have to make on them with a question which does not appear to have been satisfactorily discussed—the question of the rejection of Falstaff by the Prince on his accession to the throne. What do we feel, and what are we meant to feel, as we witness this rejection? And what does our feeling imply as to the characters of Falstaff and the new King?

1.

Sir John, you remember, is in Gloucestershire, engaged in borrowing a thousand pounds from Justice Shallow; and here Pistol, riding helter-skelter from London, brings him the great news that the old King is as dead as nail in door, and that Harry the Fifth is the man. Sir John, in wild excitement, taking any man's horses, rushes to London; and he carries Shallow with him, for he longs to reward all his friends. We find him standing with his companions just outside Westminster Abbey, in the crowd that is waiting for the King to come out after his coronation. He himself is stained with travel, and has had no time to spend any of the thousand pounds in buying new liveries for his men. But what of that? This poor show only proves his earnestness of affection, his devotion, how he could not deliberate or remember or have patience to shift himself, but rode day and night, thought of nothing else but to see Henry, and put all affairs else in oblivion, as if there were nothing else to be done but to see him. And now he stands sweating with desire to see him, and repeating and repeating this one desire of his heart—'to see him.' The moment comes. There is a shout within the Abbey like the roaring of the sea, and a clangour of trumpets, and the doors open and the procession streams out.

> *Fal.* God save thy grace, King Hal! my royal Hal!
> *Pist.* The heavens thee guard and keep, most royal imp of fame!
> *Fal.* God save thee, my sweet boy!
> *King.* My Lord Chief Justice, speak to that vain man.
> *Ch. Just.* Have you your wits? Know you what 'tis you speak?
> *Fal.* My King! my Jove! I speak to thee, my heart!
> *King.* I know thee not, old man: fall to thy prayers;

> How ill white hairs become a fool and jester!
> I have long dream'd of such a kind of man,
> So surfeit-swell'd, so old and so profane;
> But being awaked I do despise my dream.
> Make less thy body hence, and more thy grace;
> Leave gormandizing; know the grave doth gape
> For thee thrice wider than for other men.
> Reply not to me with a fool-born jest
> Presume not that I am the thing I was;
> For God doth know, so shall the world perceive,
> That I have turn'd away my former self;
> So will I those that kept me company.
> When thou dost hear I am as I have been,
> Approach me, and thou shalt be as thou wast,
> The tutor and the feeder of my riots
> Till then, I banish thee, on pain of death,
> As I have done the rest of my misleaders,
> Not to come near our person by ten mile.
> For competence of life I will allow you,
> That lack of means enforce you not to evil:
> And, as we hear you do reform yourselves,
> We will, according to your strengths and qualities,
> Give you advancement. Be it your charge, my lord,
> To see perform'd the tenour of our word.
> Set on.

The procession passes out of sight, but Falstaff and his friends remain. He shows no resentment. He comforts himself, or tries to comfort himself—first, with the thought that he has Shallow's thousand pounds, and then, more seriously, I believe, with another thought. The King, he sees, must look thus to the world; but he will be sent for in private when night comes, and will yet make the fortunes of his friends. But even as he speaks, the Chief Justice, accompanied by Prince John, returns, and gives the order to his officers:

> Go, carry Sir John Falstaff to the Fleet;
> Take all his company along with him.

Falstaff breaks out, 'My lord, my lord,' but he is cut short and hurried away; and after a few words between the Prince and the Chief Justice the scene closes, and with it the drama.

What are our feelings during this scene? They will depend on our feelings about Falstaff. If we have not keenly enjoyed the Falstaff scenes of the two plays, if we regard Sir John chiefly as an old reprobate, not only a sensualist, a liar, and a coward, but a cruel and dangerous ruffian, I suppose we enjoy his discomfiture and consider that the King has behaved magnificently. But if we *have* keenly enjoyed the Falstaff scenes, if we have enjoyed them as Shakespeare surely meant them to be enjoyed, and if, accordingly, Falstaff is not to us solely or even chiefly a reprobate and ruffian, we feel, I think, during the King's speech, a good deal of pain and some resentment; and when, without any further offence on Sir John's part, the Chief Justice returns and sends him to prison, we stare in astonishment. These, I believe, are, in greater or less degree, the feelings of most of those who really enjoy the Falstaff scenes (as many readers do not). Nor are these feelings diminished when we remember the end of the whole story, as we find it in *Henry V.*, where we learn that Falstaff quickly died, and, according to the testimony of persons not very sentimental, died of a broken heart.[2] Suppose this merely to mean that he sank under the shame of his public disgrace, and it is pitiful enough: but the words of Mrs. Quickly, 'The king has killed his heart'; of Nym, 'The king hath run bad humours on the knight; that's the even of it'; of Pistol,

> Nym, thou hast spoke the right,
> His heart is fracted and corroborate,

assuredly point to something more than wounded pride; they point to wounded affection, and remind us of Falstaff's own answer to Prince Hal's question, 'Sirrah, do I owe you a thousand pound?' 'A thousand pound, Hal? a million: thy love is worth a million: thou owest me thy love.'

Now why did Shakespeare end his drama with a scene which, though undoubtedly striking, leaves an impression so unpleasant? I will venture to put aside without discussion the idea that he meant us throughout the two plays to regard Falstaff with disgust or indignation, so that we naturally feel nothing but pleasure at his fall; for this idea implies that kind of inability to understand Shakespeare with which it is idle to argue. And there is another and a much more ingenious suggestion which must equally be rejected as impossible. According to it, Falstaff, having listened to the King's speech, did not seriously hope to be sent for by him in private; he fully realised the situation at once, and was only making game of Shallow; and in his immediate turn upon Shallow when the King goes out, 'Master Shallow, I owe you a thousand pound,' we are meant to see his humorous superiority to any rebuff, so that we end the play with the delightful feeling that, while Henry has done the right thing, Falstaff, in his outward overthrow, has still proved himself inwardly invincible. This suggestion comes from a critic who understands Falstaff, and in the suggestion itself shows that he understands him.[3] But it provides no solution, because it wholly ignores, and could not account for, that which follows the short conversation with Shallow. Falstaff's dismissal to the Fleet, and his subsequent death, prove beyond doubt that his rejection was meant by Shakespeare to be taken as a catastrophe which not even his humour could enable him to surmount.

Moreover, these interpretations, even if otherwise admissible, would still leave our problem only partly solved. For what troubles us is not only the disappointment of Falstaff, it is the conduct of Henry. It was inevitable that on his accession he should separate himself from Sir John, and we wish nothing else. It is satisfactory that Sir John should have a competence, with the hope of promotion in the highly improbable case of his reforming himself. And if Henry could not trust himself within ten miles of so fascinating a companion, by all means let him be banished that distance: we do not complain. These, arrangements would not have prevented a satisfactory ending: the King could have communicated his decision, and Falstaff could have accepted it, in a private interview rich in humour and merely touched with pathos. But Shakespeare has so contrived matters that Henry could not send a private warning to Falstaff even if he wished to, and in their public meeting Falstaff is made to behave in so infatuated and outrageous a manner that great sternness on the King's part was unavoidable. And the curious thing is that Shakespeare did not stop here. If this had been all we should have felt pain for Falstaff, but not, perhaps, resentment against Henry. But two things we do resent. Why, when this painful incident seems to be over, should the Chief Justice return and send Falstaff to prison? Can this possibly be meant for an act of private vengeance on the part of the Chief Justice, unknown to the King? No; for in that case Shakespeare would have shown at once that the King disapproved and cancelled it. It must have been the King's own act. This is one thing we resent; the other is the King's sermon. He had a right to turn away his former self, and his old companions with it, but he had no right to talk all of a sudden like a clergyman; and surely it was both ungenerous and insincere to speak of them as his 'misleaders,' as though in the days of Eastcheap and Gadshill he had been a weak and silly lad. We have seen his former self, and we know that it was nothing of the kind. He had shown himself, for all his follies, a very strong and independent young man, deliberately amusing himself among men over whom he had just as much ascendency as he chose to exert. Nay, he amused himself not only among them, but at their expense. In his first soliloquy—and first soliloquies are usually significant—he declares that he associates with them in order that, when at some future time he shows his true character, he may be the more wondered at for his previous aberrations. You may think he deceives himself here; you may believe that he frequented Sir John's company out of delight in it and not merely with this cold-blooded design; but at any rate he *thought* the design was his one motive. And, that being so, two results follow. He ought in honour long ago to have given Sir John clearly to understand that they must say good-bye on the day of his accession. And, having neglected to do this, he ought not to have lectured him as his misleader. It was not only ungenerous, it was dishonest. It looks disagreeably like an attempt to buy the praise of the respectable at the cost of honour and truth. And it succeeded. Henry *always* succeeded.

You will see what I am suggesting, for the moment, as a solution of our problem. I am suggesting that our fault lies not in our resentment at Henry's conduct, but in our surprise at it; that if we had read his character truly in the light that Shakespeare gave us, we should have been prepared for a display both of hardness and of policy at this point in his career. And although this suggestion does not suffice to solve the problem before us, I am convinced that in itself it is true. Nor is it rendered at all improbable by the fact that Shakespeare has made Henry, on the whole, a fine and very attractive character, and that here he makes no one express any disapprobation of the treatment of Falstaff. For in similar cases Shakespeare is constantly misunderstood. His readers expect him to mark in some distinct way his approval or disapproval of that which he represents; and hence where *they* disapprove and *he* says nothing, they fancy that he does *not* disapprove, and they blame his indifference, like Dr. Johnson, or at the least are puzzled. But the truth is that he shows the fact and leaves the judgment to them. And again, when he makes us like a character we expect the character to have no faults that are not expressly pointed out, and when other faults appear we either ignore them or try to explain them away. This is one of our methods of conventionalising Shakespeare. We want the world's population to be neatly divided into sheep and goats, and we want an angel by us to say, 'Look, that is a goat and this is a sheep,' and we try to turn Shakespeare into this angel. His impartiality makes us uncomfortable: we cannot bear to see him, like the sun, lighting up everything and judging nothing. And this is perhaps especially the case in his historical plays, where we are always trying to turn him into a partisan. He shows us that Richard II. was unworthy to be king, and we at once conclude that he thought Bolingbroke's usurpation justified; whereas he shows merely, what under the conditions was bound to exist, an inextricable tangle of right and unright. Or, Bolingbroke being evidently wronged, we suppose Bolingbroke's statements to be true, and are quite surprised when, after attaining his end through them, he mentions casually on his death-bed that they were lies. Shakespeare makes us admire Hotspur heartily; and accordingly, when we see Hotspur discussing with others how large his particular slice of his mother-country is to be, we either fail to recognise the monstrosity of the proceeding, or, recognising it, we complain that Shakespeare is inconsistent. Prince John breaks a tottering rebellion by practising a detestable fraud on the rebels. We are against the rebels, and have heard high praise of Prince John, but we cannot help seeing that his fraud is detestable; so we say indignantly to Shakespeare, 'Why, you told us he was a sheep'; whereas, in fact, if we had used our eyes we should have known beforehand that he was the brave, determined, loyal, cold-blooded, pitiless, unscrupulous son of a usurper whose throne was in danger.

To come, then, to Henry. Both as prince and as king he is deservedly a favourite, and particularly so with English readers, being, as he is, perhaps the most distinctively English of all Shakespeare's men. In *Henry V.* he is treated as a national hero. In this play he has lost much of the wit which in him seems to have depended on contact with Falstaff, but he has also laid aside the most serious faults of his youth. He inspires in a high degree fear, enthusiasm, and affection; thanks to his beautiful modesty he has the charm which is lacking to another mighty warrior, Coriolanus; his youthful escapades have given him an understanding of simple folk, and sympathy with them; he is the author of the saying, 'There is some soul of goodness in things evil'; and he is much more obviously religious than most of Shakespeare's heroes. Having these and other fine qualities, and being without certain dangerous tendencies which mark the tragic heroes, he is, perhaps, the most *efficient* character drawn by Shakespeare, unless Ulysses, in *Troilus and Cressida*, is his equal. And so he has been described as Shakespeare's ideal man of action; nay, it has even been declared that here for once Shakespeare plainly disclosed his own ethical creed, and showed us his ideal, not simply of a man of action, but of a man.

But Henry is neither of these. The poet who drew Hamlet and Othello can never have thought that even the ideal man of action would lack that light upon the brow which at once transfigures them and marks their doom. It is as easy to believe that, because the lunatic, the lover, and the poet are not far apart, Shakespeare would have chosen never to have loved and sung. Even poor Timon, the most inefficient of the tragic heroes, has something in him that Henry never shows. Nor is it merely that his nature is limited: if we follow Shakespeare and look closely at Henry, we shall discover with the many fine traits a few less pleasing. Henry IV. describes him as the noble image of his own youth; and, for all his superiority to his father, he is still his father's son, the son of the man whom Hotspur called a 'vile politician.' Henry's religion, for example, is genuine, it is rooted in his modesty; but it is also superstitious—an attempt to buy off supernatural vengeance for Richard's blood; and it is also in part political, like his father's projected crusade. Just as he went to war chiefly because, as his father told him, it was the way to keep factious nobles quiet and unite the nation, so when he adjures the Archbishop to satisfy him as to his right to the French throne, he knows very well that the Archbishop *wants* the war, because it will defer and perhaps prevent what he considers the spoliation of the Church. This same strain of policy is what Shakespeare marks in the first soliloquy in *Henry IV.*, where the prince describes his riotous life as a mere scheme to win him glory later. It implies that readiness to use other people as means to his own ends which is a conspicuous feature in his father; and it reminds us of his father's plan of keeping himself out of the people's sight while Richard was making himself cheap by his incessant public appearances. And if I am not mistaken there is a further likeness. Henry is kindly and pleasant to every one as Prince, to every one deserving as

King; and he is so not merely out of policy: but there is no sign in him of a strong affection for any one, such an affection as we recognise at a glance in Hamlet and Horatio, Brutus and Cassius, and many more. We do not find this in *Henry V.*, not even in the noble address to Lord Scroop, and in *Henry IV.* we find, I think, a liking for Falstaff and Poins, but no more: there is no more than a liking, for instance, in his soliloquy over the supposed corpse of his fat friend, and he never speaks of Falstaff to Poins with any affection. The truth is, that the members of the family of Henry IV. have love for one another, but they cannot spare love for any one outside their family, which stands firmly united, defending its royal position against attack and instinctively isolating itself from outside influence.

Thus I would suggest that Henry's conduct in his rejection of Falstaff is in perfect keeping with his character on its unpleasant side as well as on its finer; and that, so far as Henry is concerned, we ought not to feel surprise at it. And on this view we may even explain the strange incident of the Chief Justice being sent back to order Falstaff to prison (for there is no sign of any such uncertainty in the text as might suggest an interpolation by the players). Remembering his father's words about Henry, 'Being incensed, he's flint,' and remembering in *Henry V.* his ruthlessness about killing the prisoners when he is incensed, we may imagine that, after he had left Falstaff and was no longer influenced by the face of his old companion, he gave way to anger at the indecent familiarity which had provoked a compromising scene on the most ceremonial of occasions and in the presence alike of court and crowd, and that he sent the Chief Justice back to take vengeance. And this is consistent with the fact that in the next play we find Falstaff shortly afterwards not only freed from prison, but unmolested in his old haunt in Eastcheap, well within ten miles of Henry's person. His anger had soon passed, and he knew that the requisite effect had been produced both on Falstaff and on the world.

But all this, however true, will not solve our problem. It seems, on the contrary, to increase its difficulty. For the natural conclusion is that Shakespeare *intended* us to feel resentment against Henry. And yet that cannot be, for it implies that he meant the play to end disagreeably; and no one who understands Shakespeare at all will consider that supposition for a moment credible. No; he must have meant the play to end pleasantly, although he made Henry's action consistent. And hence it follows that he must have intended our sympathy with Falstaff to be so far weakened when the rejection-scene arrives that his discomfiture should be satisfactory to us; that we should enjoy this sudden reverse of enormous hopes (a thing always ludicrous if sympathy is absent); that we should approve the moral judgment that falls on him; and so should pass lightly over that disclosure of unpleasant traits in the King's character which Shakespeare was too true an artist to suppress. Thus our pain and resentment, if we feel them, are wrong, in the sense that they do not answer to the dramatist's intention. But it does not follow that they are wrong in a further sense. They may be right, because the dramatist has missed what he aimed at. And this, though the dramatist was Shakespeare, is what I would suggest. In the Falstaff scenes he overshot his mark. He created so extraordinary a being, and fixed him so firmly on his intellectual throne, that when he sought to dethrone him he could not. The moment comes when we are to look at Falstaff in a serious light, and the comic hero is to figure as a baffled schemer; but we cannot make the required change, either in our attitude or in our sympathies. We wish Henry a glorious reign and much joy of his crew of hypocritical politicians, lay and clerical; but our hearts go with Falstaff to the Fleet, or, if necessary, to Arthur's bosom or wheresomever he is.[4]

In the remainder of the lecture I will try to make this view clear. And to that end we must go back to the Falstaff of the body of the two plays, the immortal Falstaff, a character almost purely humorous, and therefore no subject for moral judgments. I can but draw an outline, and in describing one aspect of this character must be content to hold another in reserve.

2.

Up to a certain point Falstaff is ludicrous in the same way as many other figures, his distinction lying, so far, chiefly in the mere abundance of ludicrous traits. *Why* we should laugh at a man with a huge belly and corresponding appetites; at the inconveniences he suffers on a hot day, or in playing the footpad, or when he falls down and there are no levers at hand to lift him up again; at the incongruity of his unwieldy bulk and the nimbleness of his spirit, the infirmities of his age and his youthful lightness of heart; at the enormity of his lies and wiles, and the suddenness of their exposure and frustration; at the contrast between his reputation and his real character, seen most absurdly when, at the mere mention of his name, a redoubted rebel surrenders to him—*why*, I say, we should laugh at these and many such things, this is no place to inquire; but unquestionably we do. Here we have them poured out in endless profusion and with that air of careless ease which is so fascinating in Shakespeare; and with the enjoyment of them I believe many readers stop. But while they are quite essential to the character, there is in it much more. For these things by themselves do not explain why, beside laughing at Falstaff, we are made happy by him and laugh *with* him. He is not, like Parolles, a mere *object* of mirth.

The main reason why he makes us so happy and puts us so entirely at our ease is that he himself is happy and entirely at his ease. 'Happy' is too weak a word; he is in bliss, and we share his glory. Enjoyment—no fitful pleasure crossing a dull life, nor any vacant convulsive mirth—but a rich deep-toned chuckling enjoyment circulates continually through all his being. If you ask *what* he enjoys, no doubt the answer is, in the first place, eating and drinking, taking his ease at his inn, and the company of other merry souls. Compared with these things, what we count the graver interests of life are nothing to him. But then, while we are under his spell, it is impossible to consider these graver interests; gravity is to us, as to him, inferior to gravy; and what he does enjoy he enjoys with such a luscious and good-humoured zest that we sympathise and he makes us happy. And if any one objected, we should answer with Sir Toby Belch, 'Dost thou think, because thou art virtuous, there shall be no more cakes and ale?'

But this, again, is far from all. Falstaff's ease and enjoyment are not simply those of the happy man of appetite;[5] they are those of the humorist, and the humorist of genius. Instead of being comic to you and serious to himself, he is more ludicrous to himself than to you; and he makes himself out more ludicrous than he is, in order that he and others may laugh. Prince Hal never made such sport of Falstaff's person as he himself did. It is *he* who says that his skin hangs about him like an old lady's loose gown, and that he walks before his page like a sow that hath o'erwhelmed all her litter but one. And he jests at himself when he is alone just as much as when others are by. It is the same with his appetites. The direct enjoyment they bring him is scarcely so great as the enjoyment of laughing at this enjoyment; and for all his addiction to sack you never see him for an instant with a brain dulled by it, or a temper turned solemn, silly, quarrelsome, or pious. The virtue it instils into him, of filling his brain with nimble, fiery, and delectable shapes—this, and his humorous attitude towards it, free him, in a manner, from slavery to it; and it is this freedom, and no secret longing for better things (those who attribute such a longing to him are far astray), that makes his enjoyment contagious and prevents our sympathy with it from being disturbed.

The bliss of freedom gained in humour is the essence of Falstaff. His humour is not directed only or chiefly against obvious absurdities; he is the enemy of everything that would interfere with his ease, and therefore of anything serious, and especially of everything respectable and moral. For these things impose limits and obligations, and make us the subjects of old father antic the law, and the categorical imperative, and our station and its duties, and conscience, and reputation, and other people's opinions, and all sorts of nuisances. I say he is therefore their enemy; but I do him wrong; to say that he is their enemy implies that he regards them as serious and recognises their power, when in truth he refuses to recognise them at all. They are to him absurd; and to reduce a thing *ad absurdum* is to reduce it to nothing and to walk about free and rejoicing. This is what Falstaff does with all the would-be serious things of life, sometimes only by his words, sometimes by his actions too. He will make truth appear absurd by solemn statements, which he utters with perfect gravity and which he expects nobody to believe; and honour, by demonstrating that it cannot set a leg, and that neither the living nor the dead can possess it; and law, by evading all the attacks of its highest representative and almost forcing him to laugh at his own defeat; and patriotism, by filling his pockets with the bribes offered by competent soldiers who want to escape service, while he takes in their stead the halt and maimed and the gaol-birds; and duty, by showing how he labours in his vocation—of thieving; and courage, alike by mocking at his own capture of Colvile and gravely claiming to have killed Hotspur; and war, by offering the Prince his bottle of sack when he is asked for a sword; and religion, by amusing himself with remorse at odd times when he has nothing else to do; and the fear of death, by maintaining perfectly untouched, in the face of imminent peril and even while he *feels* the fear of death, the very same power of dissolving it in persiflage that he shows when he sits at ease in his inn. These are the wonderful achievements which he performs, not with the sourness of a cynic, but with the gaiety of a boy. And, therefore, we praise him, we laud him, for he offends none but the virtuous, and denies that life is real or life is earnest, and delivers us from the oppression of such nightmares, and lifts us into the atmosphere of perfect freedom.

No one in the play understands Falstaff fully, any more than Hamlet was understood by the persons round him. They are both men of genius. Mrs. Quickly and Bardolph are his slaves, but they know not why. 'Well, fare thee well,' says the hostess whom he has pillaged and forgiven; 'I have known thee these twenty-nine years, come peas-cod time, but an honester and truer-hearted man—well, fare thee well.' Poins and the Prince delight in him; they get him into corners for the pleasure of seeing him escape in ways they cannot imagine; but they often take him much too seriously. Poins, for instance, rarely sees, the Prince does not always see, and moralising critics never see, that when Falstaff speaks ill of a companion behind his back, or writes to the Prince that Poins spreads it abroad that the Prince is to marry his sister, he knows quite well that what he says will be repeated, or rather, perhaps, is absolutely indifferent whether it be repeated or not, being certain that it can only give him an opportunity for humour. It is the same with his lying, and almost the same with his cowardice, the two main vices laid to his charge even by sympathisers. Falstaff is neither a liar nor a coward in the usual sense, like the typical cowardly boaster of comedy. He tells his lies either for their own humour, or on purpose to get himself into a difficulty. He rarely expects to be believed, perhaps never. He abandons a statement or contradicts it the moment it is made. There is scarcely more intent in his lying than in the humorous exaggerations which he pours out in soliloquy just as much as when others are by. Poins and the Prince understand this in part. You see them waiting eagerly to convict him, not that they may really put him to shame, but in order to enjoy the greater lie that will swallow up the less. But their sense of humour lags behind his. Even the Prince seems to accept as half-serious that remorse of his which passes so suddenly into glee at the idea of taking a purse, and his request to his friend to bestride him if he should see him down in the battle. Bestride Falstaff! 'Hence! Wilt thou lift up Olympus?' Again, the attack of the Prince and Poins on Falstaff and the other thieves on Gadshill is contrived, we know, with a view to the incomprehensible lies it will induce him to tell. But when, more than rising to the occasion, he turns two men in buckram into four, and then seven, and then nine, and then eleven, almost in a breath, I believe they partly misunderstand his intention, and too many of his critics misunderstand it altogether. Shakespeare was not writing a mere farce. It is preposterous to suppose that a man of Falstaff's intelligence would utter these gross, palpable, open lies with the serious intention to deceive, or forget that, if it was too dark for him to see his own hand, he could hardly see that the three misbegotten knaves were wearing Kendal green. No doubt, if he *had* been believed, he would have been hugely tickled at it, but he no more expected to be believed than when he claimed to have killed Hotspur. Yet he is supposed to be serious even then. Such interpretations would destroy the poet's whole conception; and of those who adopt them one might ask this out of some twenty similar questions:—When Falstaff, in the men in buckram scene, begins by calling twice at short intervals for sack, and then a little later calls for more and says, 'I am a rogue if I drunk to-day,' and the Prince answers, 'O villain, thy lips are scarce wiped since thou drunk'st last,' do they think that *that* lie was meant to deceive? And if not, why do they take it for granted that the others were? I suppose they consider that Falstaff was in earnest when, wanting to get twenty-two yards of satin on trust from Master Dombledon the silk-mercer, he offered Bardolph as security; or when he said to the Chief Justice about Mrs. Quickly, who accused him of breaking his promise to marry her, 'My lord, this is a poor mad soul, and she says up and down the town that her eldest son is like you'; or when he explained his enormous bulk by exclaiming, 'A plague of sighing and grief! It blows a man up like a bladder'; or when he accounted for his voice being cracked by declaring that he had 'lost it with singing of anthems'; or even when he sold his soul on Good-Friday to the devil for a cup of Madeira and a cold capon's leg. Falstaff's lies about Hotspur and the men in buckram do not essentially differ from these statements. There is nothing serious in any of them except the refusal to take anything seriously.

This is also the explanation of Falstaff's cowardice, a subject on which I should say nothing if Maurice Morgann's essay,[6] now more than a century old, were better known. That Falstaff sometimes behaves in what we should generally call a cowardly way is certain; but that does not show that he was a coward; and if the word means a person who feels painful fear in the presence of danger, and yields to that fear in spite of his better feelings and convictions, then assuredly Falstaff was no coward. The stock bully and boaster of comedy is one, but not Falstaff. It is perfectly clear in the first place that, though he had unfortunately a reputation for stabbing and caring not what mischief he did if his weapon were out, he had not a reputation for cowardice. Shallow remembered him five-and-fifty years ago breaking Scogan's head at the court-gate when he was a crack not thus high; and Shallow knew him later a good back-swordsman. Then we lose sight of him till about twenty years after, when his association with Bardolph began; and that association implies that by the time he was thirty-five or forty he had sunk into the mode of life we witness in the plays. Yet, even as we see him there, he remains a person of consideration in the army. Twelve captains hurry about London searching for him. He is present at the Council of War in the King's tent at Shrewsbury, where the only other persons are the King, the two princes, a nobleman and Sir Walter Blunt. The messenger who brings the false report of the battle to Northumberland mentions, as one of the important incidents, the death of Sir John Falstaff. Colvile, expressly described as a famous rebel, surrenders to him as soon as he hears his name. And if his own wish that his name were not so terrible to the enemy, and his own boast of his European reputation, are not evidence of the first rank, they must not be entirely ignored in presence of these other facts. What do these facts mean? Does Shakespeare put them all in with no purpose at all, or in defiance of his own intentions? It is not credible.

And when, in the second place, we look at Falstaff's actions, what do we find? He boldly confronted Colvile, he was quite ready to fight with him, however pleased that Colvile, like a kind fellow, gave himself away. When he saw Henry and Hotspur fighting, Falstaff, instead of making off in a panic, stayed to take his chance if Hotspur should be the victor. He *led* his hundred and fifty ragamuffins where they were peppered, he did not *send* them. To draw upon Pistol and force him downstairs and wound him in the shoulder was no great feat, perhaps, but the stock coward would have shrunk from it. When the Sheriff came to the inn to arrest him for an offence whose penalty was death, Falstaff, who was hidden behind the arras, did not stand there quaking for fear, he immediately fell asleep and snored. When he stood in the battle reflecting on what would happen if the weight of his paunch should be increased by that of a bullet, he cannot have been in a tremor of craven fear. He *never* shows such fear; and surely the man who, in danger of his life, and with no one by to hear him, meditates thus: 'I like not such grinning honour as Sir Walter hath. Give me life: which if I can save, so; if not, honour comes unlooked-for, and there's an end,' is not what we commonly call a coward. 'Well,' it will be answered, 'but he ran away on Gadshill; and when Douglas attacked him he fell down and shammed dead.' Yes, I am thankful to say, he did. For of course he did not want to be dead. He wanted to live and be merry. And as he had reduced the idea of honour *ad absurdum*, had scarcely any self-respect, and only a respect for reputation as a means of life, naturally he avoided death when he could do so without a ruinous loss of reputation, and (observe) with the satisfaction of playing a colossal practical joke. For *that* after all was his first object. If his one thought had been to avoid death he would not have faced Douglas at all, but would have run away as fast as his legs could carry him; and unless Douglas had been one of those exceptional Scotchmen who have no sense of humour, he would never have thought of pursuing so ridiculous an object as Falstaff running. So that, as Mr. Swinburne remarks, Poins is right when he thus distinguishes Falstaff from his companions in robbery: 'For two of them, I know them to be as true-bred cowards as ever turned back; and for the third, if he fight longer than he sees reason, I'll forswear arms.' And the event justifies this distinction. For it is exactly thus that, according to the original stage-direction, Falstaff behaves when Henry and Poins attack him and the others. The rest run away at once; Falstaff, here as afterwards with Douglas, fights for a blow or two, but, finding himself deserted and outmatched, runs away also. Of course. He saw no reason to stay. *Any* man who had risen superior to all serious motives would have run away. But it does not follow that he would run from mere fear, or be, in the ordinary sense, a coward.[7]

3.

The main source, then, of our sympathetic delight in Falstaff is his humorous superiority to everything serious, and the freedom of soul enjoyed in it. But, of course, this is not the whole of his character. Shakespeare knew well enough that perfect freedom is not to be gained in this manner; we are ourselves aware of it even while we are sympathising with Falstaff; and as soon as we regard him seriously it becomes obvious. His freedom is limited in two main ways. For one thing he cannot rid himself entirely of respect for all that he professes to ridicule. He shows a certain pride in his rank: unlike the Prince, he is haughty to the drawers, who call him a proud Jack. He is not really quite indifferent to reputation. When the Chief Justice bids him pay his debt to Mrs. Quickly for his reputation's sake, I think he feels a twinge, though to be sure he proceeds to pay her by borrowing from her. He is also stung by any thoroughly serious imputation on his courage, and winces at the recollection of his running away on Gadshill; he knows that his behaviour there certainly looked cowardly, and perhaps he remembers that he would not have behaved so once. It is, further, very significant that, for all his dissolute talk, he has never yet allowed the Prince and Poins to *see* him as they saw him afterwards with Doll Tearsheet; not, of course, that he has any moral shame in the matter, but he knows that in such a situation he, in his old age, must appear contemptible—not a humorist but a mere object of mirth. And, finally, he has affection in him—affection, I think, for Poins and Bardolph, and certainly for the Prince; and that is a thing which he cannot jest out of existence. Hence, as the effect of his rejection shows, he is not really invulnerable. And then, in the second place, since he is in the flesh, his godlike freedom has consequences and conditions; consequences, for there is something painfully wrong with his great toe; conditions, for he cannot eat and drink for ever without money, and his purse suffers from consumption, a disease for which he can find no remedy.[8] As the Chief Justice tells him, his means are very slender and his waste great; and his answer, 'I would it were otherwise; I would my means were greater and my waist slenderer,' though worth much money, brings none in. And so he is driven to evil deeds; not only to cheating his tailor like a gentleman, but to fleecing Justice Shallow, and to highway robbery, and to cruel depredations on the poor woman whose affection he has secured.

All this is perfectly consistent with the other side of his character, but by itself it makes an ugly picture.

Yes, it makes an ugly picture when you look at it seriously. But then, surely, so long as the humorous atmosphere is preserved and the humorous attitude maintained, you do not look at it so. You no more regard Falstaff's misdeeds morally than you do the much more atrocious misdeeds of Punch or Reynard the Fox. You do not exactly ignore them, but you attend only to their comic aspect. This is the very spirit of comedy, and certainly of Shakespeare's comic world, which is one of make-believe, not merely as his tragic world is, but in a further sense—a world in which gross improbabilities are accepted with a smile, and many things are welcomed as merely laughable which, regarded gravely, would excite anger and disgust. The intervention of a serious spirit breaks up such a world, and would destroy our pleasure in Falstaff's company. Accordingly through the greater part of these dramas Shakespeare carefully confines this spirit to the scenes of war and policy, and dismisses it entirely in the humorous parts. Hence, if *Henry IV.* had been a comedy like *Twelfth Night*, I am sure that he would no more have ended it with the painful disgrace of Falstaff than he ended *Twelfth Night* by disgracing Sir Toby Belch.[9]

But *Henry IV.* was to be in the main a historical play, and its chief hero Prince Henry. In the course of it his greater and finer qualities were to be gradually revealed, and it was to end with beautiful scenes of reconciliation and affection between his father and him, and a final emergence of the wild Prince as a just, wise, stern, and glorious King. Hence, no doubt, it seemed to Shakespeare that Falstaff at last must be disgraced, and must therefore appear no longer as the invincible humorist, but as an object of ridicule and even of aversion. And probably also his poet's insight showed him that Henry, as he conceived him, *would* behave harshly to Falstaff in order to impress the world, especially when his mind had been wrought to a high pitch by the scene with his dying father and the impression of his own solemn consecration to great duties.

This conception was a natural and a fine one; and if the execution was not an entire success, it is yet full of interest. Shakespeare's purpose being to work a gradual change in our feelings towards Falstaff, and to tinge the humorous atmosphere more and more deeply with seriousness, we see him carrying out this purpose in the Second Part of *Henry IV.* Here he separates the Prince from Falstaff as much as he can, thus withdrawing him from Falstaff's influence, and weakening in our minds the connection between the two. In the First Part we constantly see them together; in the Second (it is a remarkable fact) only once before the rejection. Further, in the scenes where Henry appears apart from Falstaff, we watch him growing more and more grave, and awakening more and more poetic interest; while Falstaff, though his humour scarcely flags to the end, exhibits more and more of his seamy side. This is nowhere turned to the full light in Part I.; but in Part II. we see him as the heartless destroyer of Mrs. Quickly, as a ruffian seriously defying the Chief Justice because his position as an officer on service gives him power to do wrong, as the pike preparing to snap up the poor old dace Shallow, and (this is the one scene where Henry and he meet) as the worn-out lecher, not laughing at his servitude to the flesh but sunk in it. Finally, immediately before the rejection, the world where he is king is exposed in all its sordid criminality when we find Mrs. Quickly and Doll arrested for being concerned in the death of one man, if not more, beaten to death by their bullies; and the dangerousness of Falstaff is emphasised in his last words as he hurries from Shallow's house to London, words at first touched with humour but at bottom only too seriously meant: 'Let us take any man's horses; the laws of England are at my commandment. Happy are they which have been my friends, and woe unto my Lord Chief Justice.' His dismissal to the Fleet by the Chief Justice is the dramatic vengeance for that threat.

Yet all these excellent devices fail. They cause us momentary embarrassment at times when repellent traits in Falstaff's character are disclosed; but they fail to change our attitude of humour into one of seriousness, and our sympathy into repulsion. And they were bound to fail, because Shakespeare shrank from adding to them the one device which would have ensured success. If, as the Second Part of *Henry IV.* advanced, he had clouded over Falstaff's humour so heavily that the man of genius turned into the Falstaff of the *Merry Wives*, we should have witnessed his rejection without a pang. This Shakespeare was too much of an artist to do—though even in this way he did something—and without this device he could not succeed. As I said, in the creation of Falstaff he overreached himself. He was caught up on the wind of his own genius, and carried so far that he could not descend to earth at the selected spot. It is not a misfortune that happens to many authors, nor is it one we can regret, for it costs us but a trifling inconvenience in one scene, while we owe to it perhaps the greatest comic character in literature. For it is in this character, and not in the judgment he brings upon Falstaff's head, that Shakespeare asserts his supremacy. To show that Falstaff's freedom of soul was in part illusory, and that the realities of life refused to be conjured away by his humour—this was what we might expect from Shakespeare's unfailing sanity, but it was surely no achievement beyond the power of lesser men. The achievement was Falstaff himself, and the conception of that freedom of soul, a freedom illusory only in part, and attainable only by a mind which had received from Shakespeare's own the inexplicable touch of infinity which he bestowed on Hamlet and Macbeth and Cleopatra, but denied to Henry the Fifth.

NOTES

1. In this lecture I have mentioned the authors my obligations to whom I was conscious of in writing or have discovered since; but other debts must doubtless remain, which from forgetfulness I am unable to acknowledge.

2. See on this and other points Swinburne, *A Study of Shakespeare*, p. 106 ff.

3. Rötscher, *Shakespeare in seinen höchsten Charaktergebilden*, 1864.

4. That from the beginning Shakespeare intended Henry's accession to be Falstaff's catastrophe is clear from the fact that, when the two characters first appear, Falstaff is made to betray at once the hopes with which he looks forward to Henry's reign. See the First Part of *Henry IV.*, Act I., Scene ii.

5. Cf. Hazlitt, *Characters of Shakespear's Plays*.

6. See Note at end of lecture.

7. It is to be regretted, however, that in carrying his guts away so nimbly he 'roared for mercy'; for I fear we have no ground for rejecting Henry's statement to that effect, and I do not see my way to adopt the suggestion (I forget whose it is) that Falstaff spoke the truth when he swore that he knew Henry and Poins as well as he that made them.

8. Panurge too was 'naturally subject to a kind of disease which at that time they called lack of money'; it was a 'flux in his purse' (Rabelais, Book II., chapters xvi., xvii.).

9. I seem to remember that, according to Gervinus, Shakespeare did disgrace Sir Toby—by marrying him to Maria!

NOTE

For the benefit of readers unacquainted with Morgann's *Essay* I reproduce here, with additions, some remarks omitted from the lecture for want of time. 'Maurice Morgann, Esq. the ingenious writer of this work, descended from an ancient and respectable family in Wales; he filled the office of under Secretary of State to the late Marquis of Lansdown, during his first administration; and was afterwards Secretary to the Embassy for ratifying the peace with America, in 1783. He died at his house in Knightsbridge, in the seventy-seventh year of his age, on the 28th March, 1802' (Preface to the edition of 1825). He was a remarkable and original man, who seems to have written a good deal, but, beyond this essay and some pamphlets on public affairs, all or nearly all anonymous, he published nothing, and at his death he left orders that all his papers should be destroyed. The *Essay on the Dramatic Character of Sir John Falstaff* was first published in 1777. It arose out of a conversation in which Morgann expressed his belief that Shakespeare never meant Falstaff for a coward. He was challenged to explain and support in print what was considered an extraordinary paradox, and his essay bears on its title-page the quotation, 'I am not John of Gaunt, your grandfather: but yet no coward, Hal'—one of Falstaff's few serious sentences. But Morgann did not confine himself to the question of Falstaff's cowardice; he analysed the whole character, and incidentally touched on many points in Shakespearean criticism. 'The reader,' he observes, 'will not need to be told that this inquiry will resolve itself of course into a critique on the genius, the arts, and the conduct, of Shakespeare: for what is Falstaff, what Lear, what Hamlet, or Othello, but different modifications of Shakespeare's thought? It is true that this inquiry is narrowed almost to a single point; but general criticism is as uninstructive as it is easy: Shakespeare deserves to be considered in detail; a task hitherto unattempted.'

The last words are significant. Morgann was conscious that he was striking out a new line. The Eighteenth Century critics had done much for Shakespeare in the way of scholarship; some of them had praised him well and blamed him well; but they had done little to interpret the process of his imagination from within. This was what Morgann attempted. His attitude towards Shakespeare is that of Goethe, Coleridge, Lamb, Hazlitt. The dangers of his method might be illustrated from the *Essay*, but in his hands it yielded most valuable results. And though he did not attempt the eloquence of some of his successors, but wrote like a cultivated ironical man of the world, he wrote delightfully; so that in all respects his *Essay*, which has long been out of print, deserves to be republished and better known. [It was republished in Mr. Nichol Smith's excellent *Eighteenth Century Essays on Shakespeare*, 1903; and, in 1912, by itself, with an introduction by W. A. Gill.]

Readers of Boswell (under the year 1783) will remember that Morgann, who once met Johnson, favoured his biographer with two most characteristic anecdotes. Boswell also records Johnson's judgment of Morgann's *Essay*, which, says Mr. Swinburne, elicited from him 'as good a jest and as bad a criticism as might have been expected.' Johnson, we are told, being asked his opinion of the *Essay*, answered: 'Why, Sir, we shall have the man come forth again; and as he has proved Falstaff to be no coward, he may prove Iago to be a very good character.' The following passage from Morgann's *Essay* (p. 66 of the 1825 edition, p. 248 of Mr. Nichol Smith's book) gives, I presume, his opinion of Johnson. Having referred to Warburton, he adds: 'Another has since undertaken the custody of our author, whom he seems to consider as a sort of wild Proteus or madman, and accordingly knocks him down with the butt-end of his critical staff, as often as he exceeds that line of sober discretion, which this learned Editor appears to have chalked out for him: yet is this Editor, notwithstanding, "a man, take him for all in all," very highly respectable for his genius and his learning.'

1914—E. E. Stoll, from "Falstaff" in *Modern Philology*

E. E. Stoll, a Shakespeare scholar who taught in the Department of English at the University of Minnesota, wrote extensively about Shakespeare's plays.

. . . I have suggested that many of the "secret impressions of courage" are contradictions inherent in the type of the braggart captain. For to this type Falstaff unquestionably belongs. He has the increasing belly and decreasing leg, the diminutive page for a foil, the weapon (his pistol) that is no weapon, but a fraud, as well as most of the inner qualities of this ancient stage-figure—cowardice and outlandish bragging, gluttony and lechery, sycophancy and pride. . . . All these traits are manifest, except his sycophancy, which appears in his dependence on the Prince and his cajoling ways with him; and except his pride, which appears in his insistence on his title on every occasion [as in Part II, II, ii, 109-16], and in his reputation for a proud jack among the drawers.

In the first scene in which he appears Falstaff falters in his jollity and vows that he will give over this life, being now little better than one of the wicked. "Where shall we take a purse tomorrow, Jack?" "Zounds!" he shouts, "where thou wilt, lad!" On a blue Monday at the Boar's Head he is for repenting once more as he moodily contemplates his wasting figure. Bardolph complains of his fretfulness. "Why, there is it. Come sing me a bawdy song; make me merry!" If in this he be self-conscious, how annoying and unnatural! Those numerous critics who to keep for Falstaff his reputation as a humorist have him here play a part, seem to do so at the expense of their own. . . . Naïve, then, as well as witty, and quite as much the cause of mirth in other men when he is least aware, Falstaff is less "incomprehensible" both in his lies and, as we shall presently see, in his conduct generally. His wit is expended, not in making himself ridiculous for the sake of a joke unshared and unuttered, but, by hook or by crook, in avoiding that.

A coward, then, if ever there was one, has Falstaff a philosophy? Military freethinking has been attributed to him to lift the stigma on his name. Believing not in honor, he is not bound by it. And by the Germans [critics such as Ulrici and Gervinus] and Mr. Bradley, as we have remarked, the scope of his philosophy has been widened, and he has been turned into a practical Pyrrhonist and moral nihilist, to whom virtue is "a fig," truth absurd, and all the obligations of society stumbling-blocks and nuisances. In various ways, by the English and the Germans alike, he has been thought to deny and destroy all moral values and ideals of life, not only for his own but for our behoof. So in a certain sense he is inspired by principle—of an anarchistic sort—not void of it.

Only at one ideal—honor—does Falstaff seem to me to cavil, and that he is only shirking and dodging. How does he, as Mr. Bradley thinks, make truth absurd by lying; or law, by evading the attacks of its highest representative; or patriotism, by abusing the King's press and filling his pockets with bribes? Or matrimony (logic would not forbear to add) by consorting with Mistresses Ursula, Quickly, and Tearsheet, thus lifting us into an atmosphere of freedom indeed? It fairly makes your head turn to see a simple picaresque narrative like that of Panurge or Sir Toby Belch brought to such an upshot as that.

As it seems to me, his catechism on the battlefield and his deliverances on honor are to be taken not as coming from his heart of hearts but from his wits and to cover his shame. Like disreputable characters in mediaeval and Renaissance drama and fiction without number, he unconsciously gives himself away. His "philosophy" is but a shift and evasion, and in his catechism he eludes the calm of honor when put by his conscience just as he does when put by the Prince and Poins. When he declares discretion to be the better part of valor there is no more philosophy in him than in Panurge [a character in *Pantegruel* by Rabelais (1494-1553)] and the Franc Archier de Baignollet [in the "Ballad of Franc Archier de Baignollet, by François Villon (1431–c. 1463)] when they avow that they fear nothing but danger, or than in himself when he swears that instinct is a great matter, and purse-taking no sin but his vocation. When he cries "Give me life" and "I like not the grinning honor that Sir Walter hath," there is no more Pyrrhonism or Epicureanism in him than there is idealism when, in defending his choice of the unlikeliest men for his company, he cries, "Give me the spirit, Master Shallow," meaning, "give me the crowns and shillings, Mouldy and Bullcalf." Here as there, he only dodges and shuffles. As in his fits of remorse we have seen, he is not "dead to morality" or free from its claims; neither does he frankly oppose them, or succeed in "covering them with immortal ridicule"; but in sophistry he takes refuge from them and the ridicule rebounds on his own head.

One reason why in [Falstaff's speech on honor], we fail to penetrate this mask of unrealistic and malicious portrayal and take his words to heart, is that they are in soliloquy. A man does not banter himself. But on the stage in those times and before them a man did, and all soliloquy is phrased more as if the character were addressing himself or the audience than as if he were thinking aloud. Hence in comic soliloquy allowances are to be made, just as later, when Falstaff holds forth on sack as the cause of valor, which is another underhand confession of cowardice. . . . It is an irony which touches the speaker, not the thing spoken of, and dissolves away not all the seriousness of life but the speaker's pretenses; it is the exposure, not the expression, of his "inmost self." When Falstaff seems to be talking principle, he is, as we now say, only "putting it mildly": in his own time he gave himself away; in ours he takes the learned in.

But the main reason for our failure to penetrate the mask is that in or out of soliloquy this particular method of dramatic expression is a thing outworn, outgrown. Characters are no longer driven to banter or expose themselves, or the better audiences resent it if they are. Psychology—born of sympathy—will have none of it, as a method too external, ill-fitting, double-tongued. If the person be taken to be consciously jesting— . . . Falstaff about the vanity of honor . . . — he seems then and there to be out of character; yet it is hard to see how he can have been unconscious, either, and it is manifest that the author is more intent on the jest . . . than on the main or philosophic drift—and yet (once again) this self-consciousness and mirth surely do not imply, as in the writing of today they must needs imply, "freedom" or detachment, any measure of indifference or superiority to the pleasure of incontinently taking one's valet, keeping one's arms and legs whole, or sponging in bibulous sloth. The pith of the matter, then, is that the lines of the character are, for us, confused, the author seems to peer through and wink at the audience, and our modern sympathy and craving for reality are vexed and thwarted, somewhat as they are by the self-consciousness of the villains or by the butt-and-wit-in-one. Indeed, unless the character be taken to be unconscious, we seem here to have a case of butt-and-wit-in-one at one and the same moment. For these reasons this method of comic portrayal, which goes back at least to the Middle Ages, and occurs not only in Elizabethan comic drama but in the greatest comic drama since—in Congreve, Sheridan, not to mention Molière—has, like butt-and-wit-in-one or self-conscious villainy, been dropped by the modern spirit as a strange, ill-fitting garment....

How petty and personal Falstaff's philosophy is on the face of it!... It is the "grin" that he "likes not," and since the beginning of things no philosophy has been needed for that.

For Falstaff is simple as the dramatist and his times. By him the chivalric ideal is never questioned; Hotspur is comical only for his testiness, not for the extravagance and fanaticism of his derring-do. To some critics Falstaff seems a parody or burlesque of knighthood, and they are reminded of the contemporary Quixote and his Squire.... Falstaff is neither rebel nor critic. As clown he is supposed to have neither philosophy nor anti-philosophy, being a comic contrast and appendage to the heroes and the heroic point of view....

Falstaff... is not only subtilized but also sentimentalized! Mr. Bradley does not mind saying that he for one is glad that Falstaff ran away on Gadshill; Monsieur Stapfer declares that morally he was no worse than you or I; Hazlitt, lost in sympathy with him on the blighting of his hopes at the succession, resentfully asserts that he was a better man than the Prince; and another critic, mentioned by Sir Walter Raleigh, "takes comfort in the reflection that the thousand pounds belonging to Justice Shallow is safe in Falstaff's pocket, and will help to provide for his old age." That is, the character is lifted bodily out of the dramatist's reach. Falstaff is a rogue, and as such people cannot like him: twice Morgann protests that in order to be comical at all he must be void of evil motive. Lying for profit and jesting for profit, the cheating and swindling of your unsophisticated admirers, gluttony, lechery, extortion, highway robbery, and cowardice—pray, what is funny about all these? Hence the profit has been turned to a jest, the misdemeanours to make-believe. Not otherwise, Hercules in the *Alcestis* was thought by Browning to get roaring drunk, not for his own private satisfaction but for that of the mourners—and there is another in a play who, in the good cause of human happiness, does not mind making a fool of himself! So it must be, when we take a character to our bosom out of an old play like a pet out of the jungle—we must extract his sting. This has by the critics been duly done, to Falstaff as to Shylock. Our "white-bearded Satan" has had his claws pared.

For they that have not learned to think historically cannot stomach the picaresque. It matters not to them that nearly all the professional comic characters of Elizabethan drama, as of all drama before it, have a vein of roguery in them—Sir Toby as well as Autolycus, the Clown as well as the Vice; or that in those days high and low were rejoicing in the roguery romances, English, French, or Spanish. Such people must have delighted in Falstaff as unreservedly as does the Prince in the play. That they did not take him for an innocuous mimic and merrymaker numerous allusions in the seventeenth century, as we have already seen, attest. And Hal loved him as Morgante loved Margutte, as Baldus loved Cingar, and Pantagruel—"all his life long"—loved Panurge, not for his humour only but for his lies and deviltry. They had their notions of 'a character' as we have ours. With endless variety of repetition Rabelais revels in notions of mendacity, drunkenness, gluttony, and lasciviousness, and in tricks of cheating and cruelty, as things funny almost in themselves. With what gusto he tells of the outrages perpetrated by Panurge on the watch, the difficult Parisian lady, and Dingdong and his flock, and of Friar John's slaying and curiously and expertly mutilating his thousands with the staff of the cross in the abbey close! And yet, frowning down the facts, the critics declare that Falstaff has no malice in him, and though he laments the repayment, has had no intention of keeping the stolen money, repays Quickly full measure and running over with his company, and after all does no mentionable injury to Shallow, who has land and beeves. "Where does he cheat the weak," cries Maginn, "or prey upon the poor?" There is Quickly, poor, and weak at least before his blandishments, "made to serve his uses both in purse and in person"; and there are Bullcalf, who has a desire to stay with his friends, and Mouldy, whose dame is old and cannot help herself, both swindled in the name of the King, as Wart, Feeble, and Shadow, the unlikeliest men, are wrongfully pressed into service. All this once was funny and now is base and pitiful, but why should we either shut our eyes to it or bewail it? Surely we cannot with Morgann make allowances for his age and corpulency (how that would have staggered an Elizabethan!) and corrupting associations; or with Maginn trace the pathos of his degradation, hope after hope breaking down; or with Swinburne discover the well of tenderness within him, his heart being "fracted and corroborate," not through material disappointment, but for wounded love. With this last the present Chief Secretary for Ireland (Augustine Birrell) is properly disgusted, though in being less sentimental he is hardly more Elizabethan in spirit as he calls him "in a very real sense a terrible character, so old and so profane." About as properly "terrible" as was the nurse Sairey Gamp of late to an eminent literary critic writing for the *Times*, though truly it would have been a fearful thing to fall into the hands of the living Sairey. Yet Mr Birrell remembers Falstaff (where others have been but too glad to forget him) with Doll at the Boar's Head; and he reads an unexpurgated text. And if he does not look with the eyes of an Elizabethan, he looks honestly (though shamefacedly), with his own, and sees the old rogue and satyr in his heathen nakedness, not in the breeches that, like Volterra in the Sistine, the critics have hastened to make him.

Morals and sentiments alike, in the lapse of time, obliterate humour. Laughter is essentially a *geste social*, as Meredith and Professor Bergson have truly told us; and the immediate and necessary inference, which no doubt they themselves would have drawn, is that it languishes when the tickled *mores* change. The discussion of wit and humour and the examples of both in Castiglione's *Courtier* are illuminating. Much that was funny to the Elizabethans, or to the court of Urbino, or of the Grand Monarch, has since become pathetic, as in Shylock and Harpagon, Alceste and George Dandin; and "disgusting" or even "terrible," as in Falstaff or Tartuffe. Of this we have just seen repeated instances, and of the process of critical emasculation which ensues. Even the form and fashion of the older humour have given offense. Most of the English critics apparently have not seen Falstaff on the stage, but those who have cannot recall him without a shudder. The roaring, the falling flat, and above all the padding—"a very little stuffing under the waistcoat," one of them pleads, "would answer all the requirements of the part." And the padded bulk of his humour, as of his person—"out of all measure, out of all compass"—about his name being terrible to the enemy and known to all Europe, and Turk Gregory never doing such deeds, is so reduced by anachronizing Procrustean critics as to contain "nothing but a light ridicule." His ancestral ring seems to have been really of gold, not copper,—Morgann "believes it was really of gold" just as he "thinks he did not roar," though "probably a little too much alloyed with baser metal." And his "old ward," like his "manhood," Prince Hal might have remembered if he would. What of the multitudinous knaves in buckram and Kendal green, or of the knight himself at Hal's age not an eagle's talon in the waist or an alderman's thumb-ring, or of the nine score and odd posts he foundered as he devoured the road to battle in Gaultree Forest? Even his laugh, which must have been big as his body, riotous as his fancy, lingering and reverberating as the repetitions of his tongue, has been taken away. "The wit is from the head, not the heart. It is anything but fun." If we are to depend on the bare text or stage-directions there is no laughter in Sir Toby either, or almost any other jovial soul in Shakespeare. In robbing these fat knights of their fun critical treason has well-nigh done its worst, though before that it robbed audiences (at the cost of truth though to the profit of morals) of the fun got from Shylock, Harpagon, Dandin, and Tartuffe. On the stage and in the study much of the comedy in Shakespeare and Molière has been drained out of them from the Romantic Revival unto this day, and yet we smile at the Middle Ages Christianizing the classics.

And yet people like Falstaff, however they may interpret or explain him, as I hope my reader still can. Men do, if not women; Englishmen do, if not foreigners. It is partly, no doubt, because of the tradition that he is the supreme comic figure, and they have endeavoured and laboured to like him. But it is more because, however much in the centuries they have changed in morals, humour, and taste, Englishmen have not outlived their human nature—Shakespeare's art. Their pleasure in the picaresque they have not wholly lost: virtue cannot so inoculate our old stock but we shall relish of it. Moreover, there is something in Falstaff's appeal that is immediate and perpetual; it lies not so much in his conduct as in his speech. He talks prose but is supremely poetic, and his is in many ways the most marvellous prose ever penned. It pulses with his vast vitality and irrepressible spirit, it glows with the warmth of his friendliness and good humour, it sparkles with his fancy and wit. No prose or verse either is so heavily charged with the magnetism of a personality, or has caught so perfectly the accent and intonation of an individual human voice. It *is* a voice,—rich, full, and various. In dialogue or stage-direction there is nothing to indicate his laughter, but the words and phrases as they ripple and undulate in repetition amply suggest it or involve it. He rolls a jest as a sweet morsel upon his tongue,—food for powder, food for powder; they'll fill a pit as well as better. Tush, man, mortal men, mortal men! With that he laughs, and all the audience with him.

Englishmen cannot escape that strong infection, if Frenchmen and Germans, Spaniards and Italians may. Mézières, and perhaps most foreigners that read English no more readily than Spanish, prefer Sancho; and for a Spaniard possibly Sancho's speech may have an equal charm. The Squire, certainly, is tenderer, more naive, more moral, than the Eastcheap knight. But to Englishmen he seems much less vivid and real, less alive in every phrase and syllable, less prodigiously entertaining. Falstaff is depicted with—and endowed with—a greater gusto.

He never bores you as Sancho with his proverbs sometimes does. He is voluble but never long-winded; he is the very spirit of comradeship, the genius of converse, always ready with something to say, which provokes an answer—which provokes a better answer in turn. He both speaks and also (as some clever ones do not) listens, both sways and is swayed, and knows the mutual precipitate exhilaration—as in song and dance—of good company. Conversation is to him a thing of infinite moment: in words, not in deeds, are, not all his delights, to be sure, but all his triumphs. Time is nothing to him—he is always for making a night of it, like the moral Dr Johnson, who therefore, no doubt, forgave him. And so it is that he is the life of the party, the king of companions, the prince of good fellows, though not good. There, in the idiom, lies embedded the contradiction which justifies the contradiction in Falstaff himself. We, too, after all, like Prince Hal and Mrs Quickly, take to a man because of his charm, if it be big enough, not because of his virtue; and as for Falstaff, we are bewitched with the rogue's company, even to the point of forgetting everything else, and like Mrs Quickly even momentarily attributing to him that one thing which (none should know so well as she) he lacketh:—"Well, fare thee well! I have known thee these twenty-nine years, come peascod-time; but an honester and truer-hearted man—well, fare thee well!" What a testimony and tribute, entirely fallacious! Or, as Hal, thinking him dead, puts it more soberly and truly, "I could have better spared a better man." Under the spell of his presence and speech Mrs Quickly forgets what he owes her, for his diet and by-drinkings, the shirts bought for him and the money lent him; and, did we not stop to think, we should do the same.

But it is not merely by Falstaff's speech that we are kept under his spell; it is by all Shakespeare's comic art in the play. Here is another case of *isolation*, of comic emphasis such as we have seen in Shylock, until at the end of the Second Part he meets with the rebuff from the King. Shakespeare does not insist on Falstaff's sins and vices; he subordinates them, as we have seen, to his comic effects,—does not let them become serious, "terrible." In what Maginn says there is half a truth—"where does he cheat the weak or prey upon the poor?" His treatment of the travellers, and of Quickly, Bullcalf, Mouldy, Wart, Feeble, and Shallow, we are not suffered (or at least not expected) to take to heart or sternly remember against him. His boasting and lying is not a needless, silly, and chronic affair as it is with many braggart soldiers; it is the revival of enthusiasm after ignominious lapses, the glow of reaction after an escape. And his cowardice,—Morgann is right in insisting that it is not continual and contemptible like that of Parolles and Bobadill. That there is a difference between his and their evasions we have already noticed. In short, his roguery is not professional but human and incidental. No other coward is so attractive because none has such a variety of deportment, can in the presence of others put on such an air of dignity or pathos, or in the face of danger seem so philosophical and cool. He may run, roar, whimper, or fall flat upon the field, but so scared is he only for moments. When he hears the sheriff is at the door, he says to Prince Hal, "If you will deny the sheriff, so; if not, let him enter"; and he debates the matter of his gracing a cart and the gallows to bring tears to the eyes of others, though there are none in his own. And again, when on the eve of the engagement, he cries, "Hal, if thou see me down in the battle and bestride me, so; 'tis a point of friendship." He has the manner; he can assume a virtue, though he has it not the next moment—"I would 'twere bedtime, Hal, and all well." Yet the moment after (though for that moment only) he rallies, in soliloquy, the slender forces of manhood within him:—"Well, 'tis no matter; honour pricks me on." It is a feint—a transport—a flash in the pan! "Yea, but how if honour prick me off when I come on? How then?"

And his promptings of conscience and remorse touch us not too nearly. They are real but not too real. A quick shift of the burden to the villainous company he keeps, or a call for a bawdy song, ends them when in health; Quickly's deathbed comfort that there was no need of such thoughts yet, ends them forever. They had troubled him, though,—thoughts of honour, duty, religion; thoughts of his sins—his swearing, dicing, stealing, and lechery; thoughts of death—of God and Hell. "Peace, good Doll!" he had said in his latter heyday; "do not speak like a death's-head, do not bid me remember mine end." He winces a little when he is reminded of them, they prick him a little on the battle-field, they for a moment at the last peer in at him upon his pillow. He is not perfectly "free," not, as Professor Bradley thinks, wholly happy or at his ease, or he would not be so funny or so human. He is, as we have seen, not exalted above name and fame and duty; and the droll and delightful thing about him is the quick way he has of dodging or overriding all such obstacles and stumbling-blocks to happiness in his path. He makes shift to rise superior to his debts and duties—to all immaterial things (which, as such, are immaterial to him)— but not to circumstances. He puts on a bold face as he receives the public rebuff at the hands of the king; and he jests on gamely, perhaps brazenly, as he gives Shallow the thin satisfaction of a formal acknowledgment, *coram* Pistol and Bardolph, of his debt of a thousand pounds, assures his creditor that the king will send for his indispensable friend "soon at night," and bids him "fear no colours," punning on the word. But he does not laugh at being cast off, we have noticed, till the welkin rings, as Mr Beerbohm would have him do, and as he would do, if Rötscher's, Bulthaupt's, and Professor Bradley's conception of him quite fitted. This, at last, is to him no laughing matter; and if he have a philosophy it is not adversity's sweet milk, which fortifies. He is planted on this earth, and cannot dispense with her favours; he is not the one (if really he had it) to live on honour, on "air," like a chameleon up a tree. And prison, in his old age, without creature comforts, or company, is quite too much for him. Not that he is heart-broken—"killed his heart," we have seen, need not mean that—and though he had delighted in Prince Hal's company he on his death-bed does not remember him. Love he does not so much as crave love: Hal owes him his love, he once told him; and it pained and surprised the old fellow that Prince John, though with no particular reason to do so, did not warm up to him:—"Good faith, this same young sober-blooded boy doth not love me." He is not self-sufficient like a philosopher or a cat. Though not devoted himself, he likes the quality, insists on "good fellowship," and even on thieves being true one to another; he banks on it but all too fondly in the Prince. For he is by nature a guest, as Mr Beerbohm would say, not a host; to receive he has ever found more blessed than to give; and her guests he prays his hostess to cherish. But now the sun no longer shines; in the Fleet there is no cherishing; and while from duty he can dodge and sidle, he cannot from discomfort and cold fact. His comedy is at its period; reality, kept in the background, steps up and with disenchanting touch puts a stop to the merry make-believe; and Shakespeare is a tragic dramatist as well.

We may rightly complain of the King's priggish speech and harsh conduct; we may rightly complain perhaps that our comedy ends thus soberly; but both character and situation are true. The jig is up; the game of evasion could not last ever:—though afterwards, on his death-bed, he still contrived to evade the scruples which troubled him, and went away an it had been any christom child. But the facts, unlike the scruples and principles, that stood in the path of his happiness, he could not brush away, and he knew not how to laugh and face them. If Falstaff has, though much mirth, no philosophy, the poet has both; and Falstaff holds us under his spell not only in his own right but also in that of his maker.

1939—Mark Van Doren. "Henry IV," from *Shakespeare*

Mark Van Doren (1894-1972) was a professor of literature at Columbia University, a literary critic, a poet, and a novelist.

No play of Shakespeare's is better than "Henry IV." Certain subsequent ones may show him more settled in the maturity which he here attains almost at a single bound, but nothing that he wrote is more crowded with life or happier in its imitation of human talk. The pen that moves across these pages is perfectly free of itself. The host of persons assembled for our pleasure can say anything for their author he wants to say. The poetry of Hotspur and the prose of Falstaff have never been surpassed in their respective categories; the History as a dramatic form ripens here to a point past which no further growth is possible; and in Falstaff alone there is sufficient evidence of Shakespeare's mastery in the art of understanding style, and through style of creating men.

The vast dimensions of the comic parts should not be permitted to obscure the merit of the rest. History is enlarged here to make room for taverns and trollops and potations of sack, and the heroic drama is modified by gigantic mockery, by the roared voice of truth; but the result is more rather than less reality, just as a cathedral, instead of being demolished by merriment among its aisles, stands more august. The King of the play is more remote from the audience than any of Shakespeare's kings have been; he is more formal, and speaks with a full organ tone which as Bolingbroke he never used; but that is as it should be in a work which has so much distance to fill between laughter and law, between the alehouse and the throne. Henry wears his robes regally, and his sighs because they weigh him down are dignified and sonorous. One of his cares is that domestic rebellion keeps him from Jerusalem, where he was sworn

> To chase these pagans in those holy fields
> Over whose acres walk'd those blessed feet

Which fourteen hundred years ago were nail'd
For our advantage on the bitter cross. (1-I, i, 24–7)

He knows how to send his voice through four such lines as that, which in their lack of pause are incantation rather than speech; though in the second play, when age and illness and despair of his son have somewhat shattered his tone, he deepens his style (III, i; IV, v) to something like the complexity and variety of Shakespeare's dramatic verse at its best.

Another and the chief of his cares is the behavior of his son who will be Henry V, and who as early as the fifth act of "Richard II" was causing concern by the amount of time he spent with Falstaff's dissolute crew. The King preaches more than one sermon to the Prince, and if one were free to choose a companion for Hal one would certainly prefer the fat knight with the great belly doublet; for the sermons are heavy with state and conscious of the speaker's exalted virtue. But one is not free to choose. The King is after all the King, high away from puns and drunkenness. And Hal himself, though he will play with Falstaff through ten long acts, has secretly chosen his father all the while.

> I know you all, and will a while uphold
> The unyok'd humour of your idleness;
> Yet herein will I imitate the sun,
> Who doth permit the base contagious clouds
> To smother up his beauty from the world,
> That when he please again to be himself
> Being wanted, he may be more wonder'd at. (1-I, ii, 218–24)

If this is priggish, and it surely is, we must remember how conscious Shakespeare's princes always are of their careers, and we must remember that the uppermost drift of "Henry IV" is steadily in the direction of Hal's regeneration as Henry V. Falstaff is an interlude in his life: a circumstance from which Falstaff in fact derives much of his power. Falstaff like any other man must have his background, and it had best be a background that moves in time; if he is to be an unkempt knight, there must be banks of knights beyond him in fair dress, in full flower.

Shakespeare never permits us to forget Hal's sober side. Before Shrewsbury he confesses to his father that he has been a truant to chivalry (1-V, i, 94). And Warwick assures the King that

> The Prince but studies his companions
> Like a strange tongue, wherein, to gain the language,
> 'Tis needful that the most immodest word
> Be look'd upon and learn'd; which once attain'd,
> Your Highness knows, comes to no further use

But to be known and hated. So, like gross terms,
The Prince will in the perfectness of time
Cast off his followers. (2-IV, iv, 68–75)

Humorless as Warwick is, and much as he shocks us who have learned Falstaff's language at the Prince's side, we must recognize here the young man who had killed Hotspur in battle and who will come to such swift maturity in the scene with his dying father's crown (2-IV, v); who will commend the Chief Justice because he had imprisoned a Prince of Wales (2-V, ii); who will mock the expectation of the world and live henceforth a life of formal majesty (2-V, ii); and who at the very end will turn from Falstaff as from an old man he has never seen. This is the young man upon whom Vernon has lavished the brightest vocabulary of solemn praise; on one occasion describing to Hotspur the appearance of Hal and his comrades as they set out for Shrewsbury:

> All furnish'd, all in arms;
> All plum'd like estridges that with the wind
> Bated, like eagles having lately bath'd;
> Glittering in golden coats, like images;
> As full of spirit as the month of May,
> And gorgeous as the sun at midsummer;
> Wanton as youthful goats, wild as young bulls.
> I saw young Harry, with his beaver on,
> His cuisses on his thighs, gallantly arm'd,
> Rise from the ground like feathered Mercury,
> And vaulted with such ease into his seat,
> As if an angel dropp'd down from the clouds; (1-IV, i, 97–108)

and on another occasion crediting the Prince with every attribute of a knightly soul:

> I never in my life
> Did hear a challenge urg'd more modestly,
> Unless a brother should a brother dare
> To gentle exercise and proof of arms.
> He gave you all the duties of a man,
> Trimm'd up your praises with a princely tongue,
> Spoke your deservings like a chronicle,
> Making you ever better than his praise
> By still dispraising praise valued with you;
> And, which became him like a prince indeed,
> He made a blushing cital of himself,

And chid his truant youth with such a grace
As if he mast'red there a double spirit
Of teaching and of learning instantly.
There did he pause; but let me tell the world,
If he outlive the envy of this day,
England did never owe so sweet a hope,
So much misconstrued in his wantonness. (1-V, ii, 52–69)

We shall not end by liking Hal better than the Hotspur whom he challenges and kills, or by preferring the new king of England to the sometime prince of London's stews. The life of "Henry IV," indeed, is not in the handsome boy who will be Henry V. But he is the foil to that life, the brocaded curtain against which we watch it moving; he is the mold it is trying to break, the form of which it is the foe. If he could be broken the life would spill itself meaninglessly; whereas nothing is meaningless in "Henry IV," and least of all this pair of passages in which the first gentleman of England is so splendidly described.

Not that Hotspur is less the gentleman than Harry, but that he is more the person, the created speaking man. The King, comparing him with the Prince, pours on him the most courteous terms of praise; he is the theme of Honour's tongue, sweet Fortune's minion and her pride, the very straightest plant amongst the grove (1-I, i, 81–3). And Lady Percy, Hotspur's wife, speaks of him after his death as Ophelia speaks of the Hamlet she once knew; he was a miracle of men,

> and by his light
> Did all the chivalry of England move
> To do brave acts. He was indeed the glass
> Wherein the noble youth did dress themselves....
> In diet, in affections of delight,
> In military rules, humours of blood,
> He was the mark and glass, copy and book,
> That fashion'd others. (2-II, iii, 19–32)

But in the same speech Lady Percy lets us know something about her husband which we never know of Harry, and which Shakespeare henceforth will take the pains to publish in the case of any man who immensely interests him. Hotspur had a voice, a particular voice; one so specific in its qualities as to sound now in his widow's ears a bit abnormal. He talked "low and tardily." "Speaking thick" was the only blemish nature had given him. There was in other words a certain roughness in his throat. It went with the tartness of his tongue and with the rashness of his courage, the quick, busy directness of his purpose. It was this in him, along with his astonishing and unconventional vocabulary, that Lady Percy imitated when she called him "mad-headed ape" and "weasel," and threatened to break his little finger if he withheld his plans from her (1-II, iii). She never learned to swear as well as her master (1-III, i), but she could tell him to lie still, ye thief, as he dropped into her lap like Hamlet into the lap of Ophelia; and it can scarcely be doubted that he lived for her in his voice, as indeed he still lives for any reader of the play.

Northumberland, his father, calls him once "a wasp-stung and impatient fool." He is a high horse with dancing steel for muscles, an uncontrollable charger with gadflies ever at both flanks. It is not ambition that goads him, or any ordinary pride; it is rather a sense of his own superb mettle, a feeling of his strength, a toxin that attacks him because his energy is excessive and finds no outlet in life as most men live it. His scorn for most men takes the form of detesting their pretense; they are but apes of greatness, humbugs who profess the power he has without needing to profess it. He on the contrary, and with a certain perversity, insists furiously that he is but an ordinary fellow; there is nothing that he hates, or thinks he hates, more than the extraordinary. He even fancies that he is a silent fellow, a soldier of few words; "for I profess not talking" (1-V, ii, 92). Yet Northumberland can chide him for his "woman's mood,"

> Tying thine ear to no tongue but thine own. (1-I, iii, 238)

And the truth is that he talks all the time. He is one of Shakespeare's most copious poets, as well as one of his best.

His earliest appearance in Shakespeare was during the rebellion in "Richard II," when, entering to his father without a nod for Bolingbroke who stood by, he was asked whether he had forgotten the noble Duke. His answer was in some indefinable way impertinent, as if the contempt he was to feel for Bolingbroke as Henry IV already simmered in his blood.

> No, my good lord, for that is not forgot
> Which ne'er I did remember. To my knowledge,
> I never in my life did look on him. (II, iii, 37-9)

If there was impertinence in this it was overlooked, and the courtesy he followed with was impeccable. But now in "Henry IV" he is asked by the King why he has not delivered certain prisoners for whom a messenger has asked him, and although in a great speech of forty-one lines (1-I, iii, 29-69) he puts the reason off on the affectations of the messenger, and upon

> my impatience
> To be so pest'red with a popinjay,

we learn as soon as the King leaves that the King himself had been the reason. Hotspur's elders labor to stop his tirade; they interrupt and rebuke him as many as seven times; but he flows on, spilling his scorn in flawlessly natural lines of blank verse which he seems not to recognize as verse. And incidentally we discover the quality of his feeling towards Bolingbroke on that occasion of their first meeting.

> I'll keep them all!
> By God, he shall not have a Scot of them;
> No, if a Scot would save his soul, he shall not!
> I'll keep them, by this hand....
> Nay, I will; that's flat.
> He said he would not ransom Mortimer;
> Forbad my tongue to speak of Mortimer;
> But I will find him when he lies asleep,
> And in his ear I'll holla "Mortimer!"
> Nay,
> I'll have a starling shall be taught to speak
> Nothing but "Mortimer," and give it him,
> To keep his anger still in motion....
> All studies here I solemnly defy,
> Save how to gall and pinch this Bolingbroke;
> And that same sword-and-buckler Prince of Wales,
> But that I think his father loves him not
> And would be glad he met with some mischance,
> I would have him poison'd with a pot of ale....
> Why, look you, I am whipp'd and scourg'd with rods,
> Nettled and stung with pismires, when I hear
> Of this vile politician, Bolingbroke.
> In Richard's time,—what do you call the place?—
> A plague upon it, it is in Gloucestershire;
> 'Twas where the madcap duke his uncle kept,
> His uncle York; where I first bow'd my knee
> Unto this king of smiles, this Bolingbroke,—
> 'Sblood!—
> When you and he came back from Ravenspurgh. (1-I, iii, 213–48)

Northumberland relieves his son's agony; it was at Berkley Castle.

> You say true.
> Why, what a candy deal of courtesy
> This fawning greyhound then did proffer me?
> Look, "when his infant fortune came to age,"

And "gentle Harry Percy," and "kind cousin;"
O, the devil take such cozeners!—God forgive me!
Good uncle, tell your tale; for I have done.

His uncle Worcester cannot believe the last remark, and with ponderous irony invites him to go on till he is really done.

I have done, i' faith.

And for the time being he is done. But in the play it is not long until he has started again. The occasion is the rebels' conference at Bangor (1-III, i), and just as he had forgotten the name of Berkley Castle he now has forgotten, or thinks he has forgotten, a map that is necessary to the conference. When they find it for him he settles down to the business of the day; soon, however, to be nettled and stung by what he considers the pompous self-deception of Glendower, the tall Welshman with the deep voice who believes that he is not in the roll of common men, for at his birth the frame and huge foundation of the earth shak'd like a coward, and the heavens were all on fire because this son of Merlin had come to tread the tedious ways of art, of deep experiments. Hotspur hops about like a wasp on a hot griddle. He cannot bear such talk, and of course cannot be still. If the earth shook at Glendower's birth it must have had a kind of colic; the reason, his perverseness insists, was common and prosaic. For there is no such thing as poetry, this magnificent poet declares. His uncle Worcester had once, somewhat in the language of Theseus in "A Midsummer Night's Dream," accused him of apprehending "a world of figures" instead of the plain form of truth (1-I, iii, 209–10), but he had let that pass. Now when Glendower, roused to wrath, denies him the virtue of framing ditties lovely well as he himself has done, Hotspur explodes and cries:

Marry,
And I am glad of it with all my heart.
I had rather be a kitten and cry mew
Than one of these same metre ballad-mongers.
I had rather hear a brazen canstick turn'd,
Or a dry wheel grate on the axle-tree;
And that would set my teeth nothing on edge,
Nothing so much as mincing poetry.
'Tis like the forc'd gait of a shuffling nag. (1-III, i, 127–35)

And after Glendower has left, a speech which commences as an apology mounts quickly to the peak of wrath again:

I cannot choose. Sometime he angers me
With telling me of the moldwarp and the ant,

>   Of the dreamer Merlin and his prophecies,
>   And of a dragon and a finless fish,
>   A clip-wing'd griffin and a moulten raven,
>   A couching lion and a ramping cat,
>   And such a deal of skimble-skamble stuff
>   As puts me from my faith. I tell you what:
>   He held me last night at least nine hours
>   In reckoning up the several devils' names
>   That were his lackeys. I cried "hum," and "well, go to,"
>   But mark'd him not a word. O, he is as tedious
>   As a tired horse, a railing wife;
>   Worse than a smoky house. I had rather live
>   With cheese and garlic in a windmill, far,
>   Than feed on cates and have him talk to me
>   In any summer-house in Christendom. (1-III, i, 148–64)

"I tell you what: he held me last night at least nine hours." That is blank verse, but it is also speech, and it is as difficult to scan as a casual remark. In Hotspur Shakespeare has learned at last to make poetry as natural as the human voice—as natural, furthermore, as Falstaff's prose, or as the whole conduct of the incomparable action which is "Henry IV."

He must have been fond of his creation: of this high-strung youth who was so far above liking the art he mastered, who could be a fine poet without knowing that he was, who indeed made his poetry out of a hot love for nothing except reality and hard sense. For the paradox of Hotspur is the paradox of Shakespeare; the best poet least pampers and preens his talent, and in public at any rate would rather abuse it than take off its edge by boasting of its power to cut. Shakespeare lets Hotspur be proud of his plainness—"By God, I cannot flatter" (1-IV, i, 6)—but never of his poetry. He lets Worcester criticize his nephew for

>   Defect of manners, want of government,
>   Pride, haughtiness, opinion, and disdain, (1-III, i, 184–5)

but he will lavish two scenes of the second play upon the memory of a man whose death in the first play he must have regretted as much as the audience did. One of these scenes (II, iii) is that in which Lady Percy tells us how Hotspur had been the glass of England's fashion and charges Northumberland with his death. The charge is merited, for Northumberland's pretense of illness had been the cause of Hotspur's going unsupported into battle with Prince Hal. The other scene is the opening scene, with its elaborate business of Rumour's false news to Northumberland that his son has won the battle. Dr. Johnson dismissed this business as "wholly useless," but he was wholly wrong.

The new play pauses at the start to fix the memory of Hotspur in our minds, to render his death still more unthinkable than it had been, to honor him after his sorry mischance. Shakespeare cannot let him go without such obsequies, and without the suitable spectacle of Northumberland's frenzy once the truth has been made clear to him:

> Now let not Nature's hand
> Keep the wild flood confin'd! Let order die!
> And let this world no longer be a stage
> To feed contention in a ling'ring act;
> But let one spirit of the first-born Cain
> Reign in all bosoms, that, each heart being set
> On bloody courses, the rude scene may end,
> And darkness be the burier of the dead! (2-I, i, 153–60)

The father's turmoil of mind is more than an expression of his conscience; it is an adequate tribute to the finest figure Shakespeare has been able to carve for the serious portion of his History. For Hotspur was very serious. He was almost, indeed, insanely serious. He did not know that he was amusing. He did not understand himself—could not have named his virtues, would never have admitted his limitations. As handsome as Hamlet, and apparently as intelligent, he was not in fact intelligent at all. He was pure illusion, pure act, pure tragedy, just as Falstaff at the opposite pole of "Henry IV" is pure light, pure contemplation, pure comedy.

Falstaff understands everything and so is never serious. If he is even more amusing to himself than he is to others, that is because the truth about himself is something very obvious which he has never taken the trouble to define. His intelligence can define anything, but his wisdom tells him that the effort is not worth while. We do not know him in our words. We know him in his—which are never to the point, for they glance off his center and lead us away along tangents of laughter. His enormous bulk spreads through "Henry IV" until it threatens to leave no room for other men and other deeds. But his mind is still larger. It is at home everywhere, and it is never darkened with self-thought. Falstaff thinks only of others, and of the pleasure he can take in imitating them. He is a universal mimic; his genius is of that sort which understands through parody, and which cannot be understood except at one or more removes. He is so much himself because he is never himself; he has so much power because he has more than that maximum which for ordinary men is the condition of their identity's becoming stated. His is not stated because there is no need of proving that he has force; we feel this force constantly, in parody after parody of men he pretends to be. The parodist, the artist, is more real than most men whom we know. But we cannot fix him in a phrase, or claim more for ourselves than that we have been undeniably in his living presence.

There is a fine thread of personal idiom worked through the text of Falstaff's talk. His private voice rings out in such sentences as these:

> Indeed, you come near me now, Hal. (1-I, ii, 14)

> No; I'll give thee thy due, thou hast paid all there. (1-I, ii, 59–60)

> Indeed, I am not John of Gaunt, your grandfather; but yet no coward, Hal. (1-II, ii, 70–1)

> I'll never wear hair on my face more. (1-II, iv, 153)

> Ah, no more of that, Hal, an thou lovest me! (1-II, iv, 312–3)

> Peace, good Doll! do not speak like a death's-head. Do not bid me remember mine end. (2-II, iv, 254–5)

His native speech is casual yet pure, natural yet distinguished, easy and yet expertly wrenched out of line with the conventions of syntax; impossible to define, yet audibly his very own. We hear it, however, but seldom. Most of the time it is buried under heaps of talk delivered from a hundred assumed personalities, a hundred fictitious identities.

He is limited as a mimic only by the facts of his physique; being old and fat, he is short of breath and so must be brief of phrase.

> Tut, tut; good enough to toss; food for powder, food for powder; they'll fill a pit as well as better. Tush, man, mortal men, mortal men. (1-IV, ii, 71–3)

> How now, lad! is the wind in that door, i' faith? Must we all march? (1-III, iii, 102–3)

> How now! whose mare's dead? What's the matter? (2-II, i, 46–7)

But it will be seen at once—or heard—that he has made the most of this limitation. Artist that he is, he has accepted its challenge and employed it in effects that express his genius with a notable and economical directness. If he must gasp he will make each further gasp an echo of its fellow—an echo, but with ineffable additions. His speech then is not merely brief; it is repetitive, it rolls back on itself, it picks up its theme and tosses it to us again, with rich improvements.

> Why, Hal, 't is my vocation, Hal. 'Tis no sin for a man to labour in his vocation. (1-I, ii, 116–7)

> If the rascal have not given me medicines to make me love him, I'll be hang'd. It could not be else; I have drunk medicines. (1-II, ii, 18–20)

> A plague of all cowards, I say, and a vengeance too! marry, and amen! Give me a cup of sack, boy. . . . A plague of all cowards! Give me a cup of sack, rogue. Is there no virtue extant? (1-II, iv, 127–32)

> If I fought not with fifty of them, I am a bunch of radish. If there were not two or three and fifty upon poor old Jack, than am I no two-legg'd creature. (1-II, iv, 205–8)

> What, shall we be merry? Shall we have a play extempore? (1-II, iv, 308–9)

> Bardolph, am I not fallen away vilely since this last action? Do I not bate? Do I not dwindle? Why, my skin hangs about me like an old lady's loose gown; I am withered like an old apple-john. (1-III, iii, 1–4)

> I am not only witty in myself, but the cause that wit is in other men. I do here walk before thee like a sow that hath overwhelm'd all her litter but one. If the Prince put thee into my service for any other reason than to set me off, why then I have no judgement. Thou whoreson mandrake, thou art fitter to be worn in my cap than to wait at my heels. I was never mann'd with an agate till now. (2-I, ii, 10–9)

> What, a young knave, and begging! Is there not wars? Is there not employment? Doth not the King lack subjects? Do not the rebels need soldiers? (2-I, ii, 84–7)

> If the cook help to make the gluttony, you help to make the diseases, Doll. We catch of you, Doll, we catch of you. Grant that, my poor virtue, grant that. (2-II, iv, 48–51)

> Do you think me a swallow, an arrow, or a bullet? Have I, in my poor and old motion, the expedition of thought? (2-IV, iii, 35–7)

And, once more, its burden, its high business, is parody: imitation not always of another man who is standing by, if it is ever that, but of some man Falstaff suddenly, without warning, decides to be. Upon occasion it is the man—the bluff, successful soldier—he had been trained in his youth to be and has never become, though he knows the manner perfectly. "Tush, man, mortal men, mortal men"—there speaks the busy ghost of Sir John Falstaff, who rises again in "Whose mare's dead? What's the matter?" But there are many manners, many men. "Do not bid me remember mine end"—that is dolorously delivered, with a long face that remembers psalms. "I have drunk medicines," "Is there no virtue extant?," "I am withered like an old apple-john"—in such sighs we hear a feigned self-pity, a fooling with the music of elegy, which becomes classic in "A plague of sighing and grief! it blows a man up like a bladder" (1-II, iv, 364–5). In "We catch of you, Doll, we catch of you" there is a tickling levity, a chuckle and a poke in the ribs.

The essence of Falstaff is that he is a comic actor, most of whose roles are assumed without announcement. In at least two cases he forewarns us: when he proposes to the Prince that they take turns playing the King (1-II, iv), and when he orders his page to help him play deaf before the Lord Chief Justice (2-I, ii).

> My good lord! God give your lordship good time of day. I am glad to see your lordship abroad. I heard say your lordship was sick; I hope your lordship goes abroad by advice.

That is deliberate acting, as is the mournful gesture later on:

> Well, I cannot last ever; but it was alway yet the trick of our English nation, if they have a good thing, to make it too common.

And the mummery of Falstaff and the Prince as Henry IV provides some of the best stuff in all the play; the Prince, incidentally, showing both there and elsewhere that he has been Falstaff's aptest pupil in the school of style, for he can take off both his old master—"How now, wool-sack! what mutter you?" (1-II, iv, 149)—and his young rival in honor Hotspur (1-II, iv, 110–25). But Falstaff's stage acting, first-rate as it is, falls short of the natural acting he is incessantly busy with, whether the fiction of the moment be that he is a soldier with secret responsibilities or whether it be that he is a gay old blade of the town come to chuck the hostess under the chin and set Doll Tearsheet on his knee. Under pressure of the necessity to imitate his environment he can even break into verse, as when the Hostess's theatrical excitement over the little play of Henry IV and his son suggests to him that he treads a tragic stage:

> For God's sake, lords, convey my tristful queen;
> For tears do stop the flood-gates of her eyes; (1-II, iv, 434–5)

and as when, having so great a desire to hear what news the magnificent Pistol brings of Hal and the kingship, he knows he must fall in with the rascal's style if he is ever to get anything out of him:

> O base Assyrian knight, what is thy news?
> Let King Cophetua know the truth thereof. (2-V, iii, 105–6)

Of course he gets what he wanted; the style works like magic:

> Sir John, thy tender lambkin now is king;
> Harry the Fifth's the man. I speak the truth.
> When Pistol lies, do this, and fig me like
> The bragging Spaniard. (2-V, iii, 122–5)

And it would have been a pity if somewhere in "Henry IV" Falstaff had not added Pistol to his list of roles. For there is nothing more absurd and glorious in Shakespeare than the old-tragedy verse of Ancient Pistol:

> Fear we broadsides? No, let the fiend give fire. (2-II, iv, 196)

> There roar'd the sea, and trumpet-clangor sounds. (2-V, v, 42)

The ripest piece of Falstaff's miming is reserved, however, for a series of scenes toward the close of the second play, when Sir John, recruiting soldiers in Gloucestershire, happens upon an old friend of his London youth, the now doddering Justice Shallow. Shallow has lost all the juices that Falstaff has kept. He is thin and dry, and drones reminiscences in an old man's witless tenor.

> Come on, come on, come on, sir; give me your hand, sir, give me your hand, sir. An early stirrer, by the rood! And how doth my good cousin Silence? (2-III, ii, 1–4)

> Certain, 'tis certain; very sure, very sure. Death, as the Psalmist saith, is certain to all; all shall die. (2-III, ii, 40–2)

> I will not excuse you; you shall not be excus'd; excuses shall not be admitted; there is no excuse shall serve; you shall not be excus'd. Why, Davy! ... Davy, Davy, Davy, Davy, let me see, Davy; let me see, Davy; let me see. Yea, marry, William cook, bid him come hither. Sir John, you shall not be excus'd. (2-V, i, 5–13)

His unit of utterance is as brief as Falstaff's, and the Lord knows he repeats himself; but if any evidence were needed of the muscle in his big friend's style it could be found at once in the contrast Shallow provides. For his repetitions are relaxed, nerveless, foolish—the work of weakness, not of a still joyful strength; just as those of the Hostess are the signs of a fluttering rather than a doing mind:

> I have borne, and borne, and borne, and have been fubb'd off, and fubb'd off, and fubb'd off, from this day to that day, that it is a shame to be thought on. (2-II, i, 35–9)

> If he swagger, let him not come here; no, by my faith. I must live among my neighbours; I'll no swaggerers. I am in good name and fame with the very best. Shut the door; there comes no swaggerers here. I have not liv'd all this while, to have swaggering now. Shut the door, I pray you. (2-II, iv, 79–85)

Falstaff, whose memory of Shallow is doubtless less perfect than he says it is, takes in the truth at a glance; sees that this old forked radish, this pitiful cheese-paring of a man, lives only in the remembrance of his youth; and nobly decides—for even though he may think to have fun with Shallow later, and cash in on him as a butt for whom the Prince will pay, there is something noble in the instantaneous decision—to fall in with his way of speech, to grant him just what he desires.

> *Shallow.* O, Sir John, do you remember since we lay all night in the windmill in Saint George's field?
> *Falstaff.* No more of that, good Master Shallow, no more of that.
> *Shallow.* Ha! 'twas a merry night. And is Jane Nightwork alive?
> *Falstaff.* She lives, Master Shallow.
> *Shallow.* She never could away with me.
> *Falstaff.* Never, never; she would always say she could not abide Master Shallow.
> *Shallow.* By the mass, I could anger her to the heart. She was then a bona-roba. Doth she hold her own well?
> *Falstaff.* Old, old, Master Shallow.
> *Shallow.* Nay, she must be old; she cannot choose but be old; certain she's old; and had Robin Nightwork by old Nightwork before I came to Clement's Inn.
> *Silence.* That's fifty-five year ago.
> *Shallow.* Ha, cousin Silence, that thou hadst seen that that this knight and I have seen! Ha, Sir John, said I well?

Falstaff. We have heard the chimes at midnight, Master Shallow. (2-III, ii, 206–29)

The last and best of these sentences sums up all that Shallow could hope to say in twenty quavering years, and does it so briefly that the breath of any hearer must be taken; and expresses its speaker so completely that he can never be absent from our consciousness henceforth. We may not know the man who says this, but we know that a man says it, and we know him better than we do most members of his race. And we have not failed to note the magnanimity which after all has been from the beginning the groundwork of his humor: a magnanimity which will sound once more when, listening to the simple, bemused merriment of Silence as he sings his little songs, he generously puts in the remark:

I did not think Master Silence had been a man of this mettle. (2-V, iii, 40)

And Silence responds:

Who? I? I have been merry twice and once ere now.

The wit of Falstaff's answers when charges of cowardice, treachery, and lying are truly urged against him is the wit of a man who knows that other men are waiting to hear what he will pretend, who he will become, how he will get out of it. "Answer, thou dead elm, answer," "Come," says Poins, "your reason, Jack, your reason." Poins is thirsty for another of Jack's good reasons. He must be patient a while, for Falstaff to make time insists that though reasons were as plenty as blackberries he will give none on compulsion; but in good season it comes: "Why, hear you, my masters. Was it for me to kill the heir-apparent? Should I turn upon the true prince?" (1-II, iv, 295–7). Something like that was what Poins and the true Prince wanted, though they could not have predicted it, being no Falstaffs. Like any remark by a great man, it is at the same time surprising and in character; the form of such a man grows clearer with everything he utters, and his dimensions increase. We could not have known that he would say it; and afterwards we cannot imagine him saying anything else or better, though the next thing will be better. "Thy love is worth a million; thou ow'st me thy love" (1-III, iii, 155–6). That is better; and so is "I disprais'd him before the wicked, that the wicked might not fall in love with him; in which doing, I have done the part of a careful friend and a true subject, and thy father is to give me thanks for it" (2-II, iv, 346–50). That the King does not thank him is not surprising. Falstaff has not expected it.

What now of his vices, and why is it that they have not the sound of vices? None of them is an end in itself—that is their secret, just as Falstaff's character is his mystery. He does not live to drink or steal or lie or foin o' nights. He even does not live in order that he may be the cause of wit in other men. We do not in fact know why he lives. This great boulder is balanced lightly on the earth, and can be tipped with the lightest touch. He cannot be overturned. He knows too much, and he understands too well the art of delivering with every lie he tells an honest weight of profound and personal revelation.

1951—Harold C. Goddard. "Henry IV," from *The Meaning of Shakespeare*

> Harold C. Goddard (1878–1950) was head of the English department at Swarthmore College. One of the most important twentieth-century books on Shakespeare is his *The Meaning of Shakespeare*, published after his death.

Who at this late date can hope to say a fresh word about Falstaff? Long since, his admirers and detractors have drained language dry in their efforts to characterize him, to give expression to their fascination or detestation. Glutton, drunkard, coward, liar, lecher, boaster, cheat, thief, rogue, ruffian, villain are a few of the terms that have been used to describe a man whom others find the very incarnation of charm, one of the liberators of the human spirit, the greatest comic figure in the history of literature. "A besotted and disgusting old wretch," Bernard Shaw calls him. And isn't he?—this man who held up unprotected travelers for pastime, betrayed innocence in the person of his page, cheated a trusting and hard-working hostess, borrowed a thousand pounds from an old friend with no intention of repaying it, abused his commission by taking cash in lieu of military service, and insinuated his way into the graces of the heir apparent with an eye to later favor. And yet after three centuries there the old sinner sits, more invulnerable and full of smiles than ever, his sagging paunch shaking like a jelly, dodging or receiving full on, unperturbed, the missiles his enemies hurl at him. Which is he? A colossus of sack, sensuality, and sweat—or a wit and humorist so great that he can be compared only with his creator, a figure, to use one of Shakespeare's own great phrases, livelier than life? One might think there were two Falstaffs.

The trouble with the "besotted and disgusting old wretch" theory is that Shakespeare has given us that old wretch exactly, and he is another man: the Falstaff of *The Merry Wives of Windsor*. The disparagers of Falstaff generally make him out a mixture, in varying proportions, of this other Falstaff, Sir Toby Belch, and Parolles, each of whom was an incalculably inferior person. But to assert that

Falstaff is another man is not saying that he does not have many or even all of the vices of the "old wretch" for whom his defamers mistake him. Salt is not sodium, but that is not saying that sodium is not a component of salt. The truth is that there *are* two Falstaffs, just as there are two Henrys, the Immortal Falstaff and the Immoral Falstaff, and the dissension about the man comes from a failure to recognize that fact. That the two could inhabit one body would not be believed if Shakespeare had not proved that they could. That may be one reason why he made it so huge.

Curiously, there is no more convincing testimony to this double nature of the man than that offered by those who are most persistent in pointing out his depravity. In the very process of committing the old sinner to perdition they reveal that they have been unable to resist his seductiveness. Professor Stoll, for instance, dedicates twenty-six sections of a long and learned essay to the annihilation of the Falstaff that his congenital lovers love. And then he begins his twenty-seventh and last section with the words: "And yet people like Falstaff"! And before his first paragraph is done, all his previous labor is obliterated as we find him asserting that Falstaff is "supremely poetic" (even his most ardent admirers would hardly venture that "supremely") and that "his is in many ways the most marvellous prose ever penned." (It is, but how did the old sot, we wonder, ever acquire it?) Before his next paragraph is over, Stoll has called Falstaff "the very spirit of comradeship," "the king of companions," and "the prince of good fellows." "We, too, after all, like Prince Hal and Mrs. Quickly," he goes on, "take to a man because of his charm, if it be big enough, not because of his virtue; and as for Falstaff, we are bewitched with the rogue's company." (A Falstaff idolater could scarcely ask for more than that.) "Under the spell of his presence and speech," Stoll concludes, we should forget, as she does, the wrong he has done Mrs. Quickly, "did we not stop to think."

"Stop to think"! One may determine the orbit of the moon, or make an atomic bomb, by stopping to think, but when since the beginning of time did one man ever get at the secret of another by means of the intellect? It is all right to stop to think after we have taken a character to our hearts, but to do so before we have is fatal. Dr. Johnson stopped to think about Falstaff and as a result he decided that "he has nothing in him that can be esteemed." A child would be ashamed of such a judgment. But a child would never be guilty of it. "As for *Henry IV*," wrote one of the most imaginatively gifted young women I have ever known, "I love it. And I must have an utterly vulgar nature, for I simply adore Falstaff. He is perfectly delightful—not a fault in his nature, and the Prince is a DEVIL to reject him." That young woman evidently did not "stop to think." When she does, she will moderate that "not a fault in his nature," for that is the function of thinking—to hold our imagination within bounds and cut down its excrescences. Meanwhile, Falstaff has captured her, and she has captured Falstaff, for, as Blake said, enthusiastic admiration is the first principle of knowledge, and the last. Those who think about Falstaff before they fall in love with him may say some just things about him but they will never enter into his secret. "Would I were with him, wheresome'er he is, either in heaven or in hell!" Those words of poor Bardolph on hearing the account of Falstaff's death remain the highest tribute he ever did or ever could receive. In their stark sincerity they are worthy (irreverent as the suggestion will seem to some) to be put beside Dante's sublime incarnation of the same idea in the Paolo and Francesca incident in *The Inferno*, or even beside the words addressed to the thief who repented on the cross.

The scholars have attempted to explain Falstaff by tracing his origins. He has been found, variously, to have developed from the Devil of the miracle plays, the Vice of the morality plays, the boasting soldier of Plautine comedy, and so on. Now roots, up to a certain point, are interesting, but it takes the sun to make them grow and to illuminate the flower. And I think in this case we can find both roots and sun without going outside Shakespeare. If so, it is one of the most striking confirmations to be found of the embryological nature of his development.

If I were seeking the embryo of Falstaff in Shakespeare's imagination, I should consider the claims of Bottom—of Bottom and another character in *A Midsummer-Night's Dream*. "What!" it will be said, "the dull realistic Bottom and the lively witty Falstaff? They are nearer opposites." But embryos, it must be remembered, seldom resemble what they are destined to develop into. Bottom, like the physical Falstaff at least, is compact of the heaviness, the materiality, the reality of earth; and the ass's head that Puck bestows on him is abundantly deserved, not only in special reference to his brains but in its general implication of animality. But instead of letting himself be humiliated by it, Bottom sings, and Titania, Queen of the Fairies, her eyes anointed by the magic flower, awakening, mistakes him for an angel, and taking him in her arms, lulls him to sleep. The obvious meaning of the incident of course is that love is blind. Look at the asinine thing an infatuated woman will fall in love with! But whoever stops there, though he may have gotten the fun, has missed the beauty. The moment when Bottom emerges from his dream, as we pointed out when discussing *A Midsummer-Night's Dream*, is Shakespeare at one of his pinnacles. By a stroke of genius he turns a purely farcical incident into nothing less than a parable of the Awakening of Imagination within Gross Matter. It is the poet's way of saying that even within the head of this foolish plebeian weaver a divine light can be kindled. Bottom is conscious of transcendent things when he comes to himself. A creation has taken place within him. He struggles, in vain, to express it, and, in his very failure, succeeds:

> God's my life! . . . I have had a most rare vision. I have had a dream, past the wit of man to say what dream it was. Man is but an ass, if he go about to expound this dream. Methought I was—there is no

man can tell what. Methought I was,—and methought I had,—but man is but a patch'd fool, if he will offer to say what methought I had. The eye of man hath not heard, the ear of man hath not seen, man's hand is not able to taste, his tongue to conceive, nor his heart to report, what my dream was. I will get Peter Quince to write a ballad of this dream. It shall be called "Bottom's Dream," because it hath no bottom.

The dreamer may still be Bottom. But the dream itself is Puck. For one moment the two are one. Ass or angel? Perhaps Titania was not so deluded after all.

Do not misunderstand me. I am not suggesting that Shakespeare ever consciously connected Puck and Bottom with Falstaff in his own mind. But having achieved this inconceivable integration of the two, how easily his genius would be tempted to repeat the miracle on a grander scale: to create a perfect mountain of flesh and show how the same wonder could occur within it, not momentarily, but, humanly speaking, perpetually. That at any rate is what Falstaff is: Imagination conquering matter, spirit subduing flesh. Bottom was a weaver—a weaver of threads. "I would I were a weaver," Falstaff once exclaimed. He was a weaver—a weaver of spells. Here, if ever, is the embryology of the imagination. "Man is but a patch'd fool, if he will offer to say...." Who cannot catch the very accent of Falstaff in that?

> I'll put a girdle round about the earth
> In forty minutes.

It might have been said of Falstaff's wit. His Bottom-like body is continually being dragged down, but his Puck-like spirit can hide in a thimble or pass through a keyhole as nimbly as any fairy's. What wonder that this contradictory being—as deminatured as a satyr or a mermaid—who is forever repeating within himself the original miracle of creation, has taken on the proportions of a mythological figure. He seems at times more like a god than a man. His very solidity is solar, his rotundity cosmic. To estimate the refining power we must know the grossness of what is to be refined. To be astounded by what lifts we must know the weight of what is to be lifted. Falstaff is levitation overcoming gravitation. At his wittiest and most aerial, he is Ariel tossing the terrestrial globe in the air as if it were a ball. And yet—as we must never forget—he is also that fat old sinner fast asleep and snoring behind the arras. The sins, in fact, are the very things that make the miracle astonishing, as the chains and ropes do a Houdini's escape.

To grasp Falstaff thus *sub specie aeternitatis* we must see him, as Titania did Bottom, with our imagination, not with our senses. And that is why we shall never see Falstaff on the stage. On the stage there the monster of flesh stands—made, we know, mainly of pillows—with all his sheer material bulk and greasy beefiness, a palpable candidate for perdition. It takes rare acting to rescue him from being physically repulsive. And as for the miracle—it just refuses to happen in a theater. It would take a child to melt this too too solid flesh into spirit. It would take Falstaff himself to act Falstaff. But in a book! On the stage of our imagination! That is another matter. There the miracle can occur—and does for thousands of readers. Falstaff is a touchstone to tell whether the juice of the magic flower has been squeezed into our eyes. If it has not, we will see only his animality. To the vulgar, Falstaff will be forever just vulgar.

The problem of Falstaff himself cannot be separated from the problem of the fascination he exercises over us. Critics have long since put their fingers on the negative side of that secret. Half his charm resides in the fact that he is what we long to be and are not: *free*. Hence our delight in projecting on him our frustrated longing for emancipation. It is right here that those who do not like Falstaff score a cheap victory over those who do. The latter, say the former, are repressed or sedentary souls who go on a vicarious spree in the presence of one who commits all the sins they would like to commit but do not dare to. Like some of Falstaff's own hypotheses, the idea has an air of plausibility. But it involves a pitifully superficial view of Falstaff—as if his essence lay in his love of sack! No! it is for liberation from what all men want to be rid of, not just the bloodless few, that Falstaff stands: liberation from the tyranny of things as they are. Falstaff is immortal because he is a symbol of the supremacy of imagination over fact. He forecasts man's final victory over Fate itself. Facts stand in our way. Facts melt before Falstaff like ice before a summer sun—dissolve in the *aqua regia* of his resourcefulness and wit. He realizes the age-old dream of all men: to awaken in the morning and to know that no master, no employer, no bodily need or sense of duty calls, no fear or obstacle stands in the way—only a fresh beckoning day that is wholly ours.

But we have all awakened that way on rare occasions without becoming Falstaffs. Some men often do. An untrammeled day is not enough; we must have something to fill it with—besides lying in bed. Freedom is only the negative side of Falstaff. Possessing it, he perpetually does something creative with it. It is not enough for him to be the sworn enemy of facts. Any lazy man or fool is that. He is the sworn enemy of the factual spirit itself, of whatever is dull, inert, banal. Facts merely exist—and so do most men. Falstaff lives. And where he is, life becomes bright, active, enthralling.

Who has not been a member of some listless group on whom time has been hanging heavy when in the twinkling of an eye a newcomer has altered the face of everything as utterly as the sun, breaking through clouds, transforms the surface of a gray lake? Boredom is banished. Gaiety is restored. The most apathetic member of the company is laughing and alert and will shortly be contributing his share to the flow of good spirits. What has done it? At bottom, of course, the mysterious fluid of an infectious personality. But so far as it can be analyzed, some tall tale or personal adventure wherein a grain of fact has been worked up with a pound of fiction, some impudent assumption about the host or absurd charge against somebody present rendered plausible by a precarious resemblance to the truth. Always *something made out of nothing*, with power, when added to the facts, to get the better of them. Never an unadulterated lie, but always some monstrous perversion, some scandalous interpretation, of what actually happened. An invention, yes, but an invention attached to reality by a thread of truth—the slenderer the better, so long as it does not break. What is Falstaff but an aggrandized, universalized, individualized version of this familiar phenomenon? He makes life again worth living.

And so, whether we approach Falstaff from the mythological or the psychological angle, we reach the same goal.

But alas! we have been neglecting the other Falstaff, the old sot. Unluckily—or perhaps luckily—there is another side to the story. Having fallen in love with Falstaff, we may now "stop to think" about him without compunction. And on examining more closely this symbol of man's supremacy over nature we perceive that he is not invulnerable. He has his Achilles heel. I do not refer to his love of Hal. That is his Achilles heel in another and lovelier sense. I refer to a tiny fact, two tiny facts, that he forgets and that we would like to: the fact that his imagination is stimulated by immense potations of sack and that his victories are purchased, if necessary, at the price of an utter disregard for the rights of others. We do not remember this until we stop to think. And we do not want to stop to think. We want to identify ourselves with the Immortal Falstaff. Yet there the Immoral Falstaff is all the while. And he must be reckoned with. Shakespeare was too much of a realist to leave him out.

The Greeks incarnated in their god Dionysus the paradox of wine, its combined power to inspire and degrade. *The Bacchae* of Euripides is the profoundest treatment of this theme in Hellenic if not in any literature. "No one can hate drunkenness more than I do," says Samuel Butler, "but I am confident the human intellect owes its superiority over that of the lower animals in great measure to the stimulus which alcohol has given to imagination—imagination being little else than another name for illusion."[1] "The sway of alcohol over mankind," says William James, "is unquestionably due to its power to stimulate the mystical faculties of human nature [the imagination, that is, in its quintessence], usually crushed to earth by the cold facts and dry criticisms of the sober hour. Sobriety diminishes, discriminates, and says no; drunkenness expands, unites, and says yes. It is in fact the great exciter of the *Yes* function in man . . . it is part of the deeper mystery and tragedy of life that whiffs and gleams of something that we immediately recognize as excellent should be vouchsafed to so many of us only in the fleeting earlier phases of what in its totality is so degrading a poisoning."

James's contrast between the earlier and the later phases of alcoholic intoxication inevitably suggests the degeneration that Falstaff undergoes in the second part of *Henry IV*. That degeneration is an actual one, though several recent critics have tended to exaggerate it. Dover Wilson thinks that Shakespeare is deliberately trying to make us fall out of love with Falstaff so that we may accept with good grace his rejection by the new king. If so, for many readers he did not succeed very well. (Of that in its place.)

It is significant that we never see Falstaff drunk. His wit still scintillates practically unabated throughout the second part of the play, though some critics seem set on not admitting it. He is in top form, for instance, in his interview with the Chief Justice, and, to pick a single example from many, the reply he gives to John of Lancaster's reproach,

> When everything is ended, then you come,

is one of his pinnacles: "Do you think me a swallow, an arrow, or a bullet?" No, the degeneration of Falstaff is not so much in his wit or even in his imagination as in his moral sensibility. The company he keeps grows more continuously low, and his treatment of Shallow and of his recruits shows an increasing hardness of heart. Shakespeare inserts too many little realistic touches to let us take these scenes as pure farce, and while no one in his senses would want to turn this aspect of the play into a temperance tract it seems at times like an almost scientifically faithful account of the effect of an excess of alcohol on the moral nature. In view of what Shakespeare was at this time on the verge of saying about drunkenness in *Hamlet* and of what he was to say about it later in *Othello*, *Antony and Cleopatra*, and *The Tempest*, it is certain that he was profoundly interested in the subject; and it is not far-fetched to suppose that he had in the back of his mind in portraying the "degeneration" of Falstaff the nemesis that awaits the artificially stimulated mind. If so, the fat knight is Shakespeare's contribution, in a different key, to the same problem that is treated in *The Bacchae*, and his conclusions are close to those at which Euripides arrives.

VIII

Is there any activity of man that involves the same factors that we find present in this Falstaff: complete freedom, an all-consuming zest for life, an utter subjugation of facts to imagination, and an entire absence of moral responsibility? Obviously there is. That activity is play.

Except for that little item of moral responsibility, "play" expresses as nearly as one word can the highest conception of life we are capable of forming: life for its own sake, life as it looks in the morning to a boy with

> no more behind
> But such a day to-morrow as to-day,
> And to be boy eternal,

life for the fun of it, as against life for what you can get out of it—or whom you can knock out of it. "Play" says what the word "peace" tries to say and doesn't. "Play" brings down to the level of everyone's understanding what "imagination" conveys to more sophisticated minds. For the element of "imagination" is indispensable to true play. Play is not sport. The confusion of the two is a major tragedy of our time. A crowd of fifteen-year-old schoolboys "playing" football on a back lot are indulging in sport. They are rarely playing. The one who is playing is the child of five, all alone, pretending that dirty rag doll is the rich mother of a dozen infants—invisible to the naked eye. Even boys playing war, if they are harmonious and happy, are conducting an experiment in peace. Play is the erection of an illusion into a reality. It is not an escape from life. It is the realization of life in something like its fulness. What it *is* an escape from is the boredom and friction of existence. Like poetry, to which it is the prelude, it stands for a converting or winning-over of facts on a basis of friendship, the dissolving of them in a spirit of love, in contrast with science (at least the science of our day), which, somewhat illogically, stands first for a recognition of the absolute autonomy of facts and then for their impressment and subjection to human demands by a kind of military conquest.

Now Falstaff goes through life playing. He coins everything he encounters into play, often even into a play. He would rather have the joke on himself and make the imaginative most of it than to have it on the other fellow and let the fun stop there. Whenever he seems to be taken in because he does not realize the situation, it is safer to assume that he does realize it but keeps quiet because the imaginative possibilities are greater in that case.

Watching him, we who in dead earnest have been attending to business or doing what we are pleased to call our duty suddenly realize what we have been missing. "The object of a man's life," says Robert Henri, "should be to play as a little child plays." If that is so we have missed the object of life, while Falstaff has attained it, or at least not missed it completely, as we have. It is his glory that, like Peter Pan, he never grew up, and that glory is the greater because he is an old man. As his immense size and weight were utilized by Shakespeare as a foil for the lightness of his spirit, so his age is used to stress its youthfulness. "You that are old," he says to the Chief Justice, who has been berating him for misleading the Prince, "consider not the capacities of us that are young." The Chief Justice replies that Falstaff is in every part "blasted with antiquity," his belly increasing in size, his voice broken, "and will you yet call yourself young? Fie, fie, fie, Sir John!" Falstaff retorts that as for his belly, he was born with a round one; as for his voice, he has lost it hollaing and singing of anthems; and as for his age, he is old only in judgment and understanding. Though the Lord Chief Justice has all the facts on his side, Falstaff has the victory. There has seldom been a more delicious interview.

As this scene suggests, the right way to take the Falstaff whom we love is to take him as a child. Mrs. Quickly did that in her immortal account of his death: he went away, she said, "an it had been any christom child." To call him a liar and let it go at that is like being the hardheaded father of a poetic little son who punishes him for falsehood when he has only been relating genuine imaginative experiences—as Blake's father thrashed him for saying he had seen angels in a tree. And to call him a coward and let it go at *that* is being no profounder.

But if it is the glory of the Immortal Falstaff that he remained a child, it is the shame of the Immoral Falstaff that he never became a man—for it is a child's duty to become a man no less than it is a man's duty to become a child. Falstaff detoured manhood instead of passing through it into a higher childhood. He is like the character in *The Pilgrim's Progress* who tried to steal into Paradise by climbing over the wall near its entrance instead of passing through the wicket gate and undergoing the trials that it is the lot of man to endure. He wanted the victory without paying the price. He wanted to be an individual regardless of the social consequences, to persist in the prerogatives of youth without undertaking the responsibilities of maturity. But if his virtues are those of a child rather than those of a man, that does not prevent him from being immensely superior to those in these plays who possess the virtues of neither man nor child, or from giving us gleams of a life beyond good and evil.

Dover Wilson[2] would have us take *Henry IV* as a morality play wherein a madcap prince grows up into an ideal king. Falstaff is the devil who temps the Prince to Riot. Hotspur and especially the Lord Chief Justice are the good angels representing Chivalry and justice or the Rule of Law. It is a struggle between Vanity and Government for the possession of the Royal Prodigal.

The scheme is superbly simple and as moral as a Sunday-school lesson. But it calmly leaves the Immortal Falstaff quite out of account! If Falstaff were indeed just the immoral creature that in part he admittedly is, Wilson's parable would be more plausible, though even then the words he picks to characterize Falstaff are singularly unfortunate. "Vanity" by derivation means emptiness or absence of substance, and "riot" quarrelsomeness. Imagine calling even the Immoral Falstaff empty or lacking in substance—or quarrelsome! He had his vices but they were not these. For either vanity or riot there is not a single good word to be said. To equate Falstaff with them is to assert that not a single good word can be said for him—a preposterous proposition. Wit, humor, laughter, good-fellowship, insatiable zest for life: are these vanity or does Falstaff *not* embody them? That is the dilemma in which Mr. Wilson puts himself. And as for the Lord Chief Justice, he is indeed an admirable man; a more incorruptible one in high position is not to be found in Shakespeare. But if the poet had intended to assign him any such crucial role as Mr. Wilson thinks, he certainly would have presented him more fully and would have hesitated to let Falstaff make him look so foolish. For the Chief Justice's sense of justice was better developed than his sense of humor. And even justice is not all.

Henry IV does have a certain resemblance to a morality play. The two, however, between whom the younger Henry stands and who are in a sense contending for the possession of his soul are not Falstaff and the Chief Justice, but Falstaff and the King. It is between Falstaff and the Father—to use that word in its generic sense—that Henry finds himself.

Now in the abstract this is indeed Youth between Revelry and Responsibility. But the abstract has nothing to do with it. Where Henry really stands is between this particular companion, Falstaff, and this particular father and king, Henry IV. Of the two, which was the better man?

Concede the utmost—that is, take Falstaff at his worst. He was a drunkard, a glutton, a profligate, a thief, even a liar if you insist, but withal a fundamentally honest man. He had two sides like a coin, but he was not a counterfeit. And Henry? He was a king, a man of "honour," of brains and ability, of good intentions, but withal a "vile politician" and respectable hypocrite. He *was* a counterfeit. Which, if it comes to the choice, is the better influence on a young man? Shakespeare, for one, gives no evidence of having an iota of doubt.

But if even Falstaff at his worst comes off better than Henry, how about Falstaff at his best? In that case, what we have is Youth standing between Imagination and Authority, between Freedom and Force, between Play and War. My insistence that Falstaff is a double man, and that the abstract has nothing to do with it, will acquit me of implying that this is the whole of the story. But it is a highly suggestive part of it.

The opposite of war is not "peace" in the debased sense in which we are in the habit of using the latter word. Peace ought to mean far more, but what it has come to mean on our lips is just the absence of war. The opposite of war is creative activity, play in its loftier implications. All through these dramas the finer Falstaff symbolizes the opposite of force. When anything military enters his presence, it instantly looks ridiculous and begins to shrink. Many methods have been proposed for getting rid of war. Falstaff's is one of the simplest: laugh it out of existence. For war is almost as foolish as it is criminal. "Laugh it out of existence"? If only we could! Which is the equivalent of saying: if only more of us were like Falstaff! These plays should be required reading in all military academies. Even the "cannon-fodder" scenes of Falstaff with his recruits have their serious implications and anticipate our present convictions on the uneugenic nature of war.

How far did Shakespeare sympathize with Falstaff's attitude in this matter? No one is entitled to say. But much further, I am inclined to think, than he would have had his audience suspect or than the world since his time has been willing to admit. For consider the conditions under which Falstaff finds himself:

Henry has dethroned and murdered the rightful king of England. The Percys have helped him to obtain the crown, but a mutual sense of guilt engenders distrust between the two parties, and the Percys decide to dethrone the dethroner. Falstaff is summoned to take part in his defense. "Life is given but once." Why should Falstaff risk his one life on earth, which he is enjoying as not one man in a hundred million does, to support or to oppose the cause of either of two equally selfish and equally damnable seekers after power and glory? What good would the sacrifice of his life accomplish comparable to the boon that he confers daily and hourly on the world, to say nothing of himself, by merely being? This is no case of tyranny on one side and democracy on the other, with the liberty or slavery of a world at stake. This is a strictly dynastic quarrel. When two gangs of gunmen begin shooting it out on the streets of a great city, the discreet citizen will step behind a post or into a doorway. The analogy may not be an exact one, but it enables us to understand Falstaff's point of view. And there is plenty of Shakespearean warrant for it.

> See the coast clear'd, and then we will depart,

says the Mayor of London when caught, in *1 Henry VI*, between similar brawling factions,

> Good God! these nobles should such stomachs bear;
> I myself fight not once in forty year.

And Mercutio's "A plague o' both your houses!" comes to mind. Shakespeare meant more by that phrase than the dying man who coined it could have comprehended.

"But how about Falstaff's honor?" it will be asked. "Thou owest God a death," says the Prince to him before the battle of Shrewsbury. "'Tis not due yet," Falstaff answers as Hal goes out,

> I would be loath to pay him before his day. What need I be so forward with him that calls not on me? Well, 'tis no matter; honour pricks me on. Yea, but how if honour prick me off when I came on? how then? Can honour set to a leg? No. Or an arm? No. Or take away the grief of a wound? No. Honour hath no skill in surgery, then? No. What is honour? A word. What is in that word honour? What is that honour? Air; a trim reckoning! Who hath it? He that died o' Wednesday. Doth he feel it? No. Doth he hear it? No. 'Tis insensible, then? Yea, to the dead. But will it not live with the living? No. Why? Detraction will not suffer it. Therefore I'll none of it. Honour is a mere scutcheon: and so ends my catechism.

"You must be honorable to talk of honor," says a character in *A Raw Youth*, "or, if not, all you say is a lie." The word "honor," as that sentence of Dostoevsky's shows, is still an honorable word. It can still mean, and could in Shakespeare's day, the integrity of the soul before God. The Chief Justice had honor in that sense. But "honour" in its decayed feudal sense of glory, fame, even reputation, as page after page of these Chronicle Plays records, had outlived its usefulness and the time had come to expose its hollowness. The soul, lifted up, declared Saint Teresa (who died in 1582), sees in the word "honor" "nothing more than an immense lie of which the world remains a victim. . . . She laughs when she sees grave persons, persons of orison, caring for points of honor for which she now feels profoundest contempt. . . . With what friendship we would all treat each other if our interest in honor and in money could but disappear from the earth! For my own part, I feel as if it would be a remedy for all our ills."

Saint Teresa and Sir John Falstaff! an odd pair to find in agreement—about honor if not about money. In the saint's case no ambiguity is attached to the doctrine that honor is a lie. In the sinner's, there remains something equivocal and double-edged. Here, if ever, the two Falstaffs meet. The grosser Falstaff is himself a parasite and a dishonorable man, and coming from him the speech is the creed of Commodity and the height of irony. But that does not prevent the man who loved Hal and babbled of green fields at his death from revealing in the same words, as clearly as Saint Teresa, that life was given for something greater than glory or than the gain that can be gotten out of it.

"Give me life," cries Falstaff on the field of Shrewsbury. "Die all, die merrily," cries Hotspur. That is the gist of it. The Prince killed Hotspur in the battle, and Falstaff, with one of his most inspired lies, claimed the deed as his own. But Falstaff's lies, scrutinized, often turn out to be truth in disguise. So here. Falstaff, not Prince Henry, did kill Hotspur. He ended the outworn conception of honor for which Hotspur stood. The Prince killed his body, but Falstaff killed his soul—or rather what passed for his soul.

The dying Hotspur himself sees the truth. The verdict of his final breath is that life is "time's fool" and he himself dust. And the Prince, gazing down at his dead victim, sees it too, if only for a moment.

> Ill-weav'd ambition, how much art thou shrunk!
> When that this body did contain a spirit,
> A kingdom for it was too small a bound,

he exclaims, and, turning, he catches sight of another body from which life has also apparently departed:

> What, old acquaintance! could not all this flesh
> Keep in a little life? Poor Jack, farewell!
> I could have better spar'd a better man.

But nobody was ever more mistaken on this subject of life and flesh than was Henry on this occasion, as the shamming Falstaff proves a moment later, when the Prince goes out, by rising from the dead. "'Sblood," he cries,

> 'twas time to counterfeit, or that hot termagant Scot had paid me scot and lot too. Counterfeit? I lie, I am no counterfeit. To die is to be a counterfeit; for he is but the counterfeit of a man who hath not the life of a man; but to counterfeit dying, when a man thereby liveth, is to be no counterfeit, but the true and perfect image of life indeed. The better part of valour is discretion.

> I fear thou art another counterfeit,

Douglas had cried, coming on Henry IV on the field of Shrewsbury,

> Another king! they grow like Hydra's heads.
> I am the Douglas, fatal to all those
> That wear those colours on them. What art thou,
> That counterfeit'st the person of a king?

The literal reference of course is to the knights, disguised to represent the King, that Henry had sent into the battle to divert the enemy from his own person. "The better part of valour is discretion." This, and that repeated word "counterfeit," is Shakespeare's sign that he intends the contrast, and the deeper unconscious meaning of Douglas'

> What art thou,
> That counterfeit'st the person of a king?

(a king, notice, not the king) is just one more of the poet's judgments upon Henry. For all his "discretion," the Douglas would have killed this counterfeit king who tries to save his skin by the death of others if the Prince had not come to his rescue in the nick of time.

But that was earlier in the battle. At the point we had reached the Prince comes back with his brother John and discovers the "dead" Falstaff staggering along with the dead Hotspur on his back—a symbolic picture if there ever was one.

> Did you not tell me this fat man was dead?

cries Lancaster.

> I did; I saw him dead,
> Breathless and bleeding on the ground,

replies Henry. He has underrated the vitality of the Imagination, and even now thinks he sees a ghost:

> Art thou alive?
> Or is it fantasy that plays upon our eyesight?
> I prithee, speak; we will not trust our eyes
> Without our ears. Thou art not what thou seem'st.

"No: that's certain," retorts Falstaff, "I am not a double man." And to prove it, he throws down the body of Hotspur he is carrying. But beyond this obvious meaning, who can doubt that Falstaff, in the phrase "double man," is also having a thrust at the dual role of the man he is addressing, or that Shakespeare, in letting Falstaff deny his own doubleness, is thereby calling our attention to it? At the very least the expression proves that the world did not have to wait for Dostoevsky before it heard of the double man.

Truth has made it necessary to say some harsh things about Prince Henry; so it is a pleasure to recognize the character of his conduct on the field of Shrewsbury: his valor in his encounter with Hotspur, his courage and loyalty in rescuing his father from Douglas, and his generosity in letting Falstaff take credit for Hotspur's death. Dover Wilson makes much of this last point—too much, I think, for the good of his own case—declaring that it proves the Prince thought nothing of renown, of "the outward show of honour in the eyes of men, so long as he has proved himself worthy of its inner substance in his own." But if he was as self-effacing as all that, why did he cry at the moment he met Hotspur?—

> all the budding honours on thy crest
> I'll crop, to make a garland for my head.

Those words flatly contradict the "grace" he does Falstaff in surrendering to him so easily the greatest honor of his life. The paradox arises, I think, from the presence of those conflicting personalities, Hal and the Prince. Touched momentarily at the sight of what he believes to be his old companion dead at his feet, the fast-disappearing Hal returns and survives long enough after the surprise and joy of finding him still alive to accept Falstaff's lie for truth. But we wonder how much longer. Wilson's assumption that the Prince would or could have kept up the fiction permanently is refuted by the fact that Morton had observed the death of Hotspur at Henry's hands and reports the event correctly:

> these mine eyes saw him in bloody state,
> Rendering faint quittance, wearied and outbreath'd,

To Harry Monmouth; whose swift wrath beat down
The never-daunted Percy to the earth,
From whence with life he never more sprung up.

Everything, from the famous first soliloquy on, proves that the Prince not only craved renown but craved it in its most theatrical form.

NOTES

1. It is usually presumptuous to disagree with Samuel Butler's use of words. But if he had substituted "mind" for "intellect" in the foregoing quotation I think he would have been nearer the mark. And only the unwary reader will think that by "illusion" Butler means the same thing as delusion or lie.

2. Following Professor R. A. Law.

1953—William Empson. "Falstaff and Mr. Dover Wilson," from *The Kenyon Review*

William Empson (1906-1984) was a professor at Sheffield University, a poet, and one of the finest literary critics of his time. Two of his best-known books are *Seven Types of Ambiguity* and *Some Versions of Pastoral*.

I.

The theory that Shakespeare made Falstaff appear in his first draft of *Henry V*, so that our present text of that play is much revised and thereby gravely confused, seems to be accepted now by most of the competent authorities; indeed to be regarded as the most positive result of Mr. Dover Wilson's very detailed work on the Falstaff trilogy, and therefore as the main support for a narrow view of Falstaff in general. I want in this essay to ask the reader to look at the whole position again. Whether Shakespeare changed his mind about *Henry V* is perhaps not very important, but it gives a definite point to start from; and I think it is time someone pointed out how very weak the evidence for this theory is.

To be sure, the evidence offered is imposingly various; from the Epilogue of *II Hen. IV*, from some historical possibilities about censorship, and from the text of *Henry V* itself; but I think it breaks down all round. The relevant part of the Epilogue says:

> One word more, I beseech you. If you be not too much cloyed with fat meat, our humble author will continue the story, with Sir John in it, and make you merry with fair Catherine of France; where (for anything

I know) Falstaff shall die of a sweat, unless 'a be already killed with your hard opinions; for Oldcastle died a martyr, and this is not the man.

"For anything I know" and "if you want it" are a good deal more doubtful than what we are accustomed to nowadays in the way of advance publicity, and I haven't noticed anyone listing parallel Elizatebian examples. It seems to me that the speaker disclaims knowing what the author will do, beyond the broad fact that the next part of the familiar story is being considered for a play; and the Company might not want to give away the secrets of the next production, even if Shakespeare had decided on them. Mr. Dover Wilson makes the valuable point that the Quarto order for the text of this epilogue shows it is two of them jammed together; the Folio editor merely altered the order to make the combination speakable. The first was spoken by someone responsible for the performance, perhaps the author, probably at Court, and the second by a dancer before he began his jig or what not; the second therefore need not be taken very seriously, and only the second includes this little advertisement. Mr. Dover Wilson says he cannot believe that the "jesting" apology about Oldcastle was "spoken on the stage while the matter was still dangerous," but I cannot see what he deduces from that; it seems to be a matter of months rather than years. As to the main point, I think Falstaff *is* quite prominently "in the play," though not in the cast, and indeed I think the new king's hard opinion, which Falstaff does die of, *is* a kind of "public opinion," so that there is no inconsistency at all. Of course this would be "stretching a point" if anyone gave it as an official explanation, but it is the kind of thing the Elizabethan mind would put up with, and the whole trick of this advertisement is to tease the audience by ostentatiously refusing to satisfy their curiosity. Shakespeare could have let it be spoken if he had already decided to kill Falstaff; it is as likely that he hadn't yet started on the new effort (one would expect he dallied till he knew he had to work fast) but either way it is no proof that he wrote out two whole versions.

Mr. Dover Wilson's argument in his edition of *Henry V* (1947) was that there was nobody to act Falstaff because Kemp had suddenly left the Company. I gather that this line of effort has now been abandoned. There was a Court performance of *I Hen. IV* in 1600 (described as a private one, for the Flemish Ambassador), after Kemp is supposed to have gone, and the recent attempts to decide which actor took which part do not give it to him anyway. Kemp was a low comedian (a fine chap too), whereas one of the points you needed to make clear about Falstaff was that he was a scandalous gentleman; it doesn't seem Kemp's part at all. Besides, they would have to have some kind of understudy system. The argument has now moved to a more aristocratic ground, and we are told that Falstaff was removed from Agincourt because the descendants of "Fastolfe" influenced the censor. He was not suppressed altogether; the Ambassador could hardly be shown a play recently banned for libel, and Part II was printed in 1600, and indeed *The Merry Wives* (on this view) was brought out as an alternative to showing him at Agincourt. Mr. Dover Wilson suggests that the Company hid its embarrassment by *inventing* a story that the Queen asked to see him in love, and that Shakespeare could gratify her in three weeks. This was "convenient" for them, he thinks. I do not believe it could be done. Falstaff was a very prominent object, much the most successful Shakespeare character before Hamlet; some of this would be likely to leak out. The legend that the Queen commissioned *The Merry Wives* is recorded late and not worth much; it is evidence that the terrifying old woman had laughed at Falstaff, and that her moods were watched and remembered, but not much more. As negative evidence, however, it seems to me very strong; if she had allowed her underlings to suppress Falstaff, even in part, no "publicity" arrangement would be likely to get away with the opposite story. Besides, the "embarrassed" Company would just as soon have the truth leak out. And what about the treatment of a much more real Fastolfe in *Hen. VI*? And why not deal with the new name firmly, as had been done to the previous name Oldcastle? All the same, peculiar things do happen, and the descendants of Fastolfe might have been just strong enough to keep him out of Agincourt, and to hush the suppression up, though not strong enough to suppress him elsewhere. If we found confusions in the text of *Henry V* which needed a very special explanation this theory might be plausible. But surely it is very gratuitous if we find none.

The textual arguments for revision, in Mr. Dover Wilson's edition, are as follows.

I. Pistol says at V.i.80 that he hears his doll is dead of syphilis, so he has lost his rendezvous. I agree that the author ought to have put "Nell," and the actor had better say it, because the other word confuses us with another character. But the modern Damon Runyan slang happens to have been Elizabethan slang too; the slip was an easy one for the author to make. And I think there was an extra reason for making it here. The ladies were last mentioned in Act II; we learned that Pistol had married Mrs. Quickly (Nell) and heard him express contempt for Tearsheet (Doll) as in hospital for syphilis; he had always skirmished with Doll (when on the stage with her) and had now become keen to stand by Nell, whose position was clearly more hopeful. There can be no point in assuming he has changed over without warning the audience. But we need not be surprised that Mrs. Quickly got the disease too, and there is a deserved irony if Pistol, who talked brutally about Doll's trouble at the beginning of the play, finds at the end that the same applies to his Nell. Now, if Shakespeare meant this, both women were in his mind, and that is the kind of case where a hurried writer puts down the wrong word. It comes in the Quarto, supposed to be pirated by actors, not only in the Folio, but that need only be another of the depressing bits of evidence that Shakespeare never corrected the acting text.

Such is what I would make of it, but Mr. Dover Wilson deduces that the whole speech, and much else of the part of Pistol, was written for Falstaff, to whom Doll was last seen attached. Before erecting this mountain of conjecture I think he might have answered the note here in the Arden edition, which points out four other places where the text goes wrong over proper names; one of them calls the King of England "brother Ireland" (V.ii.10), and compared to that (which Mr. Dover Wilson positively claims as a mistake in writing by Shakespeare, who must have been thinking about Essex, he says) I do not think a reasonable man need feel very solemn about these two dolls.

I also feel that, even if Shakespeare did first write this flabby blank verse for Falstaff and not for the now miserably deflated Pistol, we need not call in the machinery of censorship to explain why he changed his mind; if his first thoughts were so bad we had better keep to his second ones and be thankful. Maybe he did toy with the idea of taking Falstaff to Agincourt—he would feel the natural strength of any easy temptation—but we have no proof here that he wrote a whole draft of it.

II. The prologue to the second Act ends:

> . . . the scene
> Is now transported, gentles, to Southampton;
> There is the playhouse now, there must you sit:
> And thence to France shall we convey you safe
> And bring you back, charming the narrow seas
> To give you gentle pass; for if we may
> We'll not offend one stomach with our play.
> But, till the King come forth and not till then,
> Unto Southampton do we shift our scene.

The next four scenes are in London, Southampton, London, and France, with the London ones describing first the illness and then the death of Falstaff. The final rhymed couplet, which follows another, whereas the prologues to the other four Acts all end with one rhymed couplet, seems a rather slack attempt to clear up a muddle and only succeeds in adding a contradiction (the Arden edition remarks, with psychological but perhaps not literal accuracy, that "the negative notion, being uppermost in his mind, thrusts itself in prematurely"). Mr. Dover Wilson deduces that the scenes about the death of Falstaff were added later. But he and the other people who hold this theory assume that comic scenes about Falstaff always existed in the play and had to be put somewhere, however different the first draft of them may have been. To prove that their position has been altered does nothing to prove that their content has been altered. It is rather curious, I think, that this simple fallacy is so convincing at first blush. You might perhaps argue that the dying Falstaff could not leave London, whereas the swashbuckling

Falstaff could be shown in Southampton; but it would be almost necessary to start him off in London, if only for a farewell to the ladies. The first Act is just under four hundred lines long, and the average for the other four Acts, all a good bit longer, is just under six hundred. The technique of five "epic" prologues was new to Shakespeare, and obviously difficult to combine with his usual unbroken one; and all the Acts contain comic material except the first. Surely he might have tried to polish off Falstaff in Act I, and then found that the balance had gone wrong, as I think it would, and then corrected the second prologue rather casually. It seems to me equally possible that he had not thought of the solemn prologues as anything to do with the comedians, and had always intended a short banging first Act, and then pushed another couplet onto the prologue to Act II, of a baffling kind, merely because the Company objected that it didn't apply to them.

III. The first two arguments point out real confusions, but the third (for which Mr. Dover Wilson gives credit elsewhere) only marks a lack of understanding in the critics. The long scene IV.i, they say, must contain a huge interpolation. The king says he wants a council of lords at his tent, so they must come there "anon," but first he wants to think alone (this is at line 30); then he has three successive conversations in disguise with his other ranks; then a long soliloquy about how they don't understand his difficulties; then Erpingham, who took the message before, returns and says the lords are searching him throughout the camp; the king says that they must be called back, and adds graciously that he will be there before the messenger (this is about line 290—the exchange with Erpingham only takes five lines); all he does is to start straight off on another soliloquy—he is at last ready for his solitary prayer, and it is not at all hurried. The critics find this "awkward," and the lords would agree, but not the audience and surely the whole point of this scene, which joins very neatly onto the repeated claim that he learned to be a good king by his experience of low life, is that he thought nothing of keeping the lords waiting while he talked to the troops; talking to the troops would even keep him from his prayers, but talking to experts on strategy never would. I do not believe that this very strong dramatic effect was an accidental result of enforced revision; I should be more inclined to call it playing to the gallery; and when Mr. Dover Wilson cannot see it he throws himself under serious suspicion, as an interpreter of Falstaff as well as of King Hal, because he is missing the whole popular story about the king he claims to rehabilitate.

Some other arguments for revision given by Mr. J. H. Walter in his article "With Sir John In It" (*MLR* July 1946) should perhaps he recognized here, but they seem to me unimportant. Fluellen doesn't use "p" for "b" in talking to Pistol (III.ii) but does so to Gower just afterwards, therefore the Pistol incident was added later (but he is on his dignity in talking to Pistol); we are promised "a little touch of Harry in the night" but don't get any of the fighting we expect, only morale-building (this seems to me an absurd objection; there was assumed to be much excitement in getting a stray contact with what Pistol calls "the lovely bully," and the morale for next day was more important than any skirmishing could be); in F though not in Q a comic capture by Pistol is impossibly made the first action of the battle (but if put later it breaks the dramatic sequence); Fluellen at the beginning of Act V "relates to Gower an entirely fresh motive for his annoyance; it has no connection with Pistol's insults in III.vi" (Shakespeare always multiplies motives, and Pistol could be trusted to do the same; besides, Fluellen might not care to repeat the insults); at the end of this scene, in the "My Doll" speech, "Pistol's characteristic verse is completely absent" (of course it is; he is deflated and in soliloquy; is this Falstaff's characteristic verse, then?) and says he is old though, unlike Falstaff, he is not (he feels old); the Dauphin comes to the battle against his father's express orders (another detail to make his father look weak); there seems an intention to bring Henry and the Dauphin into opposition, but as it comes to nothing the Master of the Revels may have cut a degrading representation of royalty (then Shakespeare may have avoided going to such lengths as might have induced the Master of the Revels to make a cut); Fluellen was present when Williams told Henry about the glove, so ought to have recognised Williams later (but he is too excitable; the plot is not meant to be deep), and there is no reason why Henry should tell both separately to go and look for Gower (but it is only to make sure they meet and have an absurd quarrel; this bit of rough fooling, ending with tossing away some gold, is entirely "in character" with the Henry of the Falstaff scenes, and was very much needed to show him as the same man in his stern grandeur). I don't much like the play, and do not mean to praise it by defending the text; but the fashion for finding "joins" in the text has I think been carried to absurd lengths, though by people who agree with Mr. Dover Wilson rather than by himself, and I hope this tedious paragraph has proved it.

There is of course a reason why we find a struggle made to prove that Falstaff was originally in *Henry V*. Mr. Dover Wilson, largely out of a patriotic impulse as I understand, feels that 19th century romantic critics went badly wrong about Falstaff, and that the main source of their error was the pathetic description of his death. If it can be shown that this description was only thrown in as a "job," to cheat the audience and hide a bit of truckling to high officials, then we need no longer smear false sentiment over him and (what is more) the modern royalist is safe in revering Hal as the ideal king. I should agree that there has been some false sentiment about Falstaff (and some of Mr. Dover Wilson's remarks about him seem to me very valuable), but this feeling of distaste should not send one in headlong flight to the opposite extreme; the main fact about Falstaff, I think, is that it is hard to get one's mind all round him.

In trying to weaken the story of his death, Mr. Dover Wilson descends to such arguments as that "neither ague nor 'sweat' has anything to do with a broken heart," whereas when Henry IV dies the critic is eager to explain that apoplexy was not always due to over-eating but sometimes (as here) to cares of state. He jeers at the bad language in which Nym and Pistol, unsentimental characters one would think, echo the plain statement by Mrs. Quickly, "the king has killed his heart," at which he dare not jeer. To be sure, their language is funny, and after Mrs. Quickly's great description of his death they only say "Shall we shog?" like fleas. But they understand what has happened; the excuse for Hal made by Nym, "The king is a good king, but it must be as it may; he passes some humours and careers," is stuffed full of the obvious coarse sentiment about Hal which seems unable to enter Mr. Dover Wilson's mind. The hero is expected to kill his tutor, in fact it proves that the tutor had the real magical skill to produce a hero; we are to be reminded later that Alexander also killed his friend. It is no use for Mr. Dover Wilson to "play down" the death of Falstaff, because it was once for all "written up," and indeed he is in a logical dilemma there; how could the passage do what he supposes, swing over an audience resentful at being cheated, if they would only think it ridiculous? We can all imagine them taking it rather casually; it is Mr. Dover Wilson who needs to argue that they didn't.

His attitude to the death, I think, could almost be called mean, which is very surprising from him, but one must realize that this comes from a conviction that the story demands reverence; that any idea of Shakespeare as "stating the case for Falstaff" should be met with indignation:

> Shakespeare plays no tricks with his public; he did not, like Euripides, dramatize the stories of his race and religion in order to subvert the traditional ideals those stories were first framed to set forth. Prince Hal is the prodigal, and his repentance is to be taken seriously; it is to be admired and commended. . . .

and so forth. It seems to me that, in this generous impulse of defence, he is rather under-rating the traditional ideals of his race and religion. They do not force you to ascribe every grace and virtue to this rather calculating type of prodigal, merely because he defeated the French. So far from that, if you take the series as a whole (and here we are greatly indebted to Dr. Tillyard, another of these rather royalist critics), the main point of the story is that he was doomed because he was a usurper; France had to be lost again, and much worse civil wars had to break out, till at last the legitimate line was restored. The insistence on this is fierce in *Richard II* and both parts of *Henry IV*. Henry V has a very inspiring kind of merit, and I think Shakespeare meant us to love him, though in an open-eyed manner; but the idea that Shakespeare presents him as an ideal king seems to me to show a certain lack of moral delicacy, which need not be described as a recall to the higher morality of an earlier world. And then again, it may be said that the audience were not thinking of such things; the intention of the series was a simple and patriotic one, whether "high" or not. But I should say that the popular story about the prodigal was itself complex (and by the way "Renaissance" not "medieval"), so that the whole of this defence for Hal is off the point—he did not need it. Of course I don't deny that there was plenty of patriotism about the thing, and that Shakespeare took that seriously, but it left room for other sentiments.

I think indeed that the whole Falstaff series needs to be looked at in terms of Dramatic Ambiguity, before one can understand what was happening in the contemporary audience; and I think that if this is done the various problems about Falstaff and Prince Hal, so long discussed, are in essence solved. Nor would this approach seem strange to Mr. Dover Wilson, who has done much the most interesting recent work on the subject. Most of this essay has the air of an attack on him, but my complaints are supposed to show cases where he has slipped back into taking sides between two viewpoints instead of letting both be real. Slipped back, because on at least one occasion he uses explicitly and firmly the principle I want to recommend; and perhaps I will look more plausible if I begin with that illustration of it.

The question whether Falstaff is a coward may be said to have started the whole snowball of modern Shakespearean criticism; it was the chief topic of Morgann's essay nearly two hundred years ago, the first time a psychological paradox was dug out of a Shakespeare text. Mr. Dover Wilson, discussing the plot about the robbery in the first three scenes where we meet Falstaff, says that the question whether Falstaff sees through the plot against him, and if so at what point he sees through it—for instance, whether he runs away from the Prince on purpose or only tells increasingly grotesque lies to him afterwards on purpose—is *meant* to be a puzzle, one that the audience are challenged to exercise their wits over; and that this had an important practical effect (it is not a matter of deep intellectual subtlety of course) because you would pay to see the play again with your curiosity undiminished. The whole joke of the great rogue is that *you* can't see through him, any more than the Prince could. I think that Mr. Dover Wilson's analysis of the text here is the final word about the question, because he shows that you aren't meant to find anything more; the dramatic effect simply *is* the doubt, and very satisfying too. Mr. Dover Wilson is a rich mine of interesting points, and it seems rather parasitic of me to keep on repeating them as weapons against him; but it seems important to urge that the method he has established here should be tried out on adjoining cases.

However, I recognise that this approach is liable to become tiresomely intellectualistic; a man who takes it into his head that he is too smart to look for the answer, on one of these points, because he knows the author means to cheat him, is likely to miss getting any real experience from the play. Besides, the actor and producer have to work out their own "conception" of Falstaff, in each case, and are sometimes felt to have produced an interesting or "original" one; it would be fatuous for the theoretical critic to say that they are merely deluding themselves, because there isn't any such thing. I do not mean that; the dramatic ambiguity is the source of these new interpretations, the reason why you can go on finding new ones, the reason why the effect is so rich. And of course there must be a basic theme which the contradictions of the play are dramatizing, which some interpretations handle better than others; after planting my citadel on the high ground of the Absolute Void, I still feel at liberty to fight in the plains against Mr. Dover Wilson at various points of his detailed interpretation. But this way of putting it is still too glib. The basic argument of Mr. Dover Wilson is that the plays ought to be taken to mean what the first audiences made of them (and they took not merely a moral but a very practical view of the importance of social order and a good king). I agree with all of that, and merely answer that the reaction of an audience is not such a simple object as he presumed. No doubt he succeeds in isolating what the first audiences would find obvious; but we may still believe that other forces had to be at work behind Falstaff, both in the author and the audiences which he understood, to make this figure as Titanic as we agree to find him; nor need we plunge for them deep into the Unconscious. The plays were an enormous hit, appealing to a great variety of people, not all of them very high-minded, one would think. Obviously a certain amount of "tact" was needed, of a straightforward kind, to swing the whole of this audience into accepting the different stages of the plot. To bring out examples of this tact as evidence of the author's single intention, or of a single judgement which he wanted to impose on the audience, seems to me naïve. So far from that, I think that on several occasions he was riding remarkably near the edge; a bit breathtaking it may have been, to certain members of the first audiences.

One cannot help feeling some doubt when Mr. Dover Wilson insists that Hal was never a "sinner," only a bit wild; especially when it becomes rather doubtful, as he goes on, what even the wildness may have consisted in. Not sex, we gather; it seems only old men like Falstaff go wrong like that. The same applies to drunkenness. Even the bishops in *Henry V*, Mr. Dover Wilson maintains, do not say that he has been converted, only that he has begun working hard (actually they say more); and even his father in reproaching him only speaks of sins in others which his wildness might encourage. Robbery, the reader is now to decide, he could not possibly have committed; to suppose that he even envisaged such a thing is to misread the whole play.

It is true that the early scenes of *I Hen. IV* can be read as Mr. Dover Wilson does. I ought to admit this the more prominently because I said in my book *Pastoral* that "we hear no more" about the Prince's claim that he will repay the stolen money, which we do (III.iv.177). But after admitting this mistake I claim all the more that the dramatic effect is inherently ambiguous. Mr. Dover Wilson points out that we ought to consider the order of events on the stage, how the thing is planned to impress you; I warmly agree, but he only uses this rule for his own purpose. It is plain, surely, that we are put in doubt whether the Prince is a thief or not, at any rate in the early scenes; if you got a strong enough impression from those scenes that he was one, you would only regard the later return of the money as a last-minute escape from a major scandal. No doubt, if you felt sure from the start that he couldn't really be one, the return of the money would act as laughing the whole thing off; but even so, the dramatist has put you through a bit of uncertainty about what he will ask you to believe. So to speak, an escape from a scandal is what happens to the audience, whether it happened to the Prince or not; and a dramatic structure of this kind assumes that at least some of the audience do not know the answer beforehand. It is therefore ridiculous, I submit, for a critic to argue heatedly that he has discovered the answer by a subtle analysis of the text. Such a critic, however, could of course, turn round on me and say I am wrong to suppose it is "this kind of dramatic structure"; so far from that, he would say, he has shown the modern actor and producer how to make the play intelligible and coherent even to a fresh audience from the beginning. I therefore need to join in his labors, instead of calling them ridiculous; I need to show that the text is so arranged that the uncertainty can still not be dispelled even after the most careful study.

Among the first words of Falstaff, who is then alone with the Prince, he says "when thou art King, let not us that are squires of the night's body be called thieves of the day's beauty" and so on, and *us* is quite positively accepted by the Prince in his reply (whether for a joke or not) as including himself: "the fortune of us that are the moon's men doth ebb and flow like the sea" and so on. Of course I am not pretending that this proves he is a thief; I give it as an example of the way the dramatist starts by making us think he *may* be a thief. The next point, as the jokes turn over, is a grave appeal from Falstaff: "Do not thou, when thou art King, hang a thief." Falstaff gets much of his fun out of a parody of moral advice, especially in these earlier scenes, and the point here must be that the Prince has no right to hang a thief because he is one himself. His reply (a very sufficient one) is that Falstaff will do it. Falstaff then inverts the obvious by upbraiding the Prince for leading him astray; he threatens to reform, and the Prince's answer is, "Where shall we take a purse tomorrow, Jack?" Falstaff accepts this as if they are old partners in robbery, and is only concerned to defend his courage—"Zounds, where thou wilt, lad, I'll make one, an I do not, call me a villain and baffle me." Poins now enters and announces a scheme for robbery, and when the Prince is asked if he will join he speaks as if the idea was absurdly outside his way of life—"Who, I? rob? I a thief? Not I, by my faith." Falstaff has already assumed that the Prince knows this plan is being prepared ("Poins! Now we shall know if Gadshill hath set a match"), and Poins is the Prince's own gentleman-in-waiting; however, Mr. Dover Wilson naturally makes the most of this brief retort:

> The proposal that the Prince is to take part in the highway
> robbery is received at first with something like indignation, even with

a touch of haughtiness, and only consented to when Poins intimates, by nods and winks behind Falstaff's back, that he is planning to make a practical joke of it.

The nods and winks are invented by the critic, of course (and printed in his text of the play), but they seem plausible enough; indeed the line, "Well, then, once in my days I'll be a madcap," reads like a rather coarse attempt to keep the respectable part of the audience from being too shocked. They are welcome to decide that the Prince is not really a thief after all. The point I want to make is that another part of the audience is still quite free to think he is one; indeed, this pretence of innocence followed immediately by acceptance (followed by further riddles) is just the way Falstaff talks himself. Poins then arranges the plot against Falstaff with the Prince, and finally the Prince makes his famous soliloquy, claiming that his present behavior is the best way to get himself admired later on. I do not think that the words suggest he is doing nothing worse than play practical jokes on low characters. To be sure, the "base contagious clouds," the "foul and ugly mists," only *seem* to strangle the sun; you can still think the Prince innocent here; and he only describes his own behavior as "loose." But then we hear about a reformation of a fault, and about an offence which must apparently be redeemed (though literally it is only time which must be redeemed). It seems to me that the balance is still being kept; you can decide with relief that surely after this he can't be a thief, or you can feel, if you prefer, he has practically admitted that for the present he is one.

The more usual question about this soliloquy is whether it shows the Prince as "callous and hypocritical," determined to betray his friends. Naturally Mr. Dover Wilson argues that it does not, because "it was a convention to convey information to the audience about the general drift of the play, much as a prologue did," and in any case at this stage of the play "we ought not to be feeling that Falstaff deserves any consideration whatever." I think this carries the "sequence" principle rather too far, and most people would know the "general drift" before they came; but I don't deny, of course, that the placing of this soliloquy is meant to establish Hal as the future hero as firmly as possible. Even so, I do not see that it does anything (whether regarded as a "convention" or not) to evade the obvious moral reflection, obvious not only to the more moralising part of the audience but to all of it, that this kind of man made a very unreliable friend. Surely the Elizabethans could follow this simple duality of feeling without getting mixed; it is inevitable that if you enjoy Falstaff you feel a grudge against the eventual swing-over of Hal, even though you agree that the broad plot couldn't be different. The real problems about the rejection do not arise here; we have no reason to presume it will come as a painful shock to his present friends (though "falsify men's hopes" may be a secret mark of the author's plan). I think a fair amount can be deduced about Shakespeare's own feelings for this kind of condescending patron; but in any case it was a commonplace of his period that the friendships of great men very often were unreliable. The whole thing seems to me in the sunlight, and for that matter the fundamental machinery seems rather crude, and perhaps it had to be to carry such a powerful conflict of judgment. There does not seem much for later critics to disagree about.

Mr. Dover Wilson, however, feels that there is, because he wants to build up Hal as a high-minded creature of delicate sensibility. A brief scene with Poins (*II Hen. IV*, II.ii) is made important for this purpose. We are told about Hal that:

> The kind of reserve that springs from absence of self-regard is in point of fact one of his principal characteristics, and such a feature is difficult to represent in dialogue. . . . We have no right to assume that Hal is heartless because he does not, like Richard II, wear his heart on his sleeve. . . . Why not . . . give him a friend like Horatio to reveal himself? . . . Shakespeare gives him Poins, and the discovery of the worthlessness of this friend is the subject of one of the most moving and revealing scenes in which the Prince figures. In view of all this, to assert as Bradley does that Hal is incapable of tenderness or affection except towards members of his own family is surely a quite unwarranted assumption.

Hal begins this scene by treating Poins with insolence, as one of the butts for his habit of contempt, and Poins answers (they have just got back from Wales as part of the civil war):

> How ill it follows, after you have laboured so hard, you should talk so idly! Tell me, how many good young princes would do so, their fathers being so sick as yours at this time is?

I can't see that this is an offensive retort; he is expected to keep his end up, and there is not even an obvious insinuation that the Prince wants his father dead—he may be being advised to recover favor. No doubt it could be acted with an offensive leer, but the usual tone in these scenes is merely a rough jeering. The Prince, however, becomes offended and says that his heart bleeds inwardly at his father's illness, but that he can't show it because he keeps bad company such as Poins. It seems a fair answer to this challenge when Poins says he would indeed think the Prince a hypocrite to show sorrow at the prospect of inheriting, "because you have been so lewd, and so much engrossed to Falstaff." "And to thee," says the gay Prince with his usual brutality. Now of course I agree that the scene is meant to tell the audience that Hal is starting to repent of his bad habits; it could not be more straightforward. It could be acted with a moody sorrow, but

I don't think it need be; the main fact is that he is physically tired. But why are we supposed to think that he is "failed" by his friend in a pathetic manner, or shows affection to anyone not a member of his own family? The whole truth of this little scene, in its surly way, is to be so bare; it does nothing to put Poins in the wrong, and indeed lets him show a fair amount of dignity and good-humor; the Prince's feelings are dragging him away from his old companions, and no new fault of theirs needs to be shown. Surely Poins has much more difficulty than Hal in expressing delicate sentiments here; if he tried to condole with the Prince he would be rebuffed more harshly than ever. A production which made the Prince disillusioned at not getting sympathy would have to cut most of the words.

A more important argument of Mr. Dover Wilson for Hal is that it is extremely generous of him to let Falstaff get all the credit for killing Hotspur, especially because if Hal claimed his due he might become more acceptable to his father. We are also told that the sudden fame thus acquired by the previously unknown Falstaff goes to his head and is the cause of the gradual nemesis which gathers throughout Part II. This seems to me a valuable idea, unlike the special pleading about the Poins scene, which would mislead an actor. The trouble about the death of Hotspur, it seems to me, is that the story is deliberately left ambiguous, and we should not allow a learned argument to impose a one-sided answer. The lyrical language of Mr. Dover Wilson about the native magnanimity and high courtesy of the Prince, "which would seem of the very essence of nobility to the Elizabethans," really does I think bring out part of the intended stage effect at the end of Part I, though the text is silent. The question is whether it is meant to go on reverberating all through Part II. To do the right thing at a dramatic moment is very different from going on telling an absurd and inconvenient lie indefinitely. Mr. Dover Wilson's view of the matter, I think, really would be picked on by spectators who preferred it that way, but other spectators could find quite different pointers. I do not want, therefore, to refute his view but to show that it is only one alternative, and I thus give myself an easy task.

The claim of Falstaff to have killed Hotspur is made to Prince Henry in the presence of Prince John, who says, "This is the strangest tale that e'er I heard." Prince Henry says:

> This is the strangest fellow, brother John.
> Come, bring your luggage nobly on your back.
> For my part, if a lie may do thee grace,
> I'll gild it with the happiest terms I have.

In Mr. Dover Wilson's edition, of course, "aside to Falstaff" has to introduce the last two lines. But I don't see Hal nipping about the stage to avoid being overheard by John, whom he despises; his business here is to stand midcenter and utter fine sentiments loud and bold. Just what lie was told, and what John made of it, we don't hear. It seems to me that the Second Part begins by throwing a lot of confusion into the matter, and that Mr. Dover Wilson merely selects points that suit him. At the start of the play three messengers come to the rebel Northumberland; the first with good news—the Prince has been killed outright and "(his) brawn,[1] the hulk Sir John" taken prisoner by Hotspur. Five other people are mentioned, but it is assumed that Falstaff was worth attention before he was believed to have killed Hotspur, and even that Hotspur had done well to capture him. The second messenger says that Hotspur is dead, the third that he was killed by the Prince. Mr. Dover Wilson admits this shows that the facts of his death "had been observed by at least one man," but adds that no other witness is quoted. But nobody at all, in the Second Part, says that Falstaff killed Hotspur. The King himself appears not to know that the Prince did it, says Mr. Dover Wilson; but the King has other things to talk about whenever we see him, and never implies that Hal can't fight. "The Lord Chief Justice grudgingly praises Falstaff's day's service at Shrewsbury," says Mr. Dover Wilson, so he must think Falstaff killed Hotspur. He says that day's service "hath a little gilded over your night's exploits at Gadshill," which hardly fits a personal triumph over the chief enemy hero. Certainly people think he fought well somehow (perhaps because he got his troop killed to keep their pay); the joke of this is driven home in Part II when Coleville surrenders to him on merely hearing his name. But even Coleville does not say, what would be so natural an excuse, that he is surrendering to the man who killed Hotspur. What is more, Falstaff himself does not once say it, and he is not prone to hide his claims. Surely the solution of this puzzle is clear; Shakespeare is deliberately *not* telling us the answer, so that an ingenious argument which forces an answer out of the text only misrepresents his intention.

Consider how difficult it is for a dramatist, especially with a mass audience, to run a second play on the mere assumption that everybody in the audience knows the first one. On Mr. Dover Wilson's view, they are assumed to know that all the characters in the Second Part hold a wrong belief derived from the First Part, although the Second Part begins by letting a man express the right belief and never once lets anybody express the wrong belief. This is incredible. But if some of the audience are expected to *wonder* how the Prince's bit of chivalry worked out, their interest is not rebuffed; they may observe like Mr. Dover Wilson that Falstaff is getting above himself. In the main the theme is simply dropped; perhaps because some of the audience would not like the Prince to be so deeply in cahoots with Falstaff, perhaps because Shakespeare did not care to make the Prince so generous, but chiefly because it would only clutter up the new play, which had other material. The puzzle is not beyond resolution; it is natural to guess (if you worry about it) that the Prince waited till the truth came out and then said that Falstaff had been useful to him at the time—thus the claim of Falstaff did not appear a mere lie after the Prince had gilded it in his happiest terms, but had to be modified. This would have been the only sensible lie for the Prince to tell, and indeed Mr. Dover Wilson hints at it when he says people thought Falstaff had "slain, *or helped to slay*" Hotspur, which has no source in the text. You may now feel that I have made a lot of unnecessary fuss, when it turns out that I agree with Mr. Dover Wilson; but I think that his treatment ignores the dramatic set-up and the variety of views possible in the audience.

The next step in his argument is that Falstaff only becomes "a person of consideration in the army" because of the Prince's lies (whatever they were) about the Battle of Shrewsbury; "in Part I he is Jack Falstaff with his familiars; in Part II he is Sir John with all Europe." This is why he over-reaches himself; the final effect of the Prince's generosity at the end of Part I is that he is forced to reject Falstaff at the end of Part II. Now, on the general principle that one should accept all theories, however contradictory, which add to the total effect, this must certainly be accepted; it pulls the whole sequence together. But it must not be carried so far as to make Falstaff "nobody" at the beginning, because that would spoil another effect, equally important for many of the audience. Falstaff is the first major joke by the English against their class system; he is a picture of how badly you can behave, and still get away with it, if you are a gentleman—a mere common rogue would not have been nearly so funny. As to the question of fact, of course, we are told he is a knight the first time he appears, and it is natural to presume he got knighted through influence; Slender eventually lets drop that he started his career as page to the Duke of Norfolk. The Stage History section of Mr. Dover Wilson's edition has some interesting hints, from both the eighteenth and twentieth centuries, to show that he has always been expected to be a gentleman; the dissentient voice is from a nineteenth-century American actor, who wrote a pamphlet claiming that he was right *not* to make the old brute a gentleman. Rather in the same way, I remember some American critic complaining that Evelyn Waugh shows an offensive snobbery about Captain Grimes, since he despises him merely for not being a real gentleman. So far from that, the whole joke about Grimes is that he is an undeniable public school man, and therefore his invariably appalling behavior must always be retrieved, though it always comes as a great shock to the other characters. This English family joke, as from inside an accepted class system, may well not appeal to Americans, but in the case of Falstaff I think English critics have rather tended to wince away from it too.

Maintaining that he was nobody till after the Battle of Shrewsbury, Mr. Dover Wilson has to explain his presence at the council of commanders just before it, and says it was simply because Shakespeare needed him on the stage. This lame argument would not apply to the Elizabethan stage. At the actual council he only makes one unneeded joke; he is needed for talk with the Prince afterwards, in what our texts call the same scene, but the back curtain will already have closed on the royal coat-of-arms and so forth; Falstaff could simply walk onto the apron. He is at the council because that adds to the joke about him, or rather because some of the audience will think so. However, it is clear anyhow that the Prince brought him; the battle itself gives a more striking case of this line of argument from Mr. Dover Wilson. A. C. Bradley had argued that Falstaff shows courage by hanging around in the battle till the Prince kills Hotspur, and the reply has to be: "To establish his false claim to the slaying of Hotspur he must be brought into the thick of the fight." Surely this makes Shakespeare a much less resourceful dramatist than he is; even I could think of a funny device to trick the great coward into his great opportunity, after he had imagined he had found a safe place. Shakespeare does not "have to" give false impressions; and what we do gather from Falstaff is that he regards a battle as a major occasion for misusing his social position (e.g. "God be thanked for these rebels; they offend none but the virtuous"). I don't deny that those spectators who would resent the social satire are given an opportunity to evade it, and take him as the "cowardly swashbuckler" of the Latin tradition; but they aren't given very much. Over the crux at the start of Part II, I think, the indignant special pleading of Mr. Dover Wilson reaches actual absurdity:

> The special mention of [Falstaff's] capture in the false report of the battle that first reaches the ears of Northumberland . . . are all accounted for by the indecent stab which the dastard gives the corpse of Hotspur as it lies stricken on the bleeding field.

To be sure, Falstaff "goes a bit too far" when he does that; it is his role. (By the way, the reason why we feel it so strongly is that the rebels have been made to look rather better than the royal family.) But really, how are we to imagine that the sight of Falstaff stabbing a recumbent Hotspur (in another play) made a messenger report that Hotspur was safe and Falstaff captured? No doubt almost any confusion can happen to a real messenger, but how can a dramatist expect his successive audiences to invent the extraordinary subtle confusion imputed here? The fact is, surely, that these pointers represent Falstaff as already a prominent figure, though an embarrassingly scandalous one; they could easily be ignored by members of the audience who were using a different line of assumption, but they would give great assurance to members who started with this one.

The interesting thing here, I think, is that Mr. Dover Wilson is partly right; but in the next case I think he is simply wrong. Nobody, whichever way up he took Falstaff, was meant to think him too abject a coward even to be able to bluster. Mr. Dover Wilson refuses to let him drive Pistol out of the inn; chiefly, I suppose, because his theory needs Falstaff to be degenerating in Part II. At II.iv.185 Doll wants Pistol thrown out, so Falstaff says "Quoit him down, Bardolph," and Bardolph says "Come, get you downstairs," but Pistol still makes a threatening harangue; Falstaff then asks for his rapier (196) and himself says

"Get you downstairs," while Doll says "I pray thee, Jack, do not draw"; then the Hostess makes a fuss about "naked weapons," then Doll says "Jack, be quiet, the rascal's gone. Ah, you whoreson little valiant villain, you," then the Hostess says "Are you not hurt i' the groin? Methought a' made a shrewd thrust at your belly"; Falstaff says to Bardolph, who must return, "Have you thrust him out of doors?" and Bardolph says "Yea, sir, The rascal's drunk, you have hurt him, sir, in the shoulder"; Falstaff says "A rascal! To brave me!" and Doll in the course of a fond speech says he is as valorous as Hector of Troy. It is unusual to have to copy out so much text to answer a commentator. This is the textual evidence on which Mr. Dover Wilson decides that Falstaff dared not fight Pistol at all, and he actually prints as part of the play two stage directions saying that Bardolph has got to do all the work. It must be about the most farcical struggle against the obvious intentions of an author that a modern scholarly editor has ever put up.

This view of Falstaff is supported by a theory about Doll, rather obscure to me: "We have, I think, to look forward to 19th-century French literature to find a match for this study of mingled sentimentality and brutal insentience, characteristic of the prostitute class." I thought at first, not going further afield than *The Beggar's Opera*, that this meant some criminal plot for gain; but the audience could not know of it (this is the first we hear of Pistol), and I suppose it means that she likes watching fighting. The argument, therefore, is that she jeers at Falstaff for shirking the fight she had encouraged, so this proves he didn't fight. After Pistol has gone he boasts, "the rogue fled from me like quicksilver" and she answers (on his knee) "I'faith, and thou followedst him like a church." Mr. Dover Wilson has to push "aside" into the text before this remark and "sits on his knee" afterwards, before he can let it go on with her praise of his courage. She does not hide her remarks from him anywhere else. I take it she means that he followed like a massive worthy object, though too fat to do it fast; to find sadism here seems to me wilful. The same trick is used against Mrs. Quickly in *Henry V*, II.i.36, over the textual crux "if he be not hewn now," which Mr. Dover Wilson refuses to change to "drawn"—"as Nym draws Q screams to her bridegroom to cut the villain down, lest the worst befall." But this frank blood-thirst is not at all in her style, and if it was she could hardly keep her house open. It seems that this picture of the ladies is drawn from the sombre vignette at the end of Part II, just before the rejection, when they are dragged across the front stage by beadles because "the man is dead that you and Pistol beat among you." He is breaking his own rules about the order of scenes, if he makes this imply that they were in a plot with Pistol at his first appearance. What we do gather before his entry is that they are afraid he may kill somebody in the house, and know they will get into trouble if he does. He starts threatening death as soon as he comes, whether as a bawdy joke or not ("I will discharge upon her, sir, with two bullets"). Also Doll had just begun a pathetic farewell to Falstaff, who is going to the wars; she is cross at their being interrupted. Also she came on for this scene already elegantly unwell from too much drink. I need to list the reasons for her anger, because Mr. Dover Wilson comments on the line "Sweet knight, I kiss thy neaf" that Pistol "is ready to go quietly, but Doll will have him thrown out"—that is, she insists on having a fight. It is hard for Mrs. Quickly to turn her own customers out, and Doll will be helping her to avoid serious danger if she can scare the bully away permanently; this, if anything, is what is underlined by the beadle scene, though by the time of *Henry V*, as we needn't be surprised, he has become a valuable protector. Such is what I would call her motive, if I looked for one, but she may well simply be too drunk and cross to realize that he is already going quietly. Either way there is no need to drag in sadism.

Mr. Dover Wilson has still another argument from this scene to prove Falstaff's increasing degeneration. After Pistol has been thrown out the Prince arrives and eavesdrops on Falstaff, who is making some rather justified remarks against him, so that Falstaff again has to find a quick excuse; he says he dispraised the Prince before the wicked, that the wicked might not fall in love with him. "He now whines and cringes on a new note, while he is forced to have recourse to defaming Doll in turn, a shift which is neither witty nor attractive." To be sure, the words "corrupt blood" may imply that she has syphilis; it is only the editor's stage direction which makes him point at her, but the idea does give her a professional reason for displaying anger. He has long been saying he has it himself, so there doesn't seem any great betrayal in saying that she has it too (as he does soon after 1.335). I imagine that the point of the joke is to insinuate that the Prince has it; thus it is too late to save him from the wicked, and too late for him to think he can cure himself by saying he has reformed—to forestall being laughed at for being found making love, Falstaff welcomes the Prince among his fellow-sufferers. The badinage in these circles is always a bit rough, and I don't deny that it is hard to know how you are expected to take it. But in this case we have an immediate pointer from an "aside" by Poins, who as usual is in a plot with the Prince against Falstaff. (By the way, this shows what nonsense it is to suppose that the Prince made a sudden pathetic discovery of the worthlessness of Poins only two scenes before, a decisive step in his life, we are to believe; they are on just the same footing as ever.) Poins says, "My lord, he will drive you out of your revenge, and turn all to a merriment, if you take not the heat." How could this be said if Falstaff was only whining and cringing, or even if he were picking a serious quarrel with the ladies? At the end of the scene, when he is called off to the war as an important officer (a dozen captains are knocking at every tavern door for Sir John Falstaff, sweating with eagerness—so says Peto, and Bardolph corroborates about the dozen; and however much the editor insists that this is only "a summons for neglect of duty" it still treats Falstaff as worth a lot of trouble in an emergency), both the women speak with heartbreaking pathos about how much they love him, and the text requires Doll to shed tears. If we critics are to call this a "calculated degradation," I do not know what we expect our own old age to be like. The truth is, surely, that we never see the old brute more triumphant; doomed you might already feel him, but not degraded.

II.

However, I do not want simply to defend Falstaff against the reproaches of the virtuous, represented by Mr. Dover Wilson; it was always an unrewarding occupation, and even the most patient treatment of detail, in such a case, has often failed to convince a jury. I think, indeed, that Mr. Dover Wilson's points are well worth examining, being of great interest in themselves; but, what is more, I think many of them are thrown in with a broadminded indifference as to whether they fit his thesis or not. Some of them seem to me rather too hot on my side of the question, and this may serve to remind us of what is so easily forgotten in a controversy, that the final truth may be complex. For example, he has a fine remark on Mrs. Quickly's description of Falstaff's death. She says she felt his feet, and then his knees, and so upward and upward, and all as cold as any stone. The only comment that would occur to me is that this dramatist can continue unflinchingly to insert bawdy jokes while both the speaker and the audience are meant to be almost in tears. Mr. Dover Wilson, taking a more scholarly view, remarks that the detail is drawn from the death of Socrates; the symptoms are those of the gradual death from hemlock. But whatever can he have intended by this parallel? Surely it has to imply that Falstaff like Socrates was a wise teacher killed by a false accusation of corrupting young men; his patient heroism under injustice, and how right the young men were to love him, are what we have to reflect on. I hope that somebody pointed out this parallel to Shakespeare; he did, I believe, feel enough magic about Falstaff for it to have given him a mixed but keen pleasure; but that seems as far as speculation can reasonably go. To make it an intentional irony really would be like Verrall on Euripides, and it would blow Mr. Dover Wilson's picture of Falstaff into smithereens. And yet, though it seems natural to talk like this, I am not certain; the idea that Falstaff was a good tutor *somehow* was a quite public part of the play, and might conceivably have been fitted out with a learned reference. He has a similar eerie flash of imagination about a stage direction in *Henry V*, where the heroes of Agincourt are described as "poor troops." He rightly complains that modern editions omit the epithet, an important guide to the producer; the story would be mere boasting if it did not emphasize that their victory was a hairbreadth escape after being gruelled. But then he goes on: "Did the 'scarecrows' that Falstaff led to Shrewsbury return to the stage?" It seems rather likely, for the convenience of a repertory company, that they did; but what can it mean, if we suppose it means anything? What is recalled is the most unbeatable of all Falstaff's retorts to Henry—"they'll fit a pit as well as better; tush, man, mortal men, mortal men." Falstaff has just boasted that he took bribes to accept such bad recruits ("I have abused the King's press damnably"), and boasts later that he got them killed to keep their pay (by the way it is before his success has "degraded" him) but this makes his reply all the more crashing, as from one murderer to another: "that is all you Norman lords want, in your squabbles between cousins over your loot, which you make an excuse to murder the English people." This very strong joke could be implied in *Hen. IV*, as part of a vague protest against civil war, but to recall it over Henry's hereditary claim to France would surely be reckless; besides, the mere return of those stage figures could not carry so much weight. But I believe that thoughts of that kind were somewhere in the ambience of the play, however firmly they were being rebutted; it is conceivable that Mr. Dover Wilson here is being wiser than either of us know.

One gets rather the same effect, I think, from his remarks about killing the prisoners at Agincourt, though here he is making a sturdy defence, not a bold conjecture. The position is that the King comes out in IV.vi, "with prisoners," and says his side has done well but must be careful; a pathetic anecdote is told; then an alarum sounds, and the King immediately (without inquiry) says:

The French have reinforced their scattered men:
Then every soldier kill his prisoners,
Give the word through.

Mr. Dover Wilson insists that this has been misunderstood because the stage direction "with prisoners" has regularly been omitted—it should be made clear on the stage that there are more prisoners than captors. But this needed to be said, not shown; the chief effect of bringing the prisoners onto the stage could only be to make the audience in cold blood see the defenceless men killed—indeed, that is clearly the reason why the editors left it out. He goes on to argue, convincingly I think, that this incident was used in the chronicles Shakespeare drew from as an example of Henry's power to recognize a necessity at once, and that the French chroniclers do not blame him for it, though Holinshed is apologetic. But we are concerned with the effect on an audience, and here the very next words, which are from Fluellen to Gower, say:

Kill the boys and the luggage! tis expressly against the law of arms, tis as arrant a piece of knavery, look you, as can be offert.

Gower remarks that *because* the Frenchmen escaping from the battle have killed unarmed boys in the King's tent *therefore* the King "most worthily hath caused every soldier to cut his prisoner's throat. O, tis a gallant king." These experts of course have just walked on for a new scene, and do not know, as we do, that it was Henry who started killing unarmed men, not the French. "Shakespeare, who might have omitted it," says Mr. Dover Wilson, "offers no apologies, but sets the device in a framework of circumstance which makes it seem natural and inevitable." This seems to me comic; the framework not only does nothing to make us think the killing of helpless people necessary but condemns it fiercely. (Even Mr. Dover Wilson reflects that it might be rather a waste of time, under a sudden counter-attack, if one hadn't got machine-guns.) Fluellen goes on to compare Henry in detail to Alexander the Big, mispronouncing it as PIG, and the final parallel is that as "Alexander killed his friend Cleitus in his ales and his cups" so Henry—well, he only turned Falstaff away, and wasn't drunk at the time. We have already seen Nym taking the same view—one must expect a hero to be ungrateful and violent; but this is a remarkable time to recall it. Henry soon comes back saying he is angry and again demanding that prisoners be killed; and even Dr. Johnson, the patron saint of Mr. Dover Wilson's criticism, found it absurd that a man who had just killed all his prisoners should express anger by trying to kill them again. The Quarto of 1600, described by Mr. Dover Wilson as "a 'reported' version, probably supplied by traitor-actors, of performances—perhaps in a shortened form for provincial audiences—of the play as acted by Shakespeare's company," not only gives the whole prisoner sequence but adds a delighted "coupla gorge" from the coward Pistol, as he prepares to join in this really safe and agreeable form of warfare. He was already practising the phrase (almost his only acquirement in the French language) before he left London, so that it is firmly associated with his particularly sordid point of view; and if we are to believe that he is shown starting the massacre the play does everything it can to make the audience nauseated by such actions, even before it has them denounced by Fluellen. I do not see that Mr. Dover Wilson makes out his case at all (the question of course is not about the historical behavior of the Prince, for whom the opinion of the French chroniclers is a weighty support, but about an effect on the Elizabethan stage). If we accept the text we must think (1) that Shakespeare's disgust against Henry explodes here, (2) that Henry's treatment of Falstaff is recalled as part of a denunciation of his brutality and deceitfulness in general, and (3) that Shakespeare, in his contempt for his brutal audience, assumes that nobody will realize what he is doing. I agree with Mr. Dover Wilson that this vehement picture is improbable; I want the conflict of forces in the play to be real, but not secret and explosive in this way.

Surely there is an easy escape from the dilemma, which must have been suggested before. Shakespeare first followed the chroniclers about Henry's decision, without making any accusations against the French; then he felt this made Henry look too brutal and "got round it," just as he contradicted the statement of Holinshed that Henry sacked Harfleur. Instead of saying that Henry started killing unarmed men he said the French did; this propaganda device is familiar nowadays—you do not simply ignore the story against your side, in case it is floating in the minds of your hearers, but contrive to plant it on the other side. This required adding both Fluellen's remarks and Henry's speech about being angry, but cutting only the single line "Then every soldier kill his prisoners." We have then to suppose that the Company ignored the omission mark, not seeing the point of it, and that the actor of Pistol added his usual gag. We are making them pretty stupid, and assuming that Shakespeare had very little control over what they did with his texts; but Mr. Dover Wilson made a strong case elsewhere for thinking he hadn't much control. Now, after making the incident more reasonable in this way, I still think that Shakespeare must have been in a mixed frame of mind when he wrote this comic speech of Fluellen, as part of a plan to make Henry appear milder than he was. Saving Henry's face was getting to be rather an effort, surely. I do not mean that Shakespeare was secretly opposed to his work, still less that he was trying to insinuate a criticism of Henry for the wiser few; I think he felt it a duty to get into the right mood for the thing, and could manage it, but found he had to watch himself, and go back and correct himself—any author who has done propaganda knows this frame of mind. Such at least is what I would make of it, but I am not certain that the view of Mr. Dover Wilson, so much more startling than he realizes, is not the true one.

Where the possibilities are so complicated, I think, a critic needs to hold on to the basic material, the *donnée*, as Mr. Dover Wilson advises. But one also needs to realize that this story of a prodigal who became a hero was already very rich when Shakespeare took it over or "cashed in on it"; it was the most popular part of the History series and carried a variety of implications, all the more because it was taken easily as a joke. To re-plan the trilogy on the basis of leaving some of them out, and that is really what Mr. Dover Wilson is up to, is sure to mislead; also I find it odd of him to claim that a historical point of view is what makes him treat Falstaff as medieval rather than Renaissance. Of course this does not make me deny that the medieval elements are still there. Falstaff is in part simply a "Vice," that is, an energetic symbol of impulses which most people have to repress, who gives pleasure by at once releasing and externalizing them. His plausibility is amusing, and his incidental satire on the world can be accepted as true, but what he stands for is recognized as wrong, and he must be punished in the end. Also (as a minor version of this type) he is in part the "cowardly swashbuckler," of the Latin play rather than the Miracle Play, whose absurdity and eventual exposure are to comfort the audience for their frequent anxiety and humiliation from "swashbucklers." As part of the historical series, he stands for the social disorder which is sure to be produced by a line of usurpers, therefore he is a parallel to the rebel leaders though very unlike them; the good king must shake him off in the end as part of his work of reuniting the country. Also I think there is a more timeless element about him, neither tied to his period in the story nor easily called Renaissance or medieval, though it seems to start with Shakespeare; he is the scandalous upper-class man whose behaviour embarrasses his class and thereby pleases the lower class in the audience, as an "exposure"; the faint echoes of upper-class complaints about him, as in the change of his name, are I think evidence that this was felt. For these last two functions, cowardice is not the vice chiefly required of him. But surely we have no reason to doubt that there were other forces at work behind the popularity of the myth, which can more directly be called Renaissance; something to do with greater trust in the natural man or pleasure in contemplating him, which would join on to what so many critics have said about "the comic idealization of freedom." I think it needs putting in more specific terms, but I don't see that Mr. Dover Wilson can be plausible in denying it altogether.

The most important "Renaissance" aspects of Falstaff, I think, can be most quickly described as nationalism and Machiavellianism; both of them make him a positively good tutor for a prince, as he regularly claims to be, so that it is not surprising that he produced a good king or that his rejection, though necessary, could be presented as somehow tragic. The Machiavellian view (no more tied to that author then than it is now, but more novel and shocking than it is now) is mainly the familiar one that a young man is better for "sowing his wild oats," especially if he is being trained to "handle men." The sort of ruler you can trust, you being one of the ruled, the sort that can understand his people and lead them to glory, is one who has learned the world by experience, especially rather low experience; he knows the tricks, he can allow for human failings, and somehow between the two he can gauge the spirit of a situation or a period. The idea is not simply that Falstaff is debauched and tricky, though that in itself made him give Hal experience, and hardly any price was too high to pay for getting a good ruler, but that he had the breadth of mind and of social understanding which the Magnanimous Man needed to acquire. It seems a lower-class rather than an upper-class line of thought (it is, of course, militantly anti-puritan, as we can assume the groundlings tended to be), and Falstaff can be regarded as a parody of it rather than a coarse acceptance of it by Shakespeare; but surely it is obviously present; indeed I imagine that previous critics have thought it too obvious to be worth writing down—there was no need to, till Mr. Dover Wilson began preaching at us about his Medieval Vice and his Ideal King. After rejecting Falstaff Henry continues to show the popular touch and so forth that Falstaff taught him; indeed, *Henry V* limits itself rather rigidly to describing the good effects of this training, for example in his treatment of the troops and of the Princess (we hear nothing about the long-bow man who actually won the battle). One tends to think of the wooing scene as a sickeningly obvious bit of film dialogue (whereas Dr. Johnson thought it implausibly low) but this was *the first time* a good young millionaire democrat had immediately melted a "foreign aristocrat by the universal power of his earthly approach and the idea is that only his wild oats, or only Falstaff, could have taught him that important method of playing to the gallery.[2] The wooing scene also brings out the nationalist aspect of the thing in a sharp form. It is almost farcical to suppose that Henry, as a Norman Prince, could not talk his own language to his Norman bride; but it was much wanted by the play. We tend to forget that the rising power of England, in Shakespeare's time, was a little embarrassed to have been so long ruled by an invading dynasty who spoke French; but the Tudors made it an important plank in their propaganda that they were the first really "English" line. As a forerunner they had only Henry V, who had learned English by hanging about the taverns when young, and had very rightly refused to learn anything else. No wonder he can re-unite the country (though only for a time because his house is cursed); no wonder that the tedious line of joke about Englishman-Scotchman-Welshman-Irishman appears *for the first time* among the heroes of Agincourt. Nor was this myth entirely false; I noticed Mr. A.L. Rouse asserting recently that Henry V was the first King of England to use the English language for his official correspondence. (The only dates one seems to need are that Agincourt was 1415 and that Chaucer died in 1400.) This of course made a much more serious defence of Falstaff, in the mind of a realistic spectator, than any romantic idea that he had improved the Prince by showing him low life; to have made the monarchy national was a decisively big thing, however absurdly bad Falstaff was otherwise, however much he needed to be rejected. Some critics have suggested that Shakespeare privately loved Falstaff but, like the Prince, betrayed him in public or when taking an official view of affairs; no doubt that feeling was present too, for some of the audience as well as for Shakespeare; but even from the coldly political angle Falstaff could stand for something valuable—it would seem absurd to say so, but one would feel there was "something in it." To put him back in his contemporary politics is perhaps a bit remote from the needs of a modern producer, being so hard to get across to his audience, but does I think remove the suggestion of false sentiment against which Mr. Dover Wilson understandably revolted.

I want now to recommend this point of view by looking at one or two memories of the Norman Conquest which have been neglected; I only noticed them myself when looking over the text after seeing the British wartime film version of the play, to find where the cuts stood out. One would expect that the rougher propaganda of earlier days had left in some damaging admissions, but that the national hero had at any rate been patriotic all right. But when Henry is answering the French Ambassador who brought the insulting tennis balls something much odder turns up. He boasts that he will conquer and rule France, his proper heritage as a Norman, and in answering the Dauphin's jeer at his life he says he naturally lived like a beast when he had only England to live in:

We never valued this poor seat of England,

but he will live in an entirely different way when he has got hold of the much more valuable bit of property called France. Critics, so far as they attend to this, placidly call it irony; and no doubt a contemporary of Shakespeare could take it that way too. Nor is it then flat, because a patriot should always regard his country as weak but heroic, certain to win but only certain because of its virtues. But surely it would be a natural reflection to many in the first audiences that a feudal lord really did think of a country like this, without any irony. Surely it is odd, when the dramatist clearly wants to make the hero patriotic, that he gives the audience such a very strong and plausible case where he isn't. It seems to me riding very near the edge, in that audience, to make the ever-popular Hal say (may I repeat what Mr. Dover Wilson's Ideal King said),

We never valued this poor seat of England.

Of course I willingly agree that the answer is merely the familiar one of dramatic suspense; this remark comes early in the play, and by the end of it we have got Hal being almost shamingly homey. But I am sure it was meant to be a real suspense, not a thing to be thrown away at once by the nods and winks at the audience which Mr. Dover Wilson is so fond of inserting in his stage directions. That Hal turned out to be the first "English" king, unlike his ancestors, was to be presented with drama, and the dramatist gives it a certain violence (though not too frankly) by recalling the doubt which would have appeared real to a fifteenth-century audience, and perhaps did not appear very unreal to a sixteenth-century one either.

I hope this idea that the English were conscious of being ruled by the French does not strike a modern reader as far-fetched; it only seems so now, I think, because the English are good at forgetting things, and the Dauphin says it very firmly about the English lords in *Henry V*:

> Shall a few sprays of us,
> The emptying of our fathers' luxury,
> Sprit up so suddenly into the clouds,
> And overlook their grafters?

The English feudal lords are rather like French Canadians, in fact, but also half-castes. I am sure it is important to realize that this is presented as an intelligible point of view, though of course refuted with triumph.

However, it was to be refuted by displaying English superiority in general, rather than by asserting that the English could and should enslave the French; this "jingo" aspect of a superficially rather coarse play (rightly described by the Germans around 1914 as "good war reading") is a bit embarrassing, and I think it is mostly removed if you remember a political background which is not part of the text. The English had been in doubt during the sixteenth century whether to have military adventures in Europe or to compete with Spain in adventures for new worlds. Elizabeth's father had made a fool of himself in Europe, which could not be said publicly, but Elizabeth herself had quietly and penuriously shown a preference for new worlds; it would not appear recklessly unpatriotic, even in *Henry V*, to insinuate that there was something to be said for her policy. Indeed, this was the only possible line of expansion; if the English had kept France, a modern reader is likely to reflect, they would soon have been ruled from Paris; and for that matter if they had kept America (later) they would soon have been ruled from Washington—the two great losses secured national independence. I am not saying that Shakespeare was wise about this controversy, or even right (he seems remarkably little interested in new worlds, apart from some good jokes against them in *The Tempest*; however, in the *Merchant of Venice* he can see the romance of making London a world trading centre like Venice all right); only that this was the context of political controversy in which he was building up his enormously popular stage machine. After all, the only claim of Hal to France is that he is a Norman not an Englishman, and almost the only thing he is praised for is learning to be an Englishman not a Norman. Shakespeare, I think, felt that one ought to be patriotic and yet that one needn't pull a long face about not ruling France; the international angle was all right somehow, though one had better keep on the fence a bit, whereas the danger of civil war at home wasn't. In the middle of his play of conquest, therefore, he can cheerfully let Hal admit to God that he has no right to conquest, and only beg for the escape of these particular devoted troops (who by the way have been questioning the rights of the war):

> Not today, O Lord,
> No, not today, think not upon the fault
> My father made in compassing this crown,

This is the most genuine thing Henry ever says (some critic argues that even now he was trying to cheat God over the deal, if you look into the facts about his offer of chantries, but that is off the point I think); and we are to regard it as accepted by God, therefore successful in saving these troops; but it does not, of course, remove the doom from Hal himself or from his usurping lineage, or even perhaps from the Norman-English claim to rule France, and he never prays for any such enormous thing. I would not want to sentimentalize the Prince, but "Not today, O Lord" really is a noble prayer when you realize how harshly limited he knows it to be; he is hardly praying for anybody except the individual troops he has just been talking to. (Naturally it was cut from the wartime film production.) And by being genuine there (as I understand the feeling) he gets not only what he asked but a magical extra gift, never known to himself but worth celebrating for ever, as he says the battle itself will be not the conquest of France but the gradual unification of his own islands. They still had to go through a terrible slow mill, because God grinds down small; the Wars of the

Roses had still to come after his early death; but Hal deserved his moment of triumph because he had shown the right way or at any rate seen things in their right proportions, before his time. That is the "religious" or "patriotic" feeling about Hal (one can hardly say which), and I feel it myself; it is a real enough thing, though grand claims need not be made for it. On this view, of course, the play isn't interested in conquering France, but in showing a good leader getting troops from different parts of the islands to work together in a tight corner and a foreign place. You may feel that this is an absurd amount of whitewashing of the play's motive, and I don't deny that the obvious appeal was the simple drum-and-trumpet one; what I maintain is that there was a controversy about these questions of foreign policy, and the play had to satisfy the less simple-minded spectators too. For that matter, Shakespeare had made Henry's father talk with almost comic cynicism about how he would use foreign aggression, or a crusade, or something, to avoid civil war; and the one thing in politics that Shakespeare really did regard seriously was civil war. I am not imputing to him an idea which could not have come into his head.

I ought now to say something about the introductory scenes of the play which give the reasons for the war, though I can say little. The clergy first make clear that the war is to their own interest and then recite Henry's technical claim to the French throne at great length. (Modern historians, as I understand, consider that Henry had no decent reason for attacking France, except possibly the one that Shakespeare made his father give.) The wartime film handled this, rather ingeniously, by keeping us in the play-house at the beginning and turning this recitation into farce, guying old-world techniques rather than anything else. It is hard to imagine how the first audiences took it; one must remember they were well accustomed to hearing sermons. Mr. Dover Wilson's attempts to save the face of the clergy do not seem to me worth a reply, but he is right in insisting that the recitation did not seem dull, as it does now; not, however, as he thinks, because everybody took it for granted. I imagine that Shakespeare was rather ostentatiously not making up anyone's mind for them.

Assuming then that the legend about Hal and the value of his tavern life had this rather massive background. I want now to say something about the interior of Falstaff; that is, not anything which was kept secret from the first audiences, but how it was that Shakespeare's incarnation of the legend could be felt intuitively as a very real character, whom one was curious to know more about; as evidently happened. The eighteenth-century Morgann, if I may avoid appearing too "modern" at this point, has some piercing remarks about the interior of a stage character in general, and how the impression of it is built up; but is mainly concerned to say about Falstaff (after using this idea to explain how we feel he isn't a coward though he appears one) that his deeper interior is more sordid than we are encouraged to recognize, though we still somehow know it. This interior of Falstaff, rather hard to get at for most of us, is also sharply lit up by some remarks of Dr Johnson; and one could wish that Mr. Dover Wilson, who is rightly fond of pointing out that later critics have not had the firm good sense of Johnson, had profited by his master here. It is not surprising that Johnson speaks with confidence about this sort of life, because he had observed it; he could say without absurdity that he regretted not having met Falstaff. Also he himself was a man of startling appearance; a pugnaciously and robustly amusing talker, who regularly conquered but never won anything that mattered, a hero of taverns, fretted by remorse (which Falstaff makes much play with if nothing more), starved of love, unwilling to be alone. He has several comments such as that "a man feels in himself the pain of deformity"; "however, like this merry knight, he may make sport of it among those whom it is his interest to please." If we compare this with the struggles of Mr. Dover Wilson to prove that Falstaff was a Medieval Vice, with no interior at all, surely the truth of Johnson stands out like a rock. The picture of him as driven on by an obscure personal shame, of an amoral sort, has several advantages, I think. Mr. Wyndham Lewis has written well about his incessant trick of "charm," his insistence on presenting himself as a deliciously lovable old bag of guts, helpless but able to make a powerful appeal to the chivalry of the protector; one needs to add that this curious view of him made a sharp contrast to his actual wickedness—that was the joke; but both sides of it are really present. He clamours for love, and I do not see why Mr. Dover Wilson should ignore it. I made a mistake in my *Pastoral* from assuming that this line of talk was concentrated upon the Prince; in *I Hen. IV*, II.ii—"If the rascal have not given me medicines to make me love him, I'll be hanged; it could not be else—I have drunk medicines," it must be Poins, not the Prince, who is supposed to have administered the love-philtre. Poins has just told the audience (though not Falstaff) that he stole the horse whose loss creates all this amorous tumult (because Falstaff is too fat to walk) and Falstaff was shouting for Poins; to be sure, the Prince is the only person yet spoken to by Falstaff in this scene, and the Prince's usual claim to innocence has put him under suspicion—the actor could drag the words round to apply to the Prince, as I first thought, and Falstaff can hardly know which of them stole it. But even Falstaff could hardly say of the Prince, "I have forsworn his company hourly any day these two and twenty years, and yet I am bewitched by the rogue's company." The historical Hal was about sixteen here; the stage one might be regarded as twenty-two, so that Falstaff has forsworn his company since he was born, but this would be rather pointlessly absurd, and the natural view is that it applies to his (presumably older and steadier) gentleman-in-waiting. It is a rather startling cry, and comes early while the character of Falstaff is being defined to the audience; I take it the idea is that he regularly expresses love towards the young men who rob for him, and that this is a powerful means of leading them astray—it is a proud thing to become the favorite of such an expert teacher. For that matter Fagin in *Oliver*

Twist is always expressing love to flatter the Artful Dodger and suchlike; even a member of the audience who hated Falstaff from the beginning would recognize that this bit of the machine had to be there, as a normal thing. It doesn't make very much difference whether Falstaff said it about Hal or Poins. The only thing that still puzzles me here is the recurrence of the number twenty-two, which probably means some private association of Shakespeare's. When the Prince says he has repaid the money gained by robbery he adds that he has procured Falstaff a charge of foot (they can all get their faces straight, now that civil war has loosened the purse-strings) and Falstaff says: "I would it had been of horse. Where shall I find one that can steal well? O for a fine thief, of the age of two and twenty or thereabouts. I am heinously unprovided." The numbers regularly have a magical claim; consider the repeated thousand pounds; these twenty-two years of the young thief seem to me like the laborious number-magic in *Hamlet*, designed to prove not, I think, anything about Hamlet's age, which Shakespeare merely happened to think differently on different occasions, but that the First Gravedigger was appointed on the day of Hamlet's birth and has been waiting there ever since for an arrival never before seen but now due. I don't suppose the number twenty-two was meant to tell the audience anything.

Returning to Falstaff's heart, I think there is a quick answer to the idea that the old brute had no heart, and therefore could not have died of breaking it. If he had had no heart he would have had no power, not even to get a drink, and he had a dangerous amount of power. I am not anxious to present Falstaff's heart as a very attractive object; you might say that it had better be called his vanity, but we are none of us sure how we would emerge from a thorough analysis on those lines; the point is that everybody felt it obvious that he had got one—otherwise he would not be plausible even in attracting his young thieves, let alone his insanely devoted "hostess." I daresay that the wincing away from the obvious (or from Mr. Wyndham Lewis' account) which I seem to find in recent critics is due to distaste for homosexuality, which is regarded nowadays in more practical terms than the Victorian ones; the idea of Falstaff making love to the Prince, they may feel, really has to be resisted. But surely Johnson gives us the right perspective here; Falstaff felt in himself the pain of a deformity which the audience could always see; no amount of expression of love from Falstaff to his young thieves would excite suspicion on that topic from the audience, not because the audiences were innocent about it, but because they could assume that any coming thief (let alone the Prince) would be too vain to yield to such deformity. I agree that a doubt here could not have been allowed, but there was no need to guard against it. A resistance to it should not prevent us from noticing that Falstaff is rather noisily shocked if young men do not love him. It is as well to take an example from near the end of Part II, where on Mr. Dover Wilson's account there should be practically nothing left in him but degeneration. He complains about Prince John (IV.ii.82), "this same young sober-blooded boy doth not love me, nor a man cannot make him laugh," and goes on in a fairly long speech to claim that he has taught Prince Hal better humanity. This is easily thought ridiculous because it is almost entirely a praise of drink, but the mere length presumes dramatic effect; and drink was presumed to teach both sympathy and courage (it is the combination of these two ideas in a "heart," of course, which make it rather baffling to discuss what kind of heart Falstaff has); and we have just seen Prince John perform a disgusting act of cowardly treachery. This detail of structure, I think, is enough to prove that at least the popular side of the audience was assumed to agree with Falstaff. Indeed, if you compare Hal to his brother and his father, whom the plays describe so very unflinchingly, it is surely obvious that to love Falstaff was a liberal education for him.

It is hard to defend this strange figure without doing it too much. May I remind the patient reader that I am still doing what this essay started to do, trying to show that Falstaff from his first conception was not intended to arrive at Agincourt, because the Prince was intended to reach that triumph over his broken heart. The real case for rejecting Falstaff at the end of Part II is that he was dangerously strong, indeed almost a rebel leader; Mr. Dover Wilson makes many good points here, and he need not throw the drama away by pretending that the bogey was always ridiculous. He is quite right in insisting that the Prince did not appear malicious in the rejection, and did only what was necessary; because Falstaff's expectations were enormous (and were recklessly expressed, by the way, to persons who could shame him afterwards); the terrible sentence "the laws of England are at my commandment, and woe to my Lord Chief Justice" meant something so practical to the audience that they may actually have stopped cracking nuts to hear what happened next. A mob would enter the small capital to see the coronation, and how much of it Falstaff could raise would be a reasonable subject for doubt; he could become "protector" of the young king; once you admit that he is both an aristocrat and a mob leader he is a familiar very dangerous type. The "special pleading" of Mr. Dover Wilson here, that the King only gave him honor by sending him to the Fleet Prison, a place where lords were put in temporary custody while waiting for inquiry before the Privy Council and such like, instead of treating him as a common criminal, seems to me off the point; he really was important enough for the Fleet Prison, both in the eyes of the imaginary fifteenth-century and the real sixteenth-century audience. Mr. Dover Wilson argues, rightly I think, that Henry shows a good deal of forbearance in his conditions to Falstaff, so far as one can interpret them; but one must remember that the King and the dramatist both had to show forbearance, for just about the same reasons, and facing a similar mob. I do not mean that either of them privately wanted to be hard on the old man, only that they both had to get through a public event. As to why Shakespeare's play had a casual Epilogue, for some performances, saying "maybe Jack will bob up again some time," it is not hard to imagine that he might sometime need to send his audience away in a good temper by having that said. So much so, indeed, that it is not evidence of his real intentions; maybe he had suddenly become so important that he had to lie like a Foreign Office. In the same way, Henry had to get rid of Falstaff with unquestionable firmness but without any suspicion that he had behaved with malice, because a rising in favor of Falstaff was just what he needed to avoid. A bit of political understanding, I think, is enough to make this problem transparent.

However, to say that the rejection has to be done firmly if done in public does not say that it need be done so at all. The real case against Hal, in the reasonable view of A. C. Bradley, is that he was dishonest in not warning Falstaff beforehand that he would have to reject him after coronation, and still more in pretending on that occasion that Falstaff had misled him. Their separation, says Bradley, might have been shown in a private scene rich in humor and only touched with pathos; a remark which shows how very different he would like the characters to be. Mr. Dover Wilson answers that *Falstaff* makes a public rejection necessary; the Prince "first tries to avoid the encounter, begging the Lord Chief Justice to say for him what must be said. But Falstaff will not allow it. . . . Though under observation (the Prince) falters and finds it difficult to keep up," etc.; and the Prince could not have warned Falstaff at a convenient time, because "Shakespeare has been busy since Shrewsbury manoeuvring the former friends into different universes between which conversation is impossible." One is often baffled by a peculiar circularity in the arguments of Mr. Dover Wilson. This may be an adequate defence for Hal, though his claim that he was misled still looks unnecessarily shifty; but it cannot also be a defence for the dramatist; indeed, I think it brings into a just prominence the fact that Shakespeare wanted, and arranged, to end his play with this rather unnerving bang. By the way, Dr Johnson called it, so far from a bang, "a lame and impotent conclusion," and poor Mr. Dover Wilson has to argue that his master is only complaining at the absence of a final heroic couplet. He argues against a phrase of Bradley, that Hal was trying "to buy the praise of the respectable at the cost of honor and truth," that the word *respectability* had not been invented (but the *thing* is visible enough here) and that the change in Hal is "an instance of the phenomenon of 'conversion'" (this does not join well onto the previous arguments that Hal was never really a sinner). None of this, I think, is adequate ground for doubting what seems obvious, that Shakespeare was deliberately aiming at a rather peculiar dramatic effect, imposing considerable strain, as most critics have felt whether they accepted it or not. The inherent tension between the characters is given its fullest expression and then left unresolved; as G. K. Chesterton remarked, this really is a "problem play," whereas the plays so called in the 'nineties were simply propaganda plays—a man might fully recognize the merits and importance of Henry V, and still doubt, without the dramatist trying to decide for him, "whether he had not been a better man when he was a thief." Of course, the play is not obtrusively a problem, because it simply tells a popular story, but to do that so strongly brings out what is inherent in it, and the apparently coarse may be profound or at least magical thinking. There seems room for the suggestion of Mr. Stewart, that Henry was felt to require before he arrived at Agincourt the *mana* which came from sacrificing the representative of a real divinity, or a tutor of heroes.

After imposing decent enough conditions on Falstaff, Henry sweeps out with the remark that the Lord Chief Justice must "perform the tenor of his word," and this is at once interpreted by the Chief Justice throwing Falstaff and all his company into the Fleet Prison; perhaps only till the mobs have dispersed, as Mr. Dover Wilson suggested. Neither he nor any other critic that I have seen discusses what would happen to Falstaff when he got there; a thing which would seem obvious to the audience but cannot to us. Surely it is likely that he would be smashed by the Fleet Prison. It assumed the prisoner to be a rich landowner who could toss money away before he got out, and it examined his sources of money and encouraged creditors to speak up. Lords at Elizabeth's court were commonly ruined if they were sent to the Fleet, living as they did on a speculator's market, and it is hard to see how Falstaff would do better. As for his last words, "Master Shallow, I owe you a thousand pounds," which Mr. Dover Wilson calls "*the* last word," they are certainly a last boast, and I warmly agree that Shakespeare did not want to send the old boy off the stage whining and appearing broken, or even telling too much truth for that matter—nor did the King. But I think a contemporary spectator would reflect that, although ready money would be a great help to Falstaff "and his company" in the Fleet, it wouldn't take them at all far. And indeed, when the next play shows Falstaff dying as a free man in the tavern, I think this person might reflect that the King must have bought him out, paying off Shallow as well as the others. I would like to have a ruling from a historian on the point, but I suspect that the last boast of Falstaff was only just enough to get him off the stage.

I have next to argue that he was sure to die. Surely we have all met these strong old men, fixed in their habits, who seem unbreakable ("wonderful" as people say) till they get a shock, and then collapse very suddenly. And the shock given to Falstaff is very severe all round; it does not matter whether ambition or love or his pleasures mattered most to him, he had lost them all, and had also lost his *mystique*; his private war against shame had been answered by public loathing of a kind which no tongue could get round; even his "company" would be reproaching him and jeering at him. As against this, which seems ordinary human experience, we have Mr. Dover Wilson arguing *both* that he was a study in increasing degeneration *and* that "the last thing Shakespeare had in mind" when he wrote the Epilogue of Part II "was a sad death for his fat knight," who was needed as a comic at Agincourt. Now, a certain amount of petty criminality can reasonably be shown among the troops at Agincourt, where it is punished, but does Mr. Dover Wilson mean that a searching picture of the third degree of degeneration would have fitted comfortably into the scene of national triumph? It seems rather hard on the Prince; who would also, I think, prefer not to be in danger of unbeatable comic criticisms from his old tutor at such a time. The idea that the text has gone wrong, I submit, comes from not seeing the story in the round; to have brought Falstaff to Agincourt would have thrown a serious jam into the gears of a rather delicate piece of machinery.

I want finally to consider what the plays meant to Shakespeare himself, as apart from the audience; there is no very definite conclusion to be expected, but one ought not to talk as if an achievement on this scale has no personal backing. It seems that Shakespeare, though of course he won his position in the Company much earlier, already perhaps from the *Hen. VI* sequence, odd as it appears now, made his decisive position out of Falstaff. Not merely as a matter of money, which was very important, but also as a matter of trust from the audience, the triumph of Falstaff made possible the series of major tragedies; it was not merely an incident to him. I pursued the subject of the personal background to Falstaff in my *Pastoral* (pp. 102–9), and want to remark that I still agree with what I said there, though this essay is concerned with something rather different. Indeed I think that to understand the many-sidedness of the legend he was using makes it more plausible to think he felt his own experience to be an illustration of it. I proved, I think, that the first soliloquy of the Prince, assuring the audience that he was going to abandon his low friends, is drawn almost line by line from the Sonnets trying to justify the person addressed. It seems inherently probable that the humiliation of Shakespeare's dealings with his young patron, which one can guess were recently finished, would get thrown into the crucible in which the prince's friends had to be created. Falstaff looks to me like a secret come-back against aristocratic patrons, marking a recovery of nerve after a long attempt to be their hanger-on. But this was not done coarsely or with bad temper; the whole triumph of the thing, on its intimate side, was to turn his private humiliation into something very different and universally entertaining. I have been arguing that Falstaff is not meant to be socially low, even when he first appears, only to be a scandal to his rank; whereas Shakespeare of course had only a dubious profession and a suspect new gentility. There are warnings in the Sonnets that friendship with Shakespeare is bad for the patron's reputation, though we hardly ever get an actual admission of inferior social status (we do in the "dyer's hand"); he would rather talk obscurely about his "guilt." Snobbery, I think, had always seemed more real to him than self-righteousness, and even in the Sonnets we can see the beginning of the process that turned player Shakespeare into Falstaff, not a socially inferior friend but (what is much less painful) a scandalous one. Nobody would argue that the result is a life-like portrait of Shakespeare; though he must have known how to amuse, and talks in the Sonnets with a regret about his old age which was absurd even for [an] Elizabethan if he was then under thirty-five, and undoubtedly was what they called a "villainist" tutor, the type who could give broad experience to a young prince. The point is not that he was like Falstaff but that, once he could imagine he was, he could "identify" himself with a scandalous aristocrat, the sufferings of that character could be endured with positive glee. I am sure that is how he came to be liberated into putting such tremendous force into every corner of the picture.

NOTES

1. *Brawn* suggests the wild boar, a strong and savage creature, honourable to hunt, though the fatted hog is not quite out of view. A similar ambivalence can be felt I think in the incessant metaphors of heavy meat-eating around Falstaff compared to "one halfpennyworth of bread to this intolerable deal of sack," where it is assumed (already in Part I) that the drunkard has no appetite.

2. The Hal legend invented this rather than Shakespeare; it comes in a milder form into *The Famous Victories of Henry V*, the pre-Shakespearean stage version, which does give credit to the longbow-men and doesn't to the Scotch, Welsh, and Irish.

1983—A. D. Nuttall. "*Henry IV*: Prince Hal and Falstaff," from *A New Mimesis: Shakespeare and the Representation of Reality*

A. D. Nuttall (1937–2007) was a professor at Oxford and one of the most admired Shakespearean scholars of recent years. His last book was *Shakespeare the Thinker*.

I have said [elsewhere] that Shakespeare likes to take a stereotype and then work against it. The stereotype of Prince Hal in relation to his father, Henry IV, is that of the uncontrolled young man, sowing his wild oats, in rebellion against an authoritarian father. Shakespeare has no sooner set this up for us than he begins to undermine it.

First, he contrives a dramatic echo-chamber, by giving Hal a secondary father. His name is Falstaff: W. H. Auden observes [in *The Dyer's Hand*] that, if you look at Hal's associates, they are really rather odd. What sort of people would one expect to find in company with a prince out on the tiles? Every generation has its own word for the answer to this question: Corinthians, rakes, bucks, blades, *jeunesse dorée*, mashers, Bright Young Things, the Beautiful People. These are not what we find about Hal. Admittedly there is one who is certainly smooth and may be young, Poins, but thereafter the stage is engrossed by an extraordinary collection of aged and seedy persons: an obese alcoholic of advanced years, various strutting scarecrows from that strange Elizabethan underworld of discharged officers and decayed soldiers, and some superannuated prostitutes. Why?

The best answer (the reader may be surprised to find me granting this) is not one resting on psychological probability. It is thematic, It is Falstaff that Shakespeare needs and all the rest is a sort of moving cloud of circumambient Falstaffiana. Shakespeare needs him first of all, as I have suggested, as a parody-father. We saw how in *Othello* Shakespeare made use of an immediate, visual contrast to enforce the theme of the outsider—the black Othello among the shining Venetians. So here (though it is somewhat less obvious) he needs a visual tableau: a grey-haired, physically disgraced old man and a superb youngster. They should *look*, for a moment, like father and son. The point is underlined in the famous scene in which Falstaff plays the part of King Henry admonishing his errant son (*1 Henry IV*, 2.4.418–64). Here we are formally presented with the required tableau.

It does not reinforce but definitely and immediately reverses the stereotype. Instead of the stern father and the 'dropout' son, we have the exact opposite. The jaded slang of the 1960s may bring out the paradox. Falstaff is an aged hippy (fundamentally uncontrolled, given over to the pleasure principle, certainly a dropout from practical society, with his own drug—alcohol—and his own lyrical mode of speech, contemptuous of legal and other convention); meanwhile Hal, we gradually learn, is a rigidly controlled personality, dedicated to effective government and the subordination of personal pleasure to legal and political ends.

At the end of 1.2, in *Part 1*, Prince Hal is left alone on the stage, and pronounces his famous explanatory soliloquy.

> I know you all, and will a while uphold
> The unyok'd humour of your idleness;
> Yet herein will I imitate the sun,

> Who doth permit the base contagious clouds
> To smother up his beauty from the world,
> That, when he please again to be himself,
> Being wanted, he may be more wond'red at
> By breaking through the foul and ugly mists
> Of vapours that did seem to strangle him.
> If all the year were playing holidays,
> To sport would be as tedious as to work;
> But when they seldom come, they wish'd for come;
> And nothing pleaseth but rare accidents.
> So, when this loose behaviour I throw off
> And pay the debt I never promised,
> By how much better than my word I am,
> By so much shall I falsify men's hopes;
> And, like bright metal on a sullen ground,
> My reformation, glitt'ring o'er my fault,
> Shall show more goodly and attract more eyes
> Than that which hath no foil to set it off.
> I'll so offend to make offence a skill.
> Redeeming time when men think least I will. (1.2.188–210)

Is the prince making cold-blooded political use of the people who suppose him to be their friend? This is the kind of speech which Levin Schücking (*Character Problems in Shakespeare's Plays*) held up to show the primitive dramatic technique of Shakespeare; it is not naturalistic, for in naturalistic drama we are encouraged to notice not only the content of the speech but also its manner, so that when, say, Leontes tells us in *The Winter's Tale* that he knows his wife is unchaste we infer from his distracted manner that his judgement is awry. But with speeches of "direct self-explanation," such as Hal's, Schücking suggests that any such inference is out of place. They are a spoken equivalent of the programme note. The actor, though he continues to say "I" rather than "he," in effect doffs his role and comes forward to explain things to the audience. Thus the object of the prince's speech is reassurance: "Do not be anxious about this young man; he is going to be a great king in due course."

With regard to the present speech this view seems to me substantially correct. It is not of course the direct address to the audience as mankind which we find in medieval drama; nor is it the "logical joke" type of audience reference common in the Renaissance theatre. Shakespeare has the prince stand watching the retreating backs of those he has just been joking with and, once they are securely out of earshot, address them in terms which (within the drama) are intended rather to articulate his own thoughts than have any effect on them. Formally (if that is the kind of criticism we are to engage in) the speech is not a direct address to the audience but an apostrophic soliloquy (that is, a soliloquy which is formally, but only formally, addressed to another person). But, at the same time, such soliloquies are formally distinct from the dramatic texture of the rest, and the extramimetic function of reassurance is quite inescapable. Even if the actor may begin in a fairly naturalistic manner—musingly—the speech rapidly gathers formal momentum, and the element of *virtual* address to the audience grows stronger.

But it by no means follows from any of this that the speech has ceased to be mimetic. It is a rule of explanatory soliloquy that we should attend strictly to content. Very well, let us do that.

Implicit in the formal account has been a suggestion that any feeling of shock we may have felt at the prince's cold manipulation of people is removed if we refuse to infer character and restrict ourselves to information. But this speech does not say, "Though I am now keeping vile company, all will be well, since a sudden change will come over me, and the surprise which this will create will be wholly salutary for the realm and the crown." What it makes utterly clear is that Hal himself proposes to bring about this transformation deliberately. The disquieting element of cool manipulation is not something we infer from a naturalistic interpretation of Hal's manner, it is something we are told. If the speech is self-explanation and provides the audience with information, this is part of the information it provides. Everything, to be sure, depends on the meaning of the word "that" in the following lines:

> Yet herein will I imitate the sun,
> Who doth permit the base contagious clouds
> To smother up his beauty from the world
> That, when he please again to be himself,
> Being wanted, he may be more wond'red at
> By breaking through the foul and ugly mists. (1.2.190–95)

The word "that," in this context, undoubtedly means "in order that."

This insistence on an uncomfortably intrusive purposive particle where we might have expected a more neutral grammar of mere consequence is precisely what led, in the final speculation of our last section, to the "existentialist" Iago. The distance between Prince Hal and Iago is great but not, perhaps, unbridgeable. W. H. Auden (the presiding genius of this part of the book) noted a curious similarity between this speech by the prince and one of Iago's soliloquies, similarly placed, early in the play:

> For when my outward action doth demonstrate
> The native act and figure of my heart

In compliment extern, 'tis not long after
But I will wear my heart upon my sleeve
For lows to peck at: I am not what I am. (*Othello* 1.1.62–66)

Both passages are Machiavellian in style; that is, they evoke an ethos of devious cunning. This also works against the critic who believes that a formalist reading can dispel all distaste. It is an inference from the manner, but not a naturalistic inference; it is a formal one.

Let us confess that this is a strange speech, marked by a very considerable tension. Shakespeare adopts a "naïve" technique, but he does so with a complex sense of context and for a particular effect. The actor who allows the text to speak in him will find that he gradually freezes as the speech proceeds. The director who understands this process may ensure that a strong light falls on the actor's almost unmoving face, on the line, "Herein will I imitate the sun." The sun is the emblem of royalty. The office of the king may thus momentarily shine through the actor figurally, and become a felt presence on the stage.

But, when every concession has been made, the speech is not naturalistic; forms are at work which are not the transparent forms of realism; the speech purveys information rather than betraying an attitude: the result is that we find ourselves presented with an essentially mimetic statement about the *character* of Prince Hal. The presumption of twentieth-century criticism—that choric exegesis precludes characterization—is shattered when the choric information turns out itself to be, baldly and explicitly, information about character. It is never good practice with Shakespeare to ignore or repress worrying, initially unwanted complexities. Far better to assimilate them, to imagine and to think. When one is watching or reading Shakespeare, this thinking can be done almost subliminally, with a wise passiveness. When criticizing or interpreting Shakespeare, one must think explicitly.

The speech certainly contained great comfort for the Tudor audience, but it is a comfort shot through with unease. There is nothing unhistorical in the supposition that an Elizabethan could have been repelled by manipulation of people's affections. The Machiavellian "twinge" in the style is not there by chance. But (and here a Tudor would have been more perceptive than a modern audience) it is all directed to the good end of stable government. And so Prince Hal is a White Machiavel. This powerful moment of confession which is also a self-dedication and a kind of promise precedes and sets the dominant tone for what follows. It is not wiped out by Warwick's observing in *Part 2* at 4.4.68–72 (long after our conception has formed) that the prince kept low company to educate himself in the moral variety of his people.

Falstaff, who is all intelligence, knows everything about the prince except this, his chilling, profoundly moral, private plan. Nevertheless, Shakespeare illogically permits two episodes in which Falstaff learns the truth. One of them is the celebrated rejection of Falstaff by the new-made King Henry V, but that poses no problem of consistency in Falstaff because it comes at the end. The more problematic one occurs in the tableau scene with which we began, where Falstaff plays the part of the prince's father (*1 Henry IV*, 2.4). When Falstaff has had his turn, the game is reversed, Hal plays his father and Falstaff plays the prince. The fun is uproarious but through it we begin to sense a profound collision and awakening. Falstaff finds that he is pleading for the prince's love and, at the second when he discovers he can never have it, is interrupted by a loud banging on the door; breathless figures with urgent news come blundering *across* the duel between Hal and Falstaff—now at last explicit. So the moment is seen, once, in total clarity, and then muffled in extraneous noise.

> *Prince*: . . . wherein worthy, but in nothing?
> *Falstaff*: I would your Grace would take me with you; whom means your Grace?
> *Prince*: That villainous, abominable misleader of youth, Falstaff, that old white-bearded Satan.
> *Falstaff*: My lord, the man I know.
> *Prince*: I know thou dost.
> *Falstaff*: But to say I know more harm in him than in myself were to say more than I know. That he is old—the more the pity—his white hairs do witness it; but that he is, saving your reverence—a whoremaster, that I utterly deny. If sack and sugar be a fault, God help the wicked! If to be old and merry be a sin, then many an old host that I know is damn'd; if to be fat be to be hated, then Pharaoh's lean kine are to be loved. No, my good lord: banish Peto, banish Bardolph, banish Poins; but, for sweet Jack Falstaff, kind Jack Falstaff, valiant Jack Falstaff—and therefore more valiant, being, as he is, old Jack Falstaff—banish not him thy Harry's company, banish not him thy Harry's company. Banish plump Jack, and banish all the world.
> *Prince*: I do, I will. [*A knocking heard*]
> [*Re-enter* BARDOLPH, *running*]
> *Bardolph*: O, my lord, my lord! the sheriff with a most monstrous watch is at the door.
> *Falstaff*: Out, ye rogue! Play out the play: I have much to say in the behalf of Falstaff.
> [*Re-enter the* HOSTESS]
> *Hostess*: O Jesu, my lord, my lord!
> *Prince*: Heigh, heigh! the devil rides upon a fiddlestick; what's the matter?
> *Hostess*: The sheriff and all the watch are at the door; they are come to search the house. Shall I let them in?

> *Falstaff*: Dost thou hear, Hal? Never call a true piece of gold a counterfeit. Thou art essentially mad, without seeming so. (*1 Henry IV* 2.4.443–76)

Notice in this exchange how at one point a laugh is killed, or at least checked. "Valiant Jack Falstaff" raises the laugh but "old Jack Falstaff" silences it with truth. When the prince answers, from a masklike face, "I do, I will," the secret is out.

When I quoted Falstaff's words flung desperately across the violent interruption, I made use of an emendation. The First and Second Folios and the string of Quarto editions (the fifth of which was probably the copy-text for the First Folio) all give "made" where I have given "mad" at 2.4.476. The word "mad" is an emendation, but is pretty well the smallest emendation possible. This becomes clear if we imagine the passage written in an Elizabethan hand. Shakespeare almost certainly wrote a secretary hand, in which case the words might have looked something like this:

[handwritten: thou art essentially made]

In this hand *d* is written *[symbol]* and *e* is written backwards as *[symbol]*. The *d* is a little taller, may have a closed loop at the bottom and a large loop at the top, but it is undoubtedly very like an *e* and in actual specimens of secretary hand the two letters are sometimes quite indistinguishable: you can tell which is which only by context.

Let us suppose that Shakespeare wanted to write the word "mad," spelling it, as he may well have done, with two *d*'s. It might then look like this.
And of course this can be read as "made." Indeed it says "made," taken letter by letter, just as much as it says "madd."

[handwritten: madd]

All of this would become a good deal weaker if we knew that Shakespeare strongly distinguished his *d*'s and his *e*'s and avoided spellings like "madd." We have no conclusive evidence on this point, but such evidence as we possess points the other way. The only specimen of handwriting, apart from some signatures, which has a good chance of being Shakespeare's is to be found on three pages of the manuscript "Book of Sir Thomas More," the passage written in what is usually called "Hand D." This passage is one of several "additions" to the text by revisers. The word *mad* does not occur on any of these three pages, but a great deal of doubling of letters does occur. The writing of Hand D spells "got" with two *t*'s, "sit" with two *t*'s, "sin" with two *n*'s, cut with two *t*'s and "dogs" with two *g*'s. Such a man, one feels, would scarcely flinch from "mad" with two *d*'s. Moreover, several of the *d*'s in the manuscript are identical in form with the *e*'s; for example, in the upper half of Folio 9, the *d* of "God" in the first line is like the *e* of "power" in the fourth line; the *d* of "hands" (thirteenth line) is like the *e* of "kneels" (sixteenth line). The graph is very close all the time.

It might be thought that, given the fact that "made" and "mad" are common words, Shakespeare's supposed manner of writing and spelling should have led to frequent textual confusion. In fact, however, although both words are common they are very different in force and meaning; as a result context usually precludes confusion. But, for all that, there are several cases in the text of Shakespeare of possible confusion of these forms; for example, in *The Winter's Tale*, at 3.3.115, the Clown says, in the Folio, "You are a mad old man" but most modern editors accept Theobald's substitution of "made." The 1609 Quarto of Sonnet 79, "Expense of spirit in a waste of shame," gave "made in pursuit" for line 9.

Given all this it is very nearly a question of printing the reading one prefers. The Folio editors in the seventeenth century made no bones about it. It would seem that as soon as they spotted "made" they changed it to "mad." The New Arden editor in our own century was obviously tempted to do the same thing but drew back because he felt "mad" gave a difficult or impossible sense. Does it? "Essentially made"—now that is really difficult. The phrase is explained as a continuation of the previous talk about true gold and counterfeiting, and "essentially made" is supposed to mean "made of true gold." The suggestion is highly implausible. It is not Shakespearean English (or any other). No parallel usage, as far as I know, has ever been shown for *essentially* in this sense. But "essentially mad" on the other hand is obviously good Shakespearean English. Does not Hamlet say, "I essentially am not in madness, / But mad in craft" (*Hamlet*, 3.4.187–88)? The sense "mad" in this passage is both clear and powerful. Falstaff has seen that the prince does not have any friends at all and he, the semiprofessional fool, suddenly cries out, "Why, you're the crazy one; You don't look it, but you are!" Hal is inside out. Instead of concealing his human features beneath a stiff, impersonal mask, he wears the golden mask of kingship beneath an ordinary, smiling human face.

Thus the stereotype of wild son and authoritarian father is reversed. Falstaff is that other kind of archetypal old man who derives by a kind of creative misreading from Paul's *vetus homo*, the old man we must put off in order to put on the new; the old Adam, the unregenerate, the happy inhabitant of a fallen world which remains, if not Eden-like, then Arcadian, excluded from the New Jerusalem. Falstaff says, "Dost thou hear, Hal? Thou knowest in the state of innocency Adam fell; and what should poor Jack Falstaff do in the days of villainy? Thus seest I have more flesh than another man, and therefore more frailty" (*1 Henry IV* 3.3.164–67). Paul calls the old Adam "the body of Sin," an expression which immediately and naturally invites joyous elaboration from Falstaff. But what now of Hal's father? Surely there the stereotype is straightforwardly maintained?

In fact, it is not. We learn this largely from the parodic structure of the play. Falstaff cannot be a figure of authority because he is a criminal. But what if the king is himself a criminal? This is a subversive idea, and there is no doubt that it is present in the plays. The dubiety of the king's right to rule is fundamental. The prince knows that it is dubious and all his dedication hinges on the decision that it is better to maintain a usurpation than to let the realm slip into anarchy.

There is a certain sort of learned critic who loves to point out that Falstaff must be classified as an evil force, since he stands for drink, conviviality and pleasure and has no sense of his responsibility to the great cause, the putting down of rebellion. All this depends, perhaps, on the authenticity and rightness of the order which is being maintained. But these same learned critics come at length in their dogged progress upon the fact than the king's rule is inauthentic. The rebels are not more rebellious than the king himself. The effect of this is to reopen the ethical debate about Falstaff. Dr Johnson was right when he reminded the reader—who, be it noted, he assumed all those years ago, would be distressed at the departure of Falstaff—that Falstaff utters no single "sentiment of generosity" in the course of the plays. Yet Auden can see Falstaff as a parabolic figure of charity. How is this?

It is partly an effect of style. Falstaff speaks a golden Shakespearean English which makes him the centre of a small world of joy wherever he goes. Above all, in the very jaws of senility and death, he is life, and whenever he comes near there is a real danger that the great warlords will be seen for what they perhaps are—mere bloody men, agents of death.

Yet (with Falstaff one has to go on and on saying "yet" since he is "poem unlimited"), even while Falstaff impugns the practical mystique of the ruler, he is made the great expression in the plays of what we may call the impractical mystique. Falstaff, who cannot get on with live King Henry, is on the best of terms with dead King Arthur. If a sense of England as a ruined Arcadia or Eden survives at all in *Henry IV* it is because of Falstaff. This comes partly from the language of the Falstaff scenes with its preference for immemorial, rustic ways of measuring time—"I have known thee these twenty-nine years, come peascodtime" (*2 Henry IV* 2.4.368–70). There is a speech in *As You Like It* which brings Falstaff to mind, and it is possible to piece together why this is so. Charles says to Oliver,

> They say he is already in the Forest of Arden, and a many merry men
> with him; and there they live like the old Robin Hood of England. They

say many young gentlemen flock to him every day, and fleet the time
carelessly, as they did in the golden world. (*As You Like It* 1.1.105–9)

Falstaff says in his first scene, "Let us be Diana's foresters, gentlemen of the shade, minions of the moon" (*1 Henry IV* 1.2.25–26). Falstaff might almost be describing that band of Kentish poachers who stole deer from Penshurst park after blacking their faces and calling themselves the servants of the Queen of the Fairies. But notice that in Falstaff's speech we have, as in Charles's speech, the forest and the gentlemen—surely merry ones, too. Then in *Part 3* Pistol speaks of "golden times" (5.3.95) and Silence sings in a quavering voice of Robin Hood (5.3.102). And so the elements of the *As You Like It* speech are resembled.

Then there is the trail of references to King Arthur (king over the lost England). These are of increasing power. In *Part 2* at 2.4, Falstaff enters singing, "When Arthur first in court" (2.4.33) and then breaks off with a request to Francis to empty the jordan. Then in the great pastoral-comical-elegiacal scene, 3.2, Shallow says that long ago he was Sir Dagonet in Arthur's show (3.2.273). Since, according to Malory, Dagonet was Arthur's fool and Shallow here plays fool to Falstaff the effect of the allusion is to turn Falstaff for a second into a grey echo of Arthur himself. But the best comes in *Henry V*. There Pistol, the Hostess, Nym, Bardolph and the Boy are talking about the way Falstaff died and wondering whether his soul is in hell or heaven. Bardolph cries out, "Would I were with him, wheresome'er he is, either in heaven or in hell!" But the Hostess answers,

> Nay, sure, he's not in hell: he's in Arthur's bosom, if ever man went to Arthur's bosom. 'A made a finer end, and went away an it had been any christom child; 'a parted even just between twelve and one, ev'n at the turning o' th' tide. (*Henry V* 2.3.7–14)

Comic malapropism can be eagerly powerful. The Hostess has confused the story in Luke about Dives and Lazarus with the story of Arthur. To that most potent story she has joined the story Luke tells of the poor leper who was shut out from the rich man's gate, as Falstaff was shut out from the presence of Hal, and how the poor man was after death raised up to Abraham's bosom while the rich man was left in hell (is there anyone left who can believe that Shakespeare was unequivocally against Falstaff when the imagery can do things like that?). To that scriptural story the Hostess has joined the legend of the old king who lies sleeping under Snowdon or perhaps Glastonbury Tor till we need him again.

Thus the anti-father. But, as I have suggested, the prince's relation with his real father is likewise, though less obviously, subversive of the stereotype. Once again it is the old man who is the outlaw and the son is the possible agent of control. The old man looks hungrily to his son for an authority he could never attain himself. One could imagine various possible reactions in a son faced with such a father, such a kingdom: a despairing withdrawal from political life, an equally desperate ferocity. Hal falls into neither of these. Instead, he commits himself, body and soul to confirming, both morally and by force of arms, the power of the crown. He knows that he is more completely alone than anyone else, more, even, than his father. His situation requires of him more perhaps than should be asked of anyone. It requires him to extinguish his humanity in the interests of the realm. E. M. Forster once wrote that if ever he was in a position where he was forced to choose between his country and his friend he hoped he would have the guts to choose his friend. People respond warmly to the passage, but I suspect that they do so because betraying one's country is a remote abstraction to most of us. Whether or not the cause is just, whether the realm is holy or corrupt, treachery on the part of the king must mean suffering, on a horrible scale. As Angelo, the fallen archangel of *Measure for Measure*, said, the good man in office must learn to pity people he does not know, has never seen (2.2.101).

Hal's White Machiavellian speech in which he explains his strange purpose produces, in the author of this book, a distinct physical symptom, a tightening at the back of the throat. The same symptom is produced in the same subject by Sonnet 94:

> They that have power to hurt and will do none,
> That do not do the thing they most do show,
> Who, moving others, are themselves as stone,
> Unmoved, cold, and to temptation slow—
> They rightly do inherit Heaven's graces,
> And husband nature's riches from expense;
> They are the lords and owners of their faces,
> Others but stewards of their excellence.

This seems to be one of the sonnets addressed to the Friend, the young, beautiful man whom Shakespeare loves and whose unresponsiveness is seen by Shakespeare at one moment as a kind of blasphemy and at others—by an immense effort of will—as admirable.

If this were the nineteenth century I should now be permitted to speculate—to wonder whether Prince Hal was not founded on the beloved Friend, whether our difficulties with the prince may not arise from the fact that we, unlike Shakespeare, are not in love with him, so that for us he gives light but not warmth, to wonder whether the rejected Falstaff, the myriad-minded, the genius with words, the messy, disordered man, might not be an ectype of Shakespeare himself, who in this sonnet made an intense effort to give praise to the other sort, to the beautiful, reserved man. Such speculations, though untestable, are not fundamentally irrational.

It may be said that the public mimesis of possible realities is one thing, and the dark genesis of a work in the private affections of the poet another, but reality is a turbulent ocean which endlessly overflows dykes and breakwaters of this kind; the terms for interpreting even an ostentatious fictitious profession of love are modified by our sense of its source; we may strive to restrict "source" to fictional "persona" but the restriction is artificial, requires an unsleeping vigilance to enforce it; left to themselves the most literate, the most literary readers of *The Waste Land* will sense, behind the epicene Tiresias, the learned and quizzical American poet. But, for all that, the inferences have become unmanageable. It is better to stick to what we can see; and we can see a little (I am still trying to understand the tightening at the back of the throat).

The phrase "lords and owners of their faces" objectively recalls the prince, for the *face* is associated with royalty from *Richard II* smashing the looking glass to the almost surrealist speech in *Henry V* where Hal, now the king, imagines his features turning to unfeeling stone (3.1.11–14). Moreover, the preservative coldness of the Friend strongly resembles Hal's—he too husbands England's riches from expense. But the sonnet ends in a barely controlled revulsion of feeling which is not, as far as I can see anywhere reflected in the dramatic sequence from *Part 1* of *Henry IV* to *Henry V*.

In Prince Hal, Shakespeare gives us a mode of goodness which is embarrassing. The man is attractive but behind his easy manner lies something very unattractive and it is that unattractive something which is most deeply, most uncomfortably involved with real virtue. But the prince is not quite a saint and the conflict of humanity and dedication can make a fool of him (where people like Hotspur and Falstaff, oddly enough, are secure). In *Part 2*, at 4.5, the old king lies dying in the Palace of Westminster. There has been talk of Prince Hal, his way of life, of the fact that at this of all times no one knows where he is. Then Westmoreland comes with good news: the rebellion is over. The king cries out, "O Westmoreland, thou art a summer bird, / Which ever in the haunch of Winter sings / The lifting up of day" (4.4.91–3). But the shock of the good news is too great and now he is conveyed to the inner room. The crown is placed beside him. Then, out of step and out of time, the prince suddenly enters, talking in too loud a voice, for which he is politely rebuked by Warwick. The prince moderates his voice and says that he will sit beside the now sleeping king. The rest withdraw and the prince's eyes fall on the crown: "O polish'd perturbation! golden care!" (4.5.23). Then his eye strays to a downy feather which has settled by the mouth and nostrils of the king; it lies there, unmoving, and the prince is suddenly sure that his father is dead:

> My Gracious lord! my father!
> This sleep is sound indeed; this is a sleep

>   That from this golden rigol hath divorc'd
>   So many English Kings. Thy due from me
>   Is tears and heavy sorrows of the blood
>   Which nature, love and filial tenderness,
>   Shall, O dear father, pay thee plenteously.
>   My due from thee is this imperial crown,
>   Which, as immediate from thy place and blood,
>   Derives itself to me [*Putting on the crown*]
>   Lo where it sits—
>   Which God shall guard; and put the world's whole strength
>   Into one giant arm, it shall not force
>   This lineal honour from me. This from thee
>   Will I to mine leave as tis left to me. (4.5.34–47)

But the king is not dead. Again he revives, to find himself alone. He calls for Warwick and the rest. Where is the prince? And then, a moment later, "*Where is the crown?*"—"Is he so hasty that he doth suppose / My sleep my death?" (4.5.61–62). Then Warwick returns to say that he found the prince weeping in the next room and that he is coming at once. The prince enters and the king orders all the rest to leave. Hal speaks first:

> I never thought to hear you speak again. (4.5.92)

The king's answer is savage:

> Thy wish was father, Harry, to that thought.
> I stay too long by thee, I weary thee.

At last the prince is allowed to make his excuses, to explain what he has done. This he performs brilliantly and touches his father's heart:

>   There is your crown,
> And He that wears the crown immortally
> Long guard it yours! (*Kneeling*) If I affect it more
> Than as your honour and as your renown,
> Let me no more from this obedience rise. . . .
> Coming to look on you, thinking you dead—
> And dead almost, my liege, to think you were—
> I spake unto this crown, as having sense,
> And thus upbraided it: "The care on thee
>   depending
> Hath fed upon the body of my father;

> Therefore thou best of gold art worst of gold...."
>   Thus, my most royal liege,
> Accusing it, I put it on my head,
> To try with it—as with an enemy
> That had before my face murd'red my father—.

The king is won by the speech and calls his son to sit by him on the bed. This is the part which, above all, produces the constriction in the throat. For the most terrible thing about this scene is that the prince, in the most venial way, lies. He did not address the crown as an enemy, nor was it in that spirit that he took up the crown in his hands. Shakespeare, I think, does not want us to make any mistake about this, for he shows us the two things in succession, first the taking up of the crown and then the prince's account, given under pressure. We know that when the prince thought his father dead he experienced two great emotions one after the other; first real (and immense) grief for his father, and then a quite different feeling: "Now it has come; now I am the King." In the story which he tells his father he changes things, so that his thoughts are of Henry throughout.

Yet we can hardly say that we have "seen through" Hal, discovered the cold ambition that lies beneath. Shakespeare refuses to make it so easy for us. What we have seen and what the prince had dissembled is, precisely, not ambition, but dedication. This is merely the worst of his ordeals. There is indeed a fierce irony in the fact that this was the prince with the common touch, the easy manner with all sorts and conditions, for no character in Shakespeare, except perhaps Iago, is so utterly alone.

The scene between the prince and his father is very like that other great and complex scene, written about a year afterwards: the quarrel scene in *Julius Caesar* with its double version of the death of Portia. Henry dies, lives and dies again and so, in a manner, does Portia (though outside the scene). The sense of anguished back-tracking over what was said only moments before ("I said an elder soldier, not a better. / Did I say better?" *Julius Caesar* 4.3.56–57) is common to both. Strongest of all is the sense in both scenes of a good man, in a state of near disintegration, exerting all his skills, all his *art*, to prevent horror and chaos from taking over, and the audience being made, in a way which is almost unseemly, privy both to the mendacity (almost invisible with Hal, palpable with Brutus) and to the heroic effort of moral will. Both Brutus and the prince are in a manner made fools of, yet in either case the phrase "made fools of" is too coarse for the work it needs to do. Cassius's comment, extraordinary in its combination of affectionate admiration, charity and analytic intelligence,

> I have as much of this in art as you,
> But yet my nature could not bear it so.
>   (*Julius Caesar* 4.3.192–93)

corresponds to the king's answer to the prince, loving yet somehow finding space within that love to register the *rhetorical* skill of what the prince has just done:

> O my son,
> God put it in thy mind to take it hence
> That thou might'st win the more thy father's love,
> Pleading so wisely in excuse of it!
> (*2 Henry IV* 4.5.178–81)

Both scenes show us more than we are accustomed to receive. Both force on us the radical opposition of nature and art in a manner which will not permit the resolution of the "nature" half of the opposition into further covert rules of art (which is what formalist critics allege). Instead the dramatist turns the tables by reminding us that art is actually employed *in* life, by Stoic commanders or anointed princes, when life is most itself, most amorphous, most crushing. The fact that a playwright has contrived the whole impression by means of fictions in no way abolishes this point. For his fiction is unintelligible unless we permit ourselves the (wholly natural) recourse to real human behaviour. The element of recalcitrant "mere probability" is so strong in these scenes that it is not only conventions of Elizabethan drama which are subtly contested. Our own comforting conventions, in which we codify our admiration of the good and our contempt for the bad, are themselves contested, so that people do not care to say, even to themselves, that Brutus, or Prince Hal lied. More often than not the thought has actually been repressed before the spectator has left the theatre. Is it not that the mirror of nature shows us spectacular blemishes (these can be accommodated, neutralized and then enjoyed by way of an appropriate rhetoric). Shakespeare shows us the painful enmeshing of falsity with good feeling as it actually happens. The scenes, from every formal point of view, are chaotic. But they have a glaringly obvious, single, clarifying source in reality itself.

Prince Hal is a late-born man, delivered over to a world which has lost its freshness. His father obtained his crown by deposing Richard II. Richard, though in many ways a fairly repellent person, was the true, anointed king, God's regent upon earth. This fact alone has power to irradiate the England of the play, *Richard II*. The dying Gaunt rebukes the king for his betrayal of the realm, yet throughout his famous speech (2.1.31–66), except for a single phrase, the praise of England remains in the present tense. The England of the usurper, Henry, lacking its point of intersection with the divine order, is greyer, less definite, less heraldic. War is seen less in terms of its high intelligible crises and more in terms of sheer mess—"bloody noses and crack'd crowns." "I never did see such pitiful rascals . . . Tut, tut; good enough to toss; food for powder, food for powder; they'll fill a pit as well as better: tush, man, mortal men, mortal men." "There's not three of my hundred and fifty left alive, and they are for the town's end, to beg during life" (*Part 1* 2.3.90; 4.2.62f; 5.3.36f).

Part 1 of *Henry IV* opens with an overwhelming impression of weariness, of more to do than can be done—"So shaken as we are, so wan with care. . . ." *Richard II* was about the fall of a king, but it was a true king that fell, and this gives the drama a unified and spectacular tragic structure. With the two loosely joined parts of *Henry IV* we get a cooler dramatic technique, inclining more to piecemeal exploration and an agnostic pluralism. In both *Richard II* and *Henry IV*, we find scenes of meditation on the idea of England as a ruined garden but they are very different. In *Richard II* we have a tiny, jewelled allegory, in which two unnamed gardeners, in measured verse, liken the conduct of a kingdom to their own simple art. All is structured, everywhere there is correspondence and analogy, all thoughts begun are concluded. But in *Henry IV* we have instead the Gloucestershire scenes, in which Falstaff, Shallow and—name of names—Master Silence ramble on together in the orchard of Shallow's decaying farm. These scenes are extremely naturalistic—almost Chekhovian—full of inconsequential remarks, voices trailing away into nothingness, of memories, mundane queries about such things as the present price of bullocks, of a sense of imminent death. In the absence of conclusive structures we are given an atmosphere, compounded of last year's apples, the grey heads of old men, of sweetness and barrenness, and of futility.

This is the non-kingdom which Hal is to inherit from his father. Somehow he must unify the kingdom, make the crown real again. This is the proper context of the strange speech of "direct self-explanation" with which we began. He has a mission (and there can be no doubt that it is a fully moral mission—unless the country is unified the blood and suffering will be endless). He dedicates himself utterly to the mission and, in its service, to a strange plan. He needs, on his inheritance, to seize the initiative, and for this he must be master of an element of spectacular surprise. In fact the people must be surprised (in the etymological sense of the word—"taken unawares") by majesty. But if majesty is to surprise it must be preceded by its opposite—ignominy, irresponsibility. And so the bizarre logic of the situation tells Hal that he must humiliate himself in preparation for his sudden blaze. He must appear to neglect his royal responsibilities, must fritter his time away in vicious idleness, with criminals and drunks, until the moment comes. Like Kim Philby in our own time, he has proposed to himself a life of systematic duplicity; a life of endless conviviality in which he is to have no friend, no possibility of ordinary candour.

The two parts of *Henry IV* probably belong to the years 1596–98, overlapping *The Merchant of Venice*, some two years earlier than *Julius Caesar*, and about six years earlier than *Othello*. *Coriolanus* may be dated anywhere between 1605 and 1608. In each of these plays we have found some notion of cultural evolution.

We have already noticed a transformation of the context, a change in England itself at the beginning of *Henry IV*. The England of *Henry IV* is not the England of *Richard II*. While the anointed king was still on the throne, the country itself seemed still partly taken up into the supernatural. Parables, allegories, Eden, Paradise naturally express the character of this island in the older play. But the England of the usurper has been abandoned to the bleak natural order.

But in order to see whether the notion of cultural evolution is present in the two parts of *Henry IV* we must bring Hotspur into the discussion. Hotspur is culturally more primitive than Hal. Auden observes that under the old kings the country had functioned fairly loosely as a set of small baronies, earldoms and the like, in which the dominant loyalties were local, personal, feudal. This is offered as a statement of a fact available to Shakespeare. A change of mental set, a change in instinctual morality was needed before people learned that their duty to a king they never saw undercut their duty to the man who fed and protected them. It is clear that in Hotspur this change has not occurred.

His energy is half-divine, and his language breathes a freshness which no one else in the play can match. Hal looks at him with a kind of envy—the moral world in which he moves is so simple. At 2.3.1, he enters reading a letter; "He could be contented—why is he not, then?" Hotspur cannot comprehend the hypothetical. Bacon wrote, *antiquitas saeculi, iuventus mundi*, "the age of the ancients was the youth of the world." He was arguing, in a highly guarded fashion, for the moderns against the ancients and brilliantly turned the tables by saying, "If it's age you like you should read the moderns; we are far older than they, who lived in the world's infancy." So Hotspur, who belongs to the old order, is above all young. When he receives his death-wound from the prince he cries,

> O Harry, thou hast robb'd me of my youth.
> (*1 Henry IV* 5.4.77)

Responsibility, prudence, caution, strategy mean nothing to him. Honour is his watchword and honour means fighting, with a complete disregard of personal safety or the probability of victory. Only at the end, when his last battle is impending, does Hotspur begin to think (the measured, bitter reply to Blunt in 4.3 brings the change of style which marks the change of heart). Shakespeare brilliantly makes him wish (at 5.2.48) that only he and Hal might fight that day. Here Hotspur's impetuosity is fused for a moment with pity for the other victims of war. But impetuous he remains. At the end of 5.2 he will not stay to read the letters brought by the messenger. The king wishes his son were like Hotspur, but it would have been disastrous if he had been. Prince Hal is like Virgil's Aeneas in that he is burdened with a sense of history and the crushing obligations implied by the likely succession of events. Aeneas has his Hotspur in Turnus, the young, impetuous leader of the Latins. For both Aeneas and Prince Hal the most important relationships are lineal. Each is dominated by the idea of his father, by Anchises and by the king. Thus for Aeneas the lateral relation with Dido is a distraction which must be crushed.

Here, it may be thought, the analogy breaks down. Hal has no Dido, no mirror love to bear him from his purpose; in the sequence from *Part 1* of *Henry IV* to *Henry V* we have no tragic queen who dies of a broken heart.

Yet someone (if we can believe Pistol, and I think we can) lay dying of a heart "fracted and corroborate" (*Henry V* 2.1.121). The analogy with the *Aeneid* is indeed broken by an explosion of genius, yet at the same time in a manner sustained. We have come back to Falstaff. For Shakespeare has chosen to give us something hilarious: a Dido in the form of an Anchises. The great distracting love of *Henry IV* is an old man, and he drinks.

Falstaff is not like Hotspur a specimen of an earlier culture. Rather, he spans and sums in his person all change, all shocks. He is as Arthurian as he is Henrician, as Arcadian as he is English, paradisal and fallen. Introduced in *Part 1* as irrelevant to clocks ("What a devil has thou to do with the time of day?" says the prince at 1.2.7), he is, as we learn in *Part 2*, soon to die. He is an old man but he is also a sort of timeless baby. The Hostess's account of the death of Falstaff is a wonderful description of a baby: "I saw him fumble with the sheets, and play with flowers, and smile upon his finger's end" (*Henry V* 2.3.15). There is a point when the two images are held in separation, and then glimmer and join. Falstaff says, "I was born about three of the clock in the afternoon, with a white head and something a round belly" (*2 Henry IV* 1.2.176–77). We hear the words and, as we listen, what do we see? A white head and a round belly.

1983—John W. Blanpied. "Rebellion and Design in *Henry IV, Part One*," from *Time and the Artist in Shakespeare's English Histories*

John W. Blanpied has taught Shakespeare, drama, and modern literature at Susquehanna University, Smith College, and the University of Rochester.

Looking back to *Richard II*, we can see how Shakespeare wrestled with the issues of imaginative freedom and control. The play revealed the playwright exerting control not, as earlier, through a conventional structure like Providence, but much more furtively and impressively through the disguise of a regal poet endowed with truly seductive gifts. By identifying with Richard, Shakespeare had found how to generate great dramatic force, but a force that looked suspiciously like vanity. He could compel our belief in Richard's unseen inwardness, but an "inwardness" that could have been a trick of theatrical mirrors. The play's ambivalence is surely Shakespeare's. What direction will he take now? Will he strive for a more seductive central figure? For less ambivalence, greater concentration, more far-reaching control? After *Richard II* he must have known himself to be on the verge of unprecedented powers. How strong might be his will to resist the temptation of artistic tyranny?

It is clear from the opening scenes of *1 Henry IV* that the temptation has been abjured. We are greeted by a compression of familiar effects, as if to draw us forward in anticipation of a major revelation; then there is an explosion, and suddenly a world appears, densely and diversely peopled, and already in full motion.[1] It is a truly spontaneous world, its life a matter of internal and native growth, its free-speaking citizens all intricately related, not by the invisible webs of a plotting playwright, but through the verisimilitude of contending strengths.[2] The play's form is not imposed, but emerges from the cross-hatching rhythms of instinctive opposition to imposed control. Rebellion is more than the subject of the play, more even than its central metaphor. Rebellion is its *style*.

The demise of Richard induces a struggle for power whose impulses are deeply theatrical. In this new dawn one feels as if a heavy restraint on speech, the author's own injunctive hand, were suddenly lifted. Something fearful has dissolved, and the result is exhilarating and dangerous both. Identities are problematical now, but the opportunities for creating them are vastly multiplied. The world bursts into excited tongues; rich creative speech jumps from virtually every character, often for no better or no lesser reason than that, abruptly freed to talk themselves into being, they will not be silenced. Falstaff incarnates his own "superfluous" speech; Hotspur would die in silence and so lives and kills in speech:

> He said he would not ransom Mortimer,
> Forbade my tongue to speak of Mortimer,
> But I will find him when he lies asleep,
> And in his ear I'll hollo "Mortimer." (1. 3. 219–22)

Even the minor characters seem to understand instinctively that in a world "turned upside down since Robin Ostler died," speech is, literally, life. Faced with this stimulated world, they respond by extemporizing vigorous performances in a language strong with individuality. This is clearly true of the play's great encounters—Hotspur with Henry or Glendower, Hal with Falstaff or Henry—but one has only to think of, say, the gritty jargon of the thieves and carriers (2. 1) —half-code, half-euphemism—to appreciate the range of dramatizing instinct in the play.

What astonishes is the readiness of the language to the occasions. Take Gadshill's mad harangue in the inn yard (2. 1). His subjects are brigandage, scurrilous companions, hanging; his excitement over the imminent "action," the robbery, takes the form of anticipatory action—that is, the speech itself as a performance resourceful enough to contain the excitement. Apart from the outright vigorous wit of his style, its striking features are the marshalled series of extravagant epithets and coinages and the incantatory rhythms and phrasings:

> ... I am joined with no foot land-rakers, no long-staff sixpenny strikers, none of these mad mustachio purple-hued maltworms; but with nobility and tranquility, burgomasters and great oneyers, such as can hold in, such as will strike sooner than speak, and speak sooner than drink, and drink sooner than pray; ... (2. 1. 70–76)

This style links Gadshill to the major characters. Yet there is no compelling "reason" for the scene (it is usually cut in performance). Through the color, energy, and independence of their language, the minor characters simply make the world dense.

In *Richard II* this sort of impertinent low-life material was routinely suppressed, out of the play's commitment to Richard's centrality. In *1 Henry IV*, individual characters try to shape the world according to their fantasies, but the world is now too abundant to submit to any one figure's imaginative sway. Much of that abundance still occurs offstage—much, that is, of the serious political action, the "chronicle" material. But there is a cinematic quality to the swift succession of scenes. The "cutting" suggests a continuous flood of events. Foreground scenes seem to retrieve highlights of complex moments in passing; the background shifts too fast to be held and neatly lit up, nor is there a steady point of view from which "pertinent" scenes might be selected or framed.

This is the rebellion of style in *1 Henry IV*. Raw energy wonderfully assumes dramatic form, but it is the performance that often comes first, the pertinence only later. Especially in the comic scenes, *what* is being acted out is not clear *until* it is acted out. Nor is this sense of gratuitous playacting confined to the "expendable" parts, such as Gadshill's monologue. It characterizes Hal's entire relationship with Falstaff. No one thinks of the large tavern scenes as meaningless, and yet the meanings are not determined by plot, but rather emerge, like the plot itself, from the energy of "superfluous" performance. There really is no reason for Falstaff's presence in the play at all. He must justify himself as he goes.

Self-justification is a leading motive in the play's competitive world, giving a nervous edge to the most virile of performances. Henry sets the pace in his opening speech. The packed diction, the expansive periods, the regal centrality constitute an aggressive attempt to seize control of the stage from the start, as if he knows in his bones that he who commands the language commands the stage that is the realm. He attempts to shape time ceremonially, to identify the beginning of the play with the true beginning of his reign. Yet his speech is resonant with his own disbelief, the strain of having to shoulder an impossible burden.

> So shaken as we are, so wan with care,
> Find we a time for frighted peace to pant
> And breathe short-winded accents of new broils
> To be commenced in stronds afar remote.
> No more the thirsty entrance of this soil
> Shall daub her lips with her own children's blood: . . . (1. 1. 1–6)

The *actor* of this speech is elusive, either disguised by crabbed syntax ("Find we a time . . .") or displaced by the vivid personifications of war. The speaker, in other words, is content to be diffused through his performance. But that performance, which celebrates the end of civil butchery, manages to evoke a sickening disorder in the very assertion of calmness: "No more the thirsty entrance of this soil / Shall daub her lips with her own children's blood"; "No more shall trenching war channel her fields"; "no more . . . no more. . . ."[3]

Henry takes away even as he gives. In the cataract of suggestive but incomplete images we can feel the onrushing of time he is claiming to have stilled. He creates a breathing space (the "time for frighted peace to pant") that separates the past ("no more") from the future ("new broils"), and in this isolated moment he asserts his power as king to start things anew: the journey to the holy lands. But the breathing space exists only in the act of the speech itself, and even that speech is heavy with despair of its own potency. As he speaks, offstage events mock his onstage efforts to legitimize his reign through ceremony. In fact, he has already made plans that must scuttle "our holy purpose to Jerusalem." By the end of the swift scene, everything originally presented in the opening speech seems to have been withdrawn. And beneath the smooth surface of compact rhetoric and military decisiveness we apprehend a reservoir of the unsaid or the unsayable. More has been done, more is being done, "more is to be said and to be done / Than out of anger can be uttered" (106–7).

We are left, then, with a sense of powerful disturbances grimly suppressed. After his strong opening claim on the stage, Henry relinquishes it—almost, we feel, with relief. He does not pause, like Richard, to marvel that the world defies his authority, but strides pragmatically off. Pretensions to ceremonial legitimacy are easily laid by; the winning of the stage itself can wait; obliqueness is as much his natural mode as directness was Richard's. His exit strikes us as that of a realist unbeguiled by theatrical illusions of power. Yet the exit sets the stage for an explosion. For that stage now seems highly vulnerable, unclaimed, undefended, undefined, a raw space.

The second scene capitalizes upon the instability left by the first. After Henry's time-pressured exit, the stage suddenly flowers into the luxury of a world with just enough time for everything to be said that needs or wants or even is to be said.[4] Yet far from dragging, this scene delivers all the energy that was suppressed in the first. Indeed, the scene rebels against nearly all prior conventions of historical drama and against all presumptions as to what is "pertinent" in a history. Falstaff at first might seem familiar as a *miles gloriosus* or bawdyhouse wit, but his dazzling verbal gifts and rich suggestiveness quickly take him beyond such prototypes. It is clear that he is a major figure and—though sheer invention—somehow central to this "history." In the end, of course, Hal steps forward in his soliloquy to impose an order upon the extravagance. He quiets the stage. But we are now aware of its compressed power, its capacity to erupt at any time into a new adventure of disorder. After this scene all bets are off as to what shape the monster will take next. Everything is, or could be, "pertinent"—and that is both the excitement and the menace of a rebellion that has thrown off the restraints of old form without yet having found its new one.[5]

When Henry returns to the stage in the third scene he has picked up its nervousness. He seems worried about his onstage authority, his ability to translate machiavellian vigor into dramatic potency. His anxieties betray, as usual, the awkward strain of self-division. He vows to be henceforward less "my condition" (his natural self) and more "myself" (his royal self), "Mighty, / And to be feared." These are not the words of a man at home upon the royal stage. He may act "mighty" and instill fear by force: he can suppress Worcester by dismissing him. But he cannot *express* the power of a king dramatically. He does not possess the stage.

When he turns his attention, then, to Hotspur, we are aware that the confrontation proceeds on two levels. The king is struggling to assert his authority in two interdependent domains, the machiavellian or political, and the antic or dramatic. He has summoned Hotspur to explain his apparent defiance in the business of the prisoners. Hotspur, though brusque, is deferential: "My liege, I did deny no prisoners." But as we follow, or try to follow, the quarrel at the level of apparent issues—the political level—we find them changing even as we begin to grasp them, shifting aside, so to speak, to reveal the deeper bases of hostility. Thus, Hotspur in his long "popinjay" speech charms away the issue of prisoners, and yet this issue is tied to something else, indistinct to us, which Henry—uncharmed—proceeds to bring forward: "Why, yet he doth deny his prisoners. . . . " Hotspur, apparently is still trying to bargain with the king, offering up the Scottish prisoners in exchange for the ransom of Mortimer. And suddenly the issue is "Mortimer"—Henry bitterly denouncing him as traitor, Hotspur, outraged, extolling him as epic hero. We feel the ground to have shifted, but there is no way for us to judge the meaning of these excited postures. Then abruptly the king decrees the argument ended; he forbids further mention of Mortimer, orders the prisoners to be sent "or you will hear of it," and leaves the stage. Instantly the issue becomes Henry's tyrannous behavior, especially his intolerable command to silence. In a whirling fury, Hotspur vows not only to "speak of Mortimer" but also to "lift the downtrod Mortimer / As high in the air as this unthankful king." Thus the idea of rebellion is first articulated, not as a plot or design centered upon specific political issues, but as Hotspur's impulsive reaction to the king's attempt to silence him.

The rebellion in fact originates in a clash of styles that feeds upon available issues like so much tinder. If we find the apparent issues of the quarrel hard to attend to, it is only partly because they are indistinct, mired in the sprawling background matter of the play. Partly they are hard to follow because we are being distracted all the while by the *other* level of combat, the antic struggle for the stage itself.

In Hotspur's first words, overtly deferential, we can hear the accent of a self-declaring native of the theater: "My liege, I did deny no prisoners." Henry must hear it, too—brusque, direct, impatient of the king's awkward protocols and jealousies. With native ease Hotspur steps into his role centerstage, drawing upon and exciting its awakened potential for disorder. Not that he does so deliberately. He is a theatrical animal, self-absorbed and self-fulfilling in his actions, but never self-conscious (as Henry always is). Eventually he will exhaust himself, stiffening into the postures of the chivalric hero; but until then he exerts a powerful charm from the magic circle of the stage.

Hotspur's "popinjay" speech (29–69) is any young actor's dream, crackling with easy anecdotal vigor. In the king's own presence, but reducing him to an onlooker or an admirer even (for Henry has confessed to admiration of this gallant puppy), Hotspur holds the stage for forty lines of superfluous playacting. The performance is superfluous both in that it fails to address the issue of defiance it purports to address and in that it literally "spills over" its occasion, taking too much time—from time-pressured Henry's point of view—just to be impertinent. What is worse, the performance *appears* to be persuasive: in its vitality it has the power to seem absolutely central to the most pertinent needs of the moment. Sir Walter Blunt is taken in, and so are we, our attention riveted. And because we are seduced by its earnestness, delighted by its vigor, the performance in fact *becomes* central in importance.

This is the point: our collaboration with Hotspur, our attention to the actor as he discovers his true role, significantly alters the nature of the staged event.[6] In a world imperiously pressured by its future, the antic-player creates time. He swells the present, extending it outward to us, now; dramatic time overtakes the fictional time. And so the performance makes Hotspur's style and presence the real and immediate issues; it gives the character his characteristic heat and before our eyes transforms the emerging political plot into a dramatic contest for our allegiance, credulity, and assent.

Henry has no recourse at this point except, futilely, to forbid speech and then simply to turn over the stage to his young rival. Hotspur's whole style is rebellion, an instinctive reaction against form or restraint of any kind. Henry, for all his "savvy," has no way of containing such "superfluous" energies and can only attempt to suppress them—and so provoke them into organized opposition. For the time being, Worcester and Northumberland have the play's rhythms on their side. Picking carefully between Hotspur's superman fantasies and their own more mundane instincts for self-protection, they begin the delicate task of imposing a form upon his wildness. They work to reclaim him, as it were, from the antic stage, and bring him gently, but usefully, back into the frame of the political action. They do this by making Mortimer's claim, retrospectively, the form and pretext for an organized assault upon the crown.

Thus the end of this scene also subdues vitality to design, shaping from Hotspur's antic energies the political plot of the play. But the political plot, through the very process of its emergence, has become explosively dramatic. The stage is flexed for a new outburst.

The world in *1 Henry IV* is imbued with the great "as if" of drama, making for drama's disturbing doubleness of feeling. In performing is life: therefore Hal lingers with Falstaff, therefore Henry engages Hotspur in a life-and-death rivalry, not over issues but over style. But the performing inevitably seems a substitute for life as well. Repeatedly we are made to feel as if original "true" energies had once, in some mythically prior time, been violently deflected into play speech. And in the urgency of their styles the characters themselves seem responsive to this condition, always pressing their speech to become more real than whatever it is that prompts it. What makes the acting-out so fascinating is—for all its intense gratification—its deep sense of futility, as though emotionally hearkening back to a center, a "point" that is no longer there.

This anxiety about the "point" of performance disturbs the political scenes. But the Eastcheap scenes lay it out more openly. In Hal's first speech, he chides Falstaff for having "forgotten to demand that truly which thou wouldest truly know"—a provocative reply to a request for the time of day. What Falstaff may have forgotten and what he would truly know are never specified. Instead they are "dramatized" in the richly layered series of verbal performances, thrust and counterthrust, in which both characters engage with the finesse of a practiced comic team. Who either of these witty people "truly" is, apart from his membership in the team, is a slippery question. When are they masquerading, and when are they playing out "real" selves in dramatic form? When are they fabricating personas and when does the invention, however extravagant, "denote me truly," as Hamlet puts it?

The idea of a "true" self, behind or beneath the acting self, may be chimerical. Both flaunting and denying his own manifest bulk—"'Sblood, I'll not bear my own flesh so far afoot again" (as if somehow "I" were not quite the same thing as "my own flesh")—Falstaff is forever pointing both at and away from the assumed center of his huge performing power. He is one model of the live actor; the more palpably present he is on the stage, the more he seems to body forth something that is absent—a *source* of presence—and therefore, to point away from what is toward what may be. Audiences in the theater and in the study have always found enormous humanity in Falstaff, and yet there is no "secret" or undisclosed character there. Any formulation of a "true" underlying self is bound to be a reduction of the character, a denial of the very mode of prodigiousness in which he is perfected. Falstaff withholds nothing, is forever spilling his guts; his lies are certainly like the father that begets them, "gross as a mountain, open, palpable." Even his soliloquies are provocative extensions of his barroom postures, not disclosures of secret motivating factors. And yet it is undeniably part of the character that he induces belief in a "self" that beckons from a center, without ever openly revealing itself.

The purer the antic mode, the sharper the strange double vision it induces. At one moment it looks like mere frivolity—"Hostess, clap to the doors . . . What, shall we be merry?" We are sure that the hostess's doors will soon give way to a heavier, more real time. But then again the antic mode, being unpressured by the need to pattern time pragmatically, seems always to tremble on the skin of the surprisingly true, always about to yield up a vital mystery. Falstaff's buffoonery seems to mask the astonishing wisdom of ageless immediacy. After all, he is the *bacchic* fool. And because his is, or seems to be, a safe world (Hal may put down the buffoon, but never the god)—a world free from the external pressures of time—it freely allows the subterranean life to be uttered. By contrast, King Henry's world, with its suppression of language and feeling, and with its commitment to a life beyond this immediate stage-life, seems hollow, haunted by what cannot be present. Yet the very fullness of Falstaff's domain causes problems, too. The outright vigor of its inventiveness, its buoyancy, wit, and rhythm, draws us inward, toward the presumed fountainhead of its exuberant energy. At the same time, the acting itself throws up a kind of screen to thwart our access to that which we "would truly know."

In the first two acts, Falstaff seems able to recycle life into play indefinitely. Everything that comes his way from "outside" is grist for in-house performance. But of course a sense of direction does emerge; the playing itself seems to be driving toward revelation, if only through the process of festive abandonment. Caught up in the play, the players find themselves performing more "truly" than they ever could by intention. Waiting for Falstaff in the Boarshead, Hal perpetrates a "jest" on the hapless drawer, Francis. In this jest Hal gives form to the complex pressures of his situation, his alienation from the presumed center of his life as heir apparent. Thus he expresses a need to command, judge, punish, as well as a need to justify his own half-guilty freedom from "masters." And so he urges Francis to rebel against his bondage and bullies him for being unable to do so. But I think Hal also responds to a more basic need (more basic in the sense that it goes to the heart of his obscure preference for Falstaff's company over his father's), namely to "drive away the time till Falstaff come." When Poins asks him the "issue" of the jest, Hal answers in the nervously explosive style of a man whose wit is all that keeps him from being swamped by a desperate sense of his own idleness. He uses a quasi-theatrical metaphor, as if he were literally full of, and must give vent to, countless personalities: "I am now of all humors that have showed themselves humors since the old days of goodman Adam. . . ." In other words, I act because I must not stop acting. He can "explain" himself only by finding new forms to accommodate his profligate energies. Thus he goes on to parody Hotspur, thence to "Call in ribs! Call in tallow!" to play opposite him as "Dame Mortimer" (2. 4. 105).

Falstaff—held offstage until the perfect moment—enters at the climax of Hal's strained solo exertions. We can feel the stage come alive; Hal's own exuberance gathers up our own and explodes with relief. No longer laboring at his antic self, he can now afford to relax and unleash all his instincts for invention, abusiveness, moral outrage. With Falstaff—in the "men in buckram" comedy, and subsequently in the twofold performance of the Prodigal Prince—Hal becomes an intensely absorbed performer. The result is a comedy so superbly structured that the actors exist only in their personas. Is Falstaff "pretending?" Is Hal "serious?" Centuries of quarreling have not resolved these impertinent questions. The more committed the playing—the more carelessly it risks both its performers and its material—the more ambiguously "real" it becomes. Such playing has the power to use up Hal's detachment, his alienation, his need for purpose, his need to impose a design.

The playing is immediately satisfying to him, therefore to us. Yet it also conveys a reality beyond itself. When Hal plays his father, and Falstaff his son, how many selves, how many voices are there present? Wit begets wonder. In its momentum the playing leads inexorably toward the ghosts at the heart of this world.

At the end of the playing we and Hal both are ready for the real meeting with his father. Like Hal, we have been drawn toward the receding center of an absorbingly fertile world, its flesh continuously redeemed by its imagination, but we have come to rest nowhere. We are drawn by pleasure, increasingly beset by anxiety.

The play centers upon Hal's meeting with his father in 3. 2. At the simplest level, the scene is crucial to the public plot, that plane of historical action, largely derived from Holinshed, concerned with putting down rebellion and insuring lineal succession to the throne. For these ends it is necessary that the prince emerge from his wildness, reconcile with the king, and go on to prove himself the true heir by defeating his rival at Shrewsbury. The atonement of father and son provides the morale, the power of spiritual unity that translates into superior battlefield strength.

But apart from the demands of the public plot, what pulls father and son together in the middle of *1 Henry IV*? What are the internal forces? Perhaps, after all, there are none. There is no history to the relationship, not even much of a desire to imagine or insist upon one, as in *Hamlet*. No mother is ever mentioned (except once, as a generic joke). Hal was "born" at the end of *Richard II* as a problem for his father: the salient fact about him was his not being there to help legitimize the coronation. And now again his absence translates, publically at least, as the king's doubtful authority. For Hal's part, his father seems to exist chiefly as a transmitter of the crown. He expects to inherit it as his right and desert, but never appears to think of deriving it personally from Henry. In other words, the distance between father and son may signify nothing more than the temperamental coldness and mutual distrust of political rivals bound together by a powerful formality. There may be no personal relationship at all—nothing between them but this negative space that must be bridged only so far as the public plot and political interests require.

And yet we are certainly led to expect something more satisfying from the encounter than a pragmatic political pact—something, that is, more responsive to the true range of experience in the play. For of course the scene is central in more powerful ways than a cold review of the characters' motives suggests. Our expectations are roused by an artful pattern of allusions, beginning with Henry's remorseful glance at Hal's absence in the opening scene and climaxing in the great "rehearsal" at the Boarshead in 2. 4. We are never told why Hal keeps his distance, but are constantly reminded of the awkward fact that he does so. In fact, the whole play turns upon the separation of father and son. Hal's absence, after all, not only makes way for Hotspur's charismatic presence, hence the rebellion; it is also the dramatic excuse for the very existence of Falstaff as embodiment of the alternative world. Structurally, in other words, the play loads the gap between father and son, and therefore their encounter, with a terrific burden of meaning.

"Where there is a reconciliation, there must first have been a sundering."[7] Stephen Dedalus's logic seems apt. And where the reconciliation is made to seem crucial, we may imagine a sundering of commensurate importance. Yet on the origins and therefore the meaning of the separation Shakespeare maintains one of his great fruitful silences. We "ask and ask," as Matthew Arnold puts it; "Thou smil'st and art still." Surely, we insist, the separation cannot mean *nothing*—too much rides on it. Surely the drive toward atonement implies some psychic violence, some blighted or repressed affection, some remorse or pain of dislocation—some source, in other words, of the dramatic urgency. We pour our questions, expectations, and explanations into the gap between father and son. They are received without comment and without altering the mysterious fact, the plain existential fact, of the vacancy itself.

The play does not repudiate the idea of a "natural bond" but simply presents it as a cipher. The filial relationship has no prior meaning except that of king to heir. In the Boarshead rehearsal Hal tries intensely to imagine a relationship, but it all turns upon the intermediary role of Falstaff. What the relationship truly is in itself—what Hal or Henry or we will "truly know"—must wait to be created in the actual encounter onstage.

But that encounter turns out to be ambiguous. It presents us, in fact, with at least two valid but conflicting ways of understanding the scene.

The scene works centripetally, drawing us from the outside in toward the elusive center. In their first speeches Hal and Henry cling to the "Holinshed" framework while warily circling the deeper unspoken issues that would absorb them. After a characteristically convoluted opening (a mixture of guilt, reproach, self-pity), Henry sharply charges Hal with "rude society" and a betrayal of the "greatness of thy blood." Having anticipated this much in his rehearsal, Hal responds with a smoothness that if anything sounds too well rehearsed itself: neither denying nor explaining, but in a general way accepting some of the blame and reasonably suggesting that his reputation for wildness would have been exaggerated by "smiling pick-thanks and base newsmongers."[8] It is a well-balanced reply, respectful of his father's anger without inflating its importance by an undue defensiveness. It says enough, and no more—and so leaves the next move up to Henry, either to proceed at this same level to specific allegations, or to make the political pact at once. So far both men have stayed away from anything very personal.

Clearly Henry is not interested in Hal's peccadilloes, and the smoothness of Hal's first response encourages the king to move in closer toward the real issues. "Yet let me wonder, Harry, / At thy affections," he begins. The "let me" is a typically indirect command to silence, for he goes on to "wonder" for the next 100 lines (with only a single line-and-a-half interruption from Hal). Hal's silent part in this performance is crucial: he must be passive without seeming indifferent, attentive without seeming secretly busy with his own thoughts. He must be tactful without being condescending, allowing his crafty, self-deceiving and self-torturing father to trust him even as he reproaches him. And so the king is (as John Russell Brown puts it) "drawn backward and inward, to an imaginary reliving of his past, as if he seeks to convince himself that Richard's behavior is the reason why he usurped the 'sunlight majesty' of the nation he now rules."[9]

As this long and powerful speech unfolds, it becomes clear that what the king wants and needs is not to pardon, or even to understand his son, but to recreate him as a better—that is, a more legitimate and successful—version of himself. In the glorification of his own youth we hear both an attempt at self-extenuation for his sense of failure now and an appeal to Hal to be that youth, but clarified and unchallenged, and so redeem what he, the king, has become. No wonder that Hal's role in this is to remain empty, unspecified, malleable to his father's fantasy.

And yet, returning from his long, half-cunning and half-mesmerized reminiscence, Henry finds that it is not Hal but Hotspur he has invoked. "And even as I was then is Percy now" (1. 96). The true son is "my nearest and dearest enemy," while the image of the king's sunlit dream of youth mounts usurpation with the same "worthy interest to the state" as Henry himself had in supplanting Richard. Thus the king invokes a shining past upon a field of failure, confusion, and unspecified loss. He sounds clear and resolute, of course, but that is ever his style—a tough and vigorous shell around an inchoate interior. He extols Hotspur's heroic style:

> Thrice hath this Hotspur, Mars in swathling clothes,
> This infant warrior, in his enterprises
> Discomfited great Douglas; ... (3. 2. 112–14)

This is precisely the style he rebuked Hotspur for using earlier in defense of Mortimer ("Thou dost belie him, Percy!"). But now he makes it plain that for Hal to be "more myself" means for him to preempt Hotspur in just this mode. Filial identity, it seems, is to be determined by the best claim on the succession, which goes to the most Hotspurian of the claimants.

But however firm and single-minded he seems in demanding a Hotspurian son, Henry himself might be told that "thou hast forgotten to demand that truly which thou wouldest truly know." His sense of self-displacement and his strenuous efforts to subdue it that dog him to his miserable end in the Jerusalem Chamber in Part 2 are enacted in this appeal to Hal, too. "Had I so lavish of my presence been," he sneers, he had been left in "reputeless banishment, / A fellow of no mark nor likelihood." But of course he has rationed himself not only to the "vulgar company," but apparently to his son as well. And now, in the interests of atonement, he urges upon Hal just those self-hoarding, self-manipulating policies that have caused the need for the atonement in the first place.[10] On the face of it he is asking for a strictly formal relationship; he is asking Hal to play the role of Hotspurian son. But the face is strained with confusion. If it is too much to say that he "truly" is pleading for the intimacy he has always withheld and discouraged, his speech is nevertheless troubled with obscure longings and regrets, never expressly voiced but evident in the distortions of his performance:

its excessive length, its rationalizations, evasions, and contradictions, the very effortfulness of its apparent control. When after forty lines of self-absorbed revery, the king turns again to address his son, he himself seems surprised by the tumult of feelings his own performance has elicited beyond the bounds of its initial, political conditions:

> Not an eye
> But is aweary of thy common sight,
> Save mine, which hath desired to see thee more;
> Which now doth that I would not have it do—
> Make blind itself with foolish tenderness. (3. 2. 87–91)

Henry cannot be wholly sincere (one can almost hear Falstaff's lugubrious parody). Yet these lines come up so unexpectedly that they bespeak real longings underneath. By contrast, Hal's response is masklike:

I shall hereafter, my thrice-gracious lord,
Be more myself. (92–93)

Is this merely formulaic, or quietly heartfelt? We cannot be sure: it gives nothing away. Henry himself shows no sign of having heard, for now that the floodgates have opened he has much to say before he has finished flushing out his passion. And now we can appreciate the deftness of Hal's response. Empty, minimal, it simply allows his father to go on talking, and hence to be drawn once more "backward and inward" into his fantasy.

His strange outpouring arrests our attention and fills the stage. Clearly something more is being revealed here than Henry either intends or understands. And our awareness that Hal, too, must realize this intensifies the experience of a supersaturated moment. Such a moment might spill over in any number of ways; *anything* could happen. What is being dramatized is the whole mystery of the separation of father and son. When Henry ends, his bitter passion rising to an outright charge of treason, then settling with a snarl—"how much thou are degenerate" (1. 128)—the hush that follows unmistakably pinpoints the crux of the scene, and indeed the crux of the play itself.

In terms of dramatic power, Hal gains much from his patience. Unlike Hotspur, who cannot keep quiet, he understands the uses of silence to set off speech. In the Boarshead earlier, Falstaff's extrication from the men-in-buckram trap was the more marvelous for its being so long delayed by the battle of insults preceding it. Hal has played just such a role with his father, allowing him to say the worst without interruption, seemingly at unanswerable length, before he attempts a defense. Now as he rises, the "all this" that he gravely promises to redeem "on Percy's head" bears the burden of all we have heard tormenting the king, both explicitly and implicitly. In performance it is scarcely possible not to feel the power of Hal's response, its dead seriousness, its fierce concentration, its galvanically rising energy of purpose. His soliloquy in act 1 was made suspect by its callow coolness. The vow here recapitulates the plan of the soliloquy—emerging in glory, redeeming time—but it is not so much a confirmation of the earlier speech as a fleshed and fully felt version of it. Hal himself, like his father, clearly is moved by the occasion, regardless of how perfectly he had anticipated it. *Being there* is new. He cannot have foreknown, after all, the complex power of his father's voice and presence, any more than Henry could have foreknown the gratifying persuasiveness of his son's deft gifts, first of silence, then of eloquence. These things they could not have known without risking each other's presence. Now the live encounter reaches its climax in Hal's declaration. The speech gathers up personal, domestic, and dynastic history, as well as the play's major themes and connections, and packs them into a single simple yet powerful logic: I am your true not counterfeit son, therefore the prince and heir apparent; I will prove it by vanquishing Hotspur; we will thereby put down rebellion and establish succession beyond all question.

> *Hal.* And I will die a hundred thousand deaths
> Ere break the smallest parcel of this vow.
>   *Henry.* A hundred thousand rebels die in this! (158–160)

The prince, as John Russell Brown sees it, stands before the king at the end of this speech "transformed." Others will see it later, but the king and the audience have seen it while it was happening. And Hal's dramatic credibility now will be vital to his claims of legitimacy later on.

Wonderfully composed as this scene is, it remains somehow disturbing. In performance it can certainly seem a fully satisfying drama of atonement at the filial and therefore the dynastic level. But as soon as we step back, reconsider the larger context, and as soon as the action picks up again, we may well have second thoughts. Does it really do what it had seemed to promise—disclose and somehow answer to the crucial void between the father and son? Does the reconciliation grow out of a deeply sounded sundering? To answer no to these questions is not to abjure our sense of the scene's satisfying fullness. Rather, it is to raise the deeper question of the scene's—and the play's—persistent ambiguity: its capacity to excite multiple, and irreconcilable, responses in us.

Subtle differences in performance can crystallize major differences in perspective. Often in performance Hal's reply takes off from the end of Henry's with little or no pause, as if the two speeches were really one interlocking set. There is something to this. The speeches balance each other so well, Hal's so firmly reverses the emotion and momentum of Henry's, that we become aware of an orchestrated relationship. A union is dramatized, father-and-son. And no doubt our aesthetic pleasure in this harmony is enhanced by an awareness of their own. Perhaps Henry is moved just as we are by his son's sheer skill, and both of them are excited, in part, by the nimbleness with which they have skirted emotional dangers. But to see the two performances as essentially one, coordinated by tacit agreement, should not obscure the fact that a choice has been made. And the moment of choice will be clear if we postulate a hush between Henry's tirade and Hal's response. At this moment, which I have described as supersaturated, a number of possible futures present themselves. Conceivably, had the silence been extended, the moment might have deepened into something like the dream form of *2 Henry IV*, where the implications of this troubled relationship, its fears, deep distrusts, guilty desires, surface disconcertingly. At this moment, in other words, we have the possibility of an unexpected revelation of the play's defended center—of an access through its relentlessly buoyant and opaque style.

What Hal does by jumping in with his perfect timing and perfect speech is to veto those possibilities—he chooses one future and suppresses the others. Rather than succumbing to the silence, he mounts a drama upon it, inventing with brilliant resourcefulness out of the volatile materials at hand. In effect he levers the power of the moment—the bitter passion of his father's rebuke still shuddering in the air—into a play of the future. His first words, a line of firm simple monosyllables, enact the shift of tenses:

Do not think so. You shall not find it so. (129)

He reshapes Henry's sharply personal attack into this generalized forward thrust, the "it" going carefully unspecified. He does not deny the charges, the past, but merely asserts what the future will be.

And God forgive them that have so much swayed
Your majesty's good thoughts away from me. (130–31)

No denial, but an emphasis upon what Henry thinks. Hal is forming a future out of Henry's thoughts, recreating his fathers guilty past into a shining image: "wasting the former times" by a powerfully cathartic style.

I will redeem all this on Percy's head . . . (132)

"All this" means, finally, the world according to Henry IV: the past gathered up and spent in a single image, a single combat.

A hundred thousand rebels die in *this!* (160, my italics)

We are caught up, Henry is caught up. It is what he wants—at least part of what he wants, or what he thinks he wants. And in any case it is clearly what they both need to be able to command the future. But the very perfection of Hal's heroic drama closes off the possibility of intimacy, either canceling or deferring the resolution of their private business. No matter how "sincere" they are, they are settling for a simulacrum of a personal atonement.

The play's rebellious energies have driven it toward its own center. Yet the central scene leaves us with a deeply ambiguous sense of what has been discovered there. The scene seems both full and hollow, both perfect and inadequate. Nothing better could have occurred, yet something vital has failed to occur. All the elements of historical experience—personal, filial, dynastic—have been accommodated as efficiently as possible, within the imperious limits of time. But time itself—or is it the characters' submission to time?—forces them to settle for a hearty fabrication of what they "would truly know."

Father and son go forth from this scene as if their relationship were fully resolved. And from this "as if" the play takes its momentum and direction, moving toward the great Shrewsbury scenes where Hal confirms his oath. But how does the ambiguity of the reconciliation bear upon the heroic plot that grows out of it? How does our awareness of the "as if" in that plot affect the meaning of its culmination?

It is impossible to separate these questions from the more general question of Hal's nature as an "actor," with all the doubleness the term implies. For all its live complexity, the interview scene is circumscribed by Hal's own secret plot. From this point of view the reconciliation is one of a series of staged events through which he will assume his regal and "true" identity. This does not mean that he detachedly manipulates the scene or his father. His dramatic genius lies in his coolly playing the prodigal son, allowing his father's vitality to vent itself spontaneously and to give the scene its compelling edge, while still controlling the ultimate shape it will assume. It is a subtle and risky kind of manipulation in which he makes himself part of what is being manipulated, and it shows promising kingcraft as well as stagecraft. Certainly it shows a maturer sense than did his soliloquy of how his present life as an actor relates to his destiny as king. Nevertheless, there are clear limits to the risks he is willing to take as an actor growing into his destiny. To guarantee the fruition of a particular future, he has to rob the dramatic moment of its existential urgency. There can be no real possibility of its turning out tragically.

Of course, what he steals from the present he vows to make good on, gloriously, in the future. In the eschatological myth of redemption implied in his soliloquy, the old machiavellian impulse, so familiar from the earlier plays, resurfaces in its most complex form so far. Obviously Hal is no Richard III, nor is the historical vision of this play nearly so constricted as that of the early ones.¹¹ Hal's role is to bring all the rambunctious vitality of *1 Henry IV*—its vastly broadened vision of historical experience—into coherent and gratified form. His role, presumably, is to comprehend that vitality. This all implies a wise as well as skillful actor, his performing instincts capable of replenishing the ground from which he rises into glory. Yet just here Hal inspires as much doubt as confidence. Rather than transcend the play's besetting ambiguity—its twin sense of purposeful surface and thwarted interior—his acting style actually heightens it.

For Henry, language always half-reveals and half-conceals his character; we always seem to be catching him in the act of covering himself. By contrast, Hal in his heroic declarations can seem to say "all," to hold nothing back, because in fact he withholds so much:

> For my part, I may speak it to my shame,
> I have a truant been to chivalry;
> And so I hear he doth account me too.
> Yet this before my father's majesty. . . . (5. 1. 93–96)

The style is "pure" and unconflicted, rolling on with unimpeded confidence because it is so impersonal. His "I" is forthright rather than furtive like his father's because it is so purely a verbal fiction. The persona is not a lie, however, but an improvisation, nimbly fashioned for the occasion from the flood of materials on hand at the moment—the political crisis, his father, the king's past, his own past, his rival, his future, himself. He has the playwright's capacity to stand back from the very experience in which he takes part and to regard it all, including himself, as passing matter, his to shape.

The result, however impressive, is utter clarity on the one hand, utter vagueness on the other. Do the personas imply a single creative will? Certainly over the course of the two plays we gather a strong sense of continuous subtextual character. It is, as Daniel Seltzer observes, one of Shakespeare's major achievements, the creation of a figure "who contains—as do all the important creations of good playwrights—an inwardly oriented *raison d'etre*," and whom we perceive as actually growing *in* dramatic time. "The character is that of a man in flux, and we should attach more importance to that sense of changing, of continual process, than is implied in our more or less common academic understanding that this is a prince 'educating' himself."¹² Agreed. But I think it is not until Part 2 that we begin to feel a character dragging against the flow of time and struggling to come into focus. Nowhere in Part 1, except perhaps momentarily in some of the Falstaff scenes, do we feel unmistakably that Hal "himself" glints through the surface of the dense and supple verbal action. In one sense, his performing style disturbs because it is just too good. He performs perfectly in whatever context he inhabits; immerses himself so completely in the dramatic situation that we lose the distinction between actor and character.

Paradoxically, this ability to "lose" himself in the moment creates the impression of some fundamental detachment from the occasion. We never see him sweat or seem to sacrifice one thing in order to embrace another. Each of the twin Shrewsbury eulogies is effortlessly appropriate to its distinctive object—chivalry for Hotspur, mockery for Falstaff. Hal himself is the bridge between them, and yet "he" is little more at that moment than a ritual inheritor. He has no voice of his own, certainly evinces nothing like his father's struggle into a style of yoked contradictions. He responds to all occasions attentively, but with unnerving efficiency; except in the Boarshead, as when he is manically "driv[ing] away the time till Falstaff come," he squanders nothing. Thus from one angle he appears to fill the moment vividly, while from another he seems to be pushing forward some energetic pantomime of a "true" self withheld. Vigorous as his acting always is, his commitment to the dramatic present has none of that massive time-stopping self-abandonment that we find preeminently in the great tragic figures, and to some extent in *Richard II*. Hal has no wish to stop time, to enlarge the present moment by pouring himself into it. He is always busy levering the present toward the future, maintaining a sort of running negotiation with the demands of time. In itself the present has no enduring hold on him, nor is it overwhelmingly real. But as it does not profoundly exist for him, he does not profoundly exist within it. Still, to belabor the disturbing effects of Hal's acting will rightly seem a heavy-handed response to what is more immediately an invigorating performance. And after all, the performance seems to work. The myth generated between father and son is precisely what is played out so impeccably at Shrewsbury: son rescues father, is acknowledged the true son by father, then turns to face and vanquish the pretender, true Harry against false. This play (in contrast to Part 2) will not require from Hal any deeper or more personal attestation of inward character than what shows forth in the battle. In its wonderful synthesis of action and design, vitality and spontaneous form, *1 Henry IV* is decidedly a springtime play: hopeful of the future and prodigal of its past, the source of its forward-thrusting power. Hal can get by with being inventive in many moods—witty, buoyant, solemn, pious, outraged—and finds no reason for doubting the adequacy of this skill to any situation an heir apparent is likely to come up against.

And yet, just this sunny harmony of hero and play does cast a shadow, muted as it is. Hal, assuming his destiny robustly, by his own gifts as an actor in this world of rebellious energies, begins to vanish into that consumer of characters, "history." He begins to vaporize into the legend that Vernon celebrates, in a speech of nine astonished similes, before an eclipsed and despairing Hotspur (4. 1. 96–109). Hal heads toward this future with such tranquil charm that we would surely troop along with him, cheering him on, were it not for the one large and indigestible fact of Falstaff, who has the power to throw everything into question. Falstaff renders everything conditional, revokes every terminal gesture. And we look to him, I believe, to redeem Hal from the hollow triumph of his own promise to square all accounts in the future. Falstaff keeps him alive in the play, holds off time, and so preserves the hope of creating rather than succumbing to history.

Hal's career can be charted in terms of his separation from Falstaff. Whether or not we find this movement satisfying, we surely grow aware of a major shift in the play's balance of powers. In shedding Falstaff, Hal gains one kind of power, forgoes another. Their polarization in the last two acts plays out in earnest—out of doors, so to speak—the tacit terms of their partnership in the first two acts. This process, as always in Shakespeare, will seem gratifying because it clarifies and offers to resolve ambiguity. Also it will sadden, for we witness the decomposition of a wonderfully complex relationship of mutual attractions and restraints, one of Shakespeare's most successful models of creative collaboration and perhaps the only authentic one in the histories.

We do not see Hal make his original choice of Falstaff, but the ritual quality of their opening exchange (1. 2) suggests that he must repeatedly reenact the choosing. However Hal may assess his own motives, we cannot miss the enthusiasm with which he responds to what is, after all, Falstaff's invitation to enter his domain. Merely to keep up with Falstaff requires a kind of abandonment to the delight and sway of language, a submission to its rhythms, an openness to its inadvertent suggestions. Hal in a role of authority may roundly chastise Falstaff, but never (until the end of Part 2) does he try to silence him. He may remove himself from his presence, he may act as if he had ceased to exist or were dead, but in this play he does not actively deny the verbal bond. They exist together in language as a living medium; it binds them together as members of each other, even as lovers of a sort. In its power to engage Hal in this collaboration—and in Hal's willingness to be engaged—Falstaff's superfluous mode, his very gratuitousness, grow compelling.

Hal plays for freedom, for multiplicity, for re-creation, for the delights and nourishments of a world beyond the power of history to conceive, or even to tolerate. Hal is there, in other words, for a lot of reasons that are not pragmatic in the sense of having a calculated usefulness in his plans for the future. In one sense, he is there to forestall or deny the future.

But Hal also plays, of course, for some very pragmatic reasons. The crudest is the one he formulates in his soliloquy, where he casts Falstaff as the sullen field from which he will rise to glory. But Falstaff is neither sullen nor passive; it is rather the vitality of the tavern life that will provide Hal the best grounds upon which to enact his heroic drama. That drama, after all, calls for a central character unburdened by Hamlet-like doubts and the internal tumult of unsounded selves. Perhaps if Hamlet had a live Yorick to drain off antic energies he would not have to play that part, among others, himself. But Hal has his Yorick, and more. Falstaff is not only alive, but powerfully alive, and certainly no figment of Hal's fantasy. His very reality spares Hal the need of inventing him as the antic side of his own personality. In Eastcheap he can safely try out and liberate rebellious energies that would otherwise complicate the wished-for self of the heroic drama. The exertions of his "vile participation" allow him to be serene and personally unexpressive in his high style. In other words, Hal needs Falstaff so that he can eventually come free of him. This means that in Hal's eschatological myth of ascension to glory, it is Falstaff's role to be transcended. And the more compelling the clown, the greater the prince's glory.

In the early scenes, both sides of Hal's motivation—the delight in play, the rebuke of play—coexist in nervous suspension. He thrives on play but also on the expectation of its coming to an end. That is the theme of the partnership itself, enacted over and over again, the vital opposition repeatedly reformed under the pressures of the outside world. When the king's messenger arrives at the climax of the Boarshead festivities, Hal might have been thrown into confusion by his own conflicting instincts. Instead he is invigorated by the threat, and the vigor finds its natural form in a renewed intensity of play. What makes the collaboration genuinely creative is this ability to interpose, between the drumbeats of history, fantastic moments, like that of the "rehearsal," which overflow, and incorporate, and then newly body forth historical "realities."

Hal preserves the doubleness of his situation as long as possible, defying the lures of form, closure, completion. When ultimately he is forced to choose, and so dissolve the doubleness, it is not because history catches up with the playing, but because the playing catches up with history. The natural rhythms of Falstaff's world drive the comedy onto its own creative sources.

The result is the reconciliation scene, in which, as we have seen, Hal pitches the drama into the future tense, clamping the lid upon all possible outcomes except the heroic plot that he and Henry have agreed upon. Forced to choose, Hal chooses heartily: he does not even bother to deny his "vile participation" with Falstaff, but simply proceeds as if it had never happened (just as father and son march out of the scene, as I said earlier, as if they had resolved all personal matters between them). But Falstaff will not agree to "play dead" for the sake of this wishful scenario. He will not be corseted into the form of a "holiday" whose term is up. As Hal's machiavellian strain grows purer, Falstaff's role as spoiler of Hal's eschatological myth grows purer in response. From act 4 on, the play suffers a dissociation of formerly integrated elements. The heroic plot assumes a powerful autonomy, and Falstaff is forced to improvise guerilla-theater tactics for survival.

What is at stake, of course, is not simply Falstaff's survival as a character, but the credibility of his entire imaginative mode of playing as an answer to the assumptions of heroic—and ultimately historical—supremacy. What enduring claim does he make upon us? It will not do to remember only his triumphs in the great tavern scene. From that point on, as Edward Pechter puts it, "the play in effect conforms itself to Hal's version of experience, and for the first time seems decisively to define its own structure as a creature of Hal's and not Falstaff's imagination." Furthermore, Falstaff not only faces exclusion by the play's "natural" flow of events; he also faces a withdrawal of our sympathy as we are brought round to an "acceptance" of the heroic plot by "a number of strategies that make Falstaff seem a much less and Hal a more endearing figure."[13] Falstaff cannot hope to survive merely as a sentimental preference.

Let me trace the argument behind this formulation of the problem. From the end of the spacious tavern scene (2. 4), we experience a constriction of the imaginative life that Hal's festive partnership with Falstaff had so pleasurably encouraged. All along, of course, we have been prepared for an end to the festivity. The question is not whether the play would reach that end but whether it would manage to satisfy all the rebellious energies it has so urgently brought forth. This means, of course, not only Hotspur's rebellion, which exhausts itself, but Falstaff's as well. Can the play reach its appointed end only by suppressing Falstaff, or does he exhaust himself, too?

One answer is that in the last half of the play Falstaff indeed forfeits much of his claim upon our sympathies—that in the cold daylight of history we come to see the tavern charmer as a frankly unappealing figure: taking bribes from draft-dodgers, sending pitiful "rag-of-muffins" into the maw of war, scrabbling for safety, comfort and profit in a context where bravery, selflessness, and honor have become the commanding virtues. Furthermore, as Brian Vickers shows, Falstaff's language becomes more and more nakedly unscrupulous and self-serving.[14] As the heroic context reproves the festive ethic of perpetual play, we are brought to accept Falstaff's exclusion from the main action of the drama and to shift our allegiance firmly to the heroic plot itself. By the end of the Shrewsbury sequence—like Hal in his carefully affectionate eulogy—we have accustomed ourselves to the idea of a dead, or at least diminished Falstaff. Whether or not we are taken in by his counterfeit death, his expansive resurrection sends a surge of delight through any audience. It delights, that is, *because* it is illogical, paradoxical, wonderful. But for this reason it also carries a sense of vaudevillian irrelevancy—one last sportive fantasy interposed between inevitable stages in the linear, historical plot. Falstaff's rising forestalls, but by no means undoes, the fulfillment of Hal's eschatology.

My argument with this reading is that it tacitly reintroduces the idea of a manipulative Shakespeare, a "king of shadows" intervening to deck out Hal in rising glory while muddying up the one character who might credibly raise doubts about that glory. But *1 Henry IV* has operated from the beginning through the freely expressed and contending strengths of all its characters, and continues to do so through the latter half.

Falstaff's distinctive strength is, in C. L. Barber's phrase, his capacity for "humorous redefinition"—a seemingly endless ability to rename himself and the world, to recycle the threatening meanings of history through the extempore world of festivity, thence out to us to dissolve in our laughter. But from the "reconciliation" on, the play itself, aligning its structure and momentum with that of the heroic plot, appears to have gone to war against humor. Hal returns to the tavern (3. 3) and finds himself drawn into something like his erstwhile collaboration with Falstaff, but his new-minted seriousness overrides the lingering affection and pleasure. "I have come to procure thee, Jack, a charge of foot." At the end of the scene Falstaff wishes "this tavern were my drum," but the humor is weak, and the attempt at redefinition futile. The tavern fades, the play moves out of doors, and the stage becomes a field of battle.

Like all the play's conflicts, the struggle of the last two acts proceeds at two distinguishable levels: the politic or mimetic action, and the antic contention for the stage itself. In the first act we saw that Henry's soberly machiavellian instincts for drama were unavailing against the galvanic energies of Hotspur. Now, however, Henry has acquired dramatic authority as well as the military advantage of swiftly moving and loyal troops. Of course the two are connected; both in and out of Shakespeare a king may inspire loyalty through regal charisma. But a king commands the stage itself only if that charisma extends to us. By act 5 Henry can justly dismiss Worcester's rambling list of grievances as "water colors" (5. 1. 80), but the fact is that Henry's own claims of legitimacy are, prima facie, no more convincing. He is credible as king because by this time in the play we have credited him, which we do because he now carries Hal's dramatic weight.

Falstaff wars, therefore, not just against the eschatology of the heroic plot with its linear structure, hierarchical assumptions, and narrow exclusiveness, but against its claim on our imagination. Act 4, scene 1, for instance, establishes the power of the heroic plot by showing the effects of the reconciliation upon the rebels. Northampton's "sickness," the king's swift advance, Hal's transformation, Glendower's collapse: the tide of news flows all one way, relentless. Nature herself seems to be marching in step with the heroic enterprise, Hal and his comrades coming on, in Vernon's eyes, as estridges and eagles, "As full of spirit as the month of May / And gorgeous as the sun at midsummer" (101–2). The strong emotional rhythms—Hotspur's desperate ups and downs against the images of rising regal potency—give the scene immediately gratifying form. The heroic plot becomes a self-sufficient narrative structure arching inexorably from the reconciliation to Shrewsbury: "Doomsday is near. Die all, die merrily."

Falstaff's answer to this scene follows. Of course 4. 2 gives us a "realistic" view of the war to balance the heroic, and Falstaff's "food for powder, food for powder. . . . Tush, man, mortal men, mortal men" satirizes the heroic perspective of battle as a struggle between mighty opposites. But more is afoot than satire or balance. Our hunger for culmination has been aroused, and Falstaff must reassert the claims of the antic mode of experience. Therefore he works to redefine the war—though now with somewhat bated humor—as a conflict not between mighty characters in an epic plot, but between that entire plot, full of all those characters, and Falstaff himself. Against the forward pressure of the changed "brave world" he asserts his rhetorical powers of invention, conjuring up a cast of outrageously pathetic "mortal men" who obviously have no place at all in an heroic view of history.

> . . . A mad fellow met me on the way, and told me I had unloaded all the gibbets and pressed the dead bodies. No eye hath seen such scarecrows. I'll not march through Coventry with them, that's flat. Nay, and the villains march wide betwixt the legs, as if they had gyves on, for indeed I had the most of them out of prison. There's not a shirt and a half in all my company, and the half-shirt is two napkins tacked together and thrown over the shoulders like a herald's coat without sleeves; . . .
> (34–46)

For all its grimy realism, the speech swells irresistably, generating details hyperbolically, forcing our attention upon Falstaff's own theatrical presence. He not only takes the new brave world as his theme; he bodies it forth, he invokes it with deadly exuberant particularity. You want war? he says to us. I'll give you war. You want to get serious? I'll give you more than you bargained for, and make you laugh to boot at what you know is not really funny, and your laughter will acknowledge the superior reality of my inventions. In other words, Falstaff counterpunches against the powerful autonomy of the heroic plot by dramatizing war as a product of the play itself, its native rebelliousness, rather than as a product of a narrowed epic convention. As such, "war" is seen as a risky venture between audience and performers, and not a controlled and shapely process leading to a predetermined end. Falstaff manages to delay the forward thrust of the plot by intruding his own unruly self into our consciousness, forcing us to hold competing images of experience in mind as the whole meaning of this war."[15]

By act 5 the separated worlds—heroic and Falstaffian—converge with violent dramatic results. Hal's offer to meet Hotspur in single combat (5. 1. 83–100) advances the heroic plot by honing the political struggle to a fine chivalric point. The decorum of the offer, its perfect lack of Hotspurian posturing, lends the moment a natural sense of propriety and immediate theatrical pleasure. But this sense of the duly ripened moment-of-choice personally threatens Falstaff. "Thou owest God a death," Hal soberly puns. "'Tis not due yet," Falstaff returns. Upon this flat counterpremise he inflates a rhetorical alternative to the linear squeeze-play of the heroic plot. "Can honor set to a leg? No. Or an arm? No . . ." The "no's" pile up, swelling by incantation and catechizing rhythms. This is the old Boarshead strategy ("Banish plump Jack and banish all the world"), adapted to a more naked threat. Again Falstaff makes himself an irresistible target through his wildly specious logic; but before we act to deflate him (thereby, like Hal earlier, playing Falstaff's game) we are led through laughter to glimpse another kind of speciousness: the myth of "honor" as a natural ethic rather than a cultural fiction. The performance lacks the old spontaneity, but it does its work and holds our attention long enough to reestablish the authority of the conditional mode and complicate our response to the heroic.

Falstaff makes his worst appearance during the battle (5. 3), mocking Sir Walter Blunt's king-costumed corpse ("There's honor for you!") and his own slaughtered draftees:

> . . . I have led my rag-of-muffins where they are peppered. There's not three of my hundred and fifty left alive, and they are for the town's end, to beg during life. . . . (35–38)

Sour as this is, Falstaff is simply refusing to submit to heroic categories of meaning. "Grinning honor" belongs to Blunt, but is meaningless for those who do not exist in the adventure story called history. In that story, after all, Falstaff and his spawn of rag-of-muffins are merely the sullen ground for the bright heroic figures. The only existence the "mortal men" have is the one that Falstaff invokes for them as an embarrassment to the heroic ethic. And the only existence *he* has is the one he maintains for himself by his stage presence. Between their death and obscurity and his life and endurance is nothing but the performance. Quite literally, that performance is "life; which if I can save, so; if not, honor comes unlooked for, and there's an end."

Not glory, not transfiguration, just an "end." To expose Hal's smiling plot as essentially humorless, its pleasures the machiavel's means toward an end, Falstaff maneuvers to grab the stage and hold it long enough to generate some extravagant but powerful alternatives:

Honor	Life
Air	Food
Pistol	Bottle
Blunt	Rag-of-muffins
History	Play
Death	Himself

Falstaff aligns not only war but all the values represented in this war with death: the values of order, design, completion, the impulse toward transcendence, the ideal of unity, the entire heroic myth of eschatology. What is more, death itself is mockery. Life alone is real—which is to say, this moment, this place, this continuing, overflowing absurdity. Of course the polarization is fraudulent. But in dramatizing outrageous alternatives of life and death—and before we recoil to dismantle his "logic"—Falstaff forces us to register our own gut allegiances.

The resurrection sequence (5. 4) recapitulates Falstaff's re-creative mode: the ultimate "putdown," the magical rising, the extrication and revitalization as he puns and riddles himself back into a commanding and central dramatic presence. There had been signs earlier of a waning enthusiasm, but now he rebounds with wonderful energy, shattering Hal's shapely design. Superfluousness incarnate, he cheerfully collapses hierarchies and distinctions, proliferating "counterfeits" until he dazzles us into belief in the democracy of all forms of play. There are no meanings but stage meanings; the play's assumption of a separate reality, of internal coherence, is a sham: all "boy's play," swords of lath, an actor feigning the dead Hotspur:

> . . . How if he should counterfeit too, and rise? By my faith, I am afraid
> he would prove the better counterfeit.[16] (5. 4. 121–23)

Then, suddenly, the vaudevillian punster shoves the blade into Hotspur's "thigh" (meaning, almost certainly, his groin) and our gasp reconstitutes the playworld. The sword is steel, the corpse is flesh, this world is real. How could we have forgotten? Hotspur has lived hotly in our imagination. In soliciting our humorous disdain for the "counterfeit" corpse, a mere caricature of "grinning honor," Falstaff has lured our attention from what we "truly know." In stabbing Hotspur he stabs contemptuously at us—at our short memories, our fickleness, our love of single meanings, our gullibility.

"Mark how a plain tale shall put you down," says Hal in the palmy Boarshead days. Falstaff's rising in 5. 4 is his answer. His "counterfeit" speech and then his castration of Hotspur amount to a tale plainer than the heroic story implied in Hal's twin eulogies. Falstaff's answer—always a version of "I knew ye"—is both more extravagant and more direct; to call the play "boy's play" is both true and an elaborate falsehood. He reasserts the great "as if" of dramatic truth itself, the vital conditionality of playing.

"This is the strangest tale that ever I heard," says John. "This is the strangest fellow, brother John," Hal concedes, and so must we. Falstaff will not be kept down, not even in our formulizing imagination. He continues to elude not just Hal but us, who had cornered him, or so we thought, as the Spirit of Play. He is the very Heisenberg Principle: catch him as mass, he has already eluded us as mobility; catch him as motion, the play's pure vitality, he'll be stealing our purse, our trust, our good name. He undermines the play and he makes the play. He is the strangest fellow still, the double man, the pun incarnate, two-in-one, the impossible confirmed by the twin testimonies of eyes and speech:

> Art thou alive,
> Or is it fantasy that plays upon our eyesight?
> I prithee speak. We will not trust our eyes
> Without our ears. Thou art not what thou seem'st. (5. 4. 132–35)

Like the thing of great constancy, however strange and admirable, Falstaff lives only in drama, and gives drama its cogency too. But the drama bodied forth by Falstaff is something more complex than the histories have shown us before. We see it, as we see Falstaff himself, freshly, with "parted eye," like the amazed lovers in *Dream*, or by a "natural perspective" as in the end of *Twelfth Night*. For a moment at least we may glimpse the astounding depth of life that feeds him, the play, and history, too.

Is there a "natural" tendency for an action to complete itself? Or do we simply project our desire for one upon the stuff of the play and call it natural?

Falstaff can rise up to thwart completion of the heroic story not because he is inexhaustible but because he plays across limits, to us and our time. He solicits our collaboration in forestalling culmination. When he grumbles, for instance, that "I'll not bear my own flesh so far afoot again" he gives us an open laugh; but he also conveys his knowing refusal to subside into the definition of his own body. This doubleness (if we are nimble enough to catch it) enriches our pleasure in his playing; it also lights up our own mixed motives. For in addition to pleasing, Falstaff also attracts our desire to penetrate the secret center of his diffuse array of roles and meanings, to name him once and for all, and put him down. We too distrust idleness and want our time, even in play, to be well spent. We want form, we want meaning, and for these we need completion and resolution of the action. Falstaff illuminates the load of aggressiveness concealed in these "aesthetic" desires.

He can do this by standing firm against the terrific urge—ours and the playwright's—for an ending. Falstaff's demeanor in the last two acts—his ugliness, his ingenuity, his particular kinds of foolishness and intelligence—is a strategy for maintaining his distinctive importance: in a word, his body and the bodily values implicit in theater. For a contrast we might think of Richard III. In the end of his play Richard deserts us, leaving us no vital presence to be loyal to. Then we are freed to turn on him with moral indignation. Nothing substantial intervenes between our desire to judge and the historical monster Richard becomes.

Unlike Richard, Falstaff gives us an unfailing locus for our skeptical, defiant impulses. The body never fails, either in its presence or in its elusiveness. In his continuing vitality Falstaff defies our drift toward moral autocracy, our tendency to acquiesce in the convention of an End to Holiday. He reveals how deeply the play assumes that convention—how play and audience tacitly collude in a wishful ordering of experience into a "natural" culmination. In the process he exposes the aggressive impulse behind the very fashioning of "history"—the impulse to selectivity and silencing, the bias toward a hierarchical, self-justifying, single-focused view of reality. In short he brings to light the operative myth of *1 Henry IV*, that of history as a humanly fulfilling process—sunny, hopeful, whole, harmonious with the best and deepest truths of human nature.

But precisely because he holds so steady against such massive pressures of change, we come to see Falstaff differently. In the monologues of the last two acts he addresses us as an increasingly disturbing figure, speaking more and more directly out of the obscure heart of the play itself. His voice grows more abstract, less flexible; he becomes harsher, more dangerous, less personal, his allegiance going to something deeper than our good will. Through him the antic spirit emerges as more complex, a richer and darker phenomenon than we have known before. We perceive it as thriving on a darkness that presses around the lighted circle of the stage. Forestalling culmination, the triumphant antic spirit causes us to think on true endings all the more gravely.

Like Hal, frustrated and delighted, therefore amazed at this strange fellow, we do Falstaff the grace of the gilded lie. We give up our efforts to bring him down and end the story. But we do so knowing that there must be a real end, and authentic acknowledgement of the darkness in which "history" is played. What this means—since it is now abundantly clear that Falstaff cannot be brought within bounds—is that he must sooner or later be killed off. *We* must kill him off. The only real question is How? And to answer, "Not now, not yet," is to beg the question, to admit that there really is no right way. Perhaps that is the point. Hal's efforts to close the design by eliminating Falstaff are premature because they are wishful and evasive. Falstaff cannot be killed silently, passively, but only in full awareness of the costs and meaning of the act. In other words, Hal, we, and perhaps even the playwright, must suffer through a whole new process of self-knowledge. What must be learned is the meaning of completing an action: that there is no "natural" act, no "natural" design. Every act implies a cruelty. Every step into the future requires a death in the past.

By surviving, depriving us of the comfort of forward motion and finished stories, Falstaff renders the very idea of history problematical.[17] He also reveals its immense sadness. We perceive him dancing for his life upon a void; in the very density of his performing he shows us the emptiness he buffers us against. Once he stops dancing, there is only the plunge into the hollowness of history.

But meanwhile, before our eyes, he turns the tragedy comic. He sets himself against the dramatist's own deep desire to arrest the flood of time that he has tapped by his own power. Thus Falstaff is rebellious even to the end, defying his own creator's will to set a form upon the indigest of history and mount a story upon the void. Always before, Shakespeare has stepped in to shape the end, and always it has meant relinquishing the autonomy of the characters whose antic energies have been his access to the true destructive nature of his material. York, Margaret, Richard III, the Bastard, Richard II all subside. None of them succeeds in holding Shakespeare's interest against the overwhelming need for form. Falstaff alone endures. Because Shakespeare finally cares so much for him he will not sacrifice him to his need. Because he cares so much, allowing his imagination to flow without stint into that figure, he has given Falstaff the power to wreck the "history," forcing the flood of time to redefine itself upon him.

And so Falstaff transforms the play's design—or rather, brings to light its true underlying design. True design is the shape that all the play's rebellious energies, freely played-out, assume. It is the materialization of the characters' collective activities. And in *1 Henry IV* the primary activity is the stimulated response to the sense of a missing center. Thus Hal's dissociation from his father is played and replayed obsessively in various keys, both with Falstaff and with Henry himself, until we begin to hear the echoes of a killing coldness at the heart. The melancholy sense of a Past emerges, all-important but known inevitably too late, realized only dynamically in the shapes that playing takes in the present. The "design" of *1 Henry IV* is the playing-out of responses to that sense of prior deprivation.

The muted tragedy of the play, brought forward by Falstaff's irrepressible comedy, is the inability of Henry and Hal to attend truly to the vacancy between them because of the need thrust upon them by their commitment to the future. Precisely because this vacancy remains unexplored there can be no ending, no final shape to their stories. Hence Part 2.

NOTES

1. "In the two parts of *Henry IV* . . . the effects [of Richard II's self-destructive acts] are exploded to create an entire dramatic world and the many various characters who inhabit it" (Alvin B. Kernan, "The Henriad: Shakespeare's Major History Plays," in *Modern Shakespearean Criticism*, ed. Alvin B. Kernan [New York: Harcourt, Brace, and World, 1970], p. 253).

2. "It is the various strengths of a stirring world, not deficiencies, which make the conflict in *1 Henry IV*," writes C. L. Barber in *Shakespeare's Festive Comedy*, (Princeton, N.J.: Princeton University Press, 1959), p. 203. Edward Pechter adds, "But it works the other way around as well, the conflict makes for the strengths" ("Falsifying Men's Hopes: The Ending of *1 Henry IV*," *Modern Language Quarterly* 41 [1980]: 218).

3. A. R. Humphreys has a good analysis of this speech in the introduction to his revised Arden edition of the play (London: Methuen, 1961), p. lxii.

4. "The prose in which [Hal] explains why time is nothing to Sir John is wonderfully leisurely and abundant, an elegant sort of talk that has all the time in the world to enjoy the completion of its schematized patterns" (Barber, *Shakespeare's Festive Comedy*, p. 199).

5. G. R. Hibbard has deftly set out the features that make for the great originality of *1 Henry IV*. Having touched on its quantum increase in new vocabulary, its proliferation of new characters and the intricate interplay among them, the abundance of prose, the amount of sheer invention, the dramatic structure—scenes related "like a series of shifting planes, corresponding to the way in which reality presents itself to us in the actual business of living"—Hibbard comes to what he considers Shakespeare's "breakthrough" in dramatic speech: Hotspur's "unpoetic" poetry, "its responsiveness to the tones of the speaking voice, and its predilection for imagery that is exact and down to earth. . . . It is a verse that bespeaks the man. . . . " (p. 9); and of course Falstaff's prose, which is infused with the qualities we would ordinarily associate with poetry. One of the implications of this is that an original audience would have felt itself in the presence of something new and unpredictable, especially in historical drama. See "'Henry IV' and 'Hamlet,'" *Shakespeare Survey* 30 (1977): 1–12.

6. For ideas about audience collaboration I am especially indebted to Thomas Whitaker, *Fields of Play in Modern Drama* (Princeton, N.J.: Princeton University Press, 1977); e.g., "For those who are discovering their roles, and for those who are responding to the actor's gestures of discovery, a play is a collaborative miming that is lifted moment by moment into the light of the attention" (p. 16).

7. James Joyce, *Ulysses* (New York: Random House, 1961), p. 193.

8. Shakespeare picks up "pick-thanks" directly from Holinshed but suppresses his allusion to the "malicious rumours" of Hal's parricidal bloodthirstiness that these same smiling pickthanks spread. In the parallel scene in Part 2, of course, the parricide theme bursts violently through; but even in Part 1 there is at least one curious outcropping. In the very midst of the ritual of proof and acknowledgement of son by father in 5. 4, Henry cannot help adding, perhaps rather coyly, that Hal by his "fair rescue . . . showed thou mak'st some tender of my life." But Hal's response is truly startling:

> O God, they did me too much injury
> That ever said I heark'ned for your death. (50–51)

He proceeds vehemently to deny his guilt by insisting that he could have let Douglas kill the king had he wanted him dead. In view of the earlier suppression of the pickthanks' "rumours," and of its sheer gratuitousness here, the outburst is eloquent.

9. John Russell Brown, ed., *Shakespeare in Performance: An Introduction Through Six Major Plays* (New York: Harcourt, Brace, Jovanovich, 1976), p. 167.

10. The most influential piece of psychoanalytic criticism of the father–son relationship—an approach that necessarily posits a particular past—is Ernst Kris, "Prince Hal's Conflict," *Psychoanalytic Quarterly* 17 (1948): 487–505. Others are J. I. M. Stewart's "The Birth and Death of Falstaff," in *Character and Motive in Shakespeare* (London: Longmans, Green, 1949); Philip Williams' "The Birth and Death of Falstaff Reconsidered," *Shakespeare Quarterly* 8 (1957): 359–65 (William's

perspective is in part anthropological); and M.D., Faber, "Falstaff Behind the Arras," *The American Imago* 27 (1970): 197–225. But see my discussion of *2 Henry IV*, where the issues crystallize as they never really do in Part 1.

11. Some, like John Danby, think of Hal/Henry V as a "whitewashed" Richard III (*Shakespeare's Doctrine of Nature* [London: Faber and Faber, 1949], pp. 90–91). Harold C. Goddard argues from this perspective eloquently and at length in *The Meaning of Shakespeare*, vol. 1 (Chicago: University of Chicago Press, 1951), pp. 161–214.

12. Daniel Seltzer, "Prince Hal and the Tragic Style," *Shakespeare Survey* 30, (1977): 22.

13. Edward Pechter, "Falsifying Men's Hopes: The Ending of *1 Henry IV*," pp. 225–26.

14. Brian Vickers, *The Artistry of Shakespeare's Prose* (London: Methuen, 1968), pp. 114–17.

15. Pechter (See n. 13 above) argues for the essential ambiguity of *1 Henry IV* —i.e., a play that induces a pleasurable "civil war" in us, exciting our mutually exclusive rages for order and chaos. Another recent study, reaching similar conclusions, is Elizabeth Freund's "Strategies of Inconclusiveness in *Henry IV, Part 1*," in *Shakespearean Comedy: Theories and Traditions*, ed. Maurice Charney (New York: New York Literary Forum, 1980), pp. 207–16. Both studies acknowledge debts to Richard Lanham's *The Motives of Eloquence: Literary Rhetoric in the Renaissance* (New Haven, Conn.: Yale University Press, 1976).

16. Sigurd Burckhardt's reading of this scene, like so much else in his work, has been seminal: see "Swoll'n With Some Other Grief: Shakespeare's Prince Hal Trilogy," in *Shakespearean Meanings* (Princeton, N.J.: Princeton University Press, 1968), pp. 147–49. James L. Calderwood follows his lead in some interesting directions. He imagines Falstaff giving us a conspiratorial wink on "nobody sees me" (l. 25). See *Metadrama in Shakespeare's Henriad* (Berkeley: University of California Press, 1979), p. 71.

17. For an excellent exploration of the essential openendedness of the history play, see David Kastan, "The Shape of Time: Form and Value in the Shakespearean History Play," *Comparative Drama* 7 (1973).

1985—E. Talbot Donaldson. "Sublimely Ridiculous: The Wife of Bath and Falstaff," from *The Swan at the Well: Shakespeare Reading Chaucer*

E. Talbot Donaldson (1910-1987) was one of the twentieth century's most important scholars of Chaucer and pre-modern English literature.

We can never ascertain whether Shakespeare had the Wife of Bath in mind—at least in his unconscious mind—when he created Falstaff.[8] It may be merely a coincidence that Falstaff in one of his early appearances is seen on the pilgrim route to Canterbury; and it may have been merely Shakespeare's instinct that told him that a gross solipsist of enormous vitality would be the proper comic figure to provide an anti-heroic foil for a fledgling monarch and an ironic commentary on the values of English power politics, and that he never thought of that earlier large solipsist of enormous vitality who provides a foil for all the virtuous wives in fact and fiction and an ironic commentary on the Middle Ages' received ideas about marriage and the nature of women. The ironic commentaries that Falstaff and the Wife of Bath make are, because of the assurance and authority of their personalities, as persuasive as is the reality of the milieus in which they live and to which they respond. Both are supremely self-confident in their idiosyncrasy. As is often pointed out, they both use—or rather misuse—in their own defense the verse of St. Paul in the first Epistle to the Corinthians, in which he enjoins Christ's followers to remain in that vocation to which they have been called. Speaking of her total dedication to the vocation of matrimony, the Wife announces

In such a state as god hath cleped vs
I wol perseuer: I nam not precious. [D 147–48]

And when the Prince comments on Falstaff's role as a taker of purses, Falstaff replies, "Why, Hal, 'tis my vocation, Hal, 'tis no sin for a man to labor in his vocation" (I.ii.104–05). I am not suggesting that Shakespeare needed the Wife of Bath to put St. Paul's text into Falstaff's mind, for the verse from the Epistle is one of several Pauline texts that were probably often perverted in a way that would have horrified the Apostle. In the C-text of *Piers Plowman*, for example, Long Will beats off an attack by Conscience and Reason on his begging for bread for a living by citing the verse as an excuse for not performing manual labor.[9] All three characters are suggesting, with varying degrees of seriousness, that, although others may find what they do reprehensible, they find their occupations fully justified because they are *their* occupations, and they find them congenial. Their ideas of the world may be at variance with other people's ideas, but they are at home with them, and do not intend to alter their styles for anyone. And, if I may pervert Scripture myself, they speak not as the Scribes and Pharisees, but as those having authority.

Judith Kollmann has recently pointed out a number of similarities between *The Canterbury Tales* and *The Merry Wives of Windsor*,[10] and I myself wonder if that play does not make a backhanded acknowledgment of Shakespeare's awareness of *The Wife of Bath*. The merry wives are in many ways, not including wifely virtue, like the Wife of Bath—independent, resourceful, sturdy women of the same middle-class background as she. This is, indeed, as Professor Kollmann shows, a background one associates with Chaucer's *Canterbury*

Tales and hardly at all with Shakespeare's plays, which are mostly aristocratic or upper class, with bits of low life thrown in for spice. But the community of Windsor is made up of the same sort of people as the community of the Canterbury pilgrims, and is complete with the Host of the Garter Inn, whose involvement with what is going on around him is like that of the Host of the Tabard Inn, who leads the Canterbury pilgrims. The two wives of the play administer sorely needed lessons about women to two men, a jealous husband and an unlikely courtly lover, and this is an enterprise that the Wife of Bath would have cheered them on in, especially when they punished that most porcine of male chauvinist pigs, Sir John Falstaff, who had the gall to rival her in comic grandeur. And indeed, the punishment of Falstaff is effected by facsimiles of those very fairies whom the Wife of Bath tells us the Friar has blessed out of existence—one of whom teaches a lesson about women to the young rapist in *The Wife of Bath's Tale*.

Of the many traits the Wife of Bath and Falstaff share, one of the most striking is their wit. Of Falstaff, who boasts that the brain of man "is not able to invent anything that intends to laughter more than I invent or is invented upon me," and that he is "not only witty in [him]self, but the cause that wit is in other men" (*Henry IV Part 2*, I.ii.7–10), no more need be said—though it's tempting to say it anyhow. But the Wife's wit is sometimes underestimated. She is, for instance, a past-mistress of the progressively engulfing squelch, the insult that hurts the victim more the more he thinks about it. At the end of a tirade directed at one of her doddering husbands she asks him, out of the blue, "What aileth soche an old man for to chide?" (D 281). Perhaps one has to be a man of advanced—or advancing—years really to feel how this question goes on subtly cutting deeper after the first superficial wound has been felt: apparently old age cancels a man's right to complain about anything, especially a vigorous wife, for an old man ought, she implies, to feel nothing but gratitude for being allowed to clutter up the house with his useless carcass. One does not have to be a friar to savor the wit of her devastating repayment of the Friar on the pilgrimage for his patronizing comments on her learning and the length of her prologue. She explains that the friars, having blessed fairies out of existence, have taken their place: the result is that women may walk the countryside safely, for where there used to be an incubus there is now only a friar, and he'll do nothing to women—except dishonor them (857–81).

As the quotation from St. Paul suggests, both the Wife of Bath and Falstaff are adept at converting received *dicta*, whether biblical or proverbial, into slightly askew statements critical of other people's values or expressive of their own. I say "converting," for the process is not really one of twisting such texts as it is reinterpreting them by a surprising use of logic. That human flesh is frail is an observation so trite that it has lost its force as a moral warning and has become an extenuating statement. Or so Falstaff suggests when he restates it in the comparative degree: "Thou seest I have more flesh than another man, and therefore more frailty" (*Henry IV Part 1*, III.iii.166–68). "The lion will not touch the true prince" is a statement which, under Falstaff's analysis, serves to excuse Falstaff's unlion-like failure to oppose Hal and Poins when they rob him of the booty of the Gadshill theft, and also to validate both Hal's claim to be a true prince and Falstaff's to be a lion, whose instinct caused him to run away from his sovereign (II.iv.270–75). The Wife of Bath, though her *forte* is the Bible—to which I shall return—matches this refurbishment of an adage by her reinterpretation of the innocent little saying that it is too miserly for a man to refuse to let another man light a candle at his lantern, since he'll have none the less light as a result (D 333–34). When the Wife identifies the man as a husband and the lantern as his wife, the proverb takes on shocking implications, managing to justify a wife's extramarital sexual activity while dutifully preserving the medieval tenet that the wife is the husband's chattel, like any other of his tangible goods.

The Wife of Bath and Falstaff create their individual versions of reality by the protraction of their speech: they erect large verbal structures which fill the listener's mind and exclude from it all other matter. The prologue to the Wife's tale is approximately as long as the Prologue to *The Canterbury Tales*, a proportionment in which she would have found nothing to criticize. In all three of the plays in which Falstaff appears one finds long, long prose passages spoken by Falstaff, sometimes to someone else, but more often to himself, and us. He is a soliloquist more copious than Hamlet. Yet despite the fact that these solipsistic monologists are constantly explaining themselves to us, we are often not sure where to have them. Both make ironic commentaries on their milieus, but both also *are* ironic commentaries on their milieus, and as such they share, along with irony, the effect of making the reader uncertain of the exact locus from which their speeches proceed—their *locus loquendi*, if I may invent a critical term. Sturdy no-nonsense commonsense is the basis for one of their guises, though this can at any time modulate into almost frightening sophistication. And both guises can suddenly give way to childlike naiveté— the kind of thing that enables the child in the old story to see that the emperor has no clothes on. And occasionally both seem genuinely naive, becoming parodies of adult behavior in the same way that small children are. One might say that the Wife of Bath and Falstaff share a Wordsworthian child's vision, uncluttered by conventions, with intimations of immorality. And each has a fourth guise as well, though one they do not share: the Wife's is the ferocious aggressive intensity of the shrew, while Falstaff's, rather surprisingly, is that of injured innocence.

Chaucer is careful to confirm our impression of the Wife of Bath's instability of guise when, after the Pardoner's interruption, she consents to his request that she teach him about marriage with an apology, which under the color of clarification produces obfuscation:

> . . . I pray to al this company
> If that I speke after my fantasy
> As taketh not agrefe of that I say,
> For mine entent is not but to playe. [D 189–92]

We know precisely what the meanings of the word *fantasy* are, but unfortunately we do not know which of the two dominant meanings is the right one. Serious scholars—over-serious, in my opinion—have suggested that she means by *fantasy* imagination, not delight and, hence, that the whole story of her marriages is a fabrication, just as she tells us that her version of what her old husbands used to say to her when they came home drunk is a fabrication. But to deny that the Wife's account of her marriages is true is to raise the insuperable problem of evaluating the truth of a fiction in relation to the truth of a fiction within a fiction. Are the separate stories in *Don Quixote* more or less true than the story of *Don Quixote*? And, in order to complicate matters, the Wife does not quite say that she is speaking after her fantasy, but asks her hearers not to be offended *if* she speaks after her fantasy: we do not know when, if ever, the protasis of the conditional sentence begins to govern the discourse. Chaucer has been careful to give the Wife of Bath's ironies an elusiveness that makes them seem to be in perpetual motion.

The Wife tells us that her intent is only to play, and that is perhaps true most of the time of Falstaff. But as with the Wife, we are often unsure where his play begins or leaves off. The most obvious example is at the tavern after the Gadshill robbery. When Falstaff boasts of his heroic behavior, and in doing so multiplies two rogues in buckram suits into eleven and then adds three misbegotten knaves in Kendall green (II.iv.191–224), does he really expect the Prince and Poins to believe him? Actually, the question is easily answered, but answered, unhappily, as easily in the negative as in the affirmative. For Falstaff's expectations are as obscure as those of Chaucer's Pardoner, when, after fully exposing his fraudulence, he tries at the end of his tale to get the Host to buy some of his pardon (C 919–59). Critical argument is unending about whether the Pardoner really thought he could make a sale. The Host's furious response reflects his ill ease, because the Pardoner is a user and exemplifier of irony whose center the Host cannot locate. The reader is apt to be similarly ill at ease with Falstaff, and critics occasionally imitate the Host's treatment of the Pardoner by trying to reduce Falstaff's various guises to mere matter, and to gross matter at that. In a way, that is what Hal is forced to do when he finally rejects Falstaff. He did not overhear Falstaff's catechism on honor at Shrewsbury (V.i.129–41), but as King he would recognize that such playful subversions are more dangerous to his rule than any robberies at Gadshill, despite, or perhaps because of, the catechism's taking the elementary form of a schoolboy's lesson. Such an ambiguously motivated question of Falstaff's when he learns that the party they are about to rob at Gadshill consists of eight or ten men, as "'Zounds, will they not rob us?" (II.ii.65) may appear on the printed page as pure play. But spoken, it develops ambiguity. Should one say, "Will they not *rob* us?" like an honest man fearing to fall among thieves, or "Will *they* not rob *us*?" like a thief recognizing that there may be other thieves with superior numbers?

And what is one to make—and what did Hal make?—of Falstaff's soliloquy just before the robbery, which is overheard by the Prince?

> Well, I doubt not but to die a fair death for all this, if I scape hanging for killing that rogue [Prince Hal]. I have forsworn his company hourly any time this two and twenty years, and yet I am bewitch'd with the rogue's company. If the rascal have not given me medicines to make me love him, I'll be hanged. It could not be else, I have drunk medicines. [II.ii.13–20]

In order to put a consistently cynical and knowing base under Falstaff so he can be pinned down, critics have suggested that he knows Prince Hal is listening, and that he is saying what will ingratiate himself with him. But this is to explain a mystery by denying its existence: It is really another irony that the love of Falstaff for the Prince is real, though it is expressed here at once with a childlike naiveté and in the ironical language Falstaff often uses in public, with the reason for his love being assigned to, even blamed on, the Prince, a rogue who he feels has corrupted him. Is there some chance that the "reverent vice," as the Prince calls him, really has a heart that is suitable for a "goodly portly man, i' faith, and a corpulent, of a cheerful look, a pleasing eye, and a most noble carriage" (II.iv.421–23) as Falstaff describes himself? Perhaps.

The Wife of Bath's bases are equally troublesome. Her approach to the Bible and its commentators is a combination of naive literalism, a somewhat questioning sense of reverence, and plain commonsense grounded in experience. She has trouble, as moralistic critics are always pointing out, understanding that it is not the letter but the spirit that one must heed. The relevant significance of Christ's remark to the Samaritan women at the well, "Thou hast had five husbands and that man that now hath thee is not thy husband" (D 14–25), eludes her. And well it might. The proposition, of which she has been told, that the text somehow limits the number of husbands a woman can have to five (six being over the legal limit) stems from St. Jerome, who heaped his Pelion of antifeminism upon the antifeminist Ossa of St. Paul. St. Jerome's proposition was based on his misreading of the biblical story, a confusion worse confounded by the Wife when she fails to understand that Christ was referring not to a fifth husband, but to a sixth man to whom the Samaritan woman had said she was not married—a disclaimer suppressed by St. Jerome in his eagerness to see that his reading of the spirit should not be belied by the letter.[11] The tenuousness of such blatantly prejudiced spiritual readings of the Bible is equally reflected in the Wife of Bath's natural perplexity and the saint's willful inaccuracy. The absurdity is enhanced by the Wife's attempt to fit the proposition to herself by misreading St. Jerome's misreading, so that the number of husbands comes out to four plus one questionable one, instead of five plus one man unwedded. Five is her current total if, as she carefully says, the fifth was canonically legal. But she herself can think of no explanation for Christ's choice of the number four, and seems ultimately to decide that the number of consecutive husbands she may have is unlimited.

In dealing with St. Paul, the Wife uses a literalist approach worthy of a puritan reformer. She reminds him of his admission that on the subject of matrimony he had no higher authority (79–82). And she uses those texts that please her and lets the others go without notice. She knows that her husband should leave father and mother and take only unto her (30–31), and that she has power over her husband's body and not he (158–59), but she fails to mention any reciprocal obligation. Yet in so doing she is providing a naturally ironic commentary on generations of celibate experts on marriage, who endlessly repeat the woman's obligation and rarely mention the husband's. She is understandably uncertain why, if the patriarchs had a number of wives, multiplicity of spouses is now deemed reprehensible (55–58). She envies Solomon his many spouses, and suppresses—if she is aware of it—the fact that Solomon's uxoriousness in building temples to his wives' strange gods brought the Lord's wrath down on him (35–43).

She even performs a bit of sophisticated biblical interpretation of her own: first she wishes that she had Solomon's gift from God of being "refreshed" by spouses as often as he was (37–38); later she remarks that she is willing to let virgins be bread of pure wheat seed and wives barley bread; but finally she notes that with barley bread Christ "refreshed" many a man (143–46)—a mixture of letter and spirit that would do credit to a patristic, intellectually speaking, if not morally. Her culminating combining of simplicity and sophistication occurs in her lament, "Alas, alas, that euer loue was sin!" (614). Moralists sometimes seize on this as proof that the Wife was aware of her sinfulness and regretted it. But her apparent repentance is actually parody, a parody of the repentance one is led to expect. It is not Christian remorse that provokes her exclamation, but regret that because sexual love is sin its availability to her has been reduced. An old age of repentance is no more the Wife of Bath's prospectus than it ever was Falstaff's.

Both the Wife of Bath and Falstaff are, though utterly charming, perfectly horrible people. It is true that the Wife's victims are mostly husbands who deserved the abuse and exploitation she practiced on them. But she is a habitual fornicator and adulterer, and her ability to be disagreeable when her authority is challenged is not limited to the domestic scene, as any parish wife who gets to the Offering before her learns. Falstaff is not only a drunken old man, but a thief, a deadbeat, an exploiter of poor women and shallow justices from whom he borrows money that he fails to repay, an abuser of the King's press, a lecher, a liar, and heaven knows what else. And as two very dubious citizens, they should *not* be sentimentalized. I say this very sternly, for I am aware that I can never discuss them at length without sentimentalizing them. I blame this on their creators, who seem to have loved them dearly while endowing them with enough vices to supply an army of the wicked—enough vices and enough vitality. I have always supposed that *Henry IV Part 2* exists largely because Falstaff's vitality was too bountiful to be confined in *Part 1*; and surely *The Merry Wives of Windsor* exists because of him. Shakespeare originally promised that Falstaff would show up in *Henry V* (Epilogue to *Henry IV, Part 2*), but prudently changed his mind and killed him off before he could stop Hal from ever getting to Agincourt. The Wife of Bath managed to get herself into *The Merchant's Tale* (E 1685–87) and into Chaucer's "Envoy to Bukton"—also an unruly fiction who would not remain on the page where she belonged. Both characters took on life independent of their creators.

And both are associated with passages of unrivaled emotional effectiveness, passages that are as splendid tributes to human vitality as any I know. The Wife of Bath speaks hers, and Falstaff's is spoken about him. The Wife of Bath's is a digression from her account of her fourth husband:

> My fourth husbonde was a reuelour—
> This is to saie, he had a paramour.
> And I was yong, and full of ragerie,
> Stubburne and strong, and ioly as a Pie.
> Well coud I daunce to an Harpe smale,
> And sing, iwis, as a Nitingale,
> Whan I had dronken a draught of swete wine.
> Metellus, the foule churle, the swine,
> That with a staffe biraft his wife her life
> For she dronk wine, though I had be his wife,
> He should not haue daunted me fro drinke.
> And after wine of Venus must I thinke,
> For also seker as cold engendreth haile,
> A likorus mouth must haue a lecherous taile.
> In women vinolent is no defence:
> This knowe lecherous by experience.

> But lord Christ, when it remembreth me
> Vpon my youth and my iolite,
> It tickleth me about the hart roote—
> Vnto this daie is doeth my hart boote—
> That I haue had my worlde as in my time.
> But age, alas, that all woll enuenime
> Hath me biraft my beaute and my pith.
> Let go, fare well, the deuile go therwith!
> The floure is gon, ther nis no more to tell;
> The bran, as I best can, now mote I sell.
> But yet to be right merie woll I fonde.
> Now forth to tell of my fourth husbonde! [D 453–80]

I doubt that many who have spent their lives far better than the Wife are able to look back with such a sense of benediction as that with which the Wife of Bath looks back on her misspent past. She has enjoyed life, and will go on enjoying it. And although she is a very immoral woman, she has, in her enjoyment, perfect integrity.

Perhaps Falstaff was incapable of so philosophical a looking back—that was not one of his guises. But Shakespeare gives him the same kind of emotional justification in the erstwhile Mistress Quickly's account of his death in *Henry V*, a kind of apology by the dramatist for Hal's shabby treatment of him and the merry wives' triumph over him. In the scene, Bardolph has just reacted violently to Falstaff's death, wishing he were "with him, wheresome'er he is, either in heaven or hell." The Hostess replies:

> Nay sure, he's not in hell; he's in Arthur's bosom, if ever man went to Arthur's bosom. 'A made a finer end, and went away and it had been any christom child. 'A parted ev'n just between twelve and one, ev'n at the turning o' th' tide; for after I saw him fumble with the sheets, and play with flowers, and smile upon his finger's end, I knew there was but one way; for his nose was as sharp as a pen, and 'a [talk'd] of green fields. "How now, Sir John?" quoth I, "what, man? be a' good cheer." So 'a cried out, "God, God, God!" three or four times. Now I, to comfort him, bid him 'a should not think of God; I hop'd there was no need to trouble himself with any such thoughts yet. So 'a bade me lay more clothes on his feet. I put my hand into the bed and felt them, and they were as cold as any stone; then I felt to his knees, [and they were as cold as any stone;] and so up'ard and up'ard, and all was as cold as any stone.[12]

Both passages occur in marvelously comic contexts, and both are perfectly controlled in their tone, with the pathos not spoiling the humor, or vice versa.

I don't think we should worry about the Hostess' misplacement of Falstaff in Arthur's bosom, any more than we should worry about the final destination of the wife of Bath's soul—*she* never did. Both characters are in any case still very much alive, very much their creators' celebrations of life, and I can hardly think of anything better to celebrate.

NOTES

8. A number of similarities between the two characters have of course been noted in the criticism, but no actual influence of Chaucer on Shakespeare's concept of Falstaff has been shown. Ann Thompson (*Shakespeare's Chaucer*, p. 83) speaks rather scornfully of "the attempts of some critics to draw comparisons between such figures as Falstaff and the Wife of Bath as 'rich comic characters',", on the uncertain grounds that Shakespeare "seems to have thought of Chaucer *primarily* as a writer of romantic and courtly poetry rather than as a comic naturalist" (p. 82). But this is to allow a preconception to override any evidence the text may provide to the contrary. In "The Non-Comic, Non-Tragic Wife: Chaucer's Alys as Sociopath," *Chaucer Reviewed*, 12 (1978), 171, Donald Sands disallows all comparison between Falstaff and the Wife of Bath by announcing, "There is no abysm of evil in him, and such an abysm may exist in Alys." Against moralization so self-assured and so prejudiced neither the Wife of Bath nor literature itself has any defense. Perhaps the best reply to Sands is to quote an equally surprising statement by Nevill Coghill—here pulled rudely out of context but not falsifying his opinion: "Chaucer had no vision of evil": see *Elizabethan and Jacobean Studies Presented to F. P. Wilson*, p. 99.

9. See *Piers Plowman by William Langland: An Edition of the C-Text*, ed. Derek Pearsall (Berkeley and Los Angeles: University of California Press, 1978), Passus V, lines 32–57.

10. Judith J. Kollmann, "Ther is noon oother incubus but he: *The Canterbury Tales, Merry Wives of Windsor* and Falstaff," in *Chaucerian Shakespeare: Adaptation and Transformation*, ed. E. T. Donaldson and J. J. Kollmann ([Detroit:] Michigan Consortium for Medieval and Early Modern Studies, 1983), pp. 43–68.

11. See my "Designing a Camel; or, Generalizing the Middle Ages," *TSL*, 22 (1977), 1–16, for a fuller discussion of Jerome's misinterpretation.

12. *King Henry V*, II.iii.9–26. Despite its brilliance, I find Theobald's famous emendation of F1 "Table" to "babbl'd" too emotive, and prefer the conjectural emendation "talk'd." The bracketed words near the end of the passage are in Q1–3, and seem to me to have been left out of F1 through scribal error.

1986—C. L. Barber and Richard P. Wheeler. "From Mixed History to Heroic Drama: The *Henriad*," from *The Whole Journey: Shakespeare's Power of Development*

C. L. Barber was a professor of literature at the University of California, Santa Cruz. He also wrote *Shakespeare's Festive Comedy*. Richard Wheeler, a professor English for many years, is vice provost and dean of the Graduate College at the University of Illinois at Urbana-Champaign.

The two parts of *Henry IV* open out onto what seems to be the whole of English society, with a splendid development of Shakespeare's range, both in subjects and in the complexity of attitudes toward experience poised against one another. In *Shakespeare's Festive Comedy* I emphasized the way this richness, which the criticism of the last fifty years has variously recognized, is organized by the polarity of holiday and everyday in Shakespeare's culture.[1] "Mingling kings and clowns" in the native theatrical tradition Sidney deplored, the two plays are organized so that *Part One* balances Misrule against Rule, with Falstaff, as Holiday, asking to be Everyday; then *Part Two*, by a kind of Trial of Carnival, leads to the sacrifice of Falstaff, who is made to carry off bad luck and sin as the Prince makes atonement with his strong but guilty father. In my view, the dramatist resorts to magical action instead of dramatizing it, in inviting us to accept the ritual expulsion of Falstaff as scapegoat for the social and political ills of England. By setting the Sonnets against these plays, I think we can see how the expulsion of Falstaff, and with it the inhibition of Falstaffian ironies, is part of an effort to use the drama to establish a new relationship to manhood.

Old Offenses and Affections New

Sonnet 146, "Poor soul, the center of my sinful earth," can serve as an entrance into a dramatic rhythm that uses the rejection of Falstaff to try to close over the ironic perspective on heroic action the two parts of *Henry IV* have opened up. After noting in chapter 6 that many regard this poem as a "Christian palinode" that resolves the conflicts engendered by the poet's search for fulfillment in human objects of love, we argued that this sonnet cannot be fully satisfying because it simplifies so drastically the complex sensibility engaged in the affirmations of human love. If we look at Sonnet 146 in relation to the Henry IV plays, we can see it as an effort by the poet to turn away from his former self, as Hal turns away from Falstaff:

> I know thee not, old man, fall to thy prayers.
> How ill white hairs becomes a fool and jester!
> I have long dreamt of such a kind of man,
> So surfeit-swell'd, so old, and so profane;
> But being awak'd, I do despise my dream.
> Make less thy body (hence) and more thy grace,
> Leave gormandizing, know the grave doth gape
> For thee thrice wider than for other men.
> Reply not to me with a fool-born jest,
> Presume not that I am the thing I was,

> For God doth know, so shall the world perceive,
> That I have turn'd away my former self;
> So will I those that kept me company. (*2H4* V.v.47–59)

Here the newly crowned Henry V is "the soul of state" (*Troilus and Cressida* III.iii.202), and Falstaff is synoptic for its corrupted body: "Then, soul, live thou upon thy servant's loss" (Sonnet 146) is the order of the day. Hal is doing what he advises Falstaff to do, and what the poet urges on himself in the sonnet: "Buy terms divine in selling hours of dross." "Make less thy body (hence) and more thy grace" recalls the poet's repudiation of his own body in the sonnet: "let that pine to aggravate thy store." As Henry V's heroic-Christian resolve replaces the passive-Christian resolution of the sonnet, the grave that gapes for "gormandizing" Falstaff displaces the death to which the poet turns with religious resignation:

> Within be fed, without be rich no more.
>   So shalt thou feed on death, that feeds on men,
>   And death once dead, there's no more dying then.

Behind the generalizing sonnets one can often hear echoes of other poems whose attitudes are in considerable tension with the sort of simplifying finality we get in Sonnet 146 < . . . >. Just so, Henry's dismissive severity can recall Falstaff's characteristically ironic self-justifications, centered on the very surfeit-swelled excess now banished:

> Dost thou hear, Hal? Thou knowest in the state of innocency Adam fell, and what should poor Jack Falstaff do in the days of villainy? Thou seest I have more flesh than another man, and therefore more frailty. (*1H4* III.iii.164–68)

The repudiation of Falstaff, however, is serious business. Shakespeare *is* exploring the soul of state and the exigencies of political action. In the last act of *2 Henry IV* and in *Henry V* he is dramatizing the way a leader can become an organizing presence for a society by meeting needs cognate to those the poet has typically sought to fulfill, not in such Christian resignation as we find in Sonnet 146, but in the presence of the young man. In *Henry V* the Chorus gives explicit expression to the satisfaction the heroic presence of the young king provides:

> . . . every wretch, pining and pale before,
> Beholding him, plucks comfort from his looks.
> A largess universal, like the sun,
> His liberal eye doth give to every one,

Thawing cold fear, that mean and gentle all
Behold, as may unworthiness define,
A little touch of Harry in the night. (IV. Cho. 41–47)

Here the Chorus uses the same sort of imagery to describe the King's countenance, in the night before Agincourt, that the Sonnets use about the largess of the young man's countenance. On the social, historical side, the Chorus is describing the process Freud deals with in *Group Psychology and the Analysis of the Ego*, by which a charismatic leader can enter into the psychic economy of followers in a way comparable to what happens in falling in love.[2] The play *Henry V* both generalizes about this and localizes it in persons (Fluellen, for instance, as he puts his Welsh individuality in the devoted service of "your Majesty's manhood" [IV.viii.33–34]), while wrestling with what it involves in the person of the King.

Henry V also invites the audience to take its hero king in the same way that his society takes him. Just how far it goes in this direction, whether it is ironic about this, and if so, how, are questions that are perennially in dispute among good critics. In its incompletely controlled tone, *Henry V* is remarkably like such absolutely phrased but finally precarious sonnets as 146, or 116—"Let me not to the marriage of true minds"—and, I think, for the same reason: the poet is using the work to meet *part* of his need as if it met the whole of it, with part of his need and sensibility kept out. But the drama provides a crucial resource that the Sonnets do not; it allows the dramatist to throw the stress, not on the need that seeks realization in a young man who cannot be brought into the utterance directed to him, but on the realization of that need in the character who meets it in a dramatic action.

The religiousness of Sonnet 146, as was emphasized earlier, has no object of worship; the poem does not turn to God or Christ in place of the young man or mistress, as Donne, for example, turns from his dead wife to Christ. At the close of *2 Henry IV*, however, there *is* such an object, along with the prudential revulsion to piety of the sonnet; the object is Henry V, even as the dramatist rejects the part of the poet that has been in Falstaff. Although the scene of the rejection is a reprise of many similar gestures in the Sonnets, where the poet makes nothing of himself to make the beloved everything, it is taking place on the main line of Shakespeare's dramatic development, and with dramatic finality—for the moment at least. Because in the dramatic form Shakespeare can hypostatize what the Sonnets seek to hold together, it is possible to leave the Falstaff sensibility behind and still take as object a young man—in whom full manhood and authority are to be envisaged as being achieved. The sonneteer's role in realizing the life of the friend is taken over by the dramatist as dramatist. As in the Sonnets the all-or-nothing investment is not in a religious incarnation or transcendence but in a beloved friend, so here in *Henry V* Shakespeare invests in a secular hero king.

As we move from Falstaff's many-sided relationship with Hal to the celebration of Henry V's heroic virtues, the shift in dramatic perspective is akin to what we find in the Sonnets if we move from the action in poems that address Shakespeare's infidelity to the friend to the eloquent affirmation of unqualified love in Sonnet 116. I have already considered difficulties about the tone of the affirmation in this sonnet, "Let me not to the marriage of true minds," following Carol Neely in her analysis of the way certain of the sonnets attempt to stand back from the "motion in corruption" of the sequence and the way this attempt breaks down.[3] When viewed from the perspective of sonnets that explicitly bring out other, more disruptive dimensions of the love for the friend, the unqualified affirmation of love in Sonnet 116 becomes precarious. The tension between the affirmation of this sonnet and the poems around it is similar to the tensions *inside* neighboring sonnets, between their hopeful finales and the stressful acknowledgments with which they begin.

We have considered the self-knowledge such poems convey, in chapter 6. Here it is the locked-in tension of these sonnets that contrasts with the similar but different things we get with Falstaff and his way of knowing and affirming himself in relation to Hal. Falstaff certainly fits in many ways the poet's self-description in Sonnet 110, written after an interval of separation:

> Alas 'tis true, I have gone here and there,
> And made myself a motley to the view,
> Gored mine own thoughts, sold cheap what is most dear,
> Made old offences of affections new.
> Most true it is, that I have looked on truth
> Askance and strangely . . .

But instead of suffering regrets about having "sold cheap what is most dear," with the strain this puts on the poet's effort to repudiate his past self and proclaim renewal, Falstaff rejoices in selling dear what, with his powers, comes cheap:

> I will devise matter enough out of this Shallow to keep Prince Harry in continual laughter the wearing out of six fashions . . . O, it is much that a lie with a slight oath and a jest with a sad brow will do with a fellow that never had the ache in his shoulders! (*2H4* V.i.78–84)

In this instance, the self-congratulatory enthusiasm belongs to Falstaff riding for a fall in *Part Two*. We can participate fully in Falstaff's gall as he relishes future prospects for opportunistic intimacy. We can also see, as he cannot, the movement of a dramatic action that is fast putting such wishful prospects, and the Prince, out of Falstaff's range, however great the imaginative powers through which he seeks to exploit them. But with Sonnet 110—which moves in an opposite direction to this action, from self-depletion and separation to wishful renewal through the friend's love—it is hard to settle what the tone is; as often with the Sonnets, the poet is using the poetry for special pleading that is not framed by anything comparable to the controlled interplay of perspectives the drama can provide.

Like Sonnet 110, Sonnet 109 ("O never say that I was false of heart") broods over absences that have "seemed my flame to qualify." Pairing these poems as "nimble apologia," Stephen Booth sees *comic* reference to perversion in 109:

> Never believe, though in my nature reigned
> All frailties that beseige all kinds of blood,
> That it could so preposterously be stained
> To leave for nothing all thy sum of good.

Of the travel simile by which Shakespeare understands his return to his soul lodged in his beloved's breast—"That is my home of love; if I have ranged / Like him that travels I return again"—Booth comments: "Shakespeare's purpose is presumably to display a Falstaff-like gall in solemnly making a logical-sounding equation between two non-comparable things: the journeys of a traveler and the promiscuous sexual liaisons of an unfaithful lover."[4] But surely the tone of this poem is ardently conflictual: it pleads, partly by the poet's acknowledging polymorphous temptation, for reconciliation that would accept the actual complexity of the poet's nature. Sonnets 109 and 110 are as moving in their way as Sonnet 116 is in its way. But there is no freedom for Falstaff-like gall in the relationship to the young man as these poems present it—the all-or-nothing bond precludes it: "For nothing this wide universe I call, / Save thou, my rose; in it thou art my all" (Sonnet 109). Hence, surely, part of the joy in creating Falstaff.

Where "Let me not to the marriage of true minds" works to submerge disruptive possibilities within a sweeping affirmation of love, Falstaff's incantatory denials of his disabling age, whoring, drunkenness, gluttony, obesity, and cowardice become an outrageous affirmation of himself:

> My lord, the man I know.... But to say I know more harm in him than in myself, were to say more than I know. That he is old, the more the pity, his white hairs do witness it, but that he is, saving your reverence, a whoremaster, that I utterly deny. (*1H4* II.iv.464–70)

What mock-king Hal, rehearsing his interview with his father, has denounced as scandalous "impediments" to the old ruffian's claims on the young prince, Falstaff denies or turns into virtues; all are swept into the accumulating rhythm of his iterative prose, splendidly varied at the moment of climax:

No, my good lord, banish Peto, banish Bardolph, banish Poins, but for sweet Jack Falstaff, kind Jack Falstaff, true Jack Falstaff, valiant Jack Falstaff, and therefore more valiant, being as he is old Jack Falstaff, banish not him thy Harry's company, banish not him thy Harry's company—banish plump Jack, and banish all the world. (lines 474–80)

Shakespeare in Sonnet 116 ascends into poetry as though into a waking dream: one can follow him into it and feel the marriage of true minds without impediments; or, on reading it in relation to more troubled sonnets, one can glimpse under its surface what in Falstaff's waking dream is there for all to see. In the play we can, with Hal, enjoy the contradictions, which are, "like their father that begets them, gross as a mountain, open, palpable" (*1H4* II.iv.225–26). "Dost thou hear me, Hal?" "Ay, and mark thee too, Jack" (II.iv.209–10). Instead of the tensions of anxious-pleading protestation, as in "Since my appeal says I did strive to prove / The constancy and virtue of your love" (Sonnet 117), there is delightful release as we at once admire and dismiss Falstaff's excuses and evasions:

Prince Hal. Sirrah, do I owe you a thousand pound?
Falstaff. A thousand pound, Hal? a million, thy love is worth a million; thou owest me thy love. (III.iii.135–37)

In the Sonnets there is a queasiness about the latent self-love displaced onto the highborn young man:

Sin of self-love possesseth all mine eye,
. . . .
Methinks no face so gracious is as mine,
. . . .
But when my glass shows me myself indeed
Beated and chopped with tanned antiquity,
Mine own self love quite contrary I read;
    Self so self-loving were iniquity.
    'Tis thee, myself, that for myself I praise,
    Painting my age with beauty of thy days. (Sonnet 62)

Falstaff's self-love is right out in the open, and at his most winning "plump Jack" has all the charm of a little child:

Chief Justice. Do you set down your name in the scroll of youth, that are written down old with all the characters of age? . . . and every part about you blasted with antiquity? . . .

> *Falstaff.* My lord, I was born about three of the clock in the afternoon, with a white head and something of a round belly.
> (*2H4* I.ii.178–80, 184, 187–89)

Self-disabling metaphor in the Sonnets is literalized in the drama—and yet does not daunt Falstaff:

> Speak of my lameness, and I straight will halt. (Sonnet 89)

> A pox of this gout! or a gout of this pox! for the one or the other plays the rogue with my great toe. 'Tis no matter if I do halt, I have the wars for my color, and my pension shall seem the more reasonable. A good wit will make use of any thing. (*2H4* I.ii.243–48)

The marvelous autonomy of Falstaff goes with his constant relaxation into physical gluttony, as against the strain on the sonneteer's psychic "gluttoning":

> So are you to my thoughts as food to life,
> . . . .
> And by and by clean starved for a look;
> . . . .
>   Thus do I pine and surfeit day by day,
>   Or gluttoning on all, or all away. (Sonnet 75)

On one side, the sonneteer is getting his comeuppance. Decrepit Falstaff takes delight in seeing his active Hal do deeds of youth in killing Hotspur: "Well said, Hal! to it Hal! Nay, you shall find no boy's play here, I can tell you" (*1H4* V.iv.75–76). The merely vicarious enjoyment of manhood is explicit in "no boy's play here." A self-interest in love that seeks to leap over caste difference is made obvious in Falstaff; so also is overestimation of what artful wit can do across such difference: "I know the young king is sick for me. Let us take any man's horses, the laws of England are at my commandement" (*2H4* V.iii.135–37). A resentment, potential in the Sonnets, at what belonging to a higher caste can do for someone actually mediocre is expressed and then rebuked as the Prince overhears Falstaff characterize him as "A good shallow young fellow. 'A would have made a good pantler, 'a would 'a' chipp'd bread well" (*2H4* II.iv.237–38). Responding to Doll Tearsheet's question about Poins—"Why does the Prince love him so then?"—Falstaff speaks of roistering talents shared by Poins and the Prince: "gambol faculties . . . that show a weak mind and an able body, for which the Prince admits him" (*2H4* II.iv.243, 251–52). "From me far off, with others all too near" echoes from Sonnet 61. As many have noted, Falstaff seems to carry a suggestion of

Shakespeare. The buffoon's triumphant gluttonous and dramatic aggression is paid for by such playful self-mockery.

Sources of humiliation or helplessness for the Sonnets poet become resources of self-aggrandizement and (ultimately illusory) control for Falstaff.

> O for my sake do you with fortune chide,
> The guilty goddess of my harmful deeds,
> That did not better for my life provide
> Than public means which public manners breeds. (Sonnet 111)

"I am Fortune's steward," Falstaff exalts when Pistol brings news of the old king's death: "Blessed are they that have been my friends, and woe to my Lord Chief Justice" (*2H4* V.iii.130–31, 137–38). In the sonnet, "public means which public manners breeds" clearly refers to Shakespeare's gaining his livelihood in the theater:

> Thence comes it that my name receives a brand,
> And almost thence my nature is subdued
> To what it works in, like the dyer's hand.

Falstaff, for his public manners, receives one brand after another:

> *Sheriff.* One of them is well known, my gracious lord, A gross fat man....
> *Prince.* This oily rascal is known as well as Paul's.
> (*1H4* II.iv.509–526)

England is Falstaff's theater, and he takes heart that "Men of all sorts take a pride to gird at me" (*2H4* I.ii.6).

Falstaff, within the plays, is always playing, freed by (and condemned to) a theatrical existence: "Out, ye rogue, play out the play, I have much to say in the behalf of that Falstaff" (*1H4* II.iv.484–85). The poet, in writing the Sonnets, is freed and condemned in a different way to living by words and gestures, since it is by means of the poems that their author lives in his friend and his friend in him, as in Sonnet 81:

> When all the breathers of this world are dead,
>   You still shall live—such virtue hath my pen—
>   Where breath most breathes, ev'n in the mouths of men.

Such immediate consummation in utterance, as we observed in the chapter on the Sonnets, gives something like an immediate experience of immortality. We have a similar experience in the great speeches where Falstaff eludes morality and mortality: "What is honor?" "The better part of valor." But the dramatic context places the experience within limits controlled by the dramatist; with the Sonnets it is only by our assessment of the potentially conflictual relationships between poems that we can place—never fully satisfactorily—the event that is such a poem as Sonnet 81. One must add that from Morgann on down to Roy Battenhouse in his essay "Falstaff as Parodist and Perhaps Holy Fool," Falstaff has been seen as triumphing in an unqualified way, or a way that somehow transcends qualification.[5]

As he relishes his role at the beginning of *Part Two*, Falstaff makes a brag that can fit his author:

The brain of this foolish-compounded clay, man, is not able to invent
any thing that intends to laughter more than I invent or is invented
on me: I am not only witty in myself, but the cause that wit is in other
men. (I.ii.7–10)

Shakespeare of course was "the cause that wit is in other men" across the board, inventing all the parts for his fellows. There is good reason to feel uneasy in setting out to claim, as here, that Shakespeare is more in one part than in others. After all, as many have pointed out, Falstaff's role is compounded of several traditional roles: clown, fool, the Vice or Good Fellowship luring innocents to the tavern in the moralities, buffoon, Lord of Misrule, Carnival.[6] If there is Shakespeare in him, to be in everybody on stage was Shakespeare's professional job. One can add that, since Falstaff is a holiday figure, protagonist of saturnalian release, Shakespeare in animating him would be going on holiday—taking with him, as revelers do, his own everyday powers now heightened by being free to express otherwise inhibited attitudes. Moreover, Shakespeare's whole controlling dramatic construction is using Falstaff, along with Hotspur, Henry IV, and the rest, in the rhythm of the polarized action, to present the development of Hal as an inclusive royal nature. By design, the two parts of *Henry IV* are centered on the Prince, not Falstaff.

Although one must grant all this, and *gladly*, in the perspective of Shakespeare's whole development something more is going on: Shakespeare is acting out the Falstaff relationship to life in order to try to banish it—"I do, I will." The goal is to disinvest in the vicarious enjoyment of manhood in order to reinvest in Manhood itself. The exigencies of the whole development are encountered (beyond full control) in the unsatisfactoriness of the hero king who emerges from the process. Hotspur, in the scene just before the Boar's Head revels, exclaims "I could divide myself and go to buffets" (*1H4* II.iii.32). Of course this is exactly what Hotspur cannot do. Shakespeare, however, is doing just such dividing, and while the divided parts are at play or at civil war, the drama has an inclusiveness which we can feel the Prince to be sharing from behind his circumspection. But the conclusion of *Part Two*, with its rejection of Falstaff, in effect tries for the simplification of such a sonnet as 110, which puts the "old offenses" of the poet behind in the renewed affiliation to the friend: "Then give me welcome, next my heav'n the best, / Ev'n to thy pure and most most loving breast." The play asks us to put Falstaff's perspective behind as we admire the heroic enterprise of King Henry V. Like "the star to every wand'ring bark" of Sonnet 116, the young king of *Henry V* becomes "this star of England" (Epi. 6), giving direction and inspiration to a whole nation that can be renewed in his presence, after having become mired in the old offenses of previous reigns. But in *Henry V*, without the full ironic interplay of perspectives that holds until the very end of *2 Henry IV*, we are back to such conflictual submission to an idealized figure as we have in the Sonnets.

"Ev'n at the Turning o' th' Tide"

The marvelous freedom of *Henry IV* depends on a redistribution outward of the aggression which in the Sonnets is so frequently turned inward on the poet. But it is striking that Shakespeare, in dealing for the first time with the transmission of heritage across tension between father and son, alters his sources to eliminate direct expressions of the Prince's hostile or defiant feelings toward his father. In the chronicles Hal and the large retinue he maintains burst in on the court dressed in strange, outlandish costume.[7] Shakespeare's Hal seeks other targets for hostile impulses engendered in a role and a bond that, by his own royal birth, are inescapable. In *The Famous Victories of Henry the Fifth*,[8] the Prince, until his sudden, unmotivated transformation, is a street bully who does undertake to abrogate the laws of England and to make one of his riotous companions a judge when he is crowned. This crude little play dramatizes the episode of Hal's striking the Chief Justice, an incident that is only referred to by Shakespeare in retrospect during the new Henry V's atonement with him at the close of *Part Two*. All explicit reference to the son's hostility is given to the father:

> *Prince.* I never thought to hear you speak again.
> *King.* Thy wish was father, Harry, to that thought.
> (*2H4* IV.v.91–92)

The scene of atonement with the Lord Chief Justice makes explicit an orientation that will be developed (if with some strain) throughout *Henry V*: the young king's aggression is wholly a function of his commitment to the sacramental political role he now embraces. Confronted by the new king, the Chief Justice apprehensively recalls the rationale by which he had imprisoned the rebellious Hal:

> I then did use the person of your father,
> The image of his power lay then in me,

> And in th' administration of his law,
> Whiles I was busy for the commonwealth,
> Your Highness pleased to forget my place,
> The majesty and power of law and justice,
> The image of the King whom I presented.⁹ (*2H4* V.ii.73–79)

Henry V responds by addressing the episode of striking the Chief Justice in a way that makes it part of an expectable pattern of youthful wildness contained politically within harmless limits—the pattern of the two Henry IV plays. He spells out, almost unctuously, the extension of filial commitment to a more general allegiance to authority and law, here embodied in the Chief Justice:

> There is my hand.
> You shall be as a father to my youth,
> My voice shall sound as you do prompt mine ear,
> And I will stoop and humble my intents
> To your well-practic'd wise directions. (V.ii.117–21)

This is pure Henry V, as we come to know him in the next play, always careful to keep righteousness on his side, consulting with the Archbishop of Canterbury about his title to France, denying that uncontrolled passion can have any part in his aggressive action, for "We are no tyrant, but a Christian king, / Unto whose grace our passion is as subject / As is our wretches fett'red in our prisons" (*H5* II.ii.241–43).

When we see Hal at the outset of the Henry IV plays, the rebelliousness acknowledged in him only at the end is expressed by Falstaff:

> *Falstaff.* But I prithee, sweet wag, shall there be gallows standing in England when thou art King? and resolution thus fubb'd as it is with the rusty curb of old father antic the law? Do not thou, when thou art king, hang a thief.
> *Prince.* No, thou shalt.
> *Falstaff.* Shall I? O rare! By the Lord, I'll be a brave judge.
> *Prince.* Thou judgest false already. I mean thou shalt have the hanging of the thieves, and so become a rare hangman. (*1H4* I.ii.58–68)

As Ernst Kris pointed out in a pioneering psychoanalytic essay, "Prince Hal's Conflict,"[10] the Prince's problem is like Hamlet's in that he is in line to inherit from a usurper, but the Oedipal motive is repressed and displaced onto Falstaff, who both covets the power Hal will inherit when the father is dead and absorbs in his own person Hal's aggression toward a father. There is no need at this point to labor the aggressive tendency of Hal's wit in undoing Falstaff's pretensions, "dethroning" him at the Boar's Head during the extempore rehearsal of the interview with the king, enjoying a rhapsody of flyting about "that roasted Manningtree ox with the pudding in his belly, that reverent Vice, that grey Iniquity, that father ruffian, that vanity in years" (*1H4* II.iv.452–54). The aggression becomes deadly in the lines of rejection: "I know thee not, *old man*."

It is dizzying to reflect that in that final scene Shakespeare is dramatizing the kind of rejection which the poet fears in the Sonnets. He gives Falstaff, in his opportunistic eagerness—to see the new king and to control the impression he will make on him—language like the Sonnets:

I will leer upon him as 'a comes by, and do but mark the countenance that he will give me. (*2H4* V.v.6–8)

But when your countenance filled up his line,
Then lacked I matter, that enfeebled mine. (Sonnet 86)

But to stand stain'd with travel, and sweating with desire to see him, thinking of nothing else, putting all affairs else in oblivion, as if there were nothing else to be done but to see him. (*2H4* V.v.24–27)

For nothing this wide universe I call,
Save thou, my rose; in it thou art my all. (Sonnet 109)

Being your slave, what should I do but tend
Upon the hours and times of your desire? (Sonnet 57)

Falstaff then calls out to the approaching king: "God save thy Grace, King Hal! my royal Hal! . . . God save thee, my sweet boy!" (V.v.41, 43).

Of course, the patterns of "worship" in Shakespeare's society, peaking in the kind of courtier courtship lavished on Elizabeth, made common idiom of expressions somewhat like these—Shakespeare skillfully insists on the breach of decorum by Falstaff's inappropriately personal and possessive phrasing, climaxing in "sweet boy!" ("What's new to speak, what now to register, / That may express my love, or thy dear merit? / Nothing, sweet boy" [Sonnet 108].) Falstaff thinks he is calling out to Hal, but it is Henry V who is coming from his coronation. By showing Falstaff, before the king appears, calculating what effects he can hope to produce, Shakespeare demonstrates beyond any doubt how impossible, morally and politically, Falstaff would be as a royal favorite. It is all handled impeccably in social-historical perspective.

Such similarities between the Sonnets and Falstaff's language when he contemplates or addresses Hal also reflect the homogeneity of Shakespeare's idiom, his repertory of tropes and situations, regardless of whether they also reflect changing ways of investing himself in his art. To see them as surveyor's reference points in his development from work to work depends on having the whole territory in view, and on one's sense of their place in the dynamic whole of each work in which they appear. So we need to be aware of the role of the Chorus and its tension with the dramatic action in *Henry V* when we compare

> Behold, as may unworthiness define,
> A little touch of Harry in the night...

with Falstaff's great lie about the action at Gadshill, when "it was so dark thou couldest not see thy hand":

> By the Lord, I knew ye as well as he that made ye. Why, hear you, my masters, was it for me to kill the heir-apparent? Should I turn upon the true prince? Why, thou knowest I am as valiant as Hercules; but beware instinct—the lion will not touch the true prince.
> (*1H4* II.iv.223–24, 267–72)

Falstaff's lie, which Hal heartily enjoys seeing through, is a burlesque of the mystique about magical royalty that undid Richard II, who imagined that the threat to his rule would dissipate when the night-reveler Bolingbroke "Shall see us rising in our throne, the east" (*R2* III.ii.50). One finds similar imagery, expressed with comparable seriousness, when the Sonnets celebrate the renewing presence of the friend. In Sonnet 27, the young man, "like a jewel hung in ghastly night, / Makes black night beauteous." "All days are nights" when the friend is absent in Sonnet 43, "And nights bright days when dreams do show thee me."

On confronting Richard, even Bolingbroke will respond to the grandeur of the king in terms of this imagery:

> See, see, King Richard doth himself appear,
> As doth the blushing discontented sun
> From out the fiery portal of the east,
> When he perceives the envious clouds are bent
> To dim his glory and to stain... (*R2* III.iii.62–66)

Yet it is, of course, Richard's magical identification of himself with such metaphorical equations that deflects him from full confrontation with political realities Bolingbroke knows how to manipulate. The same cluster of images is taken over by Hal in the soliloquy in which he explains for the audience how he is going to make Richard's imagery work, politically, by *using* his wildness and reformation:

> I know you all, and will a while uphold
> The unyok'd humor of your idleness,
> Yet herein will I imitate the sun,
> Who doth permit the base contagious clouds
> To smother up his beauty from the world,
> That when he please again to be himself,
> Being wanted, he may be more wond'red at
> By breaking through the foul and ugly mists
> Of vapors that did seem to strangle him.[11] (*1H4* I.ii.195–203)

By contrast, in the lines of the Chorus in *Henry V* about a magical sunlike presence in the night, the royal mystique is again being used seriously. In following out Hal's project to its heroic completion, with his "largess universal, like the sun, . . . / Thawing cold fear" among his soldiers, Shakespeare's search for idealized manhood carries on in a heroic mode the effort of the Sonnets poet to live through the life of his friend. It is essential to this project that Falstaff, and with him his ironic, mocking perspective on the mystique of royalty, be left behind.

From the vantage point of Shakespeare's development, it is exactly right that he did *not* carry out the program, suggested by the epilogue for *Part Two*, to "continue the story, with Sir John in it, and make merry with fair Katherine of France, where (for any thing I know) Falstaff shall die of a sweat, unless already 'a be kill'd with your hard opinions." Certainly Falstaff was not killed in the audience's opinions, as contemporary allusions to his role, and its rehandling in *The Merry Wives of Windsor*, make clear. What we learn in *Henry V*—that "The King has kill'd his heart" (II.i.88)—fits with the deeper levels of feeling underlying all the self-love and self-aggrandizement of his buffoonery, the level of feeling in the Sonnets:

> But do thy worst to steal thyself away,
> For term of life thou art assur'd mine,
> And life no longer than thy love will stay,
> For it depends upon that love of thine. (Sonnet 92)

It is not so much that Falstaff loves Hal, but that Hal's love is for Falstaff the basis of his sense of self, however far he ranges in making himself a motley within the tavern world or sharking on Shallow in the country. On his side, Falstaff's love is as selfish *and* sincere as an infant's for its parent: "thy love is worth a million" in patronage, certainly, but also because "Thy sweet love remem'bred such wealth brings, / That then I scorn to change my state with kings" (Sonnet 29).

Sonnet 87 uses the poet's characteristic tendency toward self-effacement in an uncharacteristic reckoning with the prospect of losing the friend: "Farewell, thou art too dear for my possessing, / And like enough thou know'st thy estimate." At the end of *Part Two*, Falstaff finds that Henry V is too dear for his possessing, and very well knows his estimate. "Thus have I had thee as a dream doth flatter: / In sleep a king, but waking no such matter" (Sonnet 87) could serve to spell out the recognition we do not see banished Falstaff live to make. The poet, in the "farewell" sonnets that follow 87, can find consolation in the idea of dying if the young man abandons him:

> Thou canst not vex me with inconstant mind,
> Since that my life on thy revolt doth lie.
> O what a happy title do I find,
> Happy to have thy love, happy to die! (Sonnet 92)

But here the escape into a fantasy of dying seems too easy: by introducing the logical extreme of the self-negating tendency in the Sonnets, Shakespeare pulls back from such troubling awareness of conflict as we find in many, far richer poems that surrender self-concern to extend the relationship. The effort in Sonnet 92 to bury in death the burden of exploration and understanding contrasts sharply with the powerfully resonant dramatization of the response to Falstaff's death in *Henry V*.

But Mistress Quickly's account of that death involves us in a strange, consenting fascination:

> Nay sure, he's not in hell; he's in Arthur's bosom, if ever man went to Arthur's bosom. 'A made a finer end, and went away and it had been any christom child. 'A parted ev'n just between twelve and one, ev'n at the turning o' th' tide; for after I saw him fumble with the sheets, and play with flowers, and smile upon his finger's end, I knew there was but one way; for his nose was as sharp as a pen, and 'a babbl'd of green fields. "How now, Sir John?" quoth I, "what, man? be a' good cheer." So 'a cried out, "God, God, God!" three or four times. Now I, to comfort him, bid him 'a should not think of God; I hop'd there was no need to trouble himself with any such thoughts yet. So 'a bade me lay more clothes on his feet. I put my hand into the bed and felt them, and they were as cold as any stone; then I felt to his knees, and so up'ard and up'ard, and all was as cold as any stone. (*H5* II.iii.9–26)

Arthur's bosom, the turning of the tide, and the green fields, with or without Theobald's emendation from "a Table . . ." to "'a babbl'd of green fields," make

Falstaff almost a mythological figure. One could go on about him in *Golden Bough* language: a fertility spirit, a dying god, or a scapegoat.

Shakespeare keeps it all believably within the Hostess's idiom, right through to her characteristically modest way of describing the final failure of his potency, a theme picked up in the talk that follows:

> *Nym.* They say he cried out of sack.
> *Hostess.* Ay, that 'a did.
> *Bardolph.* And of women.
> *Hostess.* Nay, that 'a did not.
> *Boy.* Yes, that 'a did, and said they were dev'ls incarnate.
> *Hostess.* 'A could never abide carnation—'twas a color he never lik'd.
> *Boy.* 'A said once, the dev'l would have him about women.
> *Hostess.* 'A did in some sort, indeed, handle women; but then he was rheumatic, and talk'd of the whore of Babylon. (II.iii.27–39)

The "mingled yarn" (*All's Well That Ends Well* IV.iii.71) is beautifully woven here to include both Falstaff with Doll and the burlesque Puritanism in him that may go back to Oldcastle. The whole scene is an elegy, framed by the very unsavory life which, as Pistol says at the close of their previous scene, will go on:

> *Pistol.* His heart is fracted and corroborate.
> *Nym.* The King is a good king, but it must be as it may; he passes some humors and careers.
> *Pistol.* Let us condole the knight, for, lambkins, we will live.
> (II.i.124–28)

The group turn to fresh fields and pastures new at the end:

> *Boy.* Do you not remember, 'a saw a flea stick upon Bardolph's nose, and 'a said it was a black soul burning in hell?
> *Bardolph.* Well, the fuel is gone that maintain'd that fire. That's all the riches I got in his service.
> *Nym.* Shall we shog? the King will be gone from Southampton.
> (II.iii.40–46)

The acceptance of death as a way out of the tensions of all-or-nothing relationship, eroticizing death within a seasonal rhythm, is the burden of one of the greatest of the sonnets. Like Mistress Quickly's elegy, Sonnet 73 culminates with warm life's yielding to the cold of the deathbed:

> That time of year thou mayest in me behold,
> When yellow leaves, or none, or few, do hang

> Upon those boughs which shake against the cold,
> Bare ruined choirs, where late the sweet birds sang.
> In me thou seest the twilight of such day,
> As after sunset fadeth in the west,
> Which by and by black night doth take away,
> Death's second self, that seals up all in rest.
> In me thou seest the glowing of such fire,
> That on the ashes of his youth doth lie,
> As the death-bed whereon it must expire,
> Consumed with that which it was nourished by.
>   This thou perceiv'st, which makes thy love more strong,
>   To love that well which thou must leave ere long.

"Fare well, thou latter spring!" Hal called out gaily after Falstaff's exit from their first scene together, "Fare well, All-hallown summer" (*1H4* I.ii.158–59). He loves that well which he must leave ere long.

On Shakespeare's part: "Greater love hath no man than this, that a man lay down his life for his friends" (John 15:13)—or so vital a part of the life in him as animated Falstaff. To return to a significant point: the sacrifice of Falstaff's vicarious enjoyment of Hal within the Henry IV plays is made to permit vicarious realization of manhood by author and audience in admiring Henry V's "royalty of nature" (*Mac.* III.i.49). The fundamental reason that Falstaff could not go on to help us make merry with fair Katherine of France is that in *Henry V* Shakespeare shifts to using the whole theater as an "oblation" (Sonnet 125) to its hero: in Henry V's world there is no place for Falstaff as, in his strange way, a steward of his excellence. Despite the program, the sacrifice does not entirely work. However admirable the civic or patriotic commitment animating the enterprise, King Henry V, "all shining with the virtues of success," in Empson's phrase,[12] is not adequate to the possibilities for manhood Shakespeare comes to envisage in tragedy.

NOTES

1. C. L. Barber, *Shakespeare's Festive Comedy* (Princeton: Princeton University Press, 1959), pp. 192–221.

2. *The Standard Edition of the Complete Psychological Works of Sigmund Freud*, trans. and ed. James Strachey et al., 24 vols. (London: Hogarth, 1953–74), vol. 18; see esp. 111–16.

3. I am drawing here on Professor Neely's "Detachment and Engagement in Shakespeare's Sonnets: 94, 116, and 129," *PMLA* 92 (1977): 83–95, to which I am greatly indebted.

4. *Shakespeare's Sonnets*, ed. with analytic commentary by Stephen Booth (New Haven: Yale University Press, 1977), p. 351.

5. Maurice Morgann, *An Essay on the Dramatic Character of Sir John Falstaff* (London: T. Davies, 1777); Roy Battenhouse, "Falstaff as Parodist and Perhaps Holy Fool," *PMLA* 90 (1975): 32–52.

6. See *Shakespeare's Festive Comedy*, pp. 67–73 for one consideration of these roles. See also J. Mr. Dover Wilson, *The Fortunes of Falstaff* (Cambridge: Cambridge University Press, 1943).

7. See Geoffrey Bullough, ed., *Narrative and Dramatic Sources of Shakspeare*, 8 vols. (London: Routledge and Kegan Paul; and New York: Columbia University Press, 1957–75), vol. 4, pp. 179, 193–94, 216–17.

8. Reprinted in *Sources*, vol. 4, pp. 299–343.

9. The whole hopeful fusion of royal prerogative and constitutional law, which worked under Elizabeth and was to come apart under James, is invoked in Henry's reply to the Chief Justice, along with Shakespeare's respect for the institution of law and for the monarch as its sanction. The new king's response underscores the characteristically Elizabethan idea that he submits to the Justice voluntarily, that the monarch abides by law and Parliament by choice, with an absolute prerogative in reserve.

10. Ernst Kris, *Psychoanalytic Explorations in Art* (New York: International Universities Press, 1952), pp. 273–88.

11. William Empson, in his wonderful chapter on the Sonnets and *Henry IV*, observes that this is the same imagery as in Sonnet 33, "the earliest and most pathetic of the attempts to justify" the friend's infidelity: "Full many a glorious morning have I seen . . . / Anon permit the basest clouds to ride / With ugly rack on his celestial face." Empson notes that the attitude of the sonnet is "turned backwards" in Hal's soliloquy: "the sun is now to free itself from the clouds by the very act of betrayal." *Some Versions of Pastoral* (London: Chatto and Windus, 1935), p. 100.

12. *Some Versions of Pastoral*, p. 100.

1987—Harold Bloom. "Introduction," from *Henry IV, Part I* (Bloom's Modern Critical Interpretations)

Harold Bloom is a premier American literary critic and a longtime Sterling Professor the Humanities at Yale University, where he teaches Shakespeare and poetry. He has written more than 50 books and has edited numerous series and hundreds of titles. Some of his most influential and best-known books are *The Anxiety of Influence, A Map of Misreading, The Western Canon, Shakespeare: The Invention of the Human,* and *Genius: A Mosaic of One Hundred Exemplary Creative Minds.*

Falstaff is to the world of the histories what Shylock is to the comedies and Hamlet to the tragedies: *the* problematical representation. Falstaff, Shylock, Hamlet put to us the question: precisely how does Shakespearean representation differ from anything before it, and how has it overdetermined our expectations of representation ever since?

The fortunes of Falstaff in scholarship and criticism have been endlessly dismal, and I will not resume them here. I prefer Harold Goddard on Falstaff to any other commentator, and yet I am aware that Goddard appears to have sentimentalized and even idealized Falstaff. I would say better that than the endless litany absurdly patronizing Falstaff as Vice, Parasite, Fool, Braggart Soldier, Corrupt Glutton, Seducer of Youth, Cowardly Liar, and everything else that would not earn the greatest wit in all literature an honorary degree at Yale or a place on the board of the Ford Foundation.

Falstaff, I will venture, in Shakespeare rather than in Verdi, is precisely what Nietzsche tragically attempted yet failed to represent in his Zarathustra: a person without a superego, or should I say, Socrates without the *daimon*. Perhaps even better, Falstaff is not the Sancho Panza of Cervantes, but the exemplary figure of Kafka's parable "The Truth about Sancho Panza." Kafka's Sancho Panza, a free man, has diverted his *daimon* from him by many nightly feedings of chivalric romances (it would be science fiction nowadays). Diverted from Sancho, his true object, the *daimon* becomes the harmless Don Quixote, whose mishaps prove edifying entertainment for the "philosophic" Sancho, who proceeds to follow his errant *daimon*, out of a sense of responsibility. Falstaff's "failure," if it can be termed that, is that he fell in love, not with his own *daimon*, but with his bad son, Hal, who all too truly is Bolingbroke's son. The witty knight should have diverted his own *daimon* with Shakespearean comedies, and philosophically have followed the *daimon* off to the forest of Arden.

Falstaff is neither good enough nor bad enough to flourish in the world of the histories. But then he is necessarily beyond, not only good and evil, but cause and effect as well. A greater monist than the young Milton, Falstaff plays at dualism partly in order to mock all dualisms, whether Christian, Platonic, or even the Freudian dualism that he both anticipates and in some sense refutes.

Falstaff provoked the best of all critics, Dr. Johnson, into the judgment that "he has nothing in him that can be esteemed." George Bernard Shaw, perhaps out of envy, called Falstaff "a besotted and disgusting old wretch." Yet Falstaff's sole rival in Shakespeare is Hamlet; no one else, as Oscar Wilde noted, has so comprehensive a consciousness. Representation itself changed permanently because of Hamlet and Falstaff. I begin with my personal favorite among all of Falstaff's remarks, if only because I plagiarize it daily:

> O, thou has damnable iteration, and art indeed able to corrupt a saint.
> Thou hast done much harm upon me, Hal, God forgive thee for it!
> Before I knew thee, Hal, I knew nothing, and now am I, if a man should speak truly, little better than one of the wicked.

W. H. Auden, whose Falstaff essentially was Verdi's, believed the knight to be "a comic symbol for the supernatural order of charity" and thus a displacement of Christ into the world of wit. The charm of this reading, though considerable, neglects Falstaff's grandest quality, his immanence. He is as immanent a representation as Hamlet is transcendent. Better than any formulation of Freud's, Falstaff perpetually shows us that the ego indeed is always a bodily ego. And the bodily ego is always vulnerable, and Hal indeed has done much harm upon it, and will do far worse, and will need forgiveness, though no sensitive audience ever will forgive him. Falstaff, like Hamlet, and like Lear's Fool, does speak truly, and Falstaff remains, despite Hal, rather better than one of the wicked, or the good.

For what is supreme immanence in what might be called the order of representation? This is another way of asking: is not Falstaff, like Hamlet, so original a representation that he originates much of what we know or expect about representation? We cannot see how original Falstaff is because Falstaff *contains* us; we do not contain him. And though we love Falstaff, he does not need our love any more than Hamlet does. His sorrow is that he loves Hal rather more than Hamlet loves Ophelia, or even Gertrude. The Hamlet of act 5 is past loving anyone, but that is a gift (if it is a gift) resulting from transcendence. If you dwell wholly in this world, and if you are, as Falstaff is, a *pervasive* entity, or as Freud would say, "a strong egoism," then you must begin to love, as Freud also says, in order that you may not fall ill. But what if your strong egoism is not afflicted by any ego-ideal, what if you are never watched, or watched over, by what is above the ego? Falstaff is *not* subject to a power that watches, discovers, and criticizes all his intentions. Falstaff, except for his single and misplaced love, is free, is freedom itself, because he seems free of the superego.

II

Why does Falstaff (and not his parody in *The Merry Wives of Windsor*) pervade histories rather than comedies? To begin is to be free, and you cannot begin freshly in comedy any more than you can in tragedy. Both genres are family romances, at least in Shakespeare. History in Shakespeare is hardly the genre of freedom for kings and nobles, but it is for Falstaff. How and why? Falstaff is of course his own mother and his own father, begotten out of wit by caprice. Ideally he wants nothing except the audience, which he always has; who could watch anyone else on stage when Ralph Richardson was playing Falstaff? Not so ideally, he evidently wants the love of a son, and invests in Hal, the impossible object. But primarily he has what he must have, the audience's fascination with the ultimate image of freedom. His precursor in Shakespeare is not Puck or Bottom, but Faulconbridge the Bastard in *The Life and Death of King John*. Each has a way of providing a daemonic chorus that renders silly all royal and noble squabbles and intrigues. The Bastard in *John*, forthright like his father Richard the Lion Heart, is not a wicked wit, but his truth-telling brutally prophesies Falstaffs function.

There are very nearly as many Falstaffs as there are critics, which probably is as it should be. These proliferating Falstaffs tend either to be degraded or idealized, again perhaps inevitably. One of the most ambiguous Falstaffs was created by the late Sir William Empson: "He is the scandalous upper-class man whose behavior embarrasses his class and thereby pleases the lower class in the audience, as an 'exposure.'" To Empson, Falstaff also was both nationalist and Machiavel, "and he had a dangerous amount of power." Empson shared the hint of Wyndham Lewis that Falstaff was homosexual, and so presumably lusted (doubtless in vain) after Hal. To complete this portrait, Empson added that Falstaff, being both an aristocrat and a mob leader, was "a familiar dangerous type," a sort of Alcibiades one presumes.

Confronted by so ambiguous a Falstaff, I return to the sublime knight's rhetoric, which I read very differently, since Falstaff's power seems to me not at all a matter of class, sexuality, politics, or nationalism. Power it is: sublime pathos, *potentia*, the drive for life, more life, at every and any cost. I will propose that Falstaff is neither a noble synecdoche nor a grand hyperbole, but rather a metalepsis or far-fetcher, to use Puttenham's term. To exist without a super ego is to be a solar trajectory, an ever-early brightness, which Nietzsche's Zarathustra, in his bathos, failed to be. "Try to live as though it were morning," Nietzsche advises. Falstaff does not need the advice, as we discover when we first encounter him:

FALSTAFF: Now, Hal, what time of day is it, lad?
PRINCE: Thou art so fat-witted with drinking of old sack, and
unbuttoning thee after supper, and sleeping upon benches after noon,
that thou hast forgotten to demand that truly which thou wouldest
truly know. What a devil hast thou to do with the time of the day?
unless hours were cups of sack, and minutes capons, and clocks the
tongues of bawds, and dials the signs of leaping-houses, and the blessed
sun himself a fair hot wench in flame-color'd taffata, I see no reason
why thou shouldst be so superfluous to demand the time of the day.

I take it that wit here remains with Falstaff, who is not only witty in himself but the cause of wit in his ephebe, Prince Hal, who mocks his teacher, but in the teacher's own exuberant manner and mode. Perhaps there is a double meaning when Falstaff opens his reply with: "Indeed, you come near me now, Hal," since near is as close as the Prince is capable of, when he imitates the master. Master of what? is the crucial question, generally answered so badly. To take up the stance of most Shakespeare scholars is to associate Falstaff with "such inordinate and low desires, / Such poor, such bare, such lewd, such mean attempts, / Such barren pleasures, rude society." I quote King Henry the Fourth, aggrieved usurper, whose description of Falstaff's aura is hardly recognizable to the audience. We recognize rather: "Counterfeit? I lie, I am no counterfeit. To die is to be a counterfeit, for he is but the counterfeit of a man who hath not the life of a man; but to counterfeit dying, when a man thereby liveth, is to be no counterfeit, but the true and perfect image of life indeed." As Falstaff rightly says, he has saved his life by counterfeiting death, and presumably the moralizing critics would be delighted had the unrespectable knight been butchered by Douglas, "that hot termagant Scot."

The true and perfect image of life, Falstaff, confirms his truth and perfection by counterfeiting dying and so evading death. Though he is given to parodying Puritan preachers, Falstaff has an authentic obsession with the dreadful parable of the rich man and Lazarus in Luke 16:19ff. A certain rich man, a purple-clad glutton, is contrasted with the beggar Lazarus, who desired "to be fed with the crumbs which fell from the rich man's table; moreover the dogs came and licked his sores." Both glutton and beggar die, but Lazarus is carried into Abraham's bosom, and the purple glutton into hell, from which he cries vainly for Lazarus to come and cool his tongue. Falstaff stares at Bardolph, his Knight of the Burning Lamp, and affirms, "I never see thy face but I think upon hell-fire and Dives that liv'd in purple; for there he is in his robes, burning, burning." Confronting his hundred and fifty tattered prodigals, as he marches them off to be food for powder, Falstaff calls them "slaves as ragged as Lazarus in the painted cloth, where the glutton's dogs lick'd his sores." In *Henry IV, Part 2*, Falstaff's first speech again returns to this fearful text, as he cries out against one who denies him credit: "Let him be damn'd like the glutton! Pray God his tongue be hotter!" Despite the ironies abounding in Falstaff the glutton invoking Dives, Shakespeare reverses the New Testament, and Falstaff ends, like Lazarus, in Abraham's bosom, according to the convincing testimony of Mistress Quickly in *Henry V*, where Arthur Britishly replaces Abraham:

BARDOLPH: Would I were with him, wheresome'er he is, either in heaven or in hell!
HOSTESS: Nay sure, he's not in hell; he's in Arthur's bosom, if ever man went to Arthur's bosom. 'A made a finer end, and went away and it had been any christom child.

In dying, Falstaff is a newly baptized child, innocent of all stain. The pattern of allusions to Luke suggests a crossing over, with the rejected Falstaff a poor Lazarus upon his knees in front of Dives wearing the royal purple of Henry V. To a moralizing critic this is outrageous, but Shakespeare does stranger tricks with biblical texts. Juxtapose the two moments:

FALSTAFF: My King, my Jove! I speak to thee, my heart!
KING: I know thee not, old man, fall to thy prayers.

> How ill white hairs becomes a fool and jester!
> I have long dreamt of such a kind of man,
> So surfeit-swell'd, so old, and so profane;
> But being awak'd, I do despise my dream.

And here is Abraham, refusing to let Lazarus come to comfort the "clothed in purple" Dives:

> And beside all this, between us and you there is a great gulf fixed: so that they which would pass from hence to you cannot; neither can they pass to us, that would come from thence.

Wherever Henry V is, he is not in Arthur's bosom, with the rejected Falstaff.

III

I suggest that Shakespearean representation in the histories indeed demands our understanding of what Shakespeare did to history, in contrast to what his contemporaries did. Standard scholarly views of literary history, and all Marxist reductions of literature and history alike, have the curious allied trait of working very well for, say, Thomas Dekker, but being absurdly irrelevant for Shakespeare. Falstaff and the Tudor theory of kingship? Falstaff and surplus value? I would prefer Falstaff and Nietzsche's vision of the use and abuse of history for life, if it were not that Falstaff triumphs precisely where the Overman fails. One can read Freud on our discomfort in culture backwards, and get somewhere close to Falstaff, but the problem again is that Falstaff triumphs precisely where Freud denies that triumph is possible. With Falstaff as with Hamlet (and, perhaps, with Cleopatra) Shakespearean representation is so self-begotten and so influential that we can apprehend it only by seeing that it originates us. We cannot judge a mode of representation that has overdetermined our ideas of representation. Like only a few other authors—the Yahwist, Chaucer, Cervantes, Tolstoy—Shakespeare calls recent critiques of literary representation severely into doubt. Jacob, the Pardoner, Sancho Panza, Hadji Murad: it seems absurd to call them figures of rhetoric, let alone to see Falstaff, Hamlet, Shylock, Cleopatra as tropes of ethos and/or of pathos. Falstaff is not language but diction, the product of Shakespeare's will over language, a will that changes characters through and by what they say. Most simply, Falstaff is not how meaning is renewed, but rather how meaning gets started.

Falstaff is so profoundly original a representation because most truly he represents the essence of invention, which is the essence of poetry. He is a perpetual catastrophe, a continuous transference, a universal family romance. If Hamlet is beyond us and beyond our need of him, so that we require our introjection of Horatio, so as to identify ourselves with Horatio's love for

Hamlet, then Falstaff too is beyond us. But in the Falstaffian beyonding, as it were, in what I think we must call the Falstaffian sublimity, we are never permitted by Shakespeare to identify ourselves with the Prince's ambivalent affection for Falstaff. Future monarchs have no friends, only followers, and Falstaff, the man without a superego, is no one's follower. Freud never speculated as to what a person without a superego would be like, perhaps because that had been the dangerous prophecy of Nietzsche's Zarathustra. Is there not some sense in which Falstaff's whole being implicitly says to us, "The wisest among you is also merely a conflict and a hybrid between plant and phantom. But do I bid you become phantoms or plants?" Historical critics who call Falstaff a phantom, and moral critics who judge Falstaff to be a plant, can be left to be answered by Sir John himself. Even in his debased form, in *The Merry Wives of Windsor*, he crushes them thus:

> Have I liv'd to stand at the taunt of one that makes fritters of English? This is enough to be the decay of lust and late-walking through the realm.

But most of all Falstaff is a reproach to all critics who seek to demystify mimesis, whether by Marxist or deconstructionist dialectics. Like Hamlet, Falstaff is a super-mimesis, and so compels us to see aspects of reality we otherwise could never apprehend. Marx would teach us what he calls "the appropriation of human reality" and so the appropriation also of human suffering. Nietzsche and his deconstructionist descendants would teach us the necessary irony of failure in every attempt to represent human reality. Falstaff, being more of an original, teaches us himself. "No, that's certain, I am not a double man; but if I be not Jack Falstaff, then am I a Jack." A double man is either a phantom or two men, and a man who is two men might as well be a plant. Sir John is Jack Falstaff; it is the Prince who is a Jack or rascal, and so are Falstaff's moralizing critics. We are in no position then to judge Falstaff or to assess him as a representation of reality. Hamlet is too dispassionate even to *want* to contain us. Falstaff is passionate and challenges us not to bore him, if he is to deign to represent us.

1992—Harold Bloom. "Introduction," from *Falstaff* (Bloom's Major Literary Characters)

Harold Bloom is a premier American literary critic and a longtime Sterling Professor the Humanities at Yale University, where he teaches Shakespeare and poetry. He has written more than fifty books, and has edited numerous series and hundreds of titles. Some of his most influential and best-known books are *The Anxiety of Influence, A Map of Misreading, The Western Canon, Shakespeare: The Invention of the Human,* and *Genius: A Mosaic of One Hundred Exemplary Creative Minds.*

In an earlier study (*Ruin the Sacred Truths*, 1989) I ventured the judgment that Shakespeare's Falstaff was a successful representation of what Freud thought impossible, a human being without a superego. Nietzsche, I remarked, had attempted just such a representation in his Zarathustra, and rather conspicuously had failed. What I forgot then, or more likely repressed, was that Freud had commented upon Falstaff in his *Jokes and Their Relation to the Unconscious* (1905). As a fierce Falstaffian, and a rather ambivalent Freudian, I rather dislike Freud on Falstaff, and I quote it here with some distaste:

> The grandiose humorous effect of a figure like that of the fat knight Sir John Falstaff rests on an economy in contempt and indignation. We recognize him as an undeserving gormandizer and swindler, but our condemnation is disarmed by a whole number of factors. We can see that he knows himself as well as we do; he impresses us by his wit, and, besides this, his physical misproportion has the effect of encouraging us to take a comic view of him instead of a serious one, as though the demands of morality and honor must rebound from so fat a stomach. His doings are on the whole harmless, and are almost excused by the common baseness of the people he cheats. We admit that the poor fellow has a right to try to live and enjoy himself like anyone else, and we almost pity him because in the chief situations we find him a plaything in the hands of someone far his superior. So we cannot feel angry with him and we add all that we economize in indignation with him to the comic pleasure which he affords us apart from this. Sir John's own humor arises in fact from the superiority of an ego which neither his physical nor his moral defects can rob of its cheerfulness and assurance.

Freud's economics of the psyche certainly are not Shakespeare's, and I am reminded again how much we need a Shakespearean reading of Freud and how little use is a Freudian reading of Shakespeare. The cheerfulness and assurance of the greatest wit in all literature do not stem from the superiority of his ego but from his freedom, specifically freedom of his ego from the superego. It is dangerous to condescend to Falstaff (as Freud does) because there is no greater wit in a literary representation than Shakespeare invested in Falstaff, the Falstaff of the *Henry IV* plays. Fundamentally, Freud thought that the comic spirit could flourish only when the superego mitigated its severities towards the battered ego. But what of the comedy that rises where there simply is no superego, no overdetermined need for punishment, no turning of the ego against itself? Where is the superego in the magnificent Falstaff? Is there any other literary character whatsoever who seems so free, free to play, free to mock the state, free to evade time? With a few honorable exceptions, Shakespeare's critics simply seem incapable of hearing what Falstaff says, and how he says it. Not even Hamlet is endowed by Shakespeare with more wit and intellect than Falstaff. It is Falstaff's cognitive strength that should astonish us. Nearly everything he says demands subsequent meditation on our part, and rewards our reveries with fresh insights that expand our understanding of far more than Falstaff himself. I am suggesting that the disreputable Falstaff—glutton, boozer, womanizer—is a teacher of wisdom, a hilarious teacher. When I was fifteen, I saw Ralph Richardson play Falstaff (with Laurence Olivier as Hotspur), and I have carried the image of Richardson's exuberant and inventive Falstaff in my head for forty-five years now, and find the image informing the text every time I reread or teach the *Henry IV* plays. Richardson's Falstaff was neither an adorable roisterer nor a kind of counter-courtier, eager for possibilities of power. Rather, he was a veteran warrior who had seen through warfare, discarded its honor and glory as pernicious illusions, and had decided that true life was play, both as we play on stage or in games, and as we play when we are children. Falstaff, wicked and old, has become a wise child again, which is the meaning of the magnificent apologia delivered by him to the Lord Chief Justice, when that embodiment of the state's sagacity reproves him for pretending to be young:

> My lord, I was born about three of the clock in the afternoon, with a white head and something a round belly. For my voice, I have lost it with hallowing and singing of anthems. To approve my youth further, I will not. The truth is, I am only old in judgment and understanding; and he that will caper with me for a thousand marks, let him lend me the money, and have at him!

Falstaff is of the company both of the heroic wits, Rosalind and Hamlet, and of the heroic vitalists, the Wife of Bath and the Panurge of Falstaffian Rabelais. He could also ride into the world of Sancho Panza and the Don, because in some sense he is their synthesis, fusing Sancho's ribald realism and the Don's faith in his own imagination and in the order of play. The Don's chivalric madness is shared by Hotspur, and not at all by Falstaff, but Cervantes is perhaps the only author except Chaucer, and Shakespeare himself, who could have imagined Sir John Falstaff. Hazlitt charmingly remarked that the Fat Knight "is perhaps the most substantial comic character that ever was invented," and certainly Falstaff is the patron of all fat men forever. There is a great deal more to him psychically than his wit, and yet wit is more central to him than to Rosalind or Hamlet. The formidable Rosalind has a gentleness that tempers her exuberance, while Hamlet, in his bewildering complexity, has in him a savagery nearly as strong as his skepticism. Falstaff's exuberance is primal and unstoppable, while he has nothing of Hamlet's savagery, or of Hal's. If there is a mystery to Falstaff, it is in his vexed relationship to Hal, which is hardly to be understood if we refuse to imagine its prehistory. L. C. Knights and other Formalists long ago shamed most critics out of considering the long foregrounds of Shakespearean protagonists, but I am no more a Formalist than I am an Historicist, and I am happy to puzzle out how the given has been constituted each time I start on one of the plays.

Hal's ambivalence towards Falstaff evidently passed into an exasperated negativity, almost a murderousness, long before the first part of *Henry IV* opens. A Formalist or an Historicist would say there was no such "long before," but no start is an authentic genesis after Genesis itself, and Shakespeare is much the greatest master of implied foregrounds that we ever will know. When we first encounter Falstaff and Hal, their dialogue is already the death's duel it rarely ceases to be, with the Prince of Wales almost perpetually attacking, and Sir John defending with deftness and a teacher's dignity, since he is aware that the rhetoric used against him by Hal remains always his own invention. The character of the future Henry V is fortunately hardly my concern here, since this cold opportunist, so admired by scholars, is precisely what Harold Goddard termed him: a hypocritical and ambitious politician, caring only for glory and for power, his father's true son. Hal is best categorized by his own despicable couplet:

I'll so offend, to make offence a skill;
Redeeming time when men think least I will.

Redemption of time is not exactly the Falstaffian project, as Hotspur tells us, when he asks if Hal and Falstaff's gang are coming to the battle:

Where is his son,
The nimble-footed madcap Prince of Wales,
And his comrades, that daffed the world aside
And bid it pass?

Thrusting the world aside, and telling it to pass, indeed is pure Falstaff, when one translates "the world" as Hotspur's exaltation of battle. However one wants to interpret Hal's Falstaffian phrase, it is difficult to improve upon Dr. Johnson's analysis of the relationship between Falstaff and Hal:

> Yet the man thus corrupt, thus despicable, makes himself necessary to the Prince that despises him, by the most pleasing of all qualities, perpetual gaiety, by an unfailing power of exciting laughter, which is the more freely indulged as his wit is not of the splendid or ambitious kind but consists in easy escapes and sallies of levity, which make sport but raise no envy. It must be observed that he is stained with no enormous or sanguinary crimes, so that his licentiousness is not so offensive but that it may be borne for his mirth.

Johnson's ambivalence towards Falstaff only superficially resembles Hal's. Both despise Falstaff, on conventional grounds, but Johnson, afflicted by a vile melancholy, forgives Falstaff everything for his perpetual gaiety, which the great doctor so desperately sought in his companions. Hal, no melancholic, found something else in Falstaff, a teacher of wit and wisdom, but a teacher he no longer cares to need. We, the audience, find more in Falstaff, because Falstaff—more than any other character in Shakespeare, indeed in all literature—bears the Blessing, in the original Yahwistic sense of more life. Falstaff, in himself, is one of the enlargements of life, one of the intimations of a time without boundaries, of a desire that cannot be beggared by fulfillment.

It is another critical commonplace to assert that Falstaff undergoes a degeneration in moral sensibility in Part Two of *Henry IV*. His humor may be a touch coarser, I might admit, but his exuberance does not falter, and his intelligence remains triumphant. What a teacher instructs us in is at last himself, and the more attractive qualities manifested by the protagonist of *Henry V* are subtly traceable to the lesson of the master. Falstaff is more than equal to every event and to every antagonist. Hamlet's intellect has faith neither in language nor in itself; Falstaff's intellect molds language precisely to its ends, and retains a perfect confidence in the mind's triumph over every danger. Hal's obsessive need to prove Falstaff a coward tells us nothing about Falstaff, and almost too much about Hal.

Falstaff's rivals in Shakespeare are not many: Hamlet, Rosalind, and Cleopatra would complete the list unless we admit the intellectual villains, Iago and Edmund. All six of these have the rhetorical genius to overcome any disputant. Yet Falstaff stands apart from the others, because he is older than all of them, and younger than all of them, younger and older even than Cleopatra, who ends in absolute transcendence, whereas Falstaff ends in rejection and grief. The great wit has violated Freud's admonition, which is not to invest too much affection in any single person. Falstaff's tragedy (what else can we call it?) is one of misplaced love, but Shakespeare does not allow that to be our final sense of his grandest comic creation. Instead, we are given the great vision of the death of Falstaff in *Henry V*, which assures us that "he's in Arthur's bosom, if ever man went to Arthur's bosom. A' made a finer end and went away an it had been any christom child." Playing with flowers, and smiling upon his fingers' end, Sir John dies as a child, reminding us again of his total lack of hypocrisy, of what after all makes us love him, of what doubtless first drew the Machiavellian Hal to him. Freedom from the superego, authentic freedom, is the liberty to play, even as a child plays, in the very act of dying.

HENRY IV, PART I
IN THE TWENTY-FIRST CENTURY

Twenty-first-century critics of *Henry IV, Part I* have extended the deconstructions and historical contextualizations which defined much of late twentieth-century criticism, but they have not abandoned traditional character criticism or a healthy fascination with Falstaff. They have, however, reconfigured them. Hugh Grady argues that the complexity of Falstaff's character is the result of the changing social contexts in which he is defined and which he affects. Is Falstaff a carnivalesque representation of misrule, a religiously-grounded depiction of vice, or an individual contained only within his own context in a society which is beginning to celebrate individualism? It is not necessary to choose an answer. The point is to see the interplay of them all with each other as contributing to the fullness of Falstaff as he is experienced by audience and reader.

The stage popularity that Samuel Johnson noted in 1765 has continued into the twenty-first century, whether the play is being presented in amateur theater and college productions or by internationally known companies. At Loyola Marymount University in 2006, women played the male roles and men played the female roles "to explore both war and the nature of manhood, as addressed in Shakespeare's play," according to Kevin Wetmore, a professor of theater at the university and director of the play. In 2004 Kevin Kline and Ethan Hawke as Falstaff and Hotspur appeared at Lincoln Center in New York. In 2007, Nicholas Hytner staged a production of *Henry IV, Part I* at the Olivier Theatre in London, emphasizing corruption, Machiavellianism, and class conflict.

2001—Hugh Grady. "Falstaff: Subjectivity between the Carnival and the Aesthetic," from *The Modern Language Review*

Hugh L. Grady, professor of English at Arcadia University, is the author of *Shakespeare, Machiavelli, and Montaigne: Power and Subjectivity from Richard II to Hamlet* (2002), *Shakespeare's Universal Wolf* (1996), and *Modernist Shakespeare* (1992)

The Many Layers of Sir John

The new historicism and cultural materialism have not been kind to Falstaff. In fact, in many ways they have been scandalously unresponsive to the great complexity of this singular Shakespearean creation. Such underappreciation of one of Shakespeare's creative triumphs was perhaps inevitable, as Falstaff had been, since the late eighteenth century, one of the principal cases in point for late Enlightenment and Romantic notions of transcendent subjectivity, notions that have served as perhaps the chief target for the postmodernist-influenced critical methods (including new historicism and cultural materialism) that have prevailed in Shakespeare studies since about 1980. With all due respect to the exhilarating paradigm shifts in Shakespeare and Renaissance studies in the U.K. and USA over the last twenty years, the most characteristic weakness of these methods has been reductionism: in defining the influence of ideology and discourse on the subject, they have too often eliminated the subject as such, producing uneven, at times unworkably deterministic theoretical models.[1]

The answer to this weakness is not, however, what Harold Bloom has done in his recent best seller *Shakespeare: The Invention of the Human*, to revert to an outmoded Romantic bardolatry and reproduce the very notions of Romantic transcendental subjectivity that have been so effectively dismantled in recent years.[2] Instead, the solution is, I believe, to account for the historical emergence of new forms of subjectivity in Shakespeare's plays in ways that do justice both to their historicity and to their complexity. This will mean a critical look at new historical and cultural materialist accounts of subjectivity, and an advocacy of more adequate theoretical models of subjectivity than those used in recent years.

In one of the defining documents of new historicism in contemporary Shakespeare studies, Stephen Greenblatt's much reprinted 'Invisible Bullets',[3] the influence of Foucault led Greenblatt (and elsewhere other new historicists) to define all-encompassing systems of power, with little if any room for resistance, and therefore little room for those qualities that have made Falstaff repeatedly hailed over three centuries as the best of all comic characters. The power-dominated world of new historical analyses is simply not very funny. Despite the availability of Bakhtinian notions of heteroglossia and carnival to describe Falstaff's potential to invert and resist the ideologies of power into which Hal is being interpellated, Falstaff's challenge to basic tenets of 1980s newer criticisms has been underappreciated and underdefined.[4]

However, the new historicist views of the Henriad were right, in my view, in seeing these plays as centrally involved in a study of early modern political power, and as I am arguing in related work, which cannot be brought out here for reasons of space, the power in question is a specifically Machiavellian one unfolding in the secular space of emerging modernity.[5] The play that preceded the two Falstaff-dominated histories, *1 and 2 Henry IV*, was of course *Richard II*, and it portrayed a kind of crisis of Machiavellianism in depicting the triumph of skilled power, via Bolingbroke, over the crowned king's empty symbolics, but left us finally in an ethical vacuum. The two plays that follow, one might say, investigate one of modernity's characteristic responses to this vacuum, a turn to subjectivity: here specifically the potential of selves unfixed from traditional roles and world views to imagine and act out new roles and potentialities as an alternative to now outmoded religious ones. It is in this context, I believe, that Falstaff's role and characteristics should be studied. Falstaff is an experiment in a kind of imagined autonomous, autotelic subjectivity ('My lord, I was born about three of the clock in the afternoon, with a white head and something a round belly')[6] specifically designed as a refuge from (and possibly as an alternative to) the Machiavellian logic of power slowly unfolding between the high jinks of the tavern scenes.

One of Falstaff's central paradoxes, however, is the extent to which this secular simulacrum of post-Reformation subjectivity is a manifestly artificial synthesis of pre-existing theatrical, folk, and literary types. It has been one of the most popular pastimes of twentieth-century academic criticism to define and analyse them. There are, for example, the direct theatrical forebears: the *miles gloriosus* and the Plautine parasite from Latin comedy;[7] the comic Vice of the late medieval moralities;[8] the tradition of fools and folly from the Middle Ages[9] and the related carnival tradition delineated by Barber, Bakhtin, Weimann, Bristol, and Laroque, to be discussed below; the *picaro* tradition and the related discourse on Elizabethan underground or rogue literature in sixteenth-century tracts and pamphlets;[10] the Renaissance celebration of the body in Cervantes and Rabelais.[11] Early on Falstaff was, and has again recently been, also connected to the so-called anti-Marprelate tracts, a series of satirical pamphlets against the aggressive and irreverent Puritan wit of the pseudonymous Martin Marprelate, including lampooning plays whose texts have not survived but which, according to the allusions to them in surviving pamphlets and tracts, were designed to satirize Puritanism as a grotesque, hypocritical carnival.[12] Many of these traditions, it can be presumed, were directly embodied in the comic style of the celebrated performer who created the role of Falstaff, William Kempe, himself an apprentice to the famous Dick Tarlton, and through him to an older popular comic tradition.[13]

Complex and contradictory as all these different attempts to conceptualize Falstaff are, they also overlap and suggest some themes in the present context and should not simply be relegated to the status of what Stephen Greenblatt called 'the traditional pieties' of that most dreary precinct of Shakespeare studies, source studies. We should recognize that Falstaff's rapid referencing of numerous stage, literary, and cultural types is the paradoxical key to what Harold Bloom has called, in his inflated way, 'the invention of the human'. A less inflated approach to the function of Falstaff's protean theatricality takes one instead squarely within some of the key topics of the 'French Shakespeare' that Harold Bloom has dismissed, the post-structuralist-influenced attempts to define the impact of modernity on subjectivity. While, as I indicated above, there are significant problems with these attempts, they by no means deserve Bloom's cavalier dismissal. Jonathan Dollimore's *Radical Tragedy* in particular is valuable in defining a disjuncture between the brave new world of available social identities of early modern London and the older inflexible ideologies of social station. Dollimore delineated this growing gap between received ideologies and the new practices of developing modernity, and he thought that the ubiquitous 'malcontent' figure, epitomized by Marston's play *The Malcontent* but instanced in several other plays by Shakespeare and his contemporaries, was a crucial dramatic representation of the new dynamics.[14] However, the impact on the theatre of new modes of subjectivity goes far beyond the malcontent type. Falstaff exemplifies the same socio-historical development that Dollimore described for the malcontents, but in a very different mode. Like numerous other Shakespearean characters, he resists being tied down to any single identity and instead continually reinvents himself through a lengthy series of dramatic improvisations. In that way the theatre itself, in that fruitful *topos* that Shakespeare exploited over and over from his earliest to his latest work, becomes the model for life in a world newly open to the unfettered subjectivity created through shifting ideologies, religions, social stations, changing gender roles, and malleable sexuality.

This brave new world is of course a theatre, not only for Falstaff but for Prince Hal, whose identity crisis is, in many ways, the dramatic centre of *1 and 2 Henry IV*. However, precisely because the Prince is one of those legendary Shakespearean characters, like Brutus, Cleopatra, or Antony, who 'becomes' his legend only after a lengthy dramatic investigation of numerous alternatives, Hal is destined to lose his protean subjectivity and take up the fixed identity of his own legendary self.[15] In this context Falstaff fulfils a kind of allegorical role, figuring the unfixed or protean subjectivity Hal must banish as he takes up his burden as king.

'Subjectivity' is, of course, a word of many meanings, and there are senses of the term that seem wholly inappropriate to the case of Falstaff. For example, he is one of the least self-reflective, solitary literary creations imaginable; instead he is always involved in friendship, socializing, scheming and other gregarious acts. If by 'subjectivity' we mean the thought processes characteristic of a solitary inner life, such as in the versions of Protestant asceticism associated by Weber with an emerging modernity, then Falstaff seems the very opposite of subjective in that sense. Indeed, Kristen Poole's study of Falstaff and the anti-Marprelate materials alluded to previously suggests that he is in fact in important part designed as the very opposite of the Protestant ascetic: communal, pleasure-loving, and self-centred rather than solitary, penitential, and self-denying.

Other critics have defined subjectivity in an Althusserian sense as the formation of an identity in ideology through the processes of interpellation.[16] In this view, subjectivity is simply social discourse internalized. However, here again, Falstaff seems to embody a constant resistance to interpellation, whether to that which would make Prince Hal a dutiful son and political agent, or that which would unkindly define him as tavern parasite and superannuated, impoverished knight.

However, Falstaff embodies facets of the new post-medieval subjectivity in other, no less important ways, ways that are linked to that dynamic quality of his which some critics have called his 'theatricality'[17] and which I am calling a protean or unfixed subjectivity. This quality can also be described as a kind of counter-factual self-fictionalization. In short, what Falstaff embodies is the ability of aspects of the self to resist or surpass the specific, fixed social roles of Althusserian interpellation.

This kind of resistance to interpellation, while it has its heroic potentialities, is by no means automatically to be applauded, rife as it is with possibilities of the denial of reality, escapism, self-indulgence and self-centredness, egotism and other kinds of self-destructive behaviour. Falstaff is indeed an excellent example of many of these potentialities as well. However, in a series of plays that will feature the absorption of the playful and harmless Prince of Wales into a formidable Machiavellian politician responsible for the deaths of thousands, Falstaff's resistance to the ways of the world is not to be dismissed lightly. William Hazlitt got it exactly right: Falstaff is the better man of the two, and he is a better man because he understands that ideology need not be the be-all and end-all of human social reality. Instead, one can play with it, and against it, as Hal does for a while and as Falstaff attempts until his end. This playfulness, this ability to subvert ideological interpellation through theatricality, is Falstaff's crucial characteristic, both as foil to Prince Hal and as thematic embodiment of resistance to power in all the plays of the Prince Hal trilogy.

If this reading is correct, it must be acknowledged that there is a kind of polarity in Falstaff's role connected to the plays' complex, layered, and contradictory evaluations of the role-playing demanded and forbidden by monarchy. At first Hal's tutor in role-playing and the unfixing of identity, Falstaff becomes at the end a victim of the logic of power that fixes, as it were, Hal's mobile sense of self. In addition, however, and to complicate things further, Falstaff is also an embodiment of the destructive egoism that is one of modern subjectivity's most prominent potential outcomes. His dramatic functions, then, are as contradictory and many-layered as the rich and contradictory critical discourse on him over three centuries suggests, but while his is a multilayered dramatic function, some parts of his complex dramatic role should not be allowed to obscure others. Thus, while Falstaff is designed to be the very opposite of a Puritan saint (I come back to this below), there are clear moments in *1 and 2 Henry IV* when his very theatricality, his ability to perform different selves and roles and escape the various tight spots that continually threaten him, is highlighted as a means of resistance to early modern power, and in such moments he emerges as a kind of anti-saint in the same inverted category twentieth-century wits have formed in the designations Saint Genet and Saint Foucault. I want to call attention to these precisely because they have been overlooked due to the preoccupation of recent criticism with power *tout court*.

At these moments, refusing to be limited by his actual material and social circumstances, Saint Falstaff creates a fictional world and acts out (as far as he is able within his material constraints) a fictional counter-reality. Thus, his cultivation of subjectivity is more like that of Richard II in prison than it is like Prince Hal's, or in another mode, but with a very similar notion of the potentials of unfixed subjectivity in flux, like that of Michel de Montaigne.[18] Much less directly oriented towards success in the world than is his companion, he fulfils his ambitions by trying to be amusing to the Prince, and so cultivates imagination (even specifically Lacan's Imaginary order, that locus of a lost unity and access to the (m)Other), and creates for himself and his companions a fictional, utopian projection of self similar to that of his thin counterpart in *Don Quixote*, the knight-errant, with, of course, important similarities to Sancho Panza, for Falstaff's utopian self is a pampered, self-indulgent recipient of bodily pleasures more like Quixote's squire in that regard than like his thin master.[19] Falstaff attempts to live out a carnival ideal suffused with a libido that is among the most successfully communicated of the multiple associations swirling around the remarkable prose Shakespeare has written for him,[20] and this libidinally charged speech is perhaps the key feature behind the centuries-old legion of followers and champions of Falstaff who have responded to the multivalent and subversive richness of passages such as the following, in which his powers of self-fictionalization are fully operative:

> Marry then, sweet wag, when thou art king, let not us that are squires of the night's body be call'd thieves of the day's beauty. Let us be 'Diana's foresters', 'gentlemen of the shade', 'minions of the moon', and let men say we be men of good government, being governed, as the sea is, by our noble and chaste mistress the moon, under whose countenance we steal.
> (*1 Henry IV*, I.2.20–27)

Unlike Quixote's mad vision, however, Falstaff's seems to contain within itself some tacit knowledge of its own fictionality,[21] some unspoken acknowledgement with his fellows in fantasy that this is, after all, a grand joke, based actually on an inversion of the situation which everyone, including Falstaff, knows to be the case. Consider the following reply to Hal:

> O, thou hast damnable iteration, and art indeed able to corrupt a saint. Thou hast done much harm upon me, Hal, God forgive thee for it.

> Before I knew thee, Hal, I knew nothing; and now am I, if a man should
> speak truly, little better than one of the wicked. I must give over this life,
> and I will give it over. By the Lord, an I do not, I am a villain. I'll be
> damned for never a king's son in Christendom. (*1 Henry IV*, I.2.80–86)

With their allusions to scripture, saints, the wicked, and damnation, these lines form part of a subtext within *1 Henry IV* connecting Sir John to that Elizabethan satirical view of Puritanism which, as mentioned previously, has been unearthed by Shakespeare scholarship. However, these allusions lost a good deal of their point when the character's name was changed to Falstaff from Oldcastle, since Oldcastle had clear Puritan connections, his namesake having been made into a Proto-Protestant martyr in John Foxe's widely distributed *Actes and Monuments of Martyrs*. With the new name of Falstaff, this subtext becomes a set of veiled allusions, yet another layer of contextual complexity in Falstaff's character,[22] so that in the text as we have received it, the implied anti-Puritan satire merges unobtrusively into Falstaff's general self-fictionalizing project of creating inverted and inflated carnivalesque images of himself as a consummately good man in a grossly unfair, wicked world:

> You rogue, here's lime in this sack too. There is nothing but roguery
> to be found in villainous man [. . .]. Go thy ways, old Jack, die when
> thou wilt. If manhood, good manhood, be not forgot upon the face of
> the earth, then am I a shotten herring. There lives not three good men
> unhang'd in England, and one of them is fat and grows old, God help
> the while. A bad world, I say. (*1 Henry IV*, II.5.112–19)

This profound project of inverted fictionalizing is behind his strange assertions of youth: 'They hate us youth. Down with them, fleece them!', Falstaff cries out during the robbery (*1 Henry IV*, II.2.76–77), and when this particular fiction is so profoundly punctured near the end of *Part 2*, in the 'chimes of midnight' dialogue with Master Shallow, it is perhaps the most important of the many signs that Falstaff's carnival is coming to an end, his self-fictionalizations having reached their material limits.

The fact that the many lies of this white-bearded old Satan form the very structure of the counter-factual carnival he attempts to inhabit is crucial to our understanding the paradoxical irrelevance, insisted upon in their different ways by Morgann, Hazlitt, Bradley, and Bloom, of Falstaff's manifest vices and self-serving proclivities. If he were a murderer like Richard III, the same effect could not prevail.[23] However, his failings generally involve victims, such as Mistress Quickly, Master Shallow, the Prince and associates, even the hapless but careless robbed pilgrims at Gadshill, and the improvident inductees of the wars, who are at least partially complicit with or tolerant of their own fleecing. Falstaff makes little secret of his self-serving and weakness: 'Dost thou hear, Hal? Thou knowest in the state of innocency Adam fell, and what should poor Jack Falstaff do in the days of villainy? Thou seest I have more flesh than another man, and therefore more frailty' (*1 Henry IV*, III.3.151–54).

However, beyond the misdemeanour-like quality of most of Falstaff's failings is the ritualistic, non-rational, wish-fulfilling, and symbolic nature of the carnival discourse that forms such an important part of Falstaff's dramatic function. Much of this role, therefore, imaginatively subverts the reality principle in favour of the pleasure principle and thereby renders irrelevant objections from the real. The fuel of Falstaff's subjectivity is desire. The play of his wit and the motivation of his actions each manifest that Lacanian 'logic' of desiring that notoriously leads modern subjects from one coveted object to the next in an endless chain. This association of Falstaff, and modern subjectivity, with desire itself helps to account for the marked critical polarization of opinion about him in the long tradition of Falstaff criticism from Dryden to the present. For desire is the ultimate double-edged sword. Without it, there is no human motivation, the world is colourless and empty, and life has no joy. On the other hand, desire is that blind striving that enthrals humans to addictions and irrational cravings destructive of dignity and accomplishment. Falstaff seems to evoke both these sides of desire.

'Henry IV': From Carnival to Metatheatre

Falstaff's gargantuan body (a comedy in itself, Dryden said),[24] his love of the pleasures of the 'lower bodily stratum', and his attempt to create a timeless realm of perpetual holiday, all link him with that plebeian, subaltern tradition, inherited from the ancient and medieval worlds, that was described by Mikhail Bakhtin in one of the great critical works of the twentieth century, *Rabelais and his World*. Bakhtin linked the grotesque aspects of the carnival tradition, its emphasis on swollen bodies, beatings, even dismemberments and bodily mutilations, to a half-conscious, ancient and peasant-based vision of life as a communal, earth-oriented, materialistic but meaning-imbued process encompassing death as a condition for life's renewal and vigour. The carnival is thus a locus for an inarticulate but powerful subaltern tradition of resistance to that series of official ideologies (ancient Platonism and its allied philosophies, spiritualist Christianity, and Stalinism) that have exalted the spirit over the body, the upper classes over the lower, or the state over society. C. L. Barber of course defined the relevance of the carnival tradition to Shakespearean comedy independently of Bakhtin, and his work remains a valuable source of ideas in this area.[25] However, Barber, specifically in the case of the *Henry IV* plays, interpreted saturnalian comedy essentially as a social pressure valve, an instance of licensed merriment that, in fact, reinforced rather than challenged authority. As Michael Bristol has previously argued, Bakhtin's analysis goes deeper, taking a much longer-range view of things, one which, while not blind to carnival's escapist functions, emphasizes instead its transgressive potential, its function as a continuing locus for embodying and preserving centuries of counter-memories and challenges to authority.[26] While both Barber and Bakhtin are highly relevant to the case of Falstaff, I am relying on Bakhtin here for what I find to be his profounder sense of the long-term meaning of the carnival tradition, a meaning crucial to an understanding of how these plays embody within their complex layers challenges to, as well as celebrations of, royal authority.

In my opinion, Bakhtin survives very well the oblique attacks on him (or at least on his relevance to understanding Falstaff) in Harry Berger's recent intricate meditation on Falstaff as an embodiment of the complex mimetic effects implicit in the conventions of the stage as an illusionistic performance.[27] When Berger argues that a number of recent cultural materialist readings of the *Henry IV* plays are in danger of missing much of this complexity by viewing Falstaff strictly as an object of various social discourses, I believe he is defining an important point, particularly so since he appreciates that many of these readings have their own areas of adequacy and truth. I am intrigued when Berger goes on to insist that Falstaff must be conceptualized as a subject of his own discourse, not merely as an object of language itself (p. 62 and throughout), but the kind of subject Berger has in mind, it appears as his argument develops, is that of Falstaff as self-punishing masochist, as a subject of his own degradation and punishment who is complicit throughout *1 and 2 Henry IV* in the production of his own ultimate banishment. There is, I believe, something to this as well: Falstaff is, as Berger argues, continually imagining and proleptically parodying his own future banishment, and he is continually creating himself as the butt of jokes and japes. However, precisely because Berger downplays theatrical performance and the social functions and provenance of Falstaff's carnivalesque comedy,[28] he misses Falstaff's paradoxical triumph with the audience despite his losses within the dramatic narrative in which he is a character. An important part of Falstaff's positive impact over several centuries springs from his metatheatrical function, which allows him to stand apart as a commentator from the character he portrays in the plot, very much as in Bertolt Brecht's 'alienation effect'. In my opinion, Berger's reading robs Falstaff of much of his vitality and subversiveness by interpreting him as caught up in self-punishment and failure, and by denying his metadramatic relation with the audience. Berger thus ends up making Falstaff appear to be serving power in the vein of Greenblatt's 'Invisible Bullets', an essay of which Berger is otherwise quite critical. Here I want to give a quite different account of Sir John, and one cognizant of what seem to me his palpable metatheatrical qualities.

It is in the second half of *1 Henry IV*, as the action builds up to the climactic battle scenes and the carnival world *per se* has been left behind, that Falstaff is transformed into the most metadramatic[29] and Brechtian of Shakespeare's characters; or, to put it perhaps more precisely, he provides a dramatic precedent, itself based on older festival traditions, which Brecht learned to exploit to the hilt.[30] In these scenes, in the absence of a chiding Hal, Falstaff becomes his own accuser, and he wins the audience's sympathy because he is the character closest to the heavily plebeian popular audience of the play, pointedly exposing the corrupt manipulations of the wars, which he himself has acted out for us. In this way, too, his role is reminiscent of the medieval fool or Lord of Misrule who frequently acted as a kind of master of ceremonies at village processions or festivals. Similarly, this is another way in which he recalls the dramatic descendant of the Lord of Misrule in the medieval moralities, the Vice character, who stands, according to Robert Weimann, 'on the threshold between the play and the community occasion' and who, as an 'ambidexter', is 'both object of and spokesman for the attack' on vice (*Shakespeare and the Popular Tradition*, pp. 43, 154, 224–46).

To see these effects at work, it is worth quoting at length from this remarkable soliloquy, in which Sir John is clearly speaking directly to the audience:[31]

> I have misused the king's press damnably. I have got in exchange of a hundred and fifty soldiers three hundred and odd pounds. I press me none but good householders, yeomen's sons, inquire me out contracted bachelors, such as had been ask'd twice on the banns, such a commodity of warm slaves as had as lief hear the devil as a drum. [. . .] and they have bought out their services; and now my whole charge consists of ensigns, corporals, lieutenants, gentlemen of companies—slaves as ragged as Lazarus in the painted cloth, where the glutton's dogs lick'd his sores—and such as indeed were never soldiers, but discarded unjust servingmen, younger sons to younger brothers, revolted tapsters, and ostlers trade-fallen, the cankers of a calm world and a long peace [. . .]. A mad fellow met me on the way and told me I had unloaded all the gibbets and pressed the dead bodies. No eye hath seen such scarecrows [. . .]. Nay, and the villains march wide betwixt the legs, as if they had gyves on, for indeed I had the most of them out of prison. There's not a shirt and a half in all my company; and the half-shirt is two napkins tacked together and thrown over the shoulders like a herald's coat without sleeves; and the shirt, to say the truth, stolen from my host at Saint Albans, or the red-nose innkeeper of Daventry. But that's all one; they'll find linen enough on every hedge. (*1 Henry IV*, IV.2.11–42)

Sir John the interlocutor has stepped out of the role of Sir John the corrupt recruiter; the former in fact denounces the latter. His voice, as Weimann puts it in a passage on a group of Shakespearean characters, including Falstaff, helps to embody a 'sense of freedom from the burden of the ruling ideologies and concepts of honor, love, ambition, and revenge [. . .]. The power of negation is [thus] turned against the representatives of the *vicious world* itself: the negation of negation dialectically gives them a structural function' (p. 159).[32] The effect is one of a simultaneous condemnation of exploitation and a dark, worldly-wise acknowledgement of the world's ways. However, we begin to realize (and this is a theme amplified in the plays to come), it is a way of the world and of 'commodity' (that subject of a similar puncturing soliloquy in *King John*) showing no signs of withering, an ancient and modern outcome of warfare as an instrumentalizing incursion into the lives of communities that destroys normal inhibitions and customs and opens them up to new forms of exploitation. Thus the exposure of the abuses of early modern recruiting is also a kind of proleptic demonstration of the logic of modernization more generally. Here, Sir John is both the instrument and the critic of such an incursion.

Falstaff between the Carnival and the Aesthetic

In the passage quoted above, Robert Weimann emphasized Falstaff's role as an ideological 'negation' in the Hegelian-Marxian sense, a character who illustrates the shortcomings and untruths of an era's received ideology. In the case of his famous catechism on honour, Falstaff is negating concepts which in a sense were already critical negations, since honour, courage, and so on represented ideals against which the empirical world could be measured and found wanting. Falstaff's catechism in turn suggests how these ideals themselves are imbued with assumptions of the world they pretend to criticize. However, this leads to a further question. If, as Weimann suggests, Falstaff is a negation of a negation, can we approximate this double negativity in terms of some positivity? What do Falstaff's negations add up to?

On the one hand, it is clear (and Weimann himself seems to suggest as much) that Falstaff is allied to the ancient carnival traditions, whose function over several centuries was to serve as a continuing negation of ruling ideologies repressive of the peasantry and other labouring classes, their vision and their values. The character of Falstaff is clearly constructed in large part from carnival and related traditions, as I have shown, and he exemplifies in many ways the world of holiday and festival.

However, C. L. Barber (and a host of followers) long ago pointed out, in connection with this play, that carnival unfolds itself through Falstaff within a modernizing society, in an urban commercial enterprise in which the ancient communal pastimes are now the stuff of nostalgic remembrance. In the absence of those communal structures, Sir John's plebeian cunning and self-preservation easily become the egoistic self-maximization that is the socio-psychological linchpin of emergent systems of power and capitalism of the early modern period. A Falstaff at liberty in a land where all the laws are at his command is dangerous in a way the charming rogue at the Boar's Head decidedly is not, the complaints of his creditors notwithstanding. In short, there is an important social as well as psychological component to Sir John's emotional and ethical complexity, productive of disparate audience responses to him. Contained within the proto-communal structures of the tavern (themselves emblematic of the rural communities from which many members of the audience came, and partially recreated in new urban settings), Sir John's comic championing of the bodily self and its pleasures functions as a communal, class-conscious discourse of a plebeian social element oppressed by the idealisms of church and state. Understood, however, in terms of a new Renaissance individualism, as an atomistic ego contending in the war of each against all, he is an emblem of the community-destroying dynamics of an embryonic capitalist society just visible at the turn of the sixteenth to the seventeenth centuries. Everything depends on the social context.

Thus the exploitative side of Falstaff can be seen as enacting one of the dangerous aspects of unfixed subjectivity in the service of unchecked appetite. Here, as in several other Shakespearean plays, the limits of subjectivity and pleasure as solutions to the crisis of emerging modernity are worked out in its very earliest stages. Whereas *joie de vivre* and pleasure are crucial values to assert in an instrumentalized world, they, too, in the evacuated cultural space of modernity, can be reified and established as a system of pointless circulation and exchange capable of enthralling individuals and entire societies, as Troy illustrated in Shakespeare's jaundiced *Troilus and Cressida*,[33] and as modern consumer society demonstrates afresh in our own day. When Hal remarks early in the play 'If all the year were playing holidays, / To sport would be as tedious as to work', he is not only rationalizing his own sowing of wild oats but also enunciating the problem that Sir John lives: what are the limits of a carnival wrenched out of its setting in the cycle of the year's months and seasons and set up as an end in itself in a society of constant moral and cultural disintegration and reconfiguration, such as is constituted by modernity?

In his metatheatrical soliloquy on the king's press, as in his many fits of remorse and resolutions to repent, Sir John himself temporarily becomes his own severest, if ultimately forgiving, critic. The carnival world that he both embodies and criticizes, takes its place as a crucial piece in play of a larger puzzle of modernity represented in this drama, rather than some static solution to its problems. In short, while Falstaff is a figure from the carnival tradition, he is one given a new function within a world no longer the same as the agrarian societies in which the carnival tradition developed. Falstaff has gone beyond the carnival, which is one of his points of origin. The carnival takes on new meanings and ultimately is transformed into something different, because it begins in Shakespeare's London to function as a negation of something different from what it had negated in earlier, more stable centuries.[34] The carnivalesque character Falstaff has become in the *Henry IV* plays is a foil for the cold, value-free, Machiavellian political world. Falstaff has thus come to embody a good deal of what is repressed in the construction of a world of value-free objects by a modernizing instrumental rationality. His libido-infused, pleasure-oriented subjectivity, represented verbally and symbolically in a popular genre, but destined to become a classic successively of high bourgeois, Modernist, and postmodernist cultures, might even be said to evoke that sublime, unrepresentable 'subjectivity itself' that has been the elusive quarry of so much nineteenth-century and twentieth-century literary criticism. The carnivalesque, which had functioned as the negation of medieval ruling-class ideology, begins to lose some of its communal qualities in Falstaff, becoming by the end of *1 Henry IV* atomistic and egotistical. To understand why this is happening to Falstaff, to help understand the process of his movement out of a medieval carnival into something we can recognize as modernity, we can look to the insights of Frankfurt School critical theory on the emergence of modern subjectivity in the process called the dialectic of enlightenment.

In their depiction of modernity and its construction of an instrumental rationality that disembodies objects of their sensual qualities the better to dominate them, Max Horkheimer and Theodor W. Adorno turned to and allegorized the episode in Book XII of *The Odyssey*, when Odysseus and his crew have to sail past the Sirens. Odysseus, availing himself of the privileges of his rank, allows himself to hear the proverbial beauty of the Sirens' song, while preventing his men from doing the same by having them stop up their ears with wax. Of course, he has himself tied to the ship's mast so as to be unable to give way to the desires the Sirens' song produce in him. This story, write Horkheimer and Adorno, is a prescient representation of the dialectic of enlightenment that strips the world of all values except those of immediate utility, making its practitioners deaf to the world's beauty, except for those few modern Odysseuses who allow themselves to hear as long as they are unable to swerve from the paths of utility in which they are set. What they hear are works of modern art, which represent something of the world's beauty but in a form separating it off from all other social reality.[35]

In Falstaff, particularly in his relation to Prince Hal, Shakespeare has given us his own version of this myth, in which the tavern world is a kind of Siren song potentially seducing the Prince from the instrumental path of Machiavellian politics. In the new context of modernity, carnivalesque Falstaff and his world embody the potential for pleasure and beauty within the emerging subjectivities of modernity. No longer anchored in communal celebrations, they have become individual and subjective, freed in the process from communal forms and open to all the new possibilities and dangers of the individual imagination.

Falstaff thus manifests a version of the carnivalesque that has been recontextualized and given new meaning by the modernizing impulses of Puritanism/capitalism. Henceforth, what had been ritual and sanctioned disorder for pre-modern Europe would have to be transformed into an emerging, historically new category of autonomous, subjective art, and the London commercial theatres of Shakespeare's day were early prototypes for this development.[36]

In classical Frankfurt School theory, the aesthetic, like the other fragmentary components of modernity, entered the world in the Enlightenment, and this chronology is supported empirically by the fact that the idea of the aesthetic as we understand the term came into being in the eighteenth century. Here as elsewhere, however, the status of the Renaissance as a precursor of Enlightenment complicates the issue, and the fact that we are dealing with works of Shakespeare complicates it even further. The plays of Shakespeare were crucial documents in many of the seminal discussions of the aesthetic, particularly those of late eighteenth-century Germany, where Shakespeare had emerged as a major figure, both a vehicle for and a major instance of the new aesthetic thinking. For example, he was a key case in point in the paradigm-changing work of G. E. Lessing.[37] For Lessing and the German Enlightenment and Romantic periods generally, *Hamlet* was the key document, and much of the fascination of it centred on the elusive subjectivity of the Prince, seen as an alienated artist or near-artist whose restless subjectivity rebelled against confinement to the role of revenge-tragedy hero. Harold Bloom, as I mentioned above, is palpably arguing a version of this moment of cultural history some two hundred years after its original construction, with Bloom adding Falstaff to Hamlet as a figure for his putative 'creation of the human', but what Bloom is describing could be more accurately termed the construction of the aesthetic and the subjective. I would add that, although there is no question of identity between Shakespearean practice and Romantic aesthetic theory, they are at least sufficiently analogous to each other to have supported two hundred years dominated by the idea that reading Shakespeare is essentially an aesthetic experience. I would posit that in the case of the emerging concepts and practices of the aesthetic and subjectivity, Shakespeare broke ground that post-Enlightenment art and theory cultivated centuries later to produce much of the conceptual world we still inhabit. In short, the great impact of the characters Hamlet and Falstaff, in their own time and subsequently, is connected to their embodiment of characteristics of the subjective and the aesthetic destined to be central to the reified world of emerging modernity. However, not Harold Bloom, but the Frankfurt School, can best guide us in understanding these developments. In that theoretical context, it is not hard to see why Falstaff became a representation of what is always already missing in the disenchanted world of modernity: the modern concepts of subjectivity and the aesthetic are related categories that preserve, refunction, and mystify the sense of (eroticized) feeling and rich meaning of which the world is bereft in the visions of instrumental reason, and Falstaff is entangled in these emerging forms.

This is not the occasion to try to tease out answers to the elusive question of just where to place Shakespeare's Falstaff in the cultural continuum between the carnivalesque and the aesthetic that was developing apace in Renaissance London. What can be said is that Falstaff, in all his contradictoriness, is a beautifully constructed instance of the process whereby the carnivalesque metamorphoses into the aesthetic. This is a process above all of refunctioning and recontextualization. Because the social and intellectual contexts that had defined the carnival were crumbling, the contents of the plays' medieval materials, including the carnivalesque, took on new meanings in the new situation. One may look, for example, at the oft-repeated claim that Falstaff is a reincarnation of the Vice figure of late medieval moralities, as suggested within the text by his off-hand reference to 'a dagger of lath' (*1 Henry IV*, II.5.124), the traditional stage prop of the Vice. What has been far less often discussed in this connection is what it could mean to refunction such a figure in the secular space of the public theatres. For this particular Vice is functioning quite autonomously from any clearly fixed moral categories, in a comic grey area in which his own peccadilloes seem small change in a larger Machiavellian world of power politics, with its wars and betrayals.

What Falstaff retains from the Vice of the moralities is his libidinal energy, his wit, and zest for transgression. In the kind of cultural negotiation theorized by Greenblatt, but with an outcome quite different from those he discussed,[38] the commercial theatre has demythologized and secularized a figure from a religious tradition, replacing the certainties of the one with the prolix, shifting, and uncertain moral frames seen in play here in aesthetic space. The morally imbued cosmology of the moralities has been replaced, in short, by an emerging modern subjectivity that erects an aesthetic sphere to refunction within an otherwise bleak space of autonomous Machiavellian power the possibilities of counter-values of pleasure, community, and solidarity drawn from a declining medieval tradition.[39] Falstaff stands within this inverted secular morality play as a kind of figure from a Blakean hell, representing a libidinal counterweight (of gargantuan proportions) to the Machiavellian power dynamics that *Richard II* (and a plethora of other plays of the era) had established as the most evident of the Renaissance outcomes of an emerging modernity.

Thus, as Weimann's history of popular stage traditions perhaps makes clearest, in Falstaff's contradictory amoral, self-serving, but community-associated virtue, we are in touch with central paradoxes associated with the centuries-old traditions of clown, carnival, and plebeian mirth. As Frankfurt School aesthetic theory implies, these are also the very qualities refunctioned and uneasily contained in the modern category of the aesthetic. Because Falstaff is located precisely between these two moments, two quite different conceptual contexts can be constructed for him, one, however, for which he is too late (the carnival), the other for which he is too early (the aesthetic). What has to be said is that he is transitional between the two and thus embodies a central moment in the development of Western modernity.

Falstaff thus steps out of the boundaries of the plays in which he is featured and becomes for a subsequent modernity a figure of an almost vanished subaltern world uneasily afoot in an emerging modern one, and he becomes thereby simultaneously a dream or wish-fulfilment, within an aesthetic register. That is why this comical figure, so often bested in his wit-duels with Hal in the two plays, so often submitted to devastating deflations and humiliations in the course of three plays, and so often sullied by his own misdemeanours, finally triumphs in a cultural collective memory as a comic colossus which indeed Hal is unable to bestride.

NOTES

1. I am thinking particularly of the 'containment' theory of Stephen Greenblatt, *Renaissance Self-Fashioning: From More to Shakespeare* (Chicago: University of Chicago Press, 1980) and the influential Althusser-Foucault synthesis of two key British cultural materialist works of the 1980s, Catherine Belsey, *The Subject of Tragedy: Identity and Difference in Renaissance Drama* (London: Methuen, 1985) and Francis Barker, *The Tremulous Private Body: Essays on Subjection* (London: Methuen, 1984). All three of these works contain important insights. For a developed critique of these approaches, see my 'On the Need for a Differentiated Theory of (Early) Modern Subjectivity', *Philosophical Shakespeares*, ed. by John J. Joughin (London: Routledge, 2000).

2. Harold Bloom, *Shakespeare: The Invention of the Human* (New York: Riverhead, 1998).

3. In Greenblatt, *Shakespearean Negotiations: The Circulation of Social Energy in Renaissance England* (Berkeley: University of California Press, 1988), pp. 21–65.

4. In a single sentence Mikhail Bakhtin, *Rabelais and his World*, trans. by Hélène Iswolsky (Cambridge, MA: MIT Press, 1968), p. 143, linked Falstaff to Rabelais's treatment of the carnival, but his focus remained on Rabelais and the traditions he drew on. Michael Bristol, *Carnival and Theater: Plebeian Culture and the Structure of Authority in Renaissance England* (New York: Methuen, 1985), eloquently defined the relevance of Bakhtin and his carnival tradition for an appreciation of Shakespeare, and he writes briefly and tellingly of Falstaff (pp. 202–06), but the book presents no longer analysis of Falstaff as a carnival character. Bakhtin's relevance to Falstaff was briefly pointed out by Graham Holderness, *Shakespeare's History* (New York: St Martin's Press, 1985), pp. 83–95. Other definers of the carnivalesque in Shakespeare with little to say on Falstaff are Peter Stallybrass and Allon White, *The Politics and Poetics of Transgression* (Ithaca, NY: Cornell University Press, 1986); Leah Marcus, *The Politics of Mirth: Jonson, Herrick, Milton, Marvell, and the Defense of Old Holiday Pastimes* (Chicago: University of Chicago Press, 1986); François Laroque, *Shakespeare's Festive World: Elizabethan Seasonal Entertainment and the Professional Stage*, trans. by Janet Lloyd (Cambridge: Cambridge University Press, 1991). In the most recent collection of essays on Shakespeare and carnival, *Shakespeare and Carnival: After Bakhtin*, ed. by Ronald Knowles (Basingstoke: Macmillan, 1998), the imbalance is somewhat redressed, through a new essay by François Laroque, 'Shakespeare's

"Battle of Carnival and Lent": The Falstaff Scenes Reconsidered (*1 & 2 Henry IV*)', pp. 83–96, which makes up for the absence of Falstaff in his earlier book; and through a revised and abridged essay by Kristen Poole on Falstaff and Puritanism, 'Facing Puritanism: Falstaff, Martin Marprelate and the Grotesque Puritan', pp. 97–122. I return briefly to each of these essays below. However, further discussion of Poole's work will refer to the fuller and earlier version of this essay with a different title, 'Saints Alive! Falstaff, Martin Marprelate, and the Staging of Puritanism', *Shakespeare Quarterly*, 46.1 (Spring 1995), 47–75.

5. See my 'Shakespeare's Links to Machiavelli and Montaigne: Constructing Intellectual Modernity in Early Modern Europe', *Comparative Literature*, 52.2 (Spring 2000), 119–42.

6. William Shakespeare, *2 Henry IV*, I.2.170–71, *The Norton Shakespeare*, ed. by Stephen Greenblatt (New York: Norton, 1997). All subsequent quotations from Shakespeare plays are from this edition.

7. E. E. Stoll, 'Falstaff', *Modern Philology*, 12.4 (October 1914), 65–108.

8. Alfred Ainger, 'Sir John Falstaff', in his *Lectures and Essays*, 2 vols (London: Macmillan, 1905), I, 119–55; John W. Spargo, 'An Interpretation of Falstaff', *Washington University Studies*, 9.2 (April 1922), 119–33; T. A. Jackson, 'Letters and Documents: Marx and Shakespeare', *International Literature*, 2 (February 1936), 75–97; J. Mr. Dover Wilson, *The Fortunes of Falstaff* (Cambridge: Cambridge University Press, 1943); Robert Weimann, *Shakespeare and the Popular Tradition in the Theater: Studies in the Social Dimension of Dramatic Form and Function*, ed. by Robert Schwartz (Baltimore, MD: Johns Hopkins University Press, 1978), pp. 128–31.

9. Enid Welsford, *The Fool: His Social and Literary History* (London: Faber, 1935); Willard Farnham, 'The Mediaeval Comic Spirit in the English Renaissance', in *Joseph Quincy Adams: Memorial Studies*, ed. by James G. McManaway, Giles E. Dawson, and Wedwin E. Willoughby (Washington, DC: Folger, 1948), pp. 429–37; Walter Kaiser, *Praisers of Folly: Erasmus, Rabelais, Shakespeare* (Cambridge, MA: Harvard University Press, 1963).

10. Herbert B. Rothschild, Jr, 'Falstaff and the Picaresque Tradition', *Modern Language Review*, 68 (1973), 14–21.

11. Algernon Charles Swinburne, *A Study of Shakespeare* (London: Worthington, 1880), pp. 105–08, and Wyndham Lewis, *The Lion and the Fox. The Role of the Hero in the Plays of Shakespeare* (London: Richards, 1927), pp. 201–27.

12. Ainger, 'Sir John Falstaff'; Barrett Wendell, *William Shakespeare: A Study in Elizabethan Literature* (New York: Scribner, 1895); Poole states, 'The person of Falstaff is in and of himself a parody of the sixteenth-century puritan' ('Saints Alive!', p. 54).

13. See Weimann, *Shakespeare and the Popular Tradition*, pp. 185–92, and E. W. Talbert, *Elizabethan Drama and Shakespeare's Early Plays: An Essay in Historical Criticism* (Chapel Hill: University of North Carolina Press, 1963), pp. 7–60 and *passim*.

14. *Radical Tragedy: Religion, Ideology, and Power in the Drama of Shakespeare and his Contemporaries*, 2nd edn (London: Harvester, 1989).

15. See Linda Charnes, *Notorious Identity: Materializing the Subject in Shakespeare* (Cambridge, MA: Harvard University Press, 1993).

16. Louis Althusser, 'Ideology and Ideological State Apparatuses: Notes towards an Investigation', in his *Lenin and Philosophy and Other Essays* (New York:

Monthly Review Press, 1971), pp. 127–86. This of course has been a central text for British cultural materialist works by Belsey, Barker, Dollimore, Sinfield, and many others.

17. See, for example, Jean E. Howard, *The Stage and Social Struggle in Early Modern England* (New York: Routledge, 1994), p. 144; Jean E. Howard and Phyllis Rackin, *Engendering a Nation: A Feminist Account of Shakespeare's English Histories* (London: Routledge, 1997), p. 166.

18. See my article 'Shakespeare's Links to Machiavelli and Montaigne', for a much-expanded discussion of this parallel.

19. See Lewis, *The Lion and the Fox*, pp. 201–27. Bloom, pp. 281–82, also finds important parallels between Falstaff and Sancho Panza.

20. See Phyllis Rackin, *Stages of History: Shakespeare's English Chronicles* (Ithaca, NY: Cornell, 1990), pp. 235–36, for an argument that the use of prose for Falstaff's speech is an emblem of his freedom and a marker for the subversion his lines enact against the dignified blank verse of the so-called official historical material.

21. The text of *Don Quixote* itself is replete with such signals of fictionality, for which it has been rightly and repeatedly celebrated, but Quixote himself as a character is sublimely indifferent to virtually all these signals, and thereby depends a good measure of what Lukács once called that novel's cosmic irony.

22. Poole, 'Saints Alive!'; on the significance of the earlier name Oldcastle, see Gary Taylor, 'The Fortunes of Oldcastle', *Shakespeare Survey*, 38 (1985), 85–100; for counter-arguments to Taylor's, see Jonathan Goldberg, 'The Commodity of Names: "Falstaff" and "Oldcastle" in *1 Henry IV*', in *Reconfiguring the Renaissance: Essays in Critical Materialism*, ed. by Jonathan Crewe (Cranbury, NJ: Associated University Presses, 1992), pp. 72–88, and Harry Berger Jr, *Imaginary Audition: Shakespeare on Stage and Page* (Berkeley: University of California Press, 1989), pp. 25–42.

23. This formula echoes a similar one from Samuel Johnson, 'Notes on Shakespeare's Plays', *The Yale Edition of the Works of Samuel Johnson*, ed. by Arthur Sherbo, 16 vols (New Haven, CT: Yale University Press, 1958–), vii (1968), 522–24, and it has been repeated, and heatedly contested, many times over the centuries. Echoing the classic argument of Paul A. Jorgensen, *Shakespeare's Military World* (Berkeley: University of California Press, 1956), pp. 64–71, Charles Whitney, 'Festivity and Topicality in the Coventry Scene of *1 Henry IV*', *English Literary Renaissance*, 24.2 (Spring 1994), 410–48, attacks this viewpoint as insensitive to the plebeian response to Falstaff's recruiting abuses (pp. 438–39), but he then goes on to define a kind of festive vision in which Falstaff is seen as a plebeian symbol, his exploitations notwithstanding (pp. 439–44).

24. John Dryden, quoted in *The Shakespeare-Allusion Book: A Collection of Allusions to Shakespeare from 1591–1700*, 2 vols, ed. by John Munro (London: Oxford University Press, 1932), II, 146.

25. C. L. Barber, *Shakespeare's Festive Comedies: A Study of Dramatic Form and its Relation to Social Custom* (1959; repr. Cleveland, OH: Meridian, 1963).

26. Bristol, *Carnival and Theater*, pp. 26–39 and *passim*; Ronald Knowles, in his introduction to *Shakespeare and Carnival*, pp. 6–7, makes a similar point.

27. Harry Berger, Jr, 'The Prince's Dog: Falstaff and the Perils of Speech-Prefixity', *Shakespeare Quarterly*, 49.1 (Spring 1998), 40–73.

28. At least this is how I interpret Berger's remarks that he wishes to create a reading that 'recentralizes interpretive activity and desire in Falstaff as the

self-testing subject of his speech' (p. 62), in opposition to Whitney's interpretation of Falstaff as directly addressing an empirical audience, members of which construe him differently according to their own interests and ideologies, and as opposed to Weimann, who sees Falstaff as essentially a character with an interlocutor's relation to the audience.

29. D. A. Traversi, *Shakespeare from Richard II to Henry V* (Stanford: Stanford University Press, 1957) defined a role for Falstaff very close to the idea of the metadramatical (without using the term): 'The essence of Falstaff lies in his standing, alone in this play and [. . .] outside the categories by which those round him are respectively defined and limited [. . .]. Falstaff is, let us say, a coward who can contemplate his own cowardice with detachment' (p. 102). Twenty years later James L. Calderwood, *Metadrama in Shakespeare's Henriad: 'Richard II' to 'Henry V'* (Berkeley: University of California Press, 1979), pp. 71–75, provides an excellent discussion of these qualities for the Falstaff of *Part 1*. Unlike Calderwood, however, I believe Falstaff's metadramatic function extends into and is intensified in *Part 2*.

30. Falstaff's Brechtian dimensions in the battle scenes were first pointed out by Jan Kott, *Shakespeare Our Contemporary*, trans. by Boleslaw Taborski (New York: Doubleday, 1966), p. 43, and more recently discussed, in a somewhat different analysis from my own, by Whitney, 'Festivity and Topicality', p. 416.

31. I find unconvincing Berger's argument that the implied audience here is really one of Falstaff-the-character's imagination ('The Prince's Dog', pp. 60–62, 66–70); or, to put it another way, there is nothing in the text that requires us to preclude a metatheatrical reading and much that comes alive if we assume one.

32. Weimann discusses the porter in *Macbeth*, the gravediggers in *Hamlet*, Launce in *The Two Gentlemen of Verona*, and Falstaff, all as characters of the *platea*, that half-symbolic theatrical space which for Weimann mediates between audience and represented reality (p. 244); see pp. 224–46 for the general discussion of the *platea*.

33. I discuss this theme in *Troilus and Cressida and Othello in Shakespeare's Universal Wolf: Studies in Early Modern Reification* (Oxford: Clarendon Press, 1966), pp. 88–89 and 135–36. Other Shakespearean plays with a similar theme include *Twelfth Night, Much Ado About Nothing, Measure for Measure*, and *The Winter's Tale*.

34. Laroque, 'Shakespeare's "Battle of Carnival and Lent"', provides a detailed account of how Falstaff's numerous carnival associations involve parody (and thus negation) of authoritative discourses, but he tends to see these as producing 'the negative counterpart of the heroic dimension' (p. 88), where I would stress their socially critical functions. In the telegraphic conclusion of his article, however, Laroque seems to shift his ground and affirms Falstaff as a 'triumph of life at the expense of tragic sacrifice' (p. 95).

35. Horkheimer and Adorno, *Dialectic of Enlightenment*, trans. by John Cumming (Boston, MA: Seabury, 1972), pp. 30–80.

36. See the interesting argument in Richard Helgerson, *Forms of Nationhood: The Elizabethan Writing of England* (Chicago: University of Chicago Press, 1992), pp. 195–245, that Shakespeare and company undertook a more or less conscious strategy of making their theatre less popular and carnivalesque over the years, mirroring a larger process creative of a new national culture.

37. See, for example, Gotthold Ephraim Lessing, *Hamburgische Dramaturgie* (1769; repr. Frankfurt a.M.: Insel, 1986). Available in English as *Hamburg Dramaturgy*, trans. by Helen Zimmern (New York: Dover, 1962).

38. *Shakespearean Negotiations*, pp. 1–20.

39. If this is correct then Weimann's eloquent assertion of the crucialness of the carnivalesque popular theatrical traditions to Shakespeare's 'myriad-minded' critical rationality and richness (*Shakespeare and the Popular Tradition*, pp. 174–77), should be supplemented with the recognition that this amounted to a refunctioning of those traditions within an emerging modern category of the aesthetic.

BIBLIOGRAPHY

Baker, Christopher. "The Christian Context of Falstaff's 'Finer End'." *Explorations in Renaissance Culture*, Vol. 12, 1986, pp. 68–86.
Barker, Roberta. "Tragical-Comical-Historical Hotspur." *Shakespeare Quarterly*, Vol. 54, No. 3 (Fall 2003), pp. 288–307.
Battenhouse, Roy. "Falstaff as Parodist," in *Shakespeare's Christian Dimension*, edited by Roy Battenhouse, Indiana University Press: Bloomington & Indianapolis, 1994, pp. 303–314.
Black, James. "'Anon, Anon, Sir': Discourse of Occasion in *Henry IV*." *Cahiers Elisabethains: Late Medieval and Renaissance Studies*, Vol. 37, April 1990, pp. 27–42.
———. "Henry IV's Pilgrimage." *Shakespeare Quarterly*, Vol. 34, No. 1 (Spring 1983), pp. 18–26.
Blanpied, John W. "Rebellion and Design in *Henry IV, Part One*," in *Time and the Artist in Shakespeare's English Histories*, University of Delaware Press: Newark, 1983, pp. 145–178.
Bloom, Harold. "Falstaff," in *Shakespeare: The Invention of the Human*. New York: Riverhead Books, 1998.
Bryan, Margaret B. "'Sir Walter Blunt. There's Honor for You!'" *Shakespeare Quarterly*, Vol. 26, No. 3 (Summer 1975), pp. 292–98.
Cox, Nick. "The Great Enlargement: The Uses of Delinquency in *Henry IV Part One*." *Literature and History*, Vol. 8, No. 1 (Spring 1999), pp. 1–19.
Campbell, Lily B. *Shakespeare's "Histories": Mirrors of Elizabethan Policy*, The Huntington Library: San Marino, Calif., 1968, pp. 346.
Cattle, Graham. "'The Detested Blot': The Representation of the Northern English in Shakespeare's *Henry IV Part One*." *Parergon: Bulletin of the Australian and New Zealand Association for Medieval and Early Modern Studies*, Vol. 13, No. 1 (July 1995), pp. 25–32.
Cubeta, Paul M. "Falstaff and the Art of Dying." *SEL: Studies in English Literature, 1500–1900*, Vol. 27, No. 2 (Spring 1987), pp. 197–211.
Dickinson, Hugh. "The Reformation of Prince Hal." *Shakespeare Quarterly*, Vol. 12, No. 1 (Winter, 1961), pp. 33–46.

Dunn, Esther Cloudman. *Shakespeare in America*, The Macmillan Company: N.Y., 1939.
Efron, Arthur. "War is the Health of the State: An Anarchist Reading of *Henry IV, Part One*." *Works and Days: Essays in the Socio-Historical Dimensions of Literature and the Arts*, Vol. 10, No. 1 [19] (Spring 1992), pp. 7–75.
Evans, G. Blakemore. "Laying a Shakespearian Ghost: I Henry IV, II.iv.225." *Shakespeare Quarterly*, 5:4 (Fall 1954), p. 427.
Fehrenbach, Robert J. "The Characterization of the King in *1 Henry IV*." *Shakespeare Quarterly*, Vol. 30, No. 1 (Winter 1979), pp. 42–50.
Findlay, Heather. "Renaissance Pederasty and Pedagogy: The 'Case' of Shakespeare's Falstaff." *The Yale Journal of Criticism: Interpretation in the Humanities*, Vol. 3, No. 1 (Fall 1989), pp. 229–238.
Gillett, Peter J. "Vernon and the Metamorphosis of Hal." *Shakespeare Quarterly*, Vol. 28, No. 3 (Summer 1977), pp. 351–53.
Hawkins, Sherman H. "*Henry IV*: The Structural Problem Revisited." *Shakespeare Quarterly*, Vol. 33, No. 3 (Fall 1982), pp. 278–301.
Howe, Warren M. "The Rejection and Regeneration of Falstaff in *1 Henry IV*." *Rocky Mountain Review of Language and Literature*, Vol. 34, No. 4 (Fall 1980), pp. 217–27.
Jowett, John. "The Thieves in *1 Henry IV*." *Review of English Studies: A Quarterly Journal of English Literature and the English Language*, Vol. 38, No. 151 (August 1987), pp. 325–33.
La Branche, Anthony. "'If Thou Wert Sensible of Courtesy': Private and Public Virtue in Henry IV, Part One," *Shakespeare Quarterly*, Vol. 17, No. 4 (Autumn, 1966), pp. 371–382.
MacLean, Hugh."'Looking Before and After': Hal and Hamlet Once More." *Papers on Language and Literature: A Journal for Scholars and Critics of Language and Literature*, Vol. 23, No. 3 (Summer 1987), pp. 273–289.
McGuire, Richard L. "The Play-within-the-Play in 1 Henry IV." *Shakespeare Quarterly*, Vol. 18, No. 1 (Winter 1967), pp. 47–52.
Rauchut, E. A. "Hotspur's Prisoners and the Laws of War in *1 Henry IV*." *Shakespeare Quarterly*, Vol. 45, No.1 (Spring 1994), pp. 96–97.
Rubinstein, E. "*1 Henry IV*: The Metaphor of Liability." *SEL: Studies in English Literature, 1500–1900*, Vol. 10, No. 2 (Spring 1970), pp. 287–95.
Taylor, Mark. "*Henry IV* and Proleptic Mimesis." In *Shakespeare's Imitations*, pp. 66–106. Newark: University of Delaware Press, 2002.
Van Doren, Mark. "*Henry IV*." In *Shakespeare*, Henry Holt and Company: N.Y., 1939, pp. 116–135.
Vickers, Brian, ed. *Shakespeare: The Critical Heritage*, Vols. 2, 4, 6. Routledge & Kegan Paul: London, 1974, 1976, 1981.
Walsh, Brian. "'Unkind Division': The Double Absence of Performing History in 1 Henry IV," *Shakespeare Quarterly* Vol. 55, No. 2 (Summer 2004).

Willems, Michèle. "Misconstruction in *1 Henry IV*" *Cahiers Elisabethains: Late Medieval and Renaissance Studies*, Vol. 37 (April 1990), pp. 43–57.

Winny, James. *The Player King: A Theme of Shakespeare's Histories,* Chatto & Windus: London, 1968, pp. 219.

Yachnin, Paul. "History, Theatricality, and the 'Structural Problem' in the *Henry IV* Plays." *Philological Quarterly*, Vol. 70, No. 2 (Spring 1991), pp. 163–79.

Acknowledgments

Twentieth Century

Barber, C. L., and Richard P. Wheeler. "From Mixed History to Heroic Drama: The *Henriad*," from *The Whole Journey: Shakespeare's Power of Development* (Berkeley: University of California Press, 1986), 198–217. © 1986 The Regents of the University of California. Published by the University of California Press.

Blanpied, John W. "Rebellion and Design in *Henry IV, Part One*," from *Time and the Artist in Shakespeare's English Histories* (Newark: University of Delaware Press, 1983), 145–178. Reprinted by permission.

Bloom, Harold. "Introduction," from *Falstaff* (New York: Chelsea House, 1992), 1–4.

Bloom, Harold. "Introduction," from *Henry IV, Part I* (New York: Chelsea House, 1987), 1–7.

Bradley, A.C. "The Rejection of Falstaff," from *Oxford Lectures on Poetry* (London: Macmillan, 1909), 247–273.

Donaldson, E. Talbot. "Sublimely Ridiculous: The Wife of Bath and Falstaff," from *The Swan at the Well: Shakespeare Reading Chaucer* (New Haven: Yale University Press, 1985), 135–144. Reprinted by permission of Yale University Press.

Empson, William. "Falstaff and Mr. Dover Wilson," from *The Kenyon Review*, XV No. 2 (Spring 1953), 213–262. Reprinted by permission.

Goddard, Harold C. "Henry IV," from *The Meaning of Shakespeare* (Chicago: University of Chicago Press, 1951), 175–190. © 1951 by University of Chicago Press.

Nuttall, A.D. "*Henry IV*: Prince Hal and Falstaff," from *A New Mimesis: Shakespeare and the Representation of Reality* (New York: Methuen, 1983), 115–133. Reprinted by permission.

Stoll, Elmer Edgar. "Falstaff" [1914], from *Shakespeare Studies: Historical and Comparative in Method* (New York: Macmillan, 1927), 479–490.

Van Doren, Mark. "Henry IV," from *Shakespeare* (New York: Henry Holt and Company, 1939), 116–135.

Twenty-first Century

Grady, Hugh. "Falstaff: Subjectivity Between the Carnival and the Aesthetic," from *The Modern Language Review*, 96:3 (July), pp. 609–623. © Modern Humanities Research Association 2001. Reproduced by permission of the publisher.

INDEX

Act I
    key passages, 23–30
    summary, 6–10
Act II
    key passages, 30–31
    summary, 10–13
Act III
    key passages, 31–34
    summary, 13–17
Act IV
    key passages, 34–37
    summary, 17–18
Act V
    key passages, 37–39
    summary, 18–21
Adorno, Theodor W., 297
Aeneas, 216–217
Aesthetic theory, 298–300
Agincourt prisoners, 186–188
Alcoholic intoxication, 158–159
Alienation effect, 293
Althusserian interpellation, 289
Anti-Marprelate tracts, 287, 288
Apostrophic soliloquy, 203
Archibald, Earl of Douglas, 41
As You Like It, 208–209
Auden, W. H., 201, 203, 275
Audience collaboration, 245n6

Bakhtin, Mikhail, 292–293, 300n4
Barber, C. L., 111, 238, 244n2, 255–273, 292, 295

Bardolph, 41, 122
Battle of Shrewsbury, 6, 17–21, 180–182
Berger, Harry, 293
Biography of Shakespeare, 1–3
Blanpied, John W., 110–111, 217–246
Bloom, Harold, xi–xii, 111, 273–284, 287–288, 298
Blunt, Walter, 18
Boar's Head Tavern, 89–95
Bolingbroke, Henry, 5–6. *See also* Henry IV
Bottom, 155–156
Bradley, A. C., 109, 112–129, 182, 197
Brecht, Bertolt, 293
Bristol, Michael, 292
Brown, John Russell, 230
Burbage, James, 2
Burckhardt, Sigurd, 246n16
Butler, Samuel, 158

Canterbury Tales (Chaucer), 247–255.
Carnivalesque, 291–294, 295–300, 300n4, 303n34, 304n39
Carriers, 41
Chamberlain, 41
Chaucer, Geoffrey, 111, 247–255, 281
Chesterton, G. K., 197
Chorus, role of, 268, 269
Civil war, 186, 193
Class system, 181, 188–189
Coleridge, Samuel Taylor, 80, 83–84

Collier, Jeremy, 48, 50–51
Comedy, 126, 136, 275
Compensation, law of, 100–101
Condell, Henry, 3
Counterfeit, 165
Courage, of Falstaff, 65–73
Cowardice, of Falstaff, 54, 64–65, 83, 122, 123–125, 129–130, 174, 182–183
Crusades, 110
Cultural materialism, 286, 293
Cultural revolution, 215–216
Cumberland, Richard, 55

Daniel, Samuel, 49
Davenant, William, 48
Death
    of Falstaff, 101–103, 107, 168, 170–171, 172–173, 185, 198–199, 270–271, 277
    of Hotspur, 164–167, 179–180, 182, 241–242
    portrayal of, 18, 36
Deconstructionism, 285
Dedalus, Stephen, 226
Defoe, Daniel, 53
Dekker, Thomas, 278
Dennis, John, 47, 53, 55
Diary, The (Pepys), 49
Dido, 217
Direct address, 202–203
Dollimore, Jonathan, 288
Don Quixote (Cervantes), 274, 290, 302n21
Donaldson, E. Talbot, 111, 246–255
Douglass, David, 55
Dowden, Edward, 80, 104–106
Downes, John, 48
Dramatic technique, 202–203, 204
Drolls, 48
Drunkenness, 158–159, 175
Dryden, John, 48, 50
Earl of Westmoreland, 43

Eastcheap, 89–92
Edmund Mortimer, Earl of March, 5, 6, 42
Edward III, 5
Elizabeth (queen), 47–48, 112, 191–192
Elizabethan humor, 132–135
Emendation, 206
Empson, William, 111, 167–200, 273n11, 276
England, transformation of, 216
English class system, 181, 188–189
English history, 5–6
Enlightenment, 298
Epicurean nature, of Falstaff, 84–85, 97–103
Esteem, 100–101

Fadegen, 283
Falstaff, 6–8, 16–17, 191–193
    appeal of, 135–136, 157–158
    Blanpied on, 224–225, 236–244
    Bloom on, xi–xii, 111, 273–284
    Bradley on, 109, 112–129
    buffoonery of, 224, 262–264
    character of, 41
    childlike nature of, 160–161
    Coleridge on, 83–84
    compared to Hamlet, 111, 122, 275, 278–279, 298
    contrasted with Henry IV, 110
    courage of, 65–73
    cowardice of, 54, 64–65, 83, 122, 123–125, 129–130, 174, 182–183
    death of, 101–103, 107, 168, 170–171, 172–173, 185, 198–199, 270–271, 277
    degeneration of, 103–104, 158–159, 183–185, 195–196, 237–238, 243
    Dennis on, 55
    double nature of, 154, 158–159, 166, 289–290
    Empson on, 111, 167–168, 167–175, 180–186, 188–190

Epicurean nature of, 84–85, 97–103
Giles on, 97–103
Goddard on, 109–110, 153–167
Grady on, 285–300
Hal and, 6–7, 11, 12–13, 30–31, 37–39, 74, 149–150, 176, 204–206, 223–225, 235–236, 259–261, 269–270
Hazlitt on, 84–88
heart of, 195–196
honor of, 19–20, 130–131, 163–164
Hudson on, 103–104
irreverence of, 7
Irving on, 89–90
Johnson on, 59–60, 283
as liar, 122–123
ludicrousness of, 120
in *Merry Wives of Windsor*, 112–113, 153–154, 169
Montagu on, 60–61
Morgann on, 61–77
Morris on, 57–58
Nuttall on, 204–206, 207–209, 217
origins of, 155–156
as parody-father, 201, 208–209
philosophy of, 130–132
popularity of character, 47–48
pride of, 125, 129–130
rejection of, 112–120, 126–127, 136–138, 177–178, 196–198, 256–258, 266–267
Richardson on, 77–78
Schlegel on, 80, 82–83
self-interest of, 36–37, 97
self-love of, 261–262
Shaw on, 80, 107–108
speech of, 147–152, 208–209
Stoll on, 109, 129–138
Van Doren on, 146–153
Wife of Bath and, 246–255
wit of, 60–64, 82, 84–86, 121–122, 131–135, 148–152, 156, 280–282

Famous Victories of Henry the Fifth, The (anonymous), 48–49
First Folio, 3
First Quarto, 47
Fleet Prison, 196, 198
Forster, E. M., 210
France, 190, 191–193
Francis, 11, 41, 92–93, 225
Frankfurt School, 297–298
Freud, Sigmund, 280

Gadshill, 41, 219, 251
Gentleman, Francis, 54, 61
Gielgud, John, 111
Gildon, Charles, 53–54
Giles, Henry, 80, 96–103
Glendower. *See* Owen Glendower
Globe Theater, 2
Goddard, Harold C., 109–110, 153–167
Grady, Hugh, 285–304
Greenblatt, Stephen, 286, 287, 300n1

Hal (Henry, Prince of Wales), 6–9. *See also* Henry V
  acting self of, 223–225, 232–234
  at battle of Shrewsbury, 17–21
  Bradley on, 109, 116–120
  character of, 41–42
  compared with Aeneas, 216–217
  contrasted with Hotspur, 8–9, 14, 20–21, 81–82, 216–217, 228–230
  Dowden on, 104–106
  Empson on, 175–180
  Falstaff and, 6–7, 11, 12–13, 30–31, 37–39, 149–150, 176, 204–206, 223–225, 235–236, 259–261, 269–270
  Goddard on, 166–167
  Grady on, 288
  Johnson on, 59–60
  lack of affection in, 118–119
  mischief-making by, 7–9
  Nuttall on, 200–204, 210–217

relationship between father and, 15–16, 31–34, 209–210, 211–215, 226–233, 265–266
   Schlegel on, 79–80, 81–82
   transformation of, 20–21, 25–26, 80, 104–106, 126, 139, 203–204, 214–216, 265–266
   Van Doren on, 139–141
   Wilson on, 178
Hamlet, 111, 122, 275, 278–279, 298
Hathaway, Anne, 1
Hazlitt, William, 80, 84–88, 289
Hemings, John, 3
Henri, Robert, 160
Henry IV
   Blanpied on, 219–221
   character of, 42
   contrasted with Falstaff, 110
   Dowden on, 106
   Hazlitt on, 87
   opening speech by, 23–25
   relationship between Hal and, 15–16, 31–34, 209–210, 211–215, 226–233, 265–266
   Schlegel on, 79, 81
   self-justification by, 219–220
   as usurper, 214–215
   Van Doren on, 138–139
Henry Percy. *See* Hotspur
Henry Percy, Earl of Northumberland, 42, 87, 145–146
Henry V, 118, 169, 211, 258
Henry V
   Englishness of, 189–191
   as ideal king, 172–174
   rejection of Falstaff by, 112–120, 126–127, 136–138, 177–178, 196–198, 256–258, 266–267
Hero king, 257–258
Heroic plot, 238–239, 242
Hibbard, G. R., 245n5
Histories, 275
Holinshed, Raphael, 49

Honor, 19–20, 106, 130–131, 163–164, 264
Hook, Theodore, 102
Horkheimer, Max, 297
Hotspur (Henry Percy), 5–6, 8, 11, 264
   at battle of Shrewsbury, 17–18
   Blanpied on, 218, 221–223
   Bradley on, 117
   character of, 42
   contrasted with Hal, 8–9, 14, 20–21, 81–82, 216–217, 228–230
   death of, 39, 164–167, 179–180, 182, 241–242
   Hazlitt on, 87–88
   relationship between wife and, 10–11
   Schlegel on, 79, 81–82
   temperament of, 30
   Van Doren on, 141–146
Hudson, H. N., 80, 103–104
Humphreys, A. R., 245n3

Iago, 203–204
Idiom, 147
Imagination, 157–158, 166
Individualism, 296
Intellect, versus sensibility, 80
Irony, 190–191
Irving, Washington, 79, 88–96

James, William, 158–159
Jefferson, Thomas, 55
John of Gaunt, 79, 81
Johnson, Samuel, 23, 53, 54, 59–60, 274, 283, 302
Jonson, Ben, 3
Julius Caesar, 213–214
Justice Shallow, 150–152

Kempe, William, 287
Key passages, 23–39
Killigrew, Thomas, 48
King Arthur, 208–209, 270–271
King Henry IV. *See* Henry IV

King's Men, 2, 49
Kollmann, Judith, 247–248
Kris, Ernst, 266

Lady Mortimer, 42
Lady Percy, 43, 141–142
Language, 218–219
Lessing, G. E., 298
Lewis, Wyndham, 194
Literary history, 278
Lord Chamberlain's Men, 1–2, 49
Lord Chief Justice, 160, 161–162, 164, 198, 265–266
Lords Appellant, 5

Machiavellianism, 189, 204, 210, 221, 232–234, 286–287, 299
Mackenzie, Henry, 55
Mad/made, 206–207
Malapropism, 209
Malcontent figure, 288
Marprelate, Martin, 287
Medieval elements, 188, 194
Merry Wives of Windsor, The, 53, 80, 112–113, 153–154, 169, 247–248, 253
Metatheatre, 293–295, 296
Midsummer-Night's Dream, A, 155–156
Mistress Quickly, 43, 90–91, 102–103, 122, 127, 133, 135–136, 154, 161, 183–184, 185, 270–271
Modernity, 297
Montagu, Elizabeth, 54, 60–61
Morality play, 161–162, 264
Morgann, Maurice, 54, 61–77, 128–129, 193, 264
Morris, Corbyn, 55, 56–58
Mortimer, Edmund. *See* Edmund Mortimer, Earl of March
Mortimer, Roger, 5

Nationalism, 189–190, 191–192
Naturalistic drama, 202, 204
Ned Poins, 7–8, 43, 107, 122, 178, 194
Neely, Carol, 259

Negation, 295
New historicism, 286–287
Nietzsche, Friedrich, 276, 278, 280
Norman Conquest, 190–191
Northumberland. *See* Henry Percy, Earl of Northumberland
Nuttall, A. D., 110, 200–217

Odysseus, 297
"Of Dramatick Poesie" (Dryden), 48, 50
Oldcastle, Sir John, 49, 200n3
Olivier, Laurence, 111
Ophelia, 112
Othello, 201, 203–204
Owen Glendower, 5, 6, 14, 41, 87

Parody, 146–147, 149, 208, 264
Patriotism, 191–193
Patronage, 177–178
Pechter, Edward, 237, 246n15
Pepys, Samuel, 48, 49
Percy, Henry. *See* Hotspur
Peto, 43
Pistol, 150, 169–170, 172, 182–183, 271
Play, 159–160, 263
Plot summary, 5–21
Poins. *See* Ned Poins
Polarity, 289–290
Poole, Kristen, 288
Popularity of play, 47–48
Postmodernism, 286
Preston, Robert, 92
Prose, 135
Puck, 155–156
Puritanism, 2, 48, 287, 291

Radical Tragedy (Dollimore), 288
Realism, 204
Rebellion, 218, 219, 221, 222–223
Religion, 192–193, 258
Renaissance, 188–189, 298
Restoration period, 48
Richard II, 5, 106, 214, 214–215, 217–218, 219, 268–269

Richard III, 242–243
Richard Scroop, 43
Richardson, Ralph, 111, 281
Richardson, William, 55, 77–78
Rogues, 132–133
Rouse, A. L., 190
Rowe, Nicholas, 47
Royal prerogative, 273n9

Sancho Panza, 274, 290
Schlegel, August Wilhelm, 79, 81–83
Scott, Sir Walter, 101
Self-justification, 219–220
Self-love, 261–262
Seltzer, Daniel, 233
Sensibility, versus intellect, 80
Shakespeare, John, 1
Shakespeare, William
    biography of, 1–3
    handwriting of, 206–207
    social status of, 199–200
    sources used by, 48–49
Shaw, George Bernard, 80, 107–108, 153, 274
Sheriff, 43
Short View of the Immorality and Profaneness of the English Stage, A (Collier), 50–51
Shylock, 136
Sir John Falstaff. *See* Falstaff
Sir Michael, 42
Sir Richard Vernon, 43
Sir Walter Blunt, 41
Skits, 48
Soliloquy, 203
Sonnet 73, 271–272
Sonnet 81, 263–264
Sonnet 87, 270
Sonnet 92, 270
Sonnet 94, 210–211
Sonnet 109, 260
Sonnet 110, 259–260, 265
Sonnet 111, 263
Sonnet 116, 259, 261

Sonnet 146, 256–258
Sonnets, 3, 199, 267–268
Sources, 48–49
Speeches, 24
Stereotypes, 200–202, 207–208, 209–210
Sterne, Laurence, 101
Stoll, E. E., 109, 129–138
Subjectivity, xii, 286, 287, 288–289, 292, 296

Tarlton, Dick, 287
Textual confusion, 207
Themes, 8
Theobald, Lewis, 54
Thomas Percy, Earl of Worcester, 42
Tillich, Paul, 54
Traversi, D. A., 303n29
"True self," 223–224

Van Doren, Mark, 110, 138–153
Vanity, 161
Vice figure, 299
Vinter, 43

Walter, J. H., 171
Walworth, William, 92
War, 162, 193, 238–241
Warburton, William, 54, 56
Warwick, 139–140
Waste Land (Eliot), 211
Waugh, Evelyn, 181
Weimann, Robert, 294–295
Welles, Orson, 111
Wetmore, Kevin, 285
Wheeler, Richard P., 111, 255–273
Whipping of the Satyre, The (W. J.), 48, 49
Whitaker, Thomas, 245n6
Wife of Bath, 111, 246–255
Wilson, J. Dover, 111, 159, 161, 166, 167, 168–188, 189–200
Winter's Tale, The, 202
Wyclif, John, 49